Anonymous

Report of the Commissioners for the Revision and Reform of the Law

December 5, 1896

Anonymous

Report of the Commissioners for the Revision and Reform of the Law
December 5, 1896

ISBN/EAN: 9783337296063

Printed in Europe, USA, Canada, Australia, Japan

Cover: Foto ©Suzi / pixelio.de

More available books at **www.hansebooks.com**

REPORT OF THE COMMISSIONERS

FOR THE

Revision and Reform of the Law.

DECEMBER 5, 1896.

FRANK T. BALDWIN,   RYLAND B. WALLACE,   JAMES C. DALY,

Commissioners.

PETER J. SHIELDS, - - - SECRETARY.

SACRAMENTO:

A. J. JOHNSTON, : : : : : : SUPERINTENDENT STATE PRINTING.

1896.

OFFICE OF THE COMMISSIONERS FOR THE
REVISION AND REFORM OF THE LAW,
SACRAMENTO, CAL., December 5, 1896.

To his Excellency JAMES H. BUDD, *Governor of the State of California:*

SIR: The undersigned herewith present the report of the Commissioners for the Revision and Reform of the Law, as required by the Act of the Legislature under which they were appointed. Owing to the unavoidable absence of Hon. Frank T. Baldwin, one of the Commissioners, during the preparation of the report, it contains those recommendations which have been agreed upon by the two other Commissioners.

The general scope of the recommendations made is to embody in the Codes, as far as practicable, the many statutes in force, in their appropriate places therein. The mass and divergent character of such statutes is, however, so great, that the work of their codification is not complete. We have attempted to harmonize the many conflicting sections of the Codes, and to place all provisions appropriately therein. Many changes in the numbering of sections have been recommended, to afford numbers in proper chapters for duplicate-numbered sections, and for provisions of statutes in force which have in this revision been placed in the Codes. No disturbance has, however, been made in the numbering of those important and leading sections which have been made the subject of judicial decision. The enumeration of statutes in force has been reserved for a subsequent report. Proposed changes in the management of public institutions have been considered, and recommendations in that regard will be made to the Legislature at its coming session.

The Commissioners are under obligations to the bench and bar of this State for many valuable suggestions.

The report is submitted with the hope that it will be carefully examined by those interested, and especially by the legal profession, whose comments thereon will enable us to correct it where erroneous, and supply its deficiencies where incomplete.

Respectfully submitted.

RYLAND B. WALLACE,
J. C. DALY,
Commissioners for the Revision and Reform of the Law.

PROPOSED AMENDMENTS TO THE

PENAL CODE.

SECTION 15. To be amended to read as follows:

Sec. 15. A crime or public offense is an act committed or omitted in violation of a law forbidding or commanding it, and to which is annexed, upon conviction, either of the following punishments:

1. Death;
2. Imprisonment;
3. Fine;
4. Removal from office;
5. Disqualification to hold and enjoy any office of honor, trust, or profit in this State;
6. Other penal discipline.

> NOTE.—The amendment is the addition of, "Other penal discipline," which is desirable because in all offenses of minors the court, in its discretion, may commit the offender to a charitable institution or person willing to receive him. (See Section 1388, this Code.)

SECTION 18. To be amended to read as follows:

Sec. 18. Except in cases where a different punishment is prescribed by this Code, every offense declared to be a felony is punishable by imprisonment in the state prison not exceeding five years, or by a fine of not exceeding one thousand dollars, or by both.

> NOTE.—The amendment allows the court, in its discretion, to punish by fine, or by both fine and imprisonment.

SECTION 22. To be amended to read as follows:

Sec. 22. No act committed by a person while in a state of voluntary intoxication is less criminal by reason of his having been in such condition. But whenever the actual existence of any particular purpose, motive, or intent is a necessary element to constitute any particular species or degree of crime, the jury may take into consideration the fact that the accused was intoxicated at the time, in determining the purpose, motive, or intent with which he committed the act; but evidence of such intoxication must be received with great caution.

> NOTE.—The amendment is the addition of, "but evidence of such intoxication must be received with great caution," which makes the section conform to the decision in *People* vs. *Vincent*, 95 Cal.

SECTION 27.   To be amended to read as follows:

Sec. 27.   The following persons are liable to punishment under the laws of this State:

1.   All persons who commit, in whole or in part, any crime within this State;

2.   All who commit without this State any offense which, if committed within this State, would be larceny or robbery under the laws of this State; and bring to, or are found with, the property stolen, or feloniously appropriated, within this State;

3.   All who, being out of this State, cause or aid, advise or encourage, another person to commit a crime within this State, and are afterward found therein;

4.   All who, being out of this State, abduct or kidnap, by force or fraud, any person, contrary to the law of the place where such act is committed, and bring, send, or convey, such person within the limits of this State, and are afterward found therein;

5.   All who leave the State for the purpose of committing a crime, and actually commit the same outside this State, as provided in this Code, and are afterward found therein.

SECTION 28.   A new section to be added to read as follows:

Presumption of responsibility for acts.

Sec. 28.   A person is presumed to be responsible for his acts.   The burden of proving that he is irresponsible is upon the accused person, except as otherwise prescribed by this Code.

SECTION 29.   A new section to be added to read as follows:

Morbid criminal propensity no defense.

Sec. 29.   A morbid propensity to commit prohibited acts, existing in the mind of a person who is not shown to be incapable of knowing the wrongfulness of such acts, forms no defense to a prosecution therefor.

SECTION 63.   A new section to be added to read as follows:

Prohibiting the sale of intoxicating liquors on election day.

Sec. 63.   Every person keeping a public house, saloon, or drinking-place, either licensed or unlicensed, who shall sell, give away, or furnish spirituous or malt liquors, wine, or any other intoxicating beverages, on any part of any day set apart, or to be set apart, for any general or special election, by the citizens, in any election district or precinct, in any of the counties within this State, where an election is in progress, during the hours when by law in said district or precinct the election polls are required to be kept open, is guilty of a misdemeanor.

NOTE.—This section contains the provisions of "An Act to prevent the sale of intoxicating liquors on election days," approved March 7, 1874.

SECTION 68. To be amended to read as follows:

Sec. 68. Every executive officer, or person elected or appointed to, or a candidate or applicant for, an executive office, who asks, receives, or agrees to receive, any bribe, emolument, gratuity, or reward, upon any agreement or understanding that his vote, opinion, or action upon any matter then pending, or which may be brought before him, in his official capacity, shall be influenced thereby, is punishable by imprisonment in the state prison for a term of not less than one, nor more than fourteen, years, and in addition thereto forfeits his office, and is forever disqualified from holding any office in this State.

NOTE.—This amendment is to include in the offense prohibited by the statute the taking of bribes by a candidate, or applicant, prior to his election or appointment.

SECTION 70. To be amended to read as follows:

Sec. 70. Every executive or ministerial officer who knowingly asks or receives any bribe, emolument, gratuity, or reward, or any promise thereof, excepting such as may be authorized by law, for doing, or having theretofore done, any official act, is guilty of a misdemeanor.

NOTE.—This amendment is suggested by the case of *People* vs. *Kalloch*, 60 Cal. 117.

SECTION 76. To be amended to read as follows:

Sec. 76. Every officer whose office is abolished by law, or who, after the expiration of the time for which he may be appointed or elected, or after he has resigned or been legally removed from office, willfully and unlawfully withholds or detains from his successor, or other person entitled thereto, the records, papers, documents, or other writing appertaining or belonging to his office, or mutilates, destroys, or takes away the same, or willfully and unlawfully withholds or detains from his successor, or other person entitled thereto, any money in his custody as such officer, shall be punished by imprisonment in the state prison for not less than one, nor more than ten, years.

NOTE.—The amendment makes the section apply to moneys in the custody of an officer where he refuses to turn over the same to his successors. The present section does not apply to such moneys. (See *People* vs. *Hamilton*, 103 Cal. 495.)

SECTION 78, of Part I, Title V. A new section to be added to read as follows:

Intoxication of officers.

Sec. 78. Any State officer, or officer of a town, village, city, county, or city and county, who shall be intoxicated while in the discharge of the duties of his office, or who, by reason of intoxication, is disqualified for the discharge, or neglects the duties of his office, shall be guilty of a misdemeanor, and, on conviction of such misdemeanor, shall forfeit his office.

NOTE.—This section is taken from "An Act relating to the intoxication of officers," approved April 15, 1880.

SECTION 99.   To be amended to read as follows:

Sec. 99.   Every Superintendent of State Printing, who, during his continuance in office, shall have any interest, directly or indirectly, in any printing of any kind, binding, engraving, or lithographing, connected with the State printing, or in any contract for furnishing paper, or other printing stock or material connected with the State printing, is punishable by imprisonment in the state prison for not less than two, nor more than five, years, or by a fine of not less than one thousand nor more than three thousand dollars, or by both such fine and imprisonment.

SECTION 100.   To be amended to read as follows:

Sec. 100.   Every Superintendent of State Printing who shall corruptly collude with any person or persons furnishing paper or materials, or bidding therefor, or with any person or persons furnishing materials connected with the State printing, or who shall have a secret understanding with any person or persons to defraud the State, or by which the State shall be defrauded, or made to sustain a loss, shall, upon conviction thereof, forfeit his office and is punishable by imprisonment in the state prison for not less than two years, or by a fine of not less than one thousand nor more than three thousand dollars, or by both such fine and imprisonment.

SECTION 119.   To be amended to read as follows:

Sec. 119.   The term "oath," as used in the last section, includes an affirmation, and every other mode authorized by law of attesting the truth of that which is stated, and also the signing of an instrument with the intention that the seal of an officer, authorized to administer oaths, shall be afterward affixed thereto, so as to make such instrument appear as duly and legally sworn to by the person signing.

SECTION 124.   To be amended to read as follows:

Making depositions, etc., when deemed complete.

Sec. 124.   The making of a deposition, affidavit, or certificate is deemed to be complete within the provisions of this chapter, from the time when it is delivered by the accused to any other person, with the intent that it be uttered or published as true.

NOTE.—The effect of this amendment is to make false statements in an affidavit come under the provisions of this section.

SECTION 129. A new section to be added to read as follows:

False returns—Perjury.

Sec. 129. Every person, who, being required by law to make any return, statement, or report, under oath, willfully makes any such return, statement, or report, knowing the same to be false in any particular, is guilty of perjury.

SECTION 137. To be amended to read as follows:

Sec. 137. Every person who gives, or offers, or promises to give, to any witness, or person about to be, or who may be called, as a witness, any bribe, emolument, gratuity, or reward, upon any understanding or agreement that the testimony of such person shall be thereby influenced, or who attempts by any means fraudulently to induce any person to give false, or withhold true, testimony, is guilty of a felony.

SECTION 138. To be amended to read as follows:

Sec. 138. Every person who is a witness, or who is about to be, or who may be called as such, who receives, or offers to receive, any bribe, emolument, gratuity, or reward, upon any understanding that his testimony shall be influenced thereby, or that he will absent himself from the trial or proceeding upon which his testimony is or may be required, is guilty of a felony.

> NOTE.—The amendments proposed to the two foregoing sections place a person who may be called as a witness within the scope thereof.

SECTIONS 158 and 159 to be consolidated into Section 158, which section is to read as follows:

Sec. 158. Common barratry is the practice of exciting groundless judicial proceedings, and is punishable by imprisonment in the county jail not exceeding six months, and by a fine not exceeding five hundred dollars; *provided*, that no person can be convicted of common barratry except upon proof that he has excited suits or proceedings at law in at least three instances, and with a corrupt or malicious intent to vex and annoy.

> NOTE.—The section is amended to require only a corrupt or malicious intent, while at present it requires that the intent shall be both corrupt *and* malicious.

SECTION 159½ to be numbered 159.

SECTION 165. To be amended to read as follows :

Sec. 165. Every person who gives or offers any bribe, emolument, gratuity, or reward, to any member of any Common Council, Board of Supervisors, or Board of Trustees, of any county, city, city and county, or corporation, with intent to corruptly influence such member in his action on any matter or subject, pending before, or which may afterward be considered by, the body of which he is a member, and every member of any of the bodies mentioned in this section who receives, or offers to receive, any such bribe, emolument, gratuity, or reward, is punishable by imprisonment in the state prison for a term of not less than one, nor more than fourteen, years, and is disqualified from holding any office in this State.

NOTE.—The amendment makes the section apply to matters which may be considered after the bribe is offered or accepted.

SECTION 167. To be amended to read as follows :

Sec. 167. Every public officer authorized by law to make or give any certificate, or other writing, who makes and delivers as true any such certificate or writing, containing any statement which he knows to be false; and every officer authorized by law to administer oaths, who certifies that a person has personally appeared before him and subscribed and sworn to a document, when in fact such person did not personally appear before him and subscribe and swear to such document, is guilty of a felony.

SECTION 172. To be amended to read as follows:

Sec. 172. Every person who, within two miles of the lands belonging to this State, upon which is situated any state prison; or within one mile of any insane asylum belonging to the State, or within the state capitol, or within the limits of the grounds adjacent and belonging thereto, sells, gives away, or exposes for sale, any vinous or alcoholic liquors, is guilty of a misdemeanor.

SECTION 178. To be repealed as repugnant to the constitution of the United States, being in conflict with the treaty between the United States and China.

SECTION 179. To be repealed for the same reason as Section 178.

SECTION 178. A new section to be added to read as follows :

Prohibiting the sale of intoxicating liquors within two miles of the University of California.

Sec. 178. Any person who keeps, or exposes for sale, or sells, or gives, or permits others to take, for any consideration, directly or indirectly, any malt, spirituous, or other alcoholic liquors, upon or within two miles of the grounds belonging and adjacent to the University of California, in Alameda County, is guilty of a misdemeanor, and is punishable by imprisonment in the county jail of Alameda County for not less than thirty, nor more than ninety, days, or by a fine not less than fifty, nor more than one hundred, dollars, or by both such fine and imprisonment.

NOTE.—This section contains substantially the provisions of the Act of December 23, 1873, relating to the subject.

SECTION 179. A new section to be added to read as follows:

Communication with convicts confined in the state prison.

Sec. 179. Every person, not authorized by law, who, without the permission of the warden, or other officer in charge of either of the state prisons of this State, communicates with any convict therein, or brings into either of said state prisons any letter or writing, addressed to, or intended for, any convict therein, or carries out of either of said state prisons any letter or writing, from any convict therein, is guilty of a misdemeanor.

SECTION 180. A new section to be added to read as follows:

Furnishing noxious drugs to convicts.

Sec. 180. Every person, not authorized by law, who shall sell, give, or furnish to any convict, confined in either of the state prisons of this State, or shall place upon any of the grounds of either of said state prisons, or in the vicinity thereof, any opium, morphine, cocaine, or other noxious drugs, is guilty of a felony.

SECTION 181. A new section to be added to read as follows:

Entering state prison grounds in the night-time.

Sec. 181. Every person who shall, without the consent of the warden, or other officer in charge of either of the state prisons of this State, go or be upon the grounds of either of said prisons, or lands belonging to the State adjacent thereto, in the night-time, is guilty of a misdemeanor.

SECTION 192. To be amended to read as follows:

Sec. 192. Manslaughter is the unlawful killing of a human being, without malice. It is of two kinds:

1. Voluntary—Upon a sudden quarrel or heat of passion; but in order to constitute voluntary manslaughter, there must be a serious and highly provoking injury inflicted upon the person killing, sufficient to excite an irresistible passion in a reasonable being;

2. Involuntary—In the commission or attempt to commit an abortion unlawfully, in consequence of which, or of any disease ensuing therefrom, the woman dies, as provided in part one, title nine, chapter three of this Code; or in the commission of an unlawful act (other than an abortion or attempt to commit an abortion) not amounting to felony; or in the commission of a lawful act which might produce death, in an unlawful manner, or without due caution and circumspection.

NOTE.—The effect of the amendment is to require a serious and highly provoking injury, sufficient to excite irresistible passion in a reasonable being, to constitute voluntary manslaughter; and to include death caused by abortion in the definition of involuntary manslaughter.

SECTION 207.   To be amended to read as follows:

Sec. 207.   Every person who forcibly steals, takes, or arrests any person in this State, and carries him to any place, or who forcibly takes or arrests any person with a design to take him out of this State, without having established a claim according to the laws of the United States, or of this State, or who hires, persuades, entices, decoys, or seduces by false promises, misrepresentations, or the like, any person to go out of this State, or to be taken or removed therefrom, for the purpose and with the intent to sell such person into slavery or involuntary servitude, or otherwise employs him for his own use, or for the use of another, without the free will and consent of such persuaded person; and every person who, being out of this State, abducts or takes by force or fraud any person contrary to the law of the place where such act is committed, and brings, sends, or conveys, such person within the limits of this State, and is afterward found within the limits thereof, is guilty of kidnaping.

> NOTE.—The present section requires the taking of the person out of the county to constitute kidnaping. The object of the amendment is to make any carrying, although within a county, sufficient to constitute kidnaping.

SECTION 218.   To be amended to read as follows:

Railroad felony defined.

Sec. 218.   Every person who goes upon, or boards, any railroad train, with the intention of robbing any passenger thereon, or of taking from said train any property or money in the possession, or care, or under the control of any person thereon, or who interferes in any manner with any switch, rail, sleeper, viaduct, culvert, embankment, or structure, appertaining to, or connected with, any railroad, or places any dynamite, or other explosive substance or material, upon or near the track of any railroad, or who sets fire to any railroad bridge or trestle, or who shows, masks, extinguishes, or alters any light or other signal, or exhibits, or compels any other person to exhibit, any false light or signal, or who stops any train, or slackens the speed thereof, or who compels, or attempts to compel, any person in charge or control thereof to stop any train or slacken the speed thereof, with the intention either to rob any passenger thereon, or to take from said train any property or money in the possession or charge, or under the control of, any person thereon, is guilty of railroad felony.

SECTION 219.   A new section to be added to read as follows:

Punishment for railroad felony.

Sec. 219.   Every person guilty of railroad felony shall suffer death, or imprisonment in the state prison for life, in the discretion of the jury trying the same.

SECTION 223. A new section to be added to read as follows:

Aiding, advising, or encouraging suicide.

Sec. 223. Every person who deliberately aids, advises, or encourages another to commit suicide, is guilty of a felony.

NOTE.—This is the second of three sections number 400 of this Code.

SECTION 232. To be amended to read as follows:

Sec. 232. No person shall be excused from testifying or answering any question upon any investigation or trial for a violation of any of the provisions of this chapter, upon the ground that his testimony might tend to convict him of a crime. But no evidence given upon any examination of a person so testifying shall be received against him in any criminal prosecution or proceeding.

NOTE.—The only change made by the above amendment is substituting the word "any" for the word "either," which seems necessary, as there are more than two of such provisions.

SECTION 258. A new section to be added to Chapter X, Part I, Title VIII, to read as follows:

Slander of females.

Sec. 258. Every person who, in a public manner, or at any meeting or assemblage, where more than twenty persons are present, states or charges that any class, or portion of a class, of females in a community, professing to lead virtuous lives, is unchaste, whether such statement or charge is true or false, is guilty of a misdemeanor.

SECTION 270. A new section to be added to Chapter I, Part I, Title IX, to read as follows:

Enticement of females for immoral purposes.

Sec. 270. Every person who inveigles or entices any unmarried female, of previous chaste character, under the age of eighteen years, into any house of ill-fame, or house of assignation, or elsewhere, for the purpose of prostitution, and every person who aids or assists in such abduction for such purpose, and every person who, by any false pretenses, false representation, or other fraudulent means, procures any female to have illicit carnal connection with any man, is punishable by imprisonment in the state prison not exceeding one year, or by a fine not exceeding one thousand dollars, or by both.

NOTE.—The present Section 270 is to be numbered Section 273.

SECTION 271. A new section to be added to Chapter I, Part I, Title IX, to read as follows:

Adultery.

Sec. 271. Every person who lives in a state of open and notorious cohabitation and adultery is guilty of a misdemeanor, and is punishable by a fine not exceeding one thousand dollars, or by imprisonment in the county jail not exceeding one year, or by both.

NOTE.—The foregoing is a part of the Act of 1872, to punish adultery, and the present section is to be numbered Section 274.

SECTION 272. A new section to be added to Chapter I, Part I, Title IX, to read as follows:

Double adultery.

Sec. 272. If two persons, each being married to another, live together in a state of open and notorious cohabitation and adultery, each is guilty of a felony, and is punishable by imprisonment in the state prison not exceeding five years; and the recorded certificate of marriage, or a certified copy thereof, there being no decree of divorce, proves the marriage of the persons for the purposes of this section.

NOTE.—The present Section 272 is to be numbered Section 275.

The present Section 270 to be numbered 273 in Chapter II, Part I, Title IX.

The present Section 271 to be numbered 274 in Chapter II, Part I, Title IX.

The present Section 272 to be numbered 275 in Chapter II, Part I, Title IX.

The present Section 274 to be numbered 276 in Chapter III, Part I, Title IX.

The present Section 275 to be numbered 277 in Chapter III, Part I, Title IX.

SECTION 278. A new section to be added to be Section 278, in Chapter III, Part I, Title IX, to read as follows:

Causing death by abortion—Manslaughter.

Sec. 278. Every person who provides, supplies, or administers to any pregnant woman, or procures any such woman to take any medicine, drug, or substance, or uses or employs any instrument, or other means whatever, with the intent thereby to procure a miscarriage, unless the same is necessary to preserve her life, and said woman die in consequence thereof, or in consequence of any disease ensuing therefrom, or caused thereby, is guilty of manslaughter.

NOTE.—The addition of this section, and the change made in the definition in voluntary manslaughter (*vide* Section 192), will reduce this crime from murder in the second degree to manslaughter. Experience has demonstrated that convictions cannot be obtained in these cases where the penalty is imprisonment for life. In New York, where the crime is manslaughter, convictions are readily obtained. The change is therefore recommended, so that those who commit this crime shall not go entirely unpunished.

The present Section 278 to be numbered 279, in Chapter IV, Part I, Title IX.

SECTION 283. To be amended to read as follows:

Sec. 283. Bigamy is punishable by a fine not exceeding two thousand dollars, or by imprisonment in the state prison not exceeding ten years.

NOTE.—This amendment changes the limit of imprisonment from three to ten years, the former being grossly inadequate for many cases which might arise.

SECTION 285. To be amended to read as follows:

Sec. 285. Persons being within the degrees of consanguinity within which marriages are declared to be incestuous and void, who intermarry with each other, or who commit fornication with each other; and persons, being inhabitants of this State, who leave this State for the purpose of intermarrying with any person within the degree of consanguinity within which marriages are declared by the laws of this State to be incestuous and void, and intermarry with such person outside of this State, are punishable by imprisonment in the state prison not exceeding ten years.

SECTION 292. To be amended to read as follows:

Sec. 292. The duty of burying the body of a deceased person devolves upon the persons hereinafter specified, and in the following order:

1. If the deceased was a married person, the duty of burial devolves upon the surviving spouse;

2. If the deceased was not a married person, and left any kindred, the duty devolves upon the person or persons in the same degree nearest of kin to the deceased, being of adult age and within this State, and possessed of sufficient means to defray the necessary expenses;

3. If the deceased left no surviving spouse or kindred answering the foregoing description, the duty of burial devolves upon the persons charged with the support of the poor in the locality in which the death occurs;

4. In case the person upon whom the duty of burial is cast by the foregoing provisions omits to make such burial within a reasonable time, the duty devolves upon the person next specified, and, if all omit to act, it devolves upon the person in the actual possession of the premises where the death occurs or the body is found; or, if there is no person in the actual possession of such premises, then upon the owner thereof; when the death occurs, or the body is found, upon a vessel, by the master thereof, and, if there is no master, by the owner thereof.

5. Such burials may be made in any cemetery organized under the laws of this State, or any now existing in which interments have been made, or any that may hereafter be established or organized by the Board of Supervisors of any county, or city and county, in this State.

Section 298.   A new section to be added to Chapter VI, Part I, Title IX, to read as follows:

Relative to exhumation of bodies.

Sec. 298.   Every person who disinters, exhumes, removes, or causes to be disinterred, exhumed, or removed, from a grave, vault, or other receptacle or burial place, the body or remains of any deceased person, without a permit therefor having first been obtained from the Board of Health, or Health Officer, if such officer there be, or from the Mayor or other head of the municipal government of the city, town, or city and county; and every person who moves, transports, or causes to be moved or transported, on or over the streets or highways of any city, town, or city and county, of this State, the body or remains of a deceased person, which shall have been disinterred or exhumed without said permit, as provided in the Political Code, shall be guilty of a misdemeanor, and shall be punished by a fine not less than fifty nor more than five hundred dollars, or by imprisonment in the county jail for not less than thirty days nor more than six months, or by both such fine and imprisonment.

> Note.—The above is part of "An Act to protect public health," approved April 1, 1878.

Section 299.   A new section to be added to read as follows:

Minor under sixteen years of age not to enter saloon.

Sec. 299.   Every person who admits any minor under the age of sixteen years of age, at any time, into any saloon or place of entertainment where any spirituous liquors, or wines, or intoxicating or malt liquors are sold, exchanged, or given away, at any time, or permit him to remain therein, or permit such minor to remain at any place of amusement known as a dance-house, or concert-saloon, unless such minor is accompanied by his parent or guardian, is guilty of a misdemeanor.

> Note.—This section is Section 1 of "An Act for the protection of children," etc., approved March 30, 1878.

Section 300.   A new section to be added to read as follows:

Forbidding employing or apprenticing minors for immoral purposes.

Sec. 300.   Every person, relative, or employer, having the care, custody, or control of any child under the age of sixteen years, whether as parent, relative, guardian, employer, or otherwise, who shall permit such child to beg, or who shall exhibit, use, or employ, or who shall in any manner or under any pretense sell, apprentice, give away, let out, or otherwise dispose of such child to any person, under any name, title, or pretense, in or for the vocation, occupation, service, or purpose of singing, playing on musical instruments, rope or wire walking, dancing, begging, or peddling, or as a gymnast, acrobat, contortionist, or rider, in any place whatsoever, or for or in any obscene, indecent, or immoral purpose, exhibition, or practice whatsoever, or for or in any business, exhibition, or vocation injurious to the health or dangerous to the life or limb of such child; or who shall cause, procure, or encourage any such child to engage therein, and every person who shall take, receive, hire, employ, use, exhibit, or have in custody, any such child for any of the purposes hereinbefore in this section mentioned, shall be guilty of a misdemeanor, and upon conviction thereof shall be punished by a fine of not less than fifty, nor more than two hundred and fifty, dollars, or by imprisonment in the county jail for a term not exceeding six months, or by both such fine and imprisonment; *provided*, that nothing in this section contained shall apply to, or affect the employment or use of, any such child as a singer or musician in any church, school, or academy, or the teaching or learning of the science or practice of music; or the employment of any such child as a musician at any concert or other musical entertainment on the written consent of the Mayor of the city, or President of the Board of Trustees, of the town where such concert or entertainment shall take place.

SECTION 301. A new section to be added to read as follows:

Relating to certain minors.

Sec. 301. Any child apparently under the age of sixteen years:

1. That is found begging, or receiving or gathering alms (whether actually begging, or under the pretext of selling or offering for sale anything), or being in any street, road, or public place for the purpose of so begging, or gathering or receiving alms;

2. That is found wandering and not having any house or settled place of abode, or proper guardianship, or visible means of subsistence;

3. That is found destitute, either being an orphan, or having a vicious parent, or who is undergoing penal servitude or imprisonment;

4. That frequents the company of reputed thieves or prostitutes, or houses of prostitution or assignation, or dance-houses, concert-saloons, theaters, and varieties, without parent or guardian—is guilty of a misdemeanor.

Such misdemeanor is punishable by imprisonment, or commitment to an orphan asylum, society for the prevention of cruelty to children, or other institution, for a term not to exceed one year, in the discretion of the court or magistrate; but no child, apparently under the age of sixteen years, shall be placed in any prison or place of confinement, or in any court-room, or in any vehicle for transportation, or in any place in company with adults charged with, or convicted of, crime, except in the presence of a proper official.

> Note.—The foregoing three sections embrace a portion of the provisions of "An Act for the protection of children," etc., approved March 30, 1878, and of "An Act relating to children," etc., of the same date. The only change is that the last section limits the term of commitment to an orphan asylum, etc., to one year, while the Acts contain no limit whatever.

Section 303.   To be repealed as unconstitutional.

Section 306.   To be repealed as unconstitutional.

Section 303.   A new section to be added to read as follows:

Selling intoxicants to minors.

Sec. 303.   Every person, except a parent ministering to his child, a guardian to his ward, or a physician to his patient, who sells or gives to any minor under the age of sixteen years, to be by him drank, as a beverage, any intoxicating drink, is guilty of a misdemeanor, and is punishable by a fine not exceeding one hundred dollars, or by imprisonment in the county jail not exceeding three months.

> Note.—The provisions of the above section are contained in the Act of March 4, 1872.

Section 306.   A new section to be added to read as follows:

Causing suffering to minors.

Sec. 306.   Every person who shall willfully cause or permit any child to suffer, or who shall inflict thereon unjustifiable physical pain or mental suffering, and whoever, having the care or custody of any child, shall willfully cause or permit the life or limb of such child to be endangered, or the health of such child to be injured, or any person who shall willfully cause or permit such child to be placed in such a situation that its life or limb may be endangered, or its health shall be likely to be injured, shall be guilty of a misdemeanor.

> Note.—This section contains the provisions of Section 4, of Act of March 30, 1878.

Section 310½.   To be repealed as unconstitutional.   (See *ex parte Jentzsch*, 44 Pac. Rep. 803.)

Section 325.   To be amended to read as follows:

Sec. 325.   All moneys and property offered for sale or distribution in violation of any of the provisions of this chapter are forfeited to the State, and may be recovered by information filed, or by an action brought by the Attorney-General, or by any District Attorney, in the name of the State.   Upon the filing of the information or complaint, the clerk of the court, or if the suit is in a Justice's Court, the justice, must issue an attachment against the property mentioned in the complaint or information, which attachment has the same force and effect against such property, and is issued in the same manner, as attachments issued from the Superior Courts in civil cases.

Note.—The only change in this section is the substitution of the words "Superior Courts" for the words "District Courts."

SECTION 339. To be amended to read as follows:

Sec. 339. Every person who carries on the business, either of a pawnbroker, or a junk-dealer, who fails at the time of the transaction to enter in a register kept by him for that purpose, in the English language, the date, duration, amount, and rate of interest of every loan made by him, or an accurate description of the property pledged, or the name and residence of the pledgor, or to deliver to the pledgor a written copy of such entry, or to keep an account, in writing, of all sales made by him, is guilty of a misdemeanor.

SECTION 341. To be amended to read as follows:

Sec. 341. Every pawnbroker, or junk-dealer, who sells any article pledged to him, and unredeemed, until it has remained in his possession six months after the last day fixed by the contract for redemption, or who makes any sale, without publishing in a newspaper printed in the city, town, or county, at least five days before such sale, a notice containing a list of the articles to be sold, and specifying the time and place of sale, is guilty of a misdemeanor.

SECTION 342. To be amended to read as follows:

Sec. 342. Every pawnbroker, or junk-dealer, who willfully refuses to disclose to the pledgor, or his agent, the name of the purchaser, and the price received by him, for any article received by him in pledge, and subsequently sold, or who, after deducting from the proceeds of any sale, the amount of the loan and interest due thereon, and four per cent of the loan for expenses of sale, refuses, on demand, to pay the balance to the pledgor, or his agent, is guilty of a misdemeanor.

Note.—The amendment to the three last above sections consists in making them applicable to junk-dealers, which is the provision of Section 502. It seems proper to make the amendment rather than to have in the Code separate sections which produce that result.

SECTION 374. To be amended to read as follows:

Sec. 374. Every person who puts the carcass of any dead animal, or the offal from any slaughter-pen, corral, or butcher-shop, into any river, creek, pond, reservoir, stream, street, alley, public highway, or road in common use, or who attempts to destroy the same by fire within one fourth of a mile of any city, town, or village, except it be in a crematory, the construction and operation of which is satisfactory to the board of health in such city, town, or village; and every person who puts any water-closet or privy, or the carcass of any dead animal, or any offal of any kind, in or upon the borders of any stream, pond, lake, or reservoir, from which water is drawn for the supply of the inhabitants of any city, city and county, or any town in this State, so that the drainage from such water-closet, privy, carcass, or offal may be taken up by or in such stream, pond, lake, or reservoir; or who allows any water-closet or privy, or carcass of any dead animal, or any offal of any kind, to remain in or upon the borders of any such stream, pond, lake, or reservoir within the boundaries of any land owned or occupied by him, so that the drainage from such water-closet, privy, carcass, or offal may be taken up by or in such stream, pond, lake, or reservoir; or who keeps any horses, mules, cattle, swine, sheep, or live stock of any kind, penned, corralled, or housed on, over, or on the borders of any such stream, pond, lake, or reservoir, so that the waters thereof shall become polluted by reason thereof; or who bathes in any such stream, pond, lake, or reservoir; or who by any other means fouls or pollutes the waters of any such stream, pond, lake, or reservoir, is guilty of a misdemeanor, and upon conviction thereof shall be punished as prescribed in section three hundred and seventy-seven of this Code.

NOTE.—The amendment changes the word "cemetery" to "crematory," in the fifth line of the section.

All that portion of Title X, Part I, after Section 382, to be amended to read as follows:

Regulating sale of oleomargarine.

Sec. 383.   Every person or corporation who shall manufacture for sale, offer or expose for sale, any article of substance in semblance of butter, not the legitimate product of the dairy, and not made exclusively of milk or cream, or into which the oil or fat of animals, not produced from milk, enters as a component part, or into which the oil or fat of animals, not produced from milk, has been introduced to take the place of cream, and shall not distinctly stamp, brand, or mark, in some conspicuous place upon every parcel of such article or substance, the word "Oleomargarine," in plain letters, not less than one fourth of one inch square, each; and who shall not, in case of retail sale of such article or substance, in parcels or otherwise, in all cases, deliver therewith to the purchaser, a printed label, bearing the plainly printed word "Oleomargarine," the said word to be printed with type, each letter of which shall not be less than one fourth of one inch square;

And every person dealing, whether by wholesale or retail, in the article or substance described in this section, and every hotel or restaurant keeper, or boarding-house keeper, in whose hotel, or restaurant, or boarding-house, such article or substance is used, who shall not continuously keep conspicuously posted up, in not less than three exposed positions, in and about their respective places of business, a printed notice, in the following words, viz.: "Oleomargarine sold here," the said notice to be plainly printed, with letters not less than two inches square, each;

And each and every hotel-keeper and restaurant-keeper, boarding-house keeper, or proprietor of any other places where meals are furnished for pay, who may use, in their respective places of business, any of the article or substance described in this section, who shall not, upon the furnishing of the same to his guests, or customers, if inquiry is made, cause each and every such guest, or customer, to be distinctly informed that the said article is not butter, the genuine production of the dairy, but is "oleomargarine"—is guilty of a misdemeanor, and upon conviction thereof, shall be punished by a fine of not less than five, nor more than five hundred, dollars, or by imprisonment for not more than three months, or by both such fine and imprisonment. And it shall be the duty of the court trying said offense, to order the payment of one half of any fine which may be imposed therein, to the person giving the information upon which the prosecution was based and the conviction had, and such fine may be collected by execution as in civil cases.

SECTION 384. A new section to be added to read as follows:

Prohibiting sale of adulterated syrup.

Sec. 384. Any person who shall knowingly sell, or keep or offer for sale, or otherwise dispose of any syrup, or golden-drips syrup, silver-drips syrup, or molasses, containing muriatic or sulphuric acids, or glucose, or adulterated with any other substance to improve the color thereof, shall be guilty of a misdemeanor.

SECTION 385. A new section to be added to read as follows:

Disposing of tainted articles.

Sec. 385. Every person who knowingly sells, or keeps or offers for sale, or otherwise disposes of, any article of food, drink, drug, or medicine, knowing that the same has become tainted, decayed, spoiled, or otherwise unwholesome, or unfit to be eaten or drank, with intent to permit the same to be eaten or drank, is guilty of a misdemeanor.

SECTION 386. A new section to be added to read as follows:

Setting fire to forests.

Sec. 386. Any person or persons who shall willfully and deliberately set fire to any wooded country or forest belonging to this State or the United States, within this State, or to any place from which fire shall be communicated to any such wooded country or forest, or who shall accidentally set fire to any such wooded country or forest, or to any place from which fire shall be communicated to any such wooded country or forest, and shall not extinguish the same, or use every effort to that end, or who shall build any fire, for lawful purposes, or otherwise, in or near any such wooded country or forest, and through carelessness or neglect shall permit said fire to extend or burn through such wooded country or forest, is guilty of a misdemeanor, and upon conviction before a court of competent jurisdiction, shall be punishable by a fine not exceeding one thousand dollars, or by imprisonment not exceeding one year, or by both such fine and imprisonment; *provided*, that nothing herein contained shall apply to any person who in good faith shall set a back-fire to prevent the extension of a fire already burning. All fines collected under this section shall be paid into the county treasury for the benefit of the common school fund of the county in which they are collected.

SECTION 387.   A new section to be added to read as follows:

Setting woods on fire.

Sec. 387.   Every person who willfully or negligently sets on fire, or causes or procures to be set on fire, any woods, prairies, grasses, or grain, on any lands, is guilty of a misdemeanor.

SECTION 388.   A new section to be added to read as follows:

Obstructing attempts to extinguish fires.

Sec. 388.   Every person who, at the burning of a building, disobeys the lawful orders of any public officer, or fireman, or offers any resistance to, or interference with, the lawful efforts of any fireman, or company of firemen, to extinguish the same, or engages in any disorderly conduct calculated to prevent the same from being extinguished, or who forbids, prevents, or dissuades others from assisting to extinguish the same, is guilty of a misdemeanor.

SECTION 389.   A new section to be added to read as follows:

Maintaining bridge or ferry without authority.

Sec. 389.   Every person who demands or receives compensation for the use of any bridge or ferry, or sets up or keeps any road, bridge, ferry, or constructed ford, for the purpose of receiving any remuneration for the use of the same, without authority of law, is guilty of a misdemeanor.

SECTION 390.   A new section to be added to read as follows:

Violating condition of undertaking to keep ferry.

Sec. 390.   Every person who, having entered into an undertaking to keep or attend a ferry, violates the conditions of such undertaking, is guilty of a misdemeanor.

SECTION 391. A new section to be added to read as follows:

Riding or driving faster than a walk on toll bridges.

Sec. 391. Every person who willfully rides or drives faster than a walk, on or over any toll bridge, lawfully licensed, is punishable by a fine not exceeding twenty dollars.

The section now numbered 389 to be 392; Section 390 to be 393; Section 391 to be 394; Section 392 to be 395; Section 393 to be 396; Section 394 to be 397; Section 395 to be 398; Section 396 to be 399; Section 397 to be 400; Section 398 to be 401; Section 399 to be 402.

SECTION 403. A new section to be added to read as follows:

Prohibiting exhibitions of deformities.

Sec. 403. Every person exhibiting the deformities of another, or his own deformities, for hire, is guilty of a misdemeanor; and every person who shall, by any artificial means, give to any person the appearance of deformity, and shall exhibit such person for hire, shall be guilty of a misdemeanor.

SECTION 404. A new section to be added to read as follows:

Prohibiting sale of adulterated candies.

Sec. 404. Every person who adulterates candy, by using in its manufacture terra alba, or any other deleterious substance, or who sells or keeps for sale any candy or candies adulterated with terra alba, or any other deleterious substance, or substances, knowing the same to be adulterated, is guilty of a misdemeanor.

SECTION 405. A new section to be added to read as follows:

Keeping, using, or selling animals affected with disease.

Sec. 405. Any person who shall knowingly sell, or offer for sale, or use, or expose, or who shall cause or procure to be sold, or offered for sale, or used, or exposed, any horse, mule, or other animal having the disease known as glanders, or farcy, or who shall bring, or cause to be brought, or aid in bringing, into this State, any sheep, hog, horse, or cattle, or any domestic animal, knowing the same to be affected with any contagious or infectious disease, shall be guilty of a misdemeanor.

SECTION 406. A new section to be added to read as follows:

Killing of animals affected with disease.

Sec. 406. Every person in possession, or the owner, or having charge of, any animal affected with glanders, or farcy, who upon discovery or knowledge of its condition, omits, neglects, or refuses to deprive such animal of life, shall be guilty of a misdemeanor.

All sections in Title XI to have their number increased by adding four to each number of said sections, respectively.

> NOTE.—There are three sections numbered 400, and two sections numbered 401, in this title. The Section 400, relating to encouraging suicide, has been passed to Chapter VI, Part I, Title VIII, in a new section to be known as 223, and the other two sections 400 have been renumbered. There are so many other discrepancies in this title that we deem it advisable that the latter part of the title should be reconstructed as above proposed.

SECTION 447. To be amended to read as follows:

Sec. 447. Arson is the willful and malicious burning of a building, with intent to destroy it. Any person who willfully sets fire to his own building, whereby the building of another is set on fire, is guilty of arson.

> NOTE.—The amendment is designed to bring within the definition of arson the burning of a building which is accomplished by firing one adjacent thereto, which may be the property of the person starting the fire.

SECTION 448. To be amended to read as follows:

Sec. 448. Any house, edifice, structure, vessel, railroad car, or other erection, capable of affording shelter for human beings, or appurtenant to, or connected with, an erection so adapted, is a "building" within the meaning of this chapter.

> NOTE.—The amendment includes a car within the definition of "building," when such car is capable of affording shelter to human beings.

Chapter II, Part I, Title XIII, omit "and house-breaking" from title of the chapter.

> NOTE.—The chapter refers entirely to burglary, the former provisions of the chapter on the subject of house-breaking having been repealed.

SECTION 459. To be amended to read as follows:

Sec. 459. Every person who enters any house, room, apartment, tenement, shop, warehouse, store, mill, barn, stable, outhouse, or other building, tent, vessel, or railroad car, with intent to commit larceny or any felony, is guilty of burglary.

> NOTE.—The amendment simplifies the definition of burglary by substituting "with intent to commit larceny" for "with intent to commit grand or petit larceny."

SECTION 480. To be amended to read as follows:

Sec. 480. Every person who makes, or knowingly has in his possession, any die, plate, or apparatus, paper, metal, or machine, or other thing whatever, made use of in counterfeiting coin, current in this State, or elsewhere, or of counterfeiting gold-dust, gold or silver bars, bullion, lumps, pieces, or nuggets, or in counterfeiting bank notes or bills, foreign or domestic, current in this State or otherwise, is punishable by imprisonment in the state prison not less than one nor more than fourteen years, and all such dies, plates, apparatus, paper, metal, or machinery intended for any of the purposes aforesaid, must be destroyed.

> NOTE.—The amendment is intended to clear any doubt of the application of the section to foreign bank notes or bills, and also to make the possession of the dies or apparatus used in making counterfeit foreign coin an offense thereunder.

SECTION 484. To be amended to read as follows:

Sec. 484. Larceny is the felonious stealing, taking, carrying, leading, or driving away the personal property of another; or one's own personal property where it is in the lawful possession of a pledgee.

> NOTE.—The amendment makes it larceny for the general owner of personal property to deprive the pledgee of the possession thereof. This result was intended by the original Code Commissioners.

SECTION 487. To be amended to read as follows:

Sec. 487. Grand larceny is larceny committed in either of the following cases:

1. When the property taken is of a value exceeding fifty dollars;

2. When the property is taken from the person of another, or his immediate presence;

3. When the property taken is a horse, mare, gelding, cow, steer, bull, calf, mule, jack, or jenny.

> NOTE.—The amendment consists in the addition of the words, "or his immediate presence," to subdivision two, and is designed to avoid the questions often arising when the facts of a case make it doubtful whether the property was taken from the person of another, although clearly from his immediate presence.

SECTION 496. To be amended to read as follows:

Sec. 496. Every person who, for his own gain, or to prevent the owner from again possessing his property, buys or receives any personal property, knowing the same to have been stolen, is punishable by imprisonment in the state prison not exceeding five years, or in the county jail not exceeding six months; and it shall be presumptive evidence that such property was stolen, if the same consists of jewelry, silver or plated ware, or articles of personal ornament, if purchased or received from a person under the age of eighteen, unless said property is sold by said minor at a fixed place of business, carried on by said minor or his employer.

> NOTE.—The amendment omits "or by both," applying to imprisonment in the state prison or county jail.

SECTION 502. To be repealed.

> NOTE.—This section, making the provisions of Sections 339, 341, and 342 applicable to junk-dealers, is rendered unnecessary by the amendments to those sections already proposed.

SECTION 502½. To be renumbered 502.

SECTION 515. A new section to be added to Chapter VI, Part I, Title XIII, to read as follows:

Embezzlement by partner or joint owner.

Sec. 515. Every person who, being a member of a co-partnership, or being one of two, or more, beneficial owners of any money, goods, effects, bills, notes, securities, or other personal property of, or belonging to, any such co-partnership, or to such joint beneficial owners, who fraudulently appropriates to his own use, or secretes with a fraudulent intent to appropriate to his own use, any personal property belonging to such co-partnership, or in which he is one of two or more joint owners, which has come into his care or control, is guilty of embezzlement.

> NOTE.—This amendment is the English statute and the New York law on the subject.

SECTION 532. To be amended to read as follows:

Sec. 532. Every person who, knowingly and designedly, by false or fraudulent representation or pretenses, defrauds any other person of money or property, real or personal, or who causes or procures others to report falsely of his wealth or mercantile character, and by thus imposing upon any person obtains credit, and thereby fraudulently gets into possession of money or property, real or personal, is punishable as follows: If the value of the property exceeds fifty dollars, by imprisonment in the state prison for not less than one, nor more than ten, years; if the value of the property does not exceed fifty dollars, by a fine not exceeding five hundred dollars, or by imprisonment in the county jail not exceeding six months, or by both.

> NOTE.—This amendment is suggested by the decision in *People* vs. *Cummings*, California decisions, October 14, 1896, where it was held that the section does not apply to obtaining real property by false pretenses.

SECTION 533. A new section to be added to read as follows:

Obtaining labor under false pretenses.

Sec. 533. Every person who, knowingly and designedly, by false or fraudulent representation or pretenses, or by causing or procuring others to report falsely of his wealth or mercantile character, obtains or procures any other person to perform labor or services for him and thereafter fails to pay the said other person for the labor or services so performed, is punishable by imprisonment in the county jail not exceeding six months, or by a fine not exceeding twice the agreed price of the labor or services so obtained, or by both.

The present Section 533 to be renumbered 534; the present Section 534 to be renumbered 535; the present Section 535 to be renumbered

536 of Chapter VIII, Part I, Title XIII, and the remaining sections of said Chapter VIII, of Part I, Title XIII, to read as follows:

SECTION 537.   A new section to be added to read as follows:

False statement concerning prices of consignment—Misdemeanor.

Sec. 537.   Every commission merchant, broker, agent, factor, or consignee, who shall willfully and corruptly make, or cause to be made, to the principal or consignor of such commission merchant, agent, broker, factor, or consignee, a false statement concerning the price obtained for, or the quality or quantity of, any property consigned or intrusted to such commission merchant, agent, broker, factor, or consignee, for sale, shall be deemed guilty of a misdemeanor, and, on conviction thereof, shall be punished by fine not exceeding five hundred dollars, or imprisonment in the county jail not exceeding six months, or by both such fine and imprisonment.

SECTION 538.   A new section to be added to read as follows:

Removing certain property with intent to defraud mortgagee—Larceny.

Sec. 538.   Every person who, after mortgaging any of the property mentioned in section twenty-nine hundred and fifty-five of the Civil Code, excepting locomotives, engines, rolling-stock of a railroad, steamboat machinery in actual use, and vessels, during the existence of such mortgage, with the intent to defraud the mortgagee, his representatives or assigns, transfers, sells, takes, drives, or carries away, or otherwise disposes of, or permits the transferring, selling, taking, driving, or carrying away, or otherwise disposing of, such mortgaged property, or any part thereof, from the county where it was situated, at the time it was mortgaged, without the written consent of the mortgagee, is guilty of larceny, and shall be punished accordingly.

SECTION 539.   A new section to be added to read as follows:

Further incumbrance of certain property—Larceny.

Sec. 539.   Every person who, after mortgaging any of the property mentioned in section twenty-nine hundred and fifty-five of the Civil Code, excepting locomotives, engines, rolling-stock of a railroad, steamboat machinery in actual use, and vessels, during the existence of such mortgage, sells, transfers, or in any manner further incumbers, the said mortgaged property, or any part thereof, or causes the same to be sold, transferred, or further incumbered, is guilty of larceny, and shall be punished accordingly; unless at or before the time of making such sale, transfer, or incumbrance, such mortgagor shall inform the person to whom such sale, transfer, or incumbrance may be made, of the existence of the prior mortgage, and shall inform the prior mortgagee of the intended sale, transfer, or incumbrance, in writing, by giving the name and place of residence of the party to whom the sale, transfer, or incumbrance is to be made.

SECTION 540.   A new section to be added to read as follows:

Misrepresentation of newspaper circulation—Misdemeanor.

Sec. 540.   Every proprietor or publisher of any newspaper or periodical, who shall willfully and knowingly misrepresent the circulation of such newspaper or periodical for the purpose of securing advertising or other patronage, is guilty of a misdemeanor.

SECTION 541.   A new section to be added to read as follows:

Defrauding proprietors of hotels, inns, etc.

Sec. 541.   Any person who obtains any food or accommodation at an inn, or boarding-house, without paying therefor, with intent to defraud the proprietor or manager thereof, or who obtains credit at an inn or boarding-house by the use of any false pretense, or who, after obtaining credit or accommodation at any inn or boarding-house, absconds or surreptitiously removes his baggage therefrom, without paying for his food or accommodation, is guilty of a misdemeanor.

SECTION 542.   A new section to be added to read as follows:

Fraudulent registration of thoroughbred cattle.

Sec. 542.   Every person who shall, by any false or fraudulent pretense, obtain from any club, association, society, or company organized for the purpose of improving the breed of cattle, horses, sheep, swine, or other domestic animals, a certificate of registration of any animal in the herd register, or any other register, of any such club, association, society, or company, or a transfer of any such registration; and any person who shall, for a legal consideration, give a false pedigree of any animal, with intent to mislead, shall be guilty of a misdemeanor.

SECTION 543.   A new section to be added to read as follows:

Advertising false pedigree of animals.

Sec. 543.   Every person willfully advertising any of such animals for purposes of copulation, or profit, as having a pedigree other than the true pedigree of such animal, is guilty of a misdemeanor.

NOTE.—The changes proposed in this chapter consist of the orderly arrangement of its provisions and renumbering where necessary. There are two sections numbered 538. A section, No. 537, relating to defrauding hotel-keepers, was repealed by an amendment of that section when there were two sections of that number. The section thus repealed is the proposed new Section 540.

Section 537½, which makes the penalty of false advertising as to pedigree of animals the forfeiture of all right to collect pay for certain services of said animals, has been changed to make the same a misdemeanor, and the section renumbered 543.

SECTION 539 of Chapter IX, Part I, Title XIII, to be Section 544 of said chapter.

SECTION 540 to be Section 545 of said chapter, and Section 541 of said chapter to be Section 546.

SECTION 544 of Chapter X, Part I, Title XIII, to be Section 547 of that chapter.

SECTION 545 of said chapter to be Section 548 thereof.

SECTION 548 of Chapter XI, Part I, Title XIII, to be Section 549 of said chapter, and Section 549 of said chapter to be Section 550 thereof.

SECTION 563. To be amended to read as follows:

Sec. 563. Every director, officer, or agent of any corporation or joint-stock association, who knowingly receives or possesses himself of any property of such corporation or association, otherwise than in payment of a just demand, and who, with intent to defraud, omits to make, or cause or direct to be made, a full and true entry thereof in the books or accounts of such corporation or association, and every director, officer, agent, or member of any corporation or joint-stock association, who, with intent to defraud, destroys, alters, mutilates, or falsifies any of the books, papers, writings, or securities belonging to such corporation or association, or makes, or concurs in making, any false entries, or omits, or concurs in omitting, to make any material entry, in any book of accounts, or other record or document kept by such corporation or association, is punishable by imprisonment in the state prison not less than three, nor more than ten, years, or by a fine not exceeding five hundred dollars, or by both such fine and imprisonment.

SECTION 591. To be amended to read as follows:

Sec. 591. Every person who unlawfully and willfully cuts, removes, injures, or obstructs any line, wire, or conduit, or apparatus connected therewith, belonging to and used by any person or corporation engaged in conducting and carrying on a telegraph or telephone business, is guilty of a misdemeanor.

SECTION 599. A new section to be added to read as follows:

Leaving open inclosures passed through, and tearing down fences for passage—Misdemeanor.

Sec. 599. Every person who passes through an inclosure of another, and leaves the same open, is guilty of a misdemeanor, and is punishable by a fine of not less than twenty, nor more than fifty, dollars; and every person who willfully and maliciously tears down fences to make a passage through an inclosure of another, is guilty of a misdemeanor, and is punishable by a fine of not less than fifty, nor more than five hundred, dollars. All fines collected under the provisions of this section shall be paid into the county school fund of the county where the offense is committed.

NOTE.—This section contains the provisions of the Act of March 16, 1872, upon the subjects therein mentioned.

SECTION 602. To be amended to read as follows:

Sec. 602. Every person who willfully commits any trespass by either:

1. Cutting down, destroying, or injuring any kind of wood or timber standing or growing upon the lands of another; or,

2. Carrying away any kind of wood or timber lying on such lands; or,

3. Maliciously injuring or severing from the freehold of another anything attached thereto, or the produce thereof; or,

4. Digging, taking, or carrying away from any lot situated within the limits of any incorporated city, without the license of the owner or legal occupant thereof, any earth, soil, or stone; or,

5. Digging, taking, or carrying away from any land in any of the cities of the State, laid down on the map or plan of such city, or otherwise recognized or established, as a street, alley, avenue, or park, without the license of the proper authorities, any earth, soil, or stone; or,

6. Putting up, affixing, fastening, printing, or painting, upon any property belonging to the State, or to any city, county, town, or village, or dedicated to the public, or upon any property of any person, without license from the owner, any notice, advertisement, or designation of, or any name for, any commodity, whether for sale or otherwise, or any picture sign, sign, or device intended to call attention thereto; or,

7. Entering upon any lands owned by any other person or persons, whereon oyster or other shell-fish are planted or growing; or injuring, gathering, or carrying away any oysters or other shell-fish planted, growing, or being on any such lands, whether covered by water or not, without the license of the owner or legal occupant thereof; or destroying or removing, or causing to be removed or destroyed, any stakes, marks, fences, or signs intended to designate the boundaries and limits of any such lands; or,

8. Landing, or entering upon any land or lands owned by another person or persons, on the seashore, or on the borders of any lake, river, or other navigable water, for the purpose of hunting, fishing, or shooting thereon, without license or the permission of the owner or legal occupant thereof, or removing or destroying, or causing to be removed or destroyed, any notice or notices prohibiting such landing, hunting, fishing, or shooting—is guilty of a misdemeanor.

SECTION 604. A new section to be added to read as follows:

Injuring certain trees—Misdemeanor.

Sec. 604. Every person who shall willfully cut down, or strip of its bark, any tree "over sixteen feet in diameter," in the grove of big trees situated in the counties of Fresno, Tulare, and Kern, or shall destroy any of said trees by fire, is guilty of a misdemeanor, and is punishable by a fine of not less than fifty, nor more than three hundred, dollars, or by imprisonment in the county jail for not less than twenty-five, nor more than one hundred and fifty, days, or by both; and upon the arrest and conviction of any person or persons guilty of any of the acts hereinbefore in this section mentioned, the party informing shall be entitled to one half of any of the fines imposed and collected.

NOTE.—This section contains the provisions of "An Act to protect the groves of big trees," etc., approved March 13, 1874.

The present Section 604 to be numbered 605; the present Section 605 to be numbered 606; the present Section 606 to be numbered 607; the present Section 607 to be numbered 608; the present Section 608 to be numbered 609.

SECTION 610. A new section to be added to read as follows:

Malicious injury to saw-logs—Felony.

Sec. 610. Every person who maliciously drives into or places within any saw-log, shingle-bolt, or other wood, any iron, steel, or other substance sufficiently hard to injure saws, knowing that the said saw-log, shingle-bolt, or other wood is intended by the owner thereof to be manufactured into any kind of lumber, is guilty of a felony, and is punishable by imprisonment in the state prison for not less than one, nor more than five, years.

NOTE.—This section contains the provisions of "An Act to protect lumber manufacturers," approved February 9, 1876.

The present Section 609 to be numbered 611; the present Section 610 to be numbered 612; the present Section 611 to be numbered 613; the present Section 612 to be numbered 614; the present Section 613 to be numbered 615; the present Section 614 to be numbered 616.

Section 617. A new section to be added to read as follows:

Damaging buoys and beacons.

Sec. 617. Every person who willfully removes, damages, or destroys any buoy or beacon, or any part thereof, placed in the waters of California by authority of the United States Lighthouse Board, or who cuts down, removes, or destroys any beacon or beacons erected on any land in this State, by the authority aforesaid, is guilty of a misdemeanor, and is punishable by a fine not exceeding five hundred dollars, or by imprisonment not exceeding six months; and one third of any fines imposed and collected under this section shall be paid to the party informing, and two thirds to the lighthouse board, to be used in repairing said buoys and beacons.

> NOTE.—This section is Section 1 of "An Act for the protection of buoys and beacons," approved March 26, 1874. The second section thereof, relating to liens on vessels, is placed in the Political Code.

The present Section 615 to be numbered 618; the present Section 616 to be numbered 619; the present Section 617 to be numbered 620; the present Section 618 to be numbered 621; the present Section 619 to be numbered 622; the present Section 620 to be numbered 623; the present Section 621 to be numbered 624; the present Section 622 to be numbered 625; the present Section 623 to be numbered 626; the present Section 624 to be numbered 627; the present Section 625 to be numbered 628 of Part I, Title XIV.

Section 626 in Chap. 15, Section 626, 626a, 626b, 626c, 626d, 626e, 626f, 626g, 626h, 626i, Section 627 and Section 627a, 627b, 627c, 627d, Section 628 and Section 628a, Section 632, Section 632a, Section 632b, Section 633, Section 634, Section 635, and Section 636, to be repealed.

Section 627. A new section to be added to Chapter I, Part I, Title XV, to read as follows:

Destruction and sale of game—when prohibited.

Sec. 627. Every person who, in the State of California, between the fifteenth day of February and the fifteenth day of August, of each year, shall hunt, pursue, take, kill, or destroy, or have in his possession, whether taken or killed in this State, or shipped into the State from any other State, Territory, or foreign country, except for the purpose of propagation, any mountain quail, or grouse, without having obtained a permit, in writing, from the game warden of the county wherein said birds are to be caught; every person who, in the State of California, between the fifteenth day of February and the first day of July, in each year, shall hunt, pursue, take, kill, or destroy, or have in his possession, any dove or doves; every person who, in the State of California, shall hunt, pursue, take, kill, or destroy, or have in his possession, any male deer, between the fifteenth day of October and the fifteenth day of July of the following year; every person who, in the State of California, shall, at any time, hunt, pursue, take, kill, or destroy, or have in his possession, any spotted fawn, or an antelope, elk, mountain sheep, or female deer; every person who, in the State of California, shall buy, sell, or offer for sale, the hide or meat of any female deer, elk, antelope, or mountain sheep, whether taken or killed in the State of California, or shipped into the State from any other State or Territory; every person who, in the State of California, shall buy, sell, offer, or expose for sale, transport, or carry, or have in his possession, the skin, hide, or pelt of any deer from which the evidence of sex has been removed; every person who, in the State of California, shall buy, sell, offer, or expose for sale, the hide or meat of any female deer, elk, antelope, or mountain sheep, whether taken or killed in the State of California, or shipped into this State from any other State or Territory (except Alaska), or a foreign country; every person who, in the State of California, before the first day of March, eighteen hundred and ninety-nine, shall hunt, pursue, take, kill, or destroy, or have in his possession, except for the purpose of propagation, any pheasant; every cold-storage company, person keeping a cold-storage warehouse, tavern or hotel keeper, restaurant or eating-house keeper, marketman, or other person, who shall buy, sell, expose or offer for sale, or give away, or have in his possession, in this State, any quail, bob-white, partridge, pheasant, grouse, dove, wild duck, male deer, or any portion thereof, during the time it shall be unlawful to kill such birds, or male deer, whether taken or killed in the State of California, or shipped into the State from any other State, Territory, or foreign country; every person who, in the State of California, shall take, gather, or destroy the eggs of any quail, bob-white, partridge, pheasant, grouse, dove, or robin, or any kind of wild duck; every person who, for the purpose of shooting any kind of wild game, conceals himself behind any living animal; every person who shall use a shotgun of a larger caliber than that commonly known and designated as number ten gauge, for the purpose of killing any quail, or any species of wild duck; every person who, upon any inclosed or cultivated grounds, which are private property, and where signs are displayed forbidding such shooting, except salt-water marsh land, shall shoot any quail, bob-white, pheasant, partridge, grouse, dove, deer, or wild duck, without permission first obtained from the owner or person in possession of such grounds, or who shall maliciously tear down, or mutilate or destroy any sign, signboard, or other notice forbidding shooting on private property; every person who, in the State of California, shall at any time hunt, shoot, shoot at, take, kill, or destroy, buy, sell, give away, or have in his possession, except for the purpose of propagation, or for educational or scientific purposes, any English skylark, canary, California oriole, humming-bird, thrush, or mocking-bird, or any part of the skin, skins, or plumage of any of said birds, or who shall rob the nests, or take or destroy the eggs, of any of said birds—is guilty of a misdemeanor, and is punishable by a fine of not less than twenty dollars, or by imprisonment in the county jail of the county in which the conviction shall be had not less than ten days, or by both; and all the fines imposed and collected for any violation of any of the provisions of this section, shall be paid into the general fund of the county in which the conviction is had.

SECTION 628.   A new section to be added to read as follows:

Regulating catching of certain fish.

Sec. 628.   Every person who takes or catches, buys, sells, or has in his possession, any striped bass of less than three pounds in weight; every person who, at any time, buys, sells, offers or exposes for sale, or has in his possession, any sturgeon less than three feet in length; every person who, at any time between the first day of April and the first day of September, of each year, takes or catches, buys, sells, or has in his possession, any fresh sturgeon, whether such sturgeon is caught outside or within this State; every person who, between the first day of January and the first day of July, takes or catches, buys, sells, or has in his possession, any black bass; every person who, at any time, takes, catches, or kills, any black bass, except with hook and line; every person who shall take, catch, or kill, or sell, expose or offer for sale, or has in his possession, any lobster or crawfish, between the fifteenth day of May and the fifteenth day of July, of each year; every person who shall, at any time, buy, sell, barter, exchange, offer or expose for sale, or have in his possession, any lobster or crawfish of less than nine and one half inches in length, measured from one extremity to the other, exclusive of legs or feelers, or less than one pound in weight, whether such lobster or crawfish is caught outside or within this State; every person who takes, catches, or kills, or exposes for sale, or has in his possession, any speckled trout, brook or salmon trout, or any variety of trout, between the first day of November and the first day of April in the following year, except steel-head trout when taken with rod and line in tidewater; every person who buys, sells, or offers or exposes for sale, any steel-head trout (*Salmo gairdneri*), between the first day of December and the first day of February of the following year; every person who buys or sells, or offers or exposes for sale, within this State, any kind of trout less than six inches in length; every person who, between the thirty-first day of August and the first day of November, of each year, takes or catches, buys, sells, offers, or exposes for sale, or has in his possession, any fresh salmon; every person who, by seine or other means, shall catch the young fish of any species and shall not return the same to the water immediately, and alive, or who shall sell, or offer for sale, any such fish, fresh or dried; every person who, in the State of California, at any time, takes or catches any trout, except with hook and line; every person who shall place, or cause to be placed, in any of the waters of this State, dynamite, gunpowder, or other explosive compound, for the purpose of killing or taking fish, or who shall at any time take, procure, kill, or destroy, any fish of any kind by means of explosives; every person who shall, at any time, except with hook and line, take or catch fish of any kind, from any river or stream within the State of California, upon which a United States fish hatchery is in operation; every person who shall set or draw, or assist in setting or drawing, any net or seine for the purpose of taking or catching salmon, shad, or striped bass, in any of the public waters of this State, at any time between sunrise of each Saturday and sunset of the following Sunday; every person who shall, for the purpose of catching shad, salmon, or striped bass, in any of the public waters of this State, fish with, or use any, seine, net, drag-net, or paranzella, the meshes of which are, when drawn closely together and measured inside the knot, less then seven and one half inches in length; every person who places, or allows to pass into any of the waters of this State, any lime, gas, tar, cocculus indicus, sawdust, shavings, slabs, edgings, mill or factory refuse, or any substance deleterious to fish; every person who shall catch, take, or carry away any trout or other fish, from any stream, pond, or reservoir, controlled by the State Board of Fish Commissioners, or belonging to any person or corporation, without the consent of the owner thereof, which stream, pond, or reservoir has been stocked with fish by hatching therein eggs or spawn, or by placing the same therein; every person who shall set, use, or continue, or shall assist in setting, using, or continuing, any pond, weir, set-net, trap, or any other fixed or permanent contrivance for catching fish in the waters of this State; and every net shall be considered a set-net when fastened in any way to a fixed or stationary object; every person who shall cast, extend, or set any seine, or net of any kind, for the catching of fish in any river, stream, or slough, of this State, which shall extend more than one-third across the width of said river, stream, or slough, at the time and place of such fishing; every person who shall cast, extend, set, use, or continue, or who shall assist in casting, extending, using, or continuing, "Chinese shrimp or bag net," or net of similar character, for the catching of fish in the waters of this State; every person who shall cast, extend, set, use, or continue, or have in his possession, or who shall assist in casting, extending, using, or continuing, "Chinese-sturgeon lines," or lines of a similar character—is guilty of a misdemeanor, and is punishable by a fine not less than one hundred dollars, or by imprisonment in the county jail in the county in which the conviction shall be had, not less than fifty days, or by both such fine and imprisonment; *provided*, that nothing in this section shall prohibit the United States Fish Commissioners and the Fish Commissioners of this State from taking, at all times, such fish as they deem necessary for the purpose of artificial hatching.

SECTION 631.   To be amended to read as follows:

Sec. 631.   Every person who shall, at any time, net or pound, cage or trap, any quail, partridge, or grouse; and every person who shall sell, transport, or give away, or offer or expose for sale, or have in his possession, any quail, partridge, or grouse, that has been snared, captured, or taken by means of any net or pound, cage or trap, whether taken in the State of California, or shipped into the State from any other State, Territory, or foreign country, is guilty of a misdemeanor; *provided*, that the same may be taken for the purpose of propagation, written permission having been first obtained from the game warden of the county wherein said birds are to be taken.

> NOTE.—The amendment to this section omits the provision which makes proof of possession *prima facie* evidence of guilt in certain cases, which provision is unconstitutional.

The present Section 637 to be numbered 632 of Part I, Title XV.

SECTION 633.   A new section to be added to Part I, Title XV, to read as follows:

Killing certain seagulls—Misdemeanor.

Sec. 633.   Every person who willfully kills or destroys any of that species of sea-birds known as gulls, within five miles of the town of Santa Monica, Los Angeles County, is guilty of a misdemeanor.

> NOTE.—The foregoing amendments to the sections upon the fish and game laws incorporate in a few sections most of the provisions now contained in the numerous sections on the subject in this Code, and also the suggestions made to us by the Fish Commission. The principal change made is that the close season and the time when it is unlawful to sell game are coincident in the proposed amendments.

SECTION 637.   A new section to be added to Chapter II, Title XV, Part I, to read as follows:

Issuing fire insurance policies not of standard form a misdemeanor.

Sec. 637.   Every insurance company or person who makes, issues, delivers, or offers to deliver, any policy of fire insurance, on property in this State, on or after September first, eighteen hundred and ninety-seven, which policy does not conform to the "California Standard Policy," shall be guilty of a misdemeanor.

SECTION 638. To be amended to read as follows:

Neglect or postponement, out of regular order, of telegraphic message.

Sec. 638. Every agent, operator, or employé of any telegraph or telephone office, who willfully refuses or neglects to send any message received at such office for transmission, or willfully postpones the same out of its order, or willfully refuses or neglects to deliver any message received by telegraph or telephone; and every agent, operator, or employé of any telegraph or telephone company, who willfully refuses or neglects to transmit, or to allow to be transmitted, any telegraph or telephone message, or willfully postpones the same out of its order, is guilty of a misdemeanor. Nothing herein contained shall be construed to require any message to be received, transmitted, delivered, or permitted to be transmitted, unless the charges thereon have been paid or tendered, nor to require the transmission, receiving, or delivery of any message counseling, aiding, abetting, or encouraging treason against the government of the United States, or of this State, or other resistance to lawful authority, or any message calculated to further any fraudulent plan or purpose, or to instigate or encourage the perpetration of any unlawful act, or to facilitate the escape of any criminal or person accused of crime.

SECTION 639. To be amended to read as follows:

Agent, operator, or employé using information from messages.

Sec. 639. Every agent, operator, or employé of any telegraph or telephone office, who, in any way, uses or appropriates any information derived by him from any private message passing through his hands, or along the lines in such office, and addressed to any other person, or in any other manner acquired by him by reason of his trust as such agent, operator, or employé, or trades or speculates upon any such information so obtained, or in any manner turns, or attempts to turn, the same to his own account, profit, or advantage, is punishable by imprisonment in the state prison not exceeding five years, or by imprisonment in the county jail not exceeding one year, or by a fine not exceeding five thousand dollars, or by both such fine and imprisonment in the county jail.

SECTION 640. A new section to be added to read as follows:

Clandestinely learning the contents of message.

Sec. 640. Every person who, by means of any machine, instrument, or contrivance, or in any other manner, willfully and fraudulently reads, or attempts to read, any message, or to learn the contents thereof, while the same is being sent over any telegraph or telephone line, or willfully and fraudulently, or clandestinely, learns, or attempts to learn, the contents or meaning of any message, while the same is in any telegraph or telephone office, or is being received thereat, or sent therefrom, or

3—c

who uses, or attempts to use, or communicates to others, any information so obtained, is punishable as provided in section six hundred and thirty-nine of this Code.

SECTION 641.   To be amended to read as follows:

Bribing operator.

Sec. 641.   Every person who, by the payment or promise of any bribe, inducement, or reward, procures, or attempts to procure, any telegraph or telephone agent, operator, or employé to disclose any private message, or the contents, purport, substance, or meaning thereof, or offers to any such agent, operator, or employé any bribe, compensation, or reward, for the disclosure of any private information received by him by reason of his trust as such agent, operator, or employé, or uses, or attempts to use, any such information so obtained, is punishable as provided in section six hundred and thirty-nine of this Code.

SECTION 654 of Title XVI, Part I, to be Section 655 of that title.

SECTIONS 655 and 656 to be consolidated and numbered 656, to read as follows:

Effect of foreign law and conviction or acquittal thereunder.

Sec. 656.   An act or omission declared punishable by this Code is not less so because it is also punishable under the laws of another State, government, or country, unless the contrary is expressly declared. Whenever on the trial of an accused person it appears that, upon a criminal prosecution under the laws of another State, government, or country, founded upon the act or omission in respect to which he is on trial, he has been acquitted or convicted, it is a sufficient defense.

NOTE.—There are two sections numbered 654, and the consolidation, as above suggested, of Sections 655 and 656 into one section, to be numbered 656, permits the number 655 to be given to the second of the sections 654.

SECTION 680.   A new section to be added to read as follows:

Absentee causing crime to be committed within this State.

Sec. 680.   Every person who, being out of this State, causes, aids, advises, or encourages any person to commit a crime within this State, and is afterwards found within this State, is punishable in the same manner as if he had been within this State when he caused, aided, advised, or encouraged the commission of such crime.

SECTION 686.   To be amended to read as follows:

Sec. 686.   In a criminal action the defendant is entitled:

1. To a speedy and public trial;

2. To be allowed counsel as in civil actions, or to appear and defend in person and with counsel;

3. To produce witnesses on his behalf, and to be confronted with the witnesses against him, in the presence of the court, except that where the charge has been preliminarily examined before a committing magistrate, and the testimony taken down by question and answer in the presence of the defendant, who has, either in person or by counsel, cross-examined, or had an opportunity to cross-examine, the witness; or where the testimony of a witness on the part of the people, who is unable to give security for his appearance, has been taken conditionally in the like manner in the presence of the defendant, who has, either in person or by counsel, cross-examined, or had an opportunity to cross-examine, the witness, the deposition of such witness may be read, upon its being satisfactorily shown to the court that he is dead or insane, or cannot with due diligence be found within the State; or where the testimony of a witness has been given at a former trial, the transcript of the shorthand reporter's notes, made and certified under oath as a full, true, and correct transcription of such evidence, by the shorthand reporter who took the notes of such testimony of such witness at a former trial, may be read and received in evidence, upon it being satisfactorily shown to the court that the witness is either dead or insane, or cannot with due diligence be found within the State.

> NOTE.—This amendment allows a certified transcription of a shorthand reporter's notes of the evidence of the witness given at a former trial to be received in evidence, when it is satisfactorily shown to the court that such witness is dead, insane, or cannot with due diligence be found within the State.

SECTION 689.   To be amended to read as follows:

Sec. 689.   No person can be convicted of a public offense unless by verdict of a jury, accepted and recorded by the court, or upon a plea of guilty, or upon judgment against him upon a demurrer in the case mentioned in section ten hundred and eleven, or upon a judgment of the court, a jury having been waived in a criminal case not amounting to a felony; or upon the judgment of a court in a criminal case, where the offense charged is the violation of a municipal ordinance, as provided in section ten hundred and forty-two.

> NOTE.—The effect of the amendment is to take away the right to trial by jury for the violation of municipal ordinances.

SECTION 707.   To be amended to read as follows:

Sec. 707.   If the undertaking required by the last section is given, the party informed of must be discharged. If he does not give it, the magistrate must commit him to prison, specifying in the warrant the requirement to give security, the amount thereof, the omission to give the same, and that he be held until he give such undertaking, not exceeding six months.

SECTION 708. To be amended to read as follows:

Sec. 708.   If the person complained of is committed for not giving the undertaking required, he may be discharged by any magistrate upon giving the same, and he may be discharged at any time without giving the same, upon good cause shown therefor.

SECTION 758. To be amended to read as follows:

Sec. 758.   An accusation in writing against any officer not mentioned in section seven hundred and thirty-seven, of this Code, and against any district, county, township, or municipal officer for willful or corrupt misconduct in office, may be presented by the grand jury of the county for or in which the officer accused is elected, appointed, or performs his duties.

> NOTE.—The object of the amendment is to render all officers, other than those named in Section 737 as liable to impeachment, subject to trial for misconduct in office.

SECTION 770. To be amended to read as follows:

Sec. 770.   From a judgment of removal an appeal may be taken to the Supreme Court, in the same manner as from a judgment in a civil action; but until such judgment is reversed, the defendant is suspended from office.   Pending the appeal the office must be filled as in case of a vacancy, but the salary attached to said office shall not be payable until after the final determination of the case.

> NOTE.—The object of the amendment is to postpone the payment of the salary until the determination of the case on appeal, and is in accordance with the decision in *Ward vs. Marshall*, 96 Cal. 155.

SECTION 772. To be amended to read as follows:

Sec. 772.   When an accusation in writing, verified by the oath of any person, is presented to a Superior Court, alleging that any officer within the jurisdiction of the court has been guilty of knowingly and corruptly charging and collecting illegal fees for services rendered, or to be rendered, in his office, or has refused or neglected to perform the official duties pertaining to his office, the court must cite the party charged to appear before the court at a time not more than ten, nor less than five, days from the time the accusation was presented, and on that day, or some other subsequent day, not more than twenty days from that on which the accusation was presented, must proceed to hear, in a summary manner, the accusation, and evidence offered in support of the same, and the answer and evidence offered by the party accused; and if, on such hearing, it appears that the charge is sustained, the court must enter a decree that the party accused be deprived of his office, and must enter a judgment for five hundred dollars in favor of the informer, and such costs as are allowed in civil cases; if the charges made against the officer are not sustained, a judgment for such costs as are allowed in civil cases shall be entered against the informer in favor of the accused officer.

NOTE.—The changes in the section are, that the accusation must be that the officer has been guilty of "knowingly and corruptly" charging and collecting illegal fees for services, etc., and allowing costs against the informer where the charges are not [sustained.

SECTION 784. To be amended to read as follows:

Sec. 784. The jurisdiction of a criminal action:

1. For forcibly and without lawful authority seizing and confining another, or inveigling or kidnaping him, with intent, against his will, to cause him to be secretly confined or imprisoned, in this State, or to be sent out of this State, or from one place in this State to another, or to be sold as a slave, or in any way to be held to service; or,

2. For decoying, taking, or enticing away a child under the age of twelve years, with intent to detain and conceal it from its parents, guardian, or other person having the lawful charge of the child; or,

3. For inveigling, enticing, or taking away an unmarried female of previous chaste character, under the age of eighteen years, for the purpose of prostitution; or,

4. For taking away any female under the age of eighteen years from her father, mother, guardian, or other person having the legal charge of her person, without their consent, for the purpose either of concubinage or prostitution—Is in the county in which the offense is committed, or out of which the person upon whom the offense was committed may, in the commission of the offense, have been brought, or in which an act was done by the defendant in instigating, procuring, promoting, or aiding in the commission of the offense, or in abetting the parties concerned therein.

NOTE.—The proposed amendments of the section are in Subdivision 1, making the section conform to the amendment proposed to Section 207; and in Subdivisions 3 and 4, changing twenty-five years to eighteen years, in Subdivision 3, to conform to Section 266, and changing sixteen years to eighteen years in Subdivision 4 to conform to Section 267.

SECTION 785. To be amended to read as follows:

Sec. 785. When the offense, either of bigamy or incest, is committed in one county, and the defendant is apprehended in another, the jurisdiction is in either county; when the offense of incest is committed outside of this State, as provided in section two hundred and eighty-five, the jurisdiction is in any county in the State where the defendant is apprehended.

SECTION 789. To be amended to read as follows:

Sec. 789. The jurisdiction for committing without this State any offense which, if committed within this State, would be larceny or robbery under the laws of this State, and bringing property so obtained within this State, is in any county into or through which said property has been brought.

> Note.—The amendment is to make the section conform more strictly to the second subdivision of Section 27, and to omit therefrom any jurisdiction in our courts of the offense of knowingly receiving stolen property out of the State, and bringing the same therein, which is given by the present section. There is no section of the Code making it a crime to knowingly receive stolen goods out of the State and bring them within the State, and it is not deemed advisable to burden our courts with the trial of criminal actions in such cases.

SECTION 796.   A new section to be added to read as follows:

Jurisdiction of certain offenses committed without this State.

Sec. 796.   The jurisdiction of a criminal action for, while outside this State, causing, aiding, advising, or encouraging any person to commit a crime within this State, and of a criminal action for abduction out of this State of any person contrary to the laws of the place where such act is committed, and bringing such person within the limits of this State, is in any county in this State.

SECTION 797.   A new section to be added to read as follows:

Jurisdiction in criminal actions generally.

Sec. 797.   When not otherwise specially provided for in this Code, the jurisdiction of criminal actions for the violation of any of the provisions of this Code, is in any county in this State.

SECTION 809.   To be amended to read as follows:

Sec. 809.   When a defendant has been examined and committed, as provided in section eight hundred and seventy-two of this Code, it shall be the duty of the District Attorney, within thirty days thereafter, to file in the Superior Court of the county in which the offense is triable, an information charging the defendant with such offense, or such other offense as may be disclosed by the evidence upon which the order of commitment is made. The information shall be in the name of the People of the State of California, and subscribed by the District Attorney, and shall be in form like an indictment for the same offense.

SECTION 925.   To be amended to read as follows:

Sec. 925.   The grand jury may, at all reasonable times, ask the advice of the court, of the judge thereof, or the District Attorney; but unless such advice is asked, the judge of the court must not be present during the sessions of the grand jury. The District Attorney of the county may at all times appear before the grand jury for the purpose of giving information or advice relative to any matter cognizable by them, and may interrogate witnesses before them whenever they or he thinks it necessary; but no other person is permitted to be present during the sessions of the grand jury, except the members, and witnesses actually under examination, and no person must be permitted to be present during the expressions of their opinions or giving their votes upon any matter before them. The grand jury, or District Attorney, may however require, by subpœna, the attendance of any person before the grand jury as interpreter; and the interpreter may be present at the examination of witnesses before the grand jury.

Heading of Chapter V, Part II, Title VI, to be changed to "Designation, by Governor, of judge to try certain indictments."

SECTION 1034. To be amended to read as follows:

Sec. 1034. Application for removal must be made in open court, and in writing, verified by the affidavit of the defendant or of the District Attorney, as the case may be, a copy of which application must be served upon the adverse party at least one day prior to the hearing of the application. At the hearing the adverse party may serve and file such counter affidavits as he may deem advisable. Whenever the affidavit of the defendant shows that he cannot safely appear in person to make such application because popular prejudice is so great as to endanger his personal safety, and such statement is sustained by other testimony, such application may be made by his attorney, and shall be heard and determined in the absence of the defendant, notwithstanding the charge then pending against him be a felony, and he has not at the time of such application been arrested or given bail, or been arraigned, or pleaded or demurred to the indictment or information.

SECTION 1042. To be amended to read as follows:

Sec. 1042. The issues of fact must be tried by a jury, unless a trial by jury be waived, in criminal cases not amounting to a felony, by the consent of both parties expressed in open court, and entered in its minutes. In cases of misdemeanor arising from the violation of any municipal or county ordinance, where the offense constituted by such ordinance is neither against the public at large, nor within the legal or common law notion of a crime or misdemeanor, nor expressed in this Code, the trial shall be by the court without a jury. In other cases of misdemeanor, the jury may consist of twelve or any number less than twelve upon which the parties may agree in open court.

NOTE.—This amendment takes away the right to trial by jury in as many cases of minor offenses as is permissible under the Constitution. It is impracticable to mention all the cases to which it would apply, but the criterion given in the section will determine what offenses come within its terms. The definition is taken from the decision in *Ex parte Young You Ting*, 106 Cal. 296. The amendment to Section 689 has been proposed in this connection.

SECTION 1064. To be amended to read as follows:

Sec. 1064. When the panel is formed from persons whose names are not drawn as jurors, a challenge may be taken to the panel on account of any bias of the officer who summoned them, which would be a good ground of challenge to a juror. Such challenge must be made in the same form, and determined in the same manner, as if made to a juror; but if the court is satisfied by the oath of the officer, or otherwise, that his action has been fair and just to the defendant in summoning the jurors, the challenge shall be disallowed.

SECTION 1066 to be repealed.

NOTE.—This section provides that the defendant must be informed before a juror is called, that if he intends so to do, he must challenge an individual juror when the juror appears and before he is sworn.

SECTION 1076. To be amended to read as follows:

Sec. 1076. In a challenge for implied bias, one or more of the causes stated in section ten hundred and seventy-four must be alleged. In a challenge for actual bias, the cause stated in the second subdivision of section ten hundred and seventy-three must be alleged; but no person shall be disqualified as a juror by reason of having formed or expressed an opinion upon the matter or cause to be submitted to such jury, founded upon public rumor, statements in public journals concerning the testimony already given upon any examination, or any former trial of the case in the Superior Court, or common notoriety; *provided*, it appear to the court, upon his declaration, under oath or otherwise, that he can and will, notwithstanding such an opinion, act impartially and fairly upon the matters to be submitted to him. The challenge may be oral, but must be entered in the minutes of the court, or of the phonographic reporter.

NOTE.—The amendment renders a person competent to act as a juror, although he has read newspaper accounts of the testimony at an examination, or former trial of the case, provided that the court is satisfied he can give the defendant a fair trial.

SECTION 1121. To be amended to read as follows:

Sec. 1121. After a juror has been sworn to try the case, the court may dispense with his further attendance upon the court until the jury shall have been completed, but before being excused, he must be admonished by the court, that it is his duty not to converse with any one on any subject connected with the trial, or to form or express any opinion thereon, until the cause is finally submitted to the jury. The jurors sworn to try an action may, at any time before the submission of the cause to the jury, in the discretion of the court, be permitted to separate or be kept in charge of a proper officer. The officer must be sworn to keep the jurors together until the next meeting of the court, to suffer no person to speak to them or communicate with them, nor to do so himself, on any subject connected with the trial, and to return them into court at the next meeting thereof.

> NOTE.—The amendment gives the court the power to excuse a juror until the jury is complete. In some cases, many days are spent in obtaining a jury, and the attendance of those already selected during such time, is unnecessary.

SECTION 1171. To be amended to read as follows:

Sec. 1171. Except as provided in section eleven hundred and seventy-seven of the Code, when a party desires to have the exceptions taken at the trial settled in a bill of exceptions, the draft of the bill must be prepared by him and presented, upon notice of at least two days to the District Attorney, to the judge for settlement within ten days after judgment has been rendered against him, unless further time is granted by the judge, or by a justice of the Supreme Court, or within that period the draft must be delivered to the clerk of the court for the judge. When received by the clerk, he must deliver it to the judge, or transmit it to him at the earliest period practicable. When settled, the bill must be signed by the judge and filed with the clerk of the court. Unless presented to the judge for his signature within ten days after its settlement, or such further time as the judge, or a justice of the Supreme Court, shall grant, the bill of exceptions shall not be signed by the judge, and such bill and the presentation of the draft thereof by the party desiring its settlement, shall be disregarded.

> NOTE.—It is proposed by the amendment to make the transcription of the shorthand notes take the place of bills of exceptions in capital cases, and this amendment, with others hereinafter proposed, is intended to carry out that scheme. The amendment also requires the drafting of the bill of exceptions as settled, within ten days thereafter.

SECTION 1177. A new section to be added to read as follows:

Record in capital cases.

Sec. 1177. In every case where the judgment is of death, the official reporter, within fifteen days after the entry thereof, shall make a full and true transcription into long hand of all the evidence, including all objections, challenges, rulings thereon, and exceptions reserved at the trial, and make affidavit before an officer authorized to administer oaths, to the fullness and correctness thereof, which affidavit must be attached to such transcription and may be in the following form:

(Title of court and cause.)

State of California,

——— County of ———. } ss.

———, being first duly sworn, deposes and says: That he was the official reporter of the above-entitled court during the trial of the above-entitled action; that as such official reporter, at the trial of said action, he took full notes in shorthand of all the evidence offered by the parties thereat, including all objections, challenges, rulings thereon, and exceptions reserved, and that the foregoing transcription contains a full and correct statement of all such matters.

Subscribed and sworn to before me, this —— day of ——, 18—.

The said transcription, with the foregoing affidavit attached thereto, shall be forthwith filed with the papers in the case. Either party may, within ten days after the receipt of written notice of the filing of the said transcription, if dissatisfied therewith, move the court, upon an affidavit specifying the particulars in which it is claimed such transcription is incorrect, for an order correcting the same. Said motion shall be heard by the court at its earliest convenience, and, if granted, the court shall make an order that the transcription be amended and corrected as in said order designated, and thereupon the clerk shall amend the said transcription by making the proper changes therein in accordance with such order. If the motion is denied, an order must be made to that effect. If, for any reason, the transcription of the official reporter's notes as herein provided is not filed, a bill of exceptions may be proposed by either party within ten days after notice that such transcription has not been filed, and thereafter such proposed bill may be settled and filed, as provided in other criminal cases where the judgment is not of death.

SECTION 1180. To be amended to read as follows:

Sec. 1180. The granting of a new trial places the parties in the same position as if no trial had been had, except where the accused was charged with the commission of more than one offense, and was acquitted on such trial as to any offense charged, a new trial shall not subject him to be tried for the offense or offenses of which he was acquitted at the former trial. All the testimony must be produced anew, except as provided in section six hundred and eighty-six, and a former verdict cannot be used or referred to either in evidence or in argument.

> NOTE.—This amendment is necessary in view of the decision in *People* vs. *Gordon*, 99 Cal. 227, and in conformity with the amendment proposed of Section 686, which allows the testimony of certain witnesses given at a former trial to be offered in certain cases from the shorthand reporter's notes, taken at the former trial.

SECTION 1205. To be amended to read as follows:

Sec. 1205. A judgment that the defendant pay a fine, or that the defendant be imprisoned and also pay a fine, may also direct that he be imprisoned until the fine be satisfied, but the judgment must specify the extent of the imprisonment, which must not exceed one day for every two dollars of the fine, nor extend in any case beyond the term for which the defendant might be sentenced to imprisonment for the offense of which he has been convicted.

NOTE.—The scope of the amendment is to allow the judgment to be of both fine and imprisonment, with a provision for imprisonment to satisfy the fine, if not paid. See *Ex parte Rosenheim*, 83 Cal. 388.

SECTION 1206. To be amended to read as follows:

Sec. 1206. A judgment rendered by a Superior Court that the defendant pay a fine, with or without imprisonment, constitutes a lien as to such fine, and the clerk shall docket the same, in like manner as a judgment for money rendered in a civil action.

SECTION 1207. To be amended to read as follows:

Sec. 1207. When judgment upon a conviction is rendered, the clerk must enter the same in the minutes, stating briefly the offense for which the conviction was had, and the fact of a prior conviction (if one), and must, within five days, annex together and file the following papers, which shall constitute the record of the action:

1. The indictment or information and a copy of the minutes of the plea or demurrer;
2. A copy of the minutes of the trial;
3. The charges given or refused, and the indorsements thereon; and,
4. A copy of the judgment.

Any bill of exceptions which has been duly settled and signed by the judge, and any transcription of the evidence made and verified by the official reporter, as provided in section eleven hundred and seventy-seven of this Code, shall, when filed, or if such transcription be amended as provided in said section eleven hundred and seventy-seven, then as amended, become a part of such record.

SECTION 1214. To be amended to read as follows:

Sec. 1214. If the judgment is for a fine alone, or for a fine and imprisonment, execution may be issued thereon for the recovery of such fine, as on a judgment in a civil action.

SECTION 1217. To be amended to read as follows:

Sec. 1217. When judgment of death is rendered, a warrant signed by the judge and attested by the clerk, under the seal of the court, must be drawn and delivered to the Sheriff. It must state the conviction, the judgment, and appoint a day upon which the judgment is to be executed, which must not be less than sixty, nor more than ninety, days from the time of judgment, and must direct the Sheriff, within ten days from the time of judgment, to deliver the defendant to the warden of one of the state prisons of this State for execution, such prison to be designated in the warrant. It must also contain a direction that, if the execution be prevented from taking place at the appointed time by reason of an appeal, the judgment be executed on the third Friday of the month following the month in which the remittitur from the Supreme Court, affirming the judgment, shall be filed in the Superior Court.

SECTION 1227. To be amended to read as follows:

Sec. 1227. If, for any reason, except the taking of an appeal, or the pendency thereof, a judgment of death has not been executed, and it remains in force, the court in which the conviction is had, on the application of the District Attorney of the county in which the conviction is had, must order the defendant to be brought before it, or if he is at large, a warrant for his apprehension must be issued. Upon the defendant being brought before the court, it must inquire into the facts, and if no legal reasons exist against the execution of the judgment, must make an order that the warden of the state prison to whom the Sheriff is directed to deliver the defendant, shall execute the judgment at a specified time. The warden must execute the judgment accordingly.

SECTION 1239. To be amended to read as follows:

Sec. 1239. An appeal from a judgment must be taken within six months after its rendition, and from an order within forty days after it is made.

> NOTE.—The present section allows one year for an appeal from a judgment, and sixty days from an order.

SECTION 1243. To be amended to read as follows:

Sec. 1243. An appeal to the Supreme Court, from a judgment of conviction, stays the execution of the judgment in all criminal cases.

> NOTE.—By the amendment, an appeal stays the execution of a judgment in all criminal cases, without a certificate of probable cause. In practice, the Supreme Court always issues such certificate when the trial judge refuses to grant it. The expense of an application to a justice of the Supreme Court in such a case is considerable, especially when the conviction is had in a remote county of the State.

SECTION 1246. To be amended to read as follows:

Sec. 1246. Upon an appeal being taken, the clerk of the court with whom the notice of appeal is filed, must, without charge, transmit to the clerk of the appellate court fifteen printed copies (one of which shall be certified to and be the original) of the notice of appeal, of the record, of all bills of exceptions, and of the transcription of the official reporter, as provided in section eleven hundred and seventy-seven, within the times following:

1. Within twenty days after the filing of the notice of appeal, if before said notice is filed the bill of exceptions has been settled by the judge; but if not, then within twenty days from the settlement of the bill of exceptions;

2. Within twenty days after the filing of the notice of appeal, if a transcription of the evidence by the official reporter has been filed and the court has made an order correcting or refusing to correct the same, or the time within which notice of motion to correct the same may be given has expired, and no such motion is pending;

3. Otherwise, after the filing of such transcription and within twenty days after the expiration of the time within which a motion may be made to correct such transcription, unless a motion is made within the time allowed by law to correct such transcription, and then within twenty days from the date of the order disposing of such motion.

Upon receipt of such printed copies, the clerk of the appellate court must file the original and dispose of the copies as he is required to do in case of transcripts on appeal in civil cases. All the services of such clerks, as provided herein, must be without charge. The clerk of the lower court must also, within the time above specified, serve printed copies of the above-named papers, without charge, upon the defendant's attorney and upon the Attorney-General. The printing and transmitting of the above papers are a county charge.

SECTION 1258. To be amended to read as follows:

Sec. 1258. After hearing the appeal, the court must give judgment without regard to technical errors or defects, or to exceptions which do not affect the substantial rights of the parties; and it shall be presumed on appeal that technical errors, defects or exceptions, do not affect the substantial rights of the parties, unless the contrary clearly appears by the record on appeal.

SECTION 1305. To be amended to read as follows:

Sec. 1305. If, without sufficient excuse, the defendant neglects to appear for arraignment, or for trial, or judgment, or upon any other occasion when his presence in court may be lawfully required, or to surrender himself in execution of the judgment, the court must direct the fact to be entered upon its minutes, and the undertaking of bail, or the money deposited instead of bail, as the case may be, is thereupon forfeited. But if at any time within twenty days after such entry in the minutes, the defendant or his bail appear and satisfactorily excuse his neglect, the court may direct the forfeiture of the undertaking or of the deposit to be discharged upon such terms as may be just.

> NOTE.—The amendment proposed is to render certain within what time the defendant or his bail may excuse his neglect in failing to appear. The present section provides that they may appear "before the final adjournment of the court." The amendments proposed to the two sections following are on account of the same phraseology contained therein.

SECTION 1306. To be amended to read as follows:

Sec. 1306. If the forfeiture is not discharged, as provided in the last section, the District Attorney may, at any time after twenty days from the entry upon the minutes, as provided in the last section, proceed by action against the bail upon their undertaking.

SECTION 1307.   To be amended to read as follows:

Sec. 1307.   If, by reason of the neglect of the defendant to appear, money deposited instead of bail is forfeited, and if the forfeiture is not discharged or remitted, the clerk with whom it is deposited must immediately, upon the expiration of twenty days from the entry upon the minutes, as provided in section thirteen hundred and five, pay over the money so deposited to the County Treasurer.

SECTION 1475.   To be amended to read as follows:

Sec. 1475.   The writ of habeas corpus may be granted:

1. By the Supreme Court, or any justice thereof, upon petition by or on behalf of any person restrained of his liberty in this State.   When so issued, it may be made returnable before the court, or any justice thereof, or before any Superior Court, or any judge thereof;

2. By the Superior Court, or a judge thereof, upon petition by or on behalf of any person restrained of his liberty, in their respective counties; but where a person is restrained of his liberty, under an order made, or a judgment rendered, by any such judge, the writ must be made returnable before such judge, unless the Supreme Court, or a justice thereof, shall otherwise direct.

SECTION 1567.   To be amended to read as follows:

Sec. 1567.   When it is necessary to have a person imprisoned in the state prison brought before any court, or a person imprisoned in the county jail brought before a court sitting in another county, an order for that purpose must be made by the court, and executed by the Sheriff of the county where it is made.

PROPOSED AMENDMENTS TO THE
CIVIL CODE.

SECTION 8.   To be repealed.

NOTE.—The provisions of this section are included in Section 7.

SECTION 9.   To be amended to read as follows:

Sec. 9.   All other days than those mentioned in the preceding section, are to be deemed business days for all purposes.

SECTION 35.   To be amended to read as follows:

Sec. 35.   In all cases other than those specified in sections thirty-six and thirty-seven, the contract of a minor, if made whilst he is under the age of eighteen years, may be disaffirmed by the minor himself, either before his majority or within a reasonable time afterwards, not exceeding three years; or, in case of his death, within that period, by his heirs or personal representatives; and if the contract be made by the minor, whilst he is over the age of eighteen years, it may be disaffirmed in like manner upon restoring the consideration to the party from whom it was received, or by paying its equivalent.

NOTE.—The amendment places a limit of three years upon *what* shall be deemed a reasonable time for disaffirmance of a minor's contract, after attaining majority. ·

SECTION 105.   To be amended to read as follows:

Sec. 105.   Willful neglect is the neglect of the husband to provide for his wife the common necessaries of life, he having the ability to do so; or it is the failure to do so by reason of idleness, profligacy, or dissipation.   In no case shall the fact that the wife earns her own living, affect the question of willful neglect on the part of the husband.

NOTE.—The case of *Rycraft* vs. *Rycraft*, 42 Cal. 444, following *Washburn* vs. *Washburn*, 9 Cal. 475, establishes the rule that if the wife's earnings are sufficient to provide her with the common necessaries of life, no divorce can be granted her under either of the two classes of conduct constituting willful neglect under this section. The result of the rule is that a wife who voluntarily remains in idleness, throwing herself upon the charity of friends or relatives for the common necessaries of life, can obtain a divorce from the husband who will not provide such necessaries, while the wife who supports herself by honest labor can not legally complain.

SECTION 106. To be amended to read as follows:

Sec. 106. Habitual intemperance is that degree of intemperance from the use of intoxicating drinks, morphine, chloral, or other narcotic drugs, which disqualifies a person a great portion of the time from properly attending to business, or which would reasonably inflict a course of great mental anguish upon an innocent party.

SECTION 123. To be amended to read as follows:

Sec. 123. Condonation of a cause of divorce, shown in the answer as a recriminatory defense, is a bar to such defense, unless the condonation be revoked, as provided in section one hundred and twenty-one of this Code, or within two years after such condonation, or unless the cause of divorce against which the recrimination shall be shown shall not have accrued or become complete within two years after such condonation.

> NOTE.—The amendment renders clear the rule that condonation unrevoked for two years, without the commission of acts by the condonee, during such time, amounting to a cause of divorce, completely obliterates the condoned matrimonial offense.

SECTION 144. To be repealed.

SECTION 165. To be amended to read as follows:

Sec. 165. A full and complete inventory of the separate personal property of the wife may be made out and signed by her, acknowledged or proved in the manner required by law for the acknowledgment or proof of a grant of real property by an unmarried woman, and recorded in the office of the Recorder of the county in which the parties reside; and such making and recording shall be equivalent to the immediate delivery and actual and continued change of possession of the personal property transferred, as required by section thirty-four hundred and forty of this Code, in transfers of personal property from husband to wife, where such personal property continues to be used in common by the spouses.

> NOTE.—This amendment makes the recording of the inventory of the wife's separate property equivalent to the immediate delivery, and actual and continued change of possession, required by Section 3440, in transfers of personal property, when such transfer is made by the husband to the wife of property used in common by them. The amendment is desirable in view of the fact that thereunder, when personal property in the possession of the husband is given to the wife, and they continue to use the same together, the rights of creditors will be better protected than they are now. In *Morgan* vs. *Ball*, 81 Cal. 93, the transfer of a horse and buggy from husband to wife, accompanied with no change of possession, and no circumstance to inform the creditors of such change of possession, other than the fact that after such transfer the personal property was considered in the neighborhood as belonging to the wife, was sustained. Ordinarily, a gift of personal property by husband to wife, which they use in common, is not accompanied by any change in the possession thereof, and it is desirable to provide some means whereby intending creditors can readily determine whether such a gift has been made. The recording of the inventory will accomplish this result.

SECTION 169. To be amended to read as follows:

Sec. 169. The earnings and accumulations of the wife, and of her minor children living with her, or in her custody, while she is living separate from her husband, by agreement, or on account of any conduct of his constituting, or which, if continued, would constitute, a cause of divorce, are the separate property of the wife.

NOTE.—The present section makes the wife's earnings, when living apart from her husband without any fault of his, her separate property. At the same time, the accumulations of the husband are community property, although the wife may have deserted him. It also offers an inducement to the wife to abandon her husband, as her earnings then become her separate property.

SECTION 172. To be amended to read as follows:

Sec. 172. The husband has the management and control of the community property, with the like absolute power of disposition, other than testamentary, as he has of his separate property; except that any gift of the community property, or any part thereof, made by him with a fraudulent intent to deprive the wife of her rights therein, is void.

NOTE.—The effect of the amendment of 1891, restricting the making of gifts by the husband of community property, has been to require the joining of the wife in all deeds of the husband, where made for a valuable consideration and affecting his separate property. The amendment will obviate this necessity, and, at the same time, protect the interests of the wife.

SECTION 203. To be amended to read as follows:

Sec. 203. The abuse of parental authority is the subject of judicial cognizance in a civil action brought by the child, or by his relatives within the third degree, or by the supervisors of the county where the child resides; and when the abuse is established, the child may be freed from the dominion of the parent, and the duty of support and education enforced. In such action the court shall have power to make all such provisional orders as may be necessary to protect the interests, or insure the safety, of the child, including an order placing the child in the custody of a person other than the parent until the suit is determined.

NOTE.—By this amendment, the power of the court is made clear to take the child from the custody of the parent, pending the determination of the suit. By the amendment and that proposed to Section 1747 of the Code of Civil Procedure, all proceedings to determine the right of the parent to the custody of the child must be by action under this section. Under Section 1747 of the Code of Civil Procedure as proposed to be amended, the court has the power, in a summary manner, to appoint a guardian of the estate of a minor when deemed expedient, but not to deprive a parent of his custody.

SECTION 230. To be amended to read as follows:

Sec. 230. The father of an illegitimate child, by publicly acknowledging it as his own, receiving it as such, with the consent of his wife, if he is married, into his family, and otherwise treating it as if it were a legitimate child, thereby adopts it as such for all purposes except

4—C

succession, and such child is thereupon deemed, for all other purposes legitimate from the time of its birth. The foregoing provisions of this chapter do not apply to such an adoption.

> NOTE.—The effect of this amendment is that an illegitimate child cannot take by succession from his father unless he is adopted by judicial decree, or in accordance with Section 1387 of the Civil Code.

SECTION 264. To be amended to read as follows:

Sec. 264. Every minor of the age of fourteen years and over, with the consent of the persons or officers hereinafter mentioned, may, of his own free will, bind himself, in writing, to serve as clerk, apprentice, or servant, in any profession, trade, or employment; and such binding shall be as valid and effectual as if such minor was of full age at the time of making the engagement, except as hereinafter in this title provided.

SECTION 265. To be amended to read as follows:

Sec. 265. Such consent shall be given:

1. By the father of the minor. If he be dead, or be not of legal capacity to give his consent, or if he shall have adandoned his family for one year, without making provision for their support, or if he shall have become an habitual drunkard, or vagrant; then,

2. By the mother. · If the mother be dead, or be not of legal capacity to give such consent or refusal; then,

3. By the guardian of such minor. If such minor have no parent living, or none in a legal capacity to give such consent, and there be no guardian; then,

4. By a judge of the Superior Court of the county in which such minor resides; *provided*, that if the child be an illegitimate child, the consent of the mother alone shall be necessary; *provided further*, that the power of the mother to bind her child, whether legitimate or illegitimate, shall cease upon her subsequent marriage, and shall not be exercised by her or her husband at any time during her marriage, without the approval of a judge of the Superior Court of the county wherein he or she resides; and such consent shall be signified in writing, by the person entitled to give the same, by certificate at the end of, or indorsed upon, the indentures.

SECTION 266. To be amended to read as follows:

Sec. 266. If the right of consent of a mother to apprenticeship, because of the husband's incompetency, abandonment of his family, habitual drunkenness, or vagrancy, as provided in the preceding section, shall be disputed by the father, upon such dispute being brought to the attention of the Superior Court by petition of the father, it shall be the duty of the Superior Court to summarily try the question. If the court find that the mother had a right to give such consent, the father shall pay all the costs of the proceeding; but if the court find otherwise, the indenture of apprenticeship is void.

SECTION 268. To be amended to read as follows:

Superior Court may bind in certain cases.

Sec. 268. When any minor who is poor, homeless, chargeable to the county, or an outcast, has no visible means of obtaining an honest livelihood, the Superior Court of the county where he is found shall have power to bind him as an apprentice, subject to the provisions of this title, until, if a male, he arrives at the age of twenty-one years, and if a female, she arrives at the age of eighteen years.

SECTION 269. To be amended to read as follows:

Indentures, what to contain.

Sec. 269. Indentures shall be signed, sealed, and delivered, in duplicate, in the presence of all of the parties concerned; and when made with the approbation of the Superior Court, such approbation shall be certified in writing, indorsed upon each copy of the indenture. One copy of the indenture shall be kept for the use of the minor by his parent or guardian (when consented to by them respectively), but when made with the approbation of the Superior Court, one copy shall be deposited in the safe-keeping of the clerk of said court for the use of the minor. The other copy shall be held by the master, and delivered up to the minor at the expiration of his term of service.

SECTION 271. To be amended to read as follows:

Indentures, conditions in.

Sec. 271. Every sum of money paid or agreed for, with or in relation to the binding out of any clerk, apprentice, or servant, shall be inserted in the indentures; and all considerations of clothes or money paid or allowed by the master, are the sole property of the apprentice, and the master is accountable to him for the same, and shall pay and account to the apprentice alone therefor.

SECTION 272. To be amended to read as follows:

Indentures to contain the obligations of master.

Sec. 272. The indentures shall contain the age of the apprentice, and an agreement on the part of the person to whom such child is bound that he will cause such child to be instructed to read and write, and to be taught the general rules of arithmetic, and in lieu thereof that he will send such child to school for at least three months of each year during the period of his apprenticeship; and in all indentures approved by the Superior Court for binding out an orphan, or homeless minor, as an apprentice, there shall be inserted among other covenants, and in addition to those provided for in this title, that the master to whom such minor shall be bound shall give him requisite instructions in the different branches of his trade or calling, and at the expiration of the term of service shall give him one hundred dollars in gold coin, and suitable clothing in value not less than fifty dollars gold coin.

SECTION 273.   To be amended to read as follows:

Treatment of apprentices.

Sec. 273.   It shall be unlawful for any master to remove an apprentice out of this State, and it shall be the duty of the master to treat the apprentice with fairness.   The Superior Court shall hear the complaints of apprentices who reside within the county, alleging undeserved or immoderate correction, insufficient allowance of food, raiment, or lodging, or alleging want of instruction in the different branches of their trade or calling, or that they are in danger of being removed out of the State, or any violation of the indenture of apprenticeship; and the court may hear and determine such cases, and make such order therein as will relieve the party in the future.

SECTION 277.   A new section to be added to read as follows:

Discharge of apprentices.

Sec. 277.   No indenture of apprenticeship, made in pursuance of this title, shall bind the minor after the death of the master; but the apprenticeship shall be thenceforth discharged, and the minor may be bound out anew.

SECTION 278.   A new section to be added to read as follows:

Court may discharge apprentice.

Sec. 278.   The Superior Court shall have power, where circumstances require it, to discharge an apprentice from his apprenticeship, and in case any money, or other thing, has been paid or contracted to be paid by either party in relation to such apprenticeship, the court shall make such order concerning the same as shall seem just and reasonable. Whenever any master of an apprentice shall wish to remove out of this State, or to quit his trade or business, he shall appear with his apprentice before the Superior Court of the proper county, and if the court be satisfied that the master has done justice to the said apprentice for the time he has had charge of the same, the court shall have power to discharge the apprentice from the service of such master.

SECTION 279.   A new section to be added to read as follows:

Liability of master.

Sec. 279.   Every master shall be liable to an action on the indenture for the breach of any covenant on his part therein contained; and all damages recovered therein, after deducting the necessary charges in prosecuting the same, shall be the property of the minor, and shall be applied and appropriated to his use by the person who shall recover the same, and shall be paid to the minor upon his reaching majority; and if such action is not brought during the minority of such minor, it may be commenced in his own name at any time within two years after coming of age.

SECTION 280. A new section to be added to read as follows:

Action against apprentice for neglect.

Sec. 280. An apprentice who shall be guilty of gross misbehavior, or refusal to do his duty, or willful neglect thereof, shall render himself liable to the complaint of the master in the Superior Court of the county wherein he resides, which complaint shall set forth the circumstances of the case, and contain a prayer that the master be discharged from the indenture of apprenticeship, and for the costs of suit; and the court shall hear and determine the case, and may render judgment that the master be discharged from the indenture of apprenticeship, and for the costs of suit. An execution thereupon may be issued against the minor, and the amount thereof may be recovered in an action brought against him after he has reached his majority.

> NOTE.—The provisions of the Act of April 3, 1876, are inconsistent with nearly all of the Code provisions upon the subject of "Master and Servant." Notwithstanding their virtual repeal, the Legislature, in 1880, amended the Code sections in several particulars, leaving the law on this subject in a very indefinite condition. The above amendments, commencing with Section 264, aim to incorporate all the provisions of that Act into the Code, retaining the unrepealed sections of the Code consistent therewith.

SECTION 291. To be amended to read as follows:

Sec. 291. The articles of incorporation of any railroad, wagon-road, telegraph, or telephone organization, must also state:

1. The kind of road, or telegraph, or telephone, intended to be constructed;

2. The place from and to which it is intended to be run, and all the intermediate branches;

3. The estimated length of the road, or telegraph, or telephone line;

4. That at least ten per cent of the capital stock subscribed has been paid in to the treasurer of the intended corporation.

SECTION 293. To be amended to read as follows:

Sec. 293. Each intended corporation named in section two hundred and ninety-one, before filing articles of incorporation, must have actually subscribed to its capital stock, for each mile of the contemplated work, the following amounts, to wit:

1. One thousand dollars per mile of railroad;
2. One hundred dollars per mile of telegraph or telephone lines;
3. Three hundred dollars per mile of wagon-roads.

SECTION 299. To be amended to read as follows:

Sec. 299. No corporation hereafter formed shall purchase, locate, or hold property in any county of this State (except in the county where its articles of incorporation have been filed), without filing a copy of the copy of its articles of incorporation filed in the office of the Secretary of State, duly certified by such Secretary of State, in the office of the County Clerk of the county in which such property is situated, within sixty days after such purchase or location is made. Every corporation now in existence, whether formed under the provisions of this Code or not, must, within ninety days after the passage of this section, file such certified copy of the copy of its articles of incorporation in the office of the County Clerk of every county in this State in which it holds property (except the county where the original articles of incorporation are filed); and if any corporation hereafter acquires any property in any county other than that in which it now holds property, it must, within ninety days thereafter, file with the Clerk of such county such certified copy of the copy of its articles of incorporation. The copies so filed with the several County Clerks, and certified copies thereof, shall have the same force and effect in evidence as would the originals. Any corporation failing to comply with the provisions of this section shall not maintain or defend any action or proceeding in relation to such property, its rents, issues, or profits, until such articles of incorporation, and such certified copy of its articles of incorporation, and such certified copy of the copy of its articles of incorporation, shall be filed at the places directed by the general law and this section; *provided,* that all corporations shall be liable in damages for any and all loss that may arise by the failure of such corporation to perform any of the foregoing duties within the time mentioned in this section; *and provided further,* that the said damages may be recovered in any action brought in any court of this State of competent jurisdiction, by any party or parties suffering the same.

> NOTE.—The amendment obviates the necessity, under the present section, of filing a copy of the copy of the articles of incorporation with the County Clerk of the county where the original articles are filed, when the corporation desires to acquire property in that county.

SECTION 301. To be amended to read as follows:

Sec. 301. Every corporation formed under this title must, within one month after filing articles of incorporation, adopt a code of by-laws for its government, not inconsistent with the constitution and laws of this State, nor unreasonable in their practicable operation. The assent of stockholders representing a majority of all the subscribed capital stock, or of a majority of the members, if there be no capital stock, is necessary to adopt by-laws, if they are adopted at a meeting called for that purpose; and in the event of such meeting being called, two weeks' notice of the same, by advertisement in some newspaper published in the county in which the principal place of business of the corporation is located, or, if none is published therein, then in a paper published in an adjoining county, must be given by order of the acting president. The written assent of the holders of two thirds of the stock, or of two thirds of the members, if there be no capital stock, shall be effectual to adopt a code of by-laws without a meeting for that purpose.

NOTE.—This amendment requires the by-laws to be reasonable in their practical operation, in addition to the present requirement of the Code that they shall be consistent with the constitution and laws of this State. (*People* vs. *Home Savings Bank*, 104 Cal. 649.)

SECTION 303. To be amended to read as follows:

Sec. 303. A corporation may, by its by-laws, where no other provision is specially made, provide for—

1. The time, place, and manner of calling and conducting its meetings;

2. The number of stockholders or members constituting a quorum;

3. The mode of voting by proxy;

4. The time of the annual election for directors, and the manner of giving notice thereof;

5. Compensation and duties of officers;

6. The number, designation, manner of election, and the tenure of office of all officers other than the directors;

7. Suitable penalties for violation of by-laws, not exceeding, in any case, one hundred dollars for any one offense;

8. The time of regular meetings of directors and the mode of calling special meetings of directors;

9. The issuance of certificates for stock prior to full payment, under such restriction and for such purposes as may be proper; and the disposition of the stock of the corporation which may be purchased by it at sales to pay delinquent assessments;

10. The newspaper in which all notices of the meetings of stockholders or board of directors, notice of which is required shall be published, which must be some newspaper published in the county where the principal place of business of the corporation is located, or if none is published therein, then in a newspaper published in an adjoining county; *provided*, that when the by-laws prescribe the newspaper in which said publication shall be made, if from any cause at the time any publication is desired to be made, the publication of such newspaper shall have ceased, the board of directors may, by an order entered

on the records of the corporation, direct the publication to be made in some other newspaper published in the county, or if none is published therein, then in an adjoining county.

NOTE.—The effect of this amendment is to gather into one section the different matters which may be ordinarily provided for in the by-laws of a corporation.

SECTIONS 317 and 318 to be incorporated into one section to be numbered 317, to read as follows:

Meeting by consent, and proceedings thereat, to be binding.

Sec. 317.   When all the stockholders or members of a corporation are present at any meeting, however called or notified, and sign a written consent thereto on the record of such meeting, the acts and proceedings of such meeting are as valid as if had at a meeting regularly called and noticed.   The stockholders or members of such corporation, when so assembled, may elect officers, fill all vacancies then existing, and may act upon such other business as might lawfully be presented at regular meetings.

SECTION 319.   To be numbered 318.

SECTION 320.   To be numbered 319.

The present two sections numbered 321 to be repealed.

SECTION 320.   A new section to be added to read as follows:

Books and notice of directors and stockholders of banks.

Sec. 320.   Every corporation doing a banking business in this State must keep in its office, in a place accessible to the stockholders, depositors, and creditors thereof, and for their use, a book containing a list of all stockholders in such corporation, and the number of shares of stock held by each; and every such corporation must keep posted in its office, in a conspicuous place, accessible to the public generally, a notice signed by the president or secretary, showing:

1. The names of the directors of such corporation;
2. The number and value of shares of stock held by each director.

The entries on such book and such notice shall be made and posted within twenty-four hours after any transfer of stock, and shall be conclusive evidence against each director and stockholder of the number of shares of stock held by each.   The provisions of this section shall apply to all banking corporations formed or existing before twelve o'clock noon of the day on which this Code took effect, as well as to those formed after such time.

SECTION 321. A new section to be added to read as follows:

Change of principal place of business.

Sec. 321. Every corporation that has been, or may be, created under the general laws of this State, may change its principal place of business from one place to another in the same county, from one city or county to another city or county, within this State. Before such change is made, the consent, in writing, of the holders of two thirds of the capital stock, or a majority of the members, if there be no capital stock, must be obtained and filed in the office of the corporation. When such consent is obtained and filed, notice of the intended removal or change must be published at least once a week for three successive weeks in some newspaper published in the county wherein said principal place of business is situated, if there is one published therein, if not, in a newspaper of an adjoining county, giving the name of the county or city where it is situated, and that to which it is intended to remove it.

> NOTE.—The amendments proposed to Section 317 and the above consist merely in consolidating Sections 317 and 318, so as to leave room in the chapter for separate numbers for the two Sections 321, passed in 1876, and a change in the second Section 321, requiring the consent of a majority of the members to the change of the principal place of business of corporations, where there is no capital stock.

SECTION 323. To be amended to read as follows:

Sec. 323. All corporations for profit must issue certificates for stock when fully paid up, signed by the president and secretary, and must issue such certificates when not fully paid up under such restriction and for such purposes as their by-laws may provide.

> NOTE.—This amendment removes from the section the provision that the by-laws may provide for the issuance of certificates prior to full payment, as that provision is incorporated in Section 303 by the proposed amendment thereto.

SECTION 342. To be amended to read as follows:

Sec. 342. The person offering at such sale to pay the assessment and costs for the smallest number of shares or fraction of a share is the highest bidder, and the stock purchased must be transferred to him on the stock-books of the corporation, and a certificate issued to him thereof on payment of the assessment and costs. A certificate of any shares unsold of a certificate offered for sale shall be issued to the person whose stock has been offered for sale, and thereupon the secretary shall cancel the former certificate by proper and appropriate entries in the records of the corporation.

SECTION 349. To be amended to read as follows:

Sec. 349. On the day specified for declaring the stock delinquent, or at any time subsequent thereto, and before the sale of the delinquent stock, the board of directors may elect to waive further proceedings under this chapter for the collection of delinquent assessments, or any part or portion thereof, and may elect to proceed by action to recover the amount of the assessment and the costs and expenses already incurred, or any part or portion thereof; but the provisions of this section shall not apply to any stock fully paid.

NOTE.—The amendment takes away the right of action upon an assessment against the stockholders whose stock is fully paid, thus restricting corporations in such case to a sale of the stock to pay any delinquent assessment.

SECTION 360.   To be amended to read as follows:

Sec. 360.   No corporation shall acquire or hold any more real property than may be reasonably necessary for the transaction of its business, or the construction of its works, except as otherwise specially provided. A corporation may acquire real property, as provided in title seven, part three, Code of Civil Procedure, when needed for any of the uses and purposes mentioned in said title.   By unanimous consent of its members or stockholders, any corporation existing under the laws of this State may acquire and hold the lot and house in which its business is carried on, and may improve the same to any extent required for the convenient transaction of its business.

NOTE—The amendment adds to the section the provisions of the Act of April 1, 1876, authorizing corporations to own and improve property in which their business is carried on.

SECTION 362.   To be amended to read as follows:

Sec. 362.   Any corporation may amend its articles of incorporation by a majority vote of its board of directors or trustees, and by a vote or written assent of the stockholders representing at least two thirds of the subscribed capital stock of such corporation, or the written assent of a majority of the members, if there be no capital stock; and a copy of the articles of incorporation as thus amended, duly certified to be correct by the president and secretary of the board of directors or trustees of such corporation, shall be filed in the office where the original articles of incorporation are required by this Code to be filed, and also in the office of the Secretary of State, and from the time of so filing such copy of the amended articles of incorporation, such corporation shall have the same powers, and it, and the stockholders thereof, shall thereafter be subject to the same liabilities, as if such amendment had been embraced in the original articles of incorporation; *provided*, that the time of the existence of such corporation shall not be by such amendment extended beyond the time fixed in the original articles of incorporation; *provided further*, that such original and amended articles of incorporation shall together contain all the matters and things required by the law under which the original articles of incorporation were executed and filed; *and provided further*, that nothing herein contained shall be construed to cure or amend any defect existing in any original articles of incorporation heretofore filed by reason that such articles did not set forth the matters required to make the same valid at the time of filing; *and also provided*, that if the assent of two thirds of the stockholders to such amendment has not been obtained, a notice of the intention to make the amendment shall first be advertised for thirty days in some newspaper published in the town, or county, or city and county, in which the principal place of business of the corporation is located, before the filing of the proposed amendment; *and provided also*, that nothing in this section shall be construed to authorize any corporation to diminish its capital stock.

> NOTE.—The present section provides that any corporation may amend "its articles of association or certificate of incorporation," but, as a matter of law and fact, no corporation has any articles of association, and if there be such a thing as a certificate of incorporation, it is obviously something which the corporation has no power to amend. Section 289 mentions the only instrument by which a private corporation can be formed, and it is called "Articles of Incorporation." If there is any paper which may properly be styled a certificate of incorporation it is that certificate mentioned in Section 296, which the Secretary of State is required to issue. This certificate obviously cannot be amended by the corporation, because it is not its act, and Section 362 surely did not contemplate that upon the amendment of its articles of incorporation a new and amended certificate should be issued by the Secretary of State. Again, the section provides that "a copy of the said articles of association, or certificate of incorporation, as thus amended, shall be filed in the office or offices where the original articles of incorporation are required by the Code to be filed," but, as before intimated, the Code does not require any "articles of association," nor any "certificate of incorporation, to be filed." The amendment proposed will remove the above objections.

SECTION 388. To be amended to read as follows:

Franchises may be sold under execution.

Sec. 388. For the satisfaction of any judgment against a corporation, its franchise, and all the rights and privileges thereof, may be levied upon and sold under execution in the same manner and with like effect as any other property; except that such sale shall not relieve the franchise, or property held thereunder, from the liabilities of the judgment debtor contracted or incurred in the operation, use, or enjoyment of such franchise, or any of its privileges.

> NOTE.—This amendment permits the sale under execution of a franchise of a corporation, restricting the effect thereof as provided in Article XII, Section 10, of the Constitution.

SECTION 392. To be amended to read as follows:

Sec. 392. A corporation may, at any time within one year after such sale, redeem the franchise by paying or tendering to the purchaser thereof the sum paid therefor, with ten per cent interest thereon; and upon such payment or tender, the franchise, and all rights and privileges thereof, revert and belong to the corporation, as if no such sale had been made.

SECTION 418. To be amended to read as follows:

Sec. 418. If any insurance corporation is under liabilities for losses to an amount equal to its capital stock, and the president or directors, after knowing the same, make any new or further insurance, all who make such insurance, or assent thereto, and their heirs, executors, and administrators, are jointly and severally liable for the amount of any loss which takes place under such insurance.

SECTION 431. A new section to be added to read as follows:

Form of fire insurance policies.

Sec. 431. On and after the first day of September, eighteen hundred and ninety-seven, no fire insurance company, corporation, or association, its officers or agents, shall make, issue, use, or deliver for use, any fire insurance policy on property in this State, other than such as shall conform, in all particulars, as to blanks, size of type, context, provisions, agreements, and conditions, with the printed form of contract or policy to be filed in the office of the Insurance Commissioner, as provided for in section six hundred and thirty-five of the Political Code, and no other or different provision, condition, agreement, or clause, shall, in any manner, be made a part of said contract or policy, or be indorsed thereon, or delivered therewith, except as follows, to wit:

1. The name of the company, its location or place of business, the date of its incorporation or organization, and the state or country under which the same is organized; the amount of paid-up capital stock, whether it is a stock or mutual company, the names of its officers, the number and date of the policy; and if it be issued through a manager or agent of the company, the words "this policy shall not be valid until countersigned by the duly authorized manager or agent of the company at ——," may be printed on policies issued on property in this State;

2. Printed or written forms of description and specification or schedules of the property covered by any particular policy, and any other matter necessary to clearly express all the facts and conditions of insurance on any particular risk (which facts or conditions shall in no case be inconsistent with, or a waiver of, any of the provisions or conditions of the standard policy provided for in the Political Code), may be written upon or attached or appended to any policy issued on property in this State;

3. A company, corporation, or association, organized or incorporated under and in pursuance of the laws of this State, or elsewhere, if entitled to do business in this State, may, with the approval of the Insurance Commissioner, if the same is not already included in the standard form to be filed in the office of said commissioner, as provided for in section six hundred and thirty-five of the Political Code, print, on its policies,

any provision which it is required, by law, to insert therein, if such provision is not in conflict with the laws of this State, or of the United States, or of the provisions of the standard form provided for in the Political Code; but said provision or provisions shall be printed apart from the other provisions, agreements, or conditions of the policy, and in type not smaller than the body of the policy, and under a separate title, as follows: "Provisions required by law to be stated in this policy," and be a part of said policy;

4. There may be indorsed on the outside of any policy herein provided for, the name, with the word "agent" or "agents," and place of business of any insurance agent or agents, either by writing, printing, stamping, or otherwise;

5. Where two or more companies, each entitled to do business in this State, unite to issue a joint policy, there may be expressed in the heading of such policy the fact of the severalty of the contract; also, the proportion of premium to be paid to each company, and the proportion of liability which each company agrees to assume, and in the printed conditions of such policy the necessary change may be made from the singular to the plural number, when reference is had to the company issuing such policy;

Provided, that any policy made, issued, or delivered, not in conformity with this section, shall nevertheless be binding upon the company issuing the same, and such company shall thereafter be disqualified from doing any insurance business in this State.

NOTE.—The proposed section, taken in connection with the proposed Section 635 of the Political Code, enacts substantially the law of New York requiring all policies of fire insurance to be uniform. The desirability of such requirement is apparent when the multiplicity of forms of policies in use, and the fact that the insured seldom reads the conditions of his policy, are considered.

The effect of a uniform policy of insurance will be that, when a person once understands its provisions, he can obtain other policies with a certainty that there is nothing therein contained of which he is not aware. New York was the first State to adopt such a law, and its operation has been satisfactory.

SECTION 444. To be amended to read as follows:

Sec. 444. Life, health, and accident insurance corporations may invest their capital stock as follows:

1. In loans upon unincumbered and improved real property within the State of California, which shall be worth at the time of the investment at least forty per cent more than the sum loaned;

2. In the purchase of or loans upon interest-bearing bonds, and other securities of the United States and of the State of California;

3. In the purchase of or loans upon interest-bearing bonds of any of the other States of the Union, or of any county, or incorporated city, or city and county, or school district in the State of California;

4. In the purchase of or loans upon any stocks of corporations formed

under the laws of this State, except of mining corporations, which shall have, at the time of the investment, a value, in the City and County of San Francisco, of not less than sixty per cent of their par value, and shall be rated as first-class securities;

But no loans shall be made on any securities specified in subdivisions three and four of this section, in any amount beyond sixty per cent of the market value of the securities, nor shall any loan be made on the stock of the corporation, or notes or other obligations of its corporators.

NOTE.—The amendment allows the investment of the capital stock of life, health, and accident insurance corporations to be made in interest-bearing bonds of school districts of California.

SECTION 445. To be amended to read as follows:

Sec. 445. The corporation may, by its by-laws, limit the number of shares which may be held by any one person, and make such other provisions for the protection of the stockholders and the better security of those dealing with it as to a majority of the stockholders may seem proper, not inconsistent with the constitution and laws of the State, nor unreasonable in their practical operation.

SECTION 467. To be amended to read as follows:

Sec. 467. If at any time after the location of the line of the railroad, and the filing of the maps and profiles thereof, as provided in the preceding section, it appears that the location can be improved, the directors may, as provided in subdivision seven of section four hundred and sixty-five, alter or change the same, and cause new maps and profiles to be filed, showing such changes, in the same offices where the originals are on file, and may proceed, in the same manner as the original location was acquired, to acquire and take possession of such new line, and must sell or relinquish the lands owned by them for the original location, within five years after such change; *provided, however,* that forthwith upon such change being made, the lands acquired by the corporation under the right of eminent domain shall revert to the original owners thereof, or their successors in interest.

NOTE.—The new provision made by the amendment is that when the corporation changes the line of its road all property which was obtained by eminent domain for the portion of the road abandoned shall revert to the original owners or their successors in interest.

SECTION 472. To be amended to read as follows:

Sec. 472. Whenever the track of such railroad crosses a railroad or highway, such railroad or highway may be carried under, over, or on a level with the track, as may be most expedient; and in cases where an embankment or cutting necessitates a change in the line of such railroad or highway, the corporation may take such additional lands and material as are necessary for the construction of such road or highway on such new line. If such other necessary lands cannot be had otherwise, they may be condemned as provided in title seven, part three, Code of Civil Procedure; and when compensation is made therefor, the same becomes the property of the corporation. In all such cases it is the duty of the corporation to restore the highway to its former condition, so as not to interfere materially with its use for the convenience of the public.

SECTION 492. To be amended to read as follows:

Sec. 492. The legislative or other body to whom is intrusted the government of the county, city and county, city, or town, under such regulations, restrictions, and limitations, and upon such terms and payment of license tax as the county, city and county, city, or town authority may provide, may grant franchises for the construction of elevated or underground railroad tracks over, across, or under the streets and public highways of any such county, city and county, city, or town, for a term not exceeding fifty years; *provided*, that before granting such franchise there shall be presented to such legislative or other body a petition signed by the owners of a majority of the landed property, other than public property, on the line of said elevated portion applied for. The provisions of this section shall apply to all railroad companies heretofore or hereafter incorporated.

NOTE.—The amendment incorporates therein the provisions of Section 493.

SECTION 493. A new section to be added to read as follows:

Non-operation of railroads—Forfeiture.

Sec. 493. From and after the completion of any railroad, or the completion of such portion thereof capable of being operated, it shall be the duty of the corporation or individual owning the same, to operate it; and upon the failure of said corporation or individual so owning said road to keep the same, or any part thereof, in full operation for the period of six months, its or his right to operate the same, in whole or in part, as the case may be, shall be forfeited; and the lands occupied for the purposes of its or his road, so far as the same shall not be operated, shall revert to the original owners, or their successors in interest. A railroad shall be deemed to be in full operation when one passenger train, or one mixed train, is run over it once each day in each direction, and a sufficient number of freight trains to accommodate the traffic on said road.

SECTION 494. A new section to be added to read as follows:

Prevention of operation—Duty of Railroad Commissioners.

Sec. 494. The preceding section shall not be construed to apply to a case where the operation of the road is prevented by the act of God, nor to a case where the operation of said road, together with its branch or trunk lines, does not yield income sufficient to defray the expenses of maintaining and operating the same in connection with its said branch or trunk line. The Railroad Commissioners of the State of California shall have the power to examine and determine the question whether said road, together with its said branch and trunk lines, does or does not yield income sufficient to operate the same.

NOTE.—The two last preceding proposed sections contain the provisions of the Act of April 15, 1880, to compel railroad corporations and individuals owning railroads to operate their roads. (See Stats. 1880, p. 43.)

The heading of Title VII, Part IV, Division I, to be amended to read: "Telegraph and Telephone Corporations."

SECTION 536. To be amended to read as follows:

Sec. 536. Telegraph or telephone corporations, when they have acquired their franchises from counties, cities and counties, cities, and towns, as provided by law, and in conformity therewith, may construct lines of telegraph or telephone along and upon any public road or highway, along or across any of the waters or lands within this State, along, upon, or across which such franchises are so acquired, and may erect poles, posts, piers, or abutments for supporting the insulators, wires, and other necessary fixtures of their lines, in such manner and at such points as not to incommode the public use of the road or highway, or interrupt the navigation of the waters.

SECTION 537. To be amended to read as follows:

Persons liable for damages for injuring telegraph and telephone property.

Sec. 537. Any person who injures or destroys, through want of proper care, any necessary or useful fixtures of any telegraph or telephone corporation, is liable to the corporation owning the same for all damages sustained thereby. Any vessel which, by dragging its anchor or otherwise, breaks, injures, or destroys the sub-aqueous cable of a telegraph or telephone corporation, subjects its owner to the damages hereinbefore specified.

SECTION 538. To be amended to read as follows:

Damages, willful and malicious injury.

Sec. 538. Any person who willfully and maliciously does any injury to any telegraph or telephone property mentioned in the preceding section is liable to the corporation owning the same for one hundred times the amount of actual damages sustained thereby, to be recovered in any court of competent jurisdiction.

Section 539.   To be amended to read as follows:

Conditions on which damage to sub-aqueous cable may be recovered.

Sec. 539.   No telegraph or telephone corporation can recover damages for the breaking or injuring of any sub-aqueous telegraph or telephone cable, unless such corporation has previously erected, on either bank of the waters under which the cable is placed, a monument, indicating the place where the cable lies, and publishes for one month in some newspaper most likely to give notice to navigators, a notice giving the description and the purpose of the monuments, and the general course, landings, and termini of the cable.

Section 540 to be amended to read as follows:

May dispose of certain rights.

Sec. 540.   Any telegraph or telephone corporation may, at any time, with the consent of the persons holding two thirds of the issued stock of the corporation, sell, lease, assign, transfer, or convey any rights, privileges, franchises, or property of the corporation, except its corporate franchise; *provided,* that this section shall not be so construed as to permit the leasing or alienation of any franchise by any such corporation, so as to relieve the franchise or property held thereunder from the liabilities of the lessor or grantor, lessee or grantee, contracted or incurred in the operation, use, or enjoyment of such franchise, or any of its privileges.

> Note.—The amendments to the five preceding sections consist merely in placing telephone companies on the same footing with telegraph companies in relation to the construction and maintenance of their lines.

Section 548.   To be repealed.

> Note.—The section is in conflict with Section 19, Article XI, of the Constitution.

Section 549.   To be repealed.

> Note.—The section is unconstitutional.

Section 550.   To be repealed.

> Note.—The section is unconstitutional.

Section 565.   To be amended to read as follows:

Annual report to be published.

Sec. 565.   The actual financial condition of all homestead corporations must, by the directors thereof, be published annually in a newspaper published at the principal place of business of the corporation, for four weeks, if published in a weekly, and two weeks, if published in a daily.   The statement must be made up to the end of each year, and must be verified by the oath of the president and secretary, showing the items of property and liabilities.

5—c

SECTION 571. To be amended to read as follows:

Organization of savings and loan corporations—On what terms may loan money, how, and to whom, and how long.

Sec. 571. Corporations organized for the purpose of accumulating and loaning the funds of their members, stockholders, and depositors, may loan and invest the funds thereof, receive deposits of money, loan, invest, and collect the same, with interest, and may repay depositors with or without interest. No such corporation must loan money, except on adequate security on real or personal property, and such loan must not be for a longer period than six years. No savings and loan corporation shall do business under the same management as, or in the same banking house with, any other banking institution.

> NOTE.—The amendment prohibits savings banks from doing business in conjunction with any other banking institution.

SECTION 574. To be amended to read as follows:

Property which may be owned, and how disposed of.

Sec. 574. Savings and loan corporations may purchase, hold, and convey real and personal property, as follows:

1. The lot and building in which the business of the corporation is carried on, the cost of which must not exceed one hundred thousand dollars; except, on a vote of two thirds of the stockholders, the corporation may increase the sum to an amount not exceeding two hundred and fifty thousand dollars;

2. Such as may have been mortgaged, pledged, or conveyed to it in trust, for its benefit in good faith, for money loaned in pursuance of the regular business of the corporation;

3. Such as may have been purchased at sales under pledges, mortgages, or deeds of trust made for its benefit, for money so loaned, and such as may be conveyed to it by borrowers in satisfaction and discharge of loans made thereon;

4. No such corporation must purchase, hold, or convey real estate in any other case or for any other purpose; and all real estate described in subdivision three of this section must be sold by the corporation within five years after the title thereto is vested in it by purchase or otherwise;

5. No such corporation must purchase, own, or sell personal property, except such as may be requisite for its immediate accommodation for the convenient transaction of its business, mortgages on real estate, bonds, securities, or evidences of indebtedness, public or private, gold and silver bullion, and United States mint certificates of ascertained value, and evidences of debt issued by the United States;

6. No such corporation must purchase, hold, or convey bonds, securities, or evidences of indebtedness, public or private, except bonds of the United States, of the State of California, and of the counties, cities,

cities and counties, towns, or school districts of the State of California, unless such corporation has a capital stock or reserved fund paid in of not less than three hundred thousand dollars.

> NOTE.—The amendment authorizes the purchase of school district bonds by savings and loan corporations irrespective of the amount of their capital stock.

SECTION 585. To be repealed.

> NOTE.—The section refers to the procedure enacted by Section 584, which was repealed in 1875.

SECTION 588. A new section to be added, to read as follows:

Books and reports of mining corporations.

Sec. 588. It shall be the duty of the secretary of every corporation formed under the laws of this State for the purpose of mining, to keep a complete set of books, showing all receipts and expenditures of such corporation, the sources of such receipts, and the object of such expenditures, and also all transfers of stock. All books and papers shall at all times, during business hours, be open to the inspection of any bona fide stockholder; and if any stockholder shall at any time so request, it shall be the duty of the secretary to attend at the office of said company at least one hour in the day out of regular business hours, and exhibit such books and papers of the company as such stockholder may desire, and such stockholder shall be entitled to be accompanied by an expert; and he shall also be entitled to make copies or extracts from any such books or papers. It shall be the duty of the directors, on the first Monday of each and every month, to cause to be made an itemized account or balance-sheet for the previous month, embracing a full and complete statement of all disbursements and receipts, showing from what sources such receipts were derived, and for what and to whom such disbursements or payments were made, and for what object or purpose the same were made; also all indebtedness or liabilities incurred or existing at the time, and for what the same were incurred, and the balance of money, if any, on hand. Such account or balance-sheet shall be verified under oath by the president and secretary, and posted in some conspicuous place in the office of the company. It shall be the duty of the superintendent, on the first Monday of each month, to file with the secretary an itemized account, verified under oath, showing all receipts and disbursements made by him for the previous month, and for what said disbursements were made. It shall also be the duty of the superintendent to file with the secretary a weekly statement, under oath, showing the number of men employed under him and for what purpose, and the rate of wages paid to each one. He shall attach to such account a full and complete report, under oath, of the work done in said mine, the amount of ore extracted, from what part of the mine taken, the amount sent to mill for reduction, its assay value, the amount of bullion received, the amount of bullion shipped to the office of the company or elsewhere, and the amount, if any, retained by the superintendent. It shall also be his duty to forward to the office of the company a full report, under oath, of all discoveries of ores or mineral-bearing quartz made in said mine, whether by boring, drifting, sinking, or otherwise, together with the assay value thereof. All accounts, reports, and correspondence from the superintendent shall be kept in some conspicuous place in the office of said company, and be open to the inspection of all stockholders.

SECTION 589.   A new section to be added to read as follows:

Examination of grounds by stockholders.

Sec. 589.   Any bona fide stockholder of a corporation formed under the laws of this State for the purpose of mining shall be entitled to visit, accompanied by his expert, and examine, the mine or mines owned by such corporation, and every part thereof, at any time he may see fit to make such visit and examination; and when such stockholder shall make application to the president of such corporation, he shall immediately cause the secretary thereof to issue and deliver to such applicant an order, under the seal of the corporation, directed to the superintendent, commanding him to show and exhibit such parts of said mine or mines as the party named in said order may desire to visit and examine. It shall be the duty of the superintendent, on receiving such order, to furnish such stockholder every facility for making a full and complete inspection of said mine or mines, and of the workings therein; it shall be his duty also either to accompany said stockholder in person, or to furnish some person familiar with said mine or mines to accompany him in his visit to and through such mine or mines, and every part thereof.   In case of the failure or refusal of the superintendent to obey such order, such stockholder shall be entitled to recover in any court of competent jurisdiction, against said corporation, the sum of one thousand dollars and traveling expenses to and from said mine as liquidated damages, together with costs of suit.   In case of such refusal, it shall be the duty of the directors of such corporation forthwith to remove the officer so refusing, and thereafter he shall not be employed, directly or indirectly, by such corporation, and no salary shall be paid to him.

SECTION 590.   A new section to be added to read as follows:

Penalty for refusal to permit examination of grounds, and for failure to make and post reports.

Sec. 590.   In case of the refusal or neglect of the president to cause to be issued by the secretary the order in the preceding section mentioned, such stockholder shall be entitled to recover against said president the sum of one thousand dollars and costs. In case of the failure of the directors to have the reports and accounts current made and posted as provided in section five hundred and eighty-eight, they shall be liable, either severally or jointly, to an action by any stockholder, in any court of competent jurisdiction, complaining thereof, and on proof of such refusal or failure, such complaining stockholder shall recover judgment for one thousand dollars liquidated damages, with costs of suit.

NOTE.—The foregoing three proposed new sections contain the provisions of the Act for the protection of stockholders in California mining corporations, approved March 30, 1874 (Stats. 1873-4, p. 866).

SECTION 591. A new section to be added to read as follows:

Certain acts of directors unlawful, unless two thirds of capital stock consent thereto.

Sec. 591. It shall not be lawful for the directors of any mining corporation to sell, lease, mortgage, or otherwise dispose of the whole or any part of the mining ground owned or held by such corporation, or to purchase or obtain, in any way, any additional mining ground, unless such act be ratified by the holders of at least two thirds of the capital stock of such corporation. Such ratification may be made either in writing, signed and acknowledged by such stockholders, or by resolution, duly passed at a stockholders' meeting called for that purpose.

SECTION 592. A new section to be added to Title XI, Division I, Part IV, to read as follows:

Stock to be in the name of real owner or trustee, and how voted.

Sec. 592. All stock in each and every mining corporation in this State shall stand in the books of said company, in all cases, in the names of the real owners of such stock, or in the names of the trustees of such real owners; but in every case where such stock shall stand in the name of a trustee, the party for whom he holds such stock in trust shall be designated upon said books, and also in the body of the certificate of such stock. And it shall not be lawful for any such corporation, or the secretary thereof, to close the books of said corporation more than two days prior to the day of any election. At such election the stock of said corporation shall be voted by the bona fide owners thereof, as shown by the books of said corporation, unless the certificate of stock, duly indorsed, be produced at such election, in which case said certificates shall be deemed the highest evidence of ownership, and the holder thereof shall be entitled to vote the same.

Title XII, Division I, Part IV, to be changed to " Corporations organized for purposes other than pecuniary profit."

SECTION 602. To be amended to read as follows:

Sec. 602.   Whenever the rules, regulations, or discipline of any religious denomination, society, or church so require, for the administration of the temporalities thereof, and the management of the estate and
property thereof, it shall be lawful for the bishop, chief priest, or presiding elder of such religious denomination, society, or church to become
a sole corporation, in the manner prescribed in this title, as nearly as
may be, and with all the powers and duties, and for the uses and purposes in this title provided for religious incorporations, and subject to
all the conditions, limitations, and provisions in said title prescribed.
Every corporation sole shall, however, have power to contract in the
same manner and to the same extent as a natural person, and may sue
and be sued, and may defend, in all courts and places, in all matters
and proceedings whatever, and shall have authority to borrow money,
and give promissory notes therefor, and to secure the payment thereof
by mortgage or other lien upon property, real or personal; and to buy,
sell, lease, mortgage, and in every way deal in real and personal property to the same extent and in the same manner that a natural person
may, and without the order of any court.   The articles of incorporation to be filed shall set forth the facts authorizing such incorporation,
and declare the manner in which any vacancy occurring in the incumbency of such bishop, chief priest, or presiding elder is required by the
rules, regulations, or discipline of such denomination, society, or church
to be filled, which statement shall be verified by affidavit, and for proof
of the appointment or election of such bishop, chief priest, or presiding
elder, or of any succeeding incumbent of such corporation, it shall be
sufficient to record with the clerk of the county in which such bishop,
chief priest, or presiding elder resides the original or a copy of his
commission, or certificate, or letters of election or appointment, duly
attested; *provided*, all property held by such bishop, chief priest, or
presiding elder shall be in trust for the use, purpose, and behoof of his
religious denomination, society, or church.   The limitation in section
five hundred and ninety-five shall not apply to corporations formed
under this section, when the land is held or used for churches, hospitals,
schools, colleges, orphan asylums, parsonages, or cemetery purposes.
Any judge of the Superior Court in the county in which any corporation
is formed under this chapter shall at all times have access to the books
of such incorporation.   Any corporation sole heretofore organized and
existing under the laws of this State may elect to continue its existence
under this title by filing a certificate to that effect, under its corporate
seal and the hand of its incumbent, or amended articles of incorporation, in the form required by this title, and as prescribed by section two
hundred and eighty-seven of this Code; and from and after the filing
of such certificate or amended articles, such corporation shall be entitled

to the privileges and subject to the duties, liabilities, and provisions in this title expressed.

SECTION 603. To be repealed.

NOTE.—An attempt was made to repeal this section by the Act of March 11, 1887, the repealing Act mentioning Section 604 instead of Section 603 of the Code.

TITLE XIV. The heading thereof to be amended to read as follows:

Agricultural fair, coöperative and business corporations, and corporations for the extension and promotion of trade and commerce, and for the advancement, protection, and improvement of mechanic arts and sciences.

SECTION 623. A new section to be added to read as follows:

Coöperative business corporations, and by-laws thereof.

Sec. 623. A coöperative business corporation can be formed for the purpose of conducting any lawful business, and of dividing a portion of its profits among persons other than its stockholders, under division first, part four, title one, of this Code, and the by-laws thereof, in addition to the matters enumerated in section three hundred and three of this Code, may provide for the number of votes to which each stockholder shall be entitled, and the amount of profits which shall be divided among persons other than stockholders, and the manner in which, and the persons among whom, such division shall be made.

NOTE.—This section contains the provisions of the Act of April 1, 1878. (Stats. 1877-8, p. 883.)

SECTION 624. A new section to be added to read as follows:

Formation of chambers of commerce, boards of trade, mechanic institutes, and other kindred associations.

Sec. 624. Corporations for the organization of chambers of commerce, boards of trade, mechanic institutes, and other associations for the extension and promotion of trade and commerce, and for the advancement, promotion, and improvement of the mechanical arts and sciences, may be formed under the provisions of this title; and such corporations, and the members thereof, shall be subject to the liabilities imposed by this title, and to none other. Any twenty or more persons, who may desire to form a corporation for any of the purposes specified in this section, shall make, sign, and acknowledge, before some officer competent to take acknowledgments of deeds, and file in the office of the County Clerk of the county in which the principal place of business of the corporation is intended to be located, and a certified copy thereof in the office of the Secretary of State, articles of incorporation, in which shall be stated the corporate name of the corporation, the object for which the corporation shall be formed, the time of the existence, not to exceed fifty years, the name of the city, or town, and county, in which the principal place of business of the corporation is to be located; and, if the right to exercise the corporate powers of the corporation is confined to a board of directors, board of trustees, or to a body to be styled the executive committee of the corporation, the articles of incorporation shall state that fact, and whether the right is limited, or otherwise, and the names of those who shall have been selected to manage the affairs of the corporation for the first six months. If it is desired that such corporation shall have a capital stock, the articles of incorporation shall also contain a statement of the amount of such capital stock, and the number of shares into which it is divided. Upon the filing of a certified copy of the articles of incorporation with the Secretary of State, he must issue to the corporation, over the great seal of the State, a certificate, that a copy of the articles, containing the required statement of facts, has been filed in his office; and thereupon the persons signing the articles, and their associates and successors, shall be a body politic and corporate, by the name stated in the certificate, and for a term not to exceed fifty years.

SECTION 625. A new section to be added to read as follows:

By-laws of such corporation.

Sec. 625. The by-laws of corporations formed under the preceding section shall determine the manner of calling and conducting the meetings of the corporation, the number of members that shall constitute a quorum, the manner of levying and collecting assessments, the officers of the same, the manner of their election or appointment, and their tenure of office, and may prescribe penalties for the violation of their by-laws, not to exceed in any case one hundred dollars for any one offense. The by-laws of all corporations formed under the provisions of the preceding section, without capital stock, shall prescribe how the officers, agents, and servants shall be elected or appointed.

SECTION 626. A new section to be added to read as follows:

The rights and powers of such corporations.

Sec. 626. Corporations formed under section six hundred and twenty-four of this Code shall have power to lease, purchase, hire, hold, use, take possession of, or enjoy in fee simple, or otherwise, any personal or real estate, within this State, necessary for the uses and purposes of such corporation, and to sell, lease, deed in trust, alien, or dispose of the same at their pleasure. All real estate owned by such corporation shall be held in the name of the same, and all conveyances made by such corporation shall be signed by the president and secretary, and attested by the corporate seal; *provided*, that no such corporation shall engage in any mercantile, commercial, or mechanical business. Such corporation shall have power to confer upon the board of directors, board of trustees, or upon a body to be known as the executive committee of the corporation, the right to exercise all or any portion of the corporate powers of the corporation.

SECTION 627. A new section to be added to read as follows:

Other rights and powers of such corporations.

Sec. 627. Corporations formed under the provisions of section six hundred and twenty-four of this title shall have power:

1. To sue and be sued in any court;

2. To make and use a common seal, and alter the same at pleasure;

3. To elect or appoint such officers, agents, or servants, as the business of the corporation shall require;

4. To make by-laws not inconsistent with the constitution and laws of this State, nor unreasonable in their practical operation, for the organization of the corporation and the management of its affairs.

Corporations formed under section six hundred and twenty-four of this title, if they have a capital stock, shall determine by their by-laws the relative rights of stockholders and members at large.

NOTE.—The four proposed preceding sections contain the material provisions of the Act of March 31, 1866, to provide for the formation of chambers of commerce, boards of trade, mechanic institutes, and other kindred associations. (See Stats. 1866, p. 469.)

SECTION 628. To be repealed.

NOTE.—The section conflicts with Article XI, Section 19, of the Constitution.

TITLE XVI. To be amended to read as follows:

TITLE XVI.

BUILDING AND LOAN ASSOCIATIONS.

SECTION 633. *What are building and loan associations—Commissioners may determine.*

Sec. 633. The name ".building and loan association," and all reference to the same as "association" or "associations," as used in this title, shall include all corporations, societies, or organizations, investment companies, or associations, whether organized in this State or represented by agents, doing a savings and loan or investment business, and which are not under the direct supervision of the Bank Commissioners or the Insurance Commissioner, and whether issuing certificates of stock which mature at a time fixed in advance or not, and shall also include any association or company which is based on the plan of building and loan associations, and which contains features similar to

such associations, and the Commissioners of the Building and Loan
Associations are hereby vested with the power of determining whether
such association or associations contain such features as are based on
plans similar to those of building and loan associations, and whether
they properly come within the purview of this title.

SECTION 634. *Corporations may be formed—What articles shall contain—Capital stock, and how paid in.*

Sec. 634. Corporations may be formed subject to the provisions of
this title, and with all the rights, duties, and powers herein specified.
Such corporations shall be known as mutual building and loan associations, and the words "mutual building and loan association" shall
form part of the name of every such corporation. The articles of incorporation, in setting forth the purposes for which the corporation is
formed, shall state that it is formed to encourage industry, frugality,
home building among the stockholders; the accumulation of savings;
the loan to its stockholders of the funds so accumulated, with the profits
and earnings; and the repayment to each stockholder of his savings
and profits when they have accumulated to a certain sum, or at any
time when he shall desire the same, as provided in the by-laws, or when
the corporation shall desire to repay the same; and shall also state that
it is formed for all the purposes specified in this title.

The capital stock of such corporations shall be paid in by the stockholders in regular, equal, periodical payments, at such times and in
such amounts as shall be provided in the by-laws. Such periodical
payments shall be called dues. And at or before a time to be stated in
the by-laws, each stockholder shall pay to the corporation, upon each
share of stock held by him, such an amount of dues as the by-laws
shall provide; and the payment of dues shall so continue on each share
of stock issued till it reaches its matured value, or is withdrawn, canceled, or forfeited. The capital stock shall consist, primarily, of the
accumulated dues paid in, and secondarily, of such profits as may be
apportioned to such shares whenever such dues and profits shall be
sufficient to mature the shares of any particular series. The full-paid
capital stock of such association shall in no case exceed two million
dollars. It shall be divided into shares of matured or par value of one
hundred dollars or two hundred dollars each, as shall be provided in
the articles of incorporation and fixed by the by-laws. Certificates of
stock shall be issued to each stockholder on the first payment of dues
by him. The shares shall be issued in yearly, half-yearly, or quarterly
series, in such amounts in each series, and at such times, as shall be
determined by the board of directors. No shares of a prior series shall
be issued after the issuing of shares in a new series. Shares which have
not been pledged as a security for the repayments of a loan shall be

called free shares. Shares that have been so pledged shall be called pledged shares. All stock matured and surrendered or canceled in any series shall become the property of the corporation, and may be issued in any subsequent series. Payment of dues on shares of stock in each series shall commence from the time that shares began to be issued in such series. Any such corporation shall have power by its by-laws to impose and collect a fine from each stockholder, not exceeding ten per cent of the defaulted amount, for any failure, neglect, or refusal to make his payments of dues on the regular payday specified. On any default in the payment of interest, premium, or fees, or on the failure, neglect, or refusal of any borrower to refund any moneys advanced by the association to protect the mortgaged property from the action of mechanics' liens or tax liens (other than taxes on said mortgage), or a failure or refusal to repay money advanced for the payment of insurance premiums or other similar charges against the mortgaged property, the association shall have power to levy a fine, not exceeding five per cent on such defaulted amount. On the cumulative amount of such dues, delinquencies, and advances upon which a first fine of five or ten per cent may have been imposed, the association shall have power to levy a fine, not exceeding two per cent, on each succeeding regular payday after the first, during such default. Every such corporation shall also have power to charge an entrance fee upon each share of stock issued, not exceeding ten cents on each share, and may also charge a transfer fee, not exceeding ten cents on each share, all of which shall be paid into the treasury and accounted for as all other funds of the association. Payment of dues or interest may be made in advance, but no association shall allow interest on such advance payments at a greater rate than six per cent per annum, nor for a longer period than one year.

SECTION 635. *Free shares—How may be withdrawn.*

Sec. 635. The directors may, at their discretion, under the regulations prescribed in their by-laws, retire the free shares of any series of stock, at any time after four years from the date of their issue, by enforcing the withdrawal of the same; but whenever there shall remain in any series at the expiration of five years after the date of its issue, an excess above one hundred free shares of the par value of two hundred dollars each, or two hundred free shares of the par value of one hundred dollars each, then it shall be the duty of the directors to retire annually twenty-five per cent of such excess existing at said expiration of five years after the date of its issue, so that no more than one hundred free shares shall remain in such series at the expiration of nine years from the date of its issue; *provided,* that no more than one half of the monthly receipts shall be used for that purpose; and thereafter the directors may, in their discretion, retire such other free shares as they consider it to the best interest of the association to retire; *provided,* that whenever, under the provisions of this section, the withdrawal of shares is to be enforced, the shares to be retired shall be determined by lot, drawn from all free shares in the series, as shall be regulated by the by-laws, and the holders thereof shall be paid the amount actually paid in, and the full amount of earnings at the date of last apportionment of profits.

SECTION 636.   *Proceedings when stock matured—Moneys, how loaned—Premium—Interest.*

Sec. 636.   When the stock in any series shall have reached its matured value, payment of dues thereon shall cease, and all the stockholders in such series who have borrowed from the association shall be entitled to have their securities returned to them, and a satisfaction of the mortgages made by them to the association; and the holders of free shares of stock in such series shall be paid, out of the funds of the association, the matured value thereof, with such rate of interest as shall be determined by the by-laws, from the time the board of directors shall declare such shares to have been matured, until paid; but at no time shall more than one third of the receipts of the association be applicable to the payment of matured shares without the consent of the board of directors.   The order of the payment of the matured shares shall be determined by the by-laws.

The moneys in the hands of the treasurer, and such sums as may be borrowed by the corporation for the purpose, shall be loaned out in open meeting to the member who shall bid the highest premium, or may be loaned out at such premium as may be fixed, from time to time, by the board of directors; and the premium may be deducted from the amount of the loan, or such proportion may be deducted as the by-laws shall provide, and in that case the balance of said premium shall be payable in such installments as the by-laws shall determine; *provided, however,* that where the premium is payable in installments, the number of installments into which the same is divided shall be uniformly applicable to all loans made by the corporation, and shall be payable at the times and in the manner as provided in the by-laws; *and provided further,* that in no case shall the amount loaned exceed the matured value of the shares pledged to secure the loan.

The rate of interest on all loans may be fixed by the by-laws, but in case the by-laws fail to fix the rate, then it shall be fixed from time to time by the board of directors.   For every loan made, a note or obligation secured by a first mortgage upon unincumbered real estate shall be given, accompanied by a transfer and pledge to the association of the shares borrowed upon, as collateral security for the repayment of the loan; or, in lieu of the mortgage, there may be pledged and transferred to the association, for the payment of the loan, free shares, the withdrawal value of which under the by-laws, at the time of such borrowing, shall exceed the amount borrowed and interest thereon for six months. At the discretion of the board of directors, a borrower may repay a loan, and all arrears of interest and fines thereon at any time upon the surrender of the shares pledged for the loan.

SECTION 637. *Member in arrears—Proceedings on.*

Sec. 637. Whenever any member shall be six months in arrears in the payment of his dues upon free shares, the secretary shall give him notice thereof, in writing, and a statement of his arrearages, by mailing the same to him at the last post office address given by him to the association, and if he shall not pay the same within two months thereafter, the board of directors may, at their option, declare his shares forfeited; and at the time of such forfeiture the withdrawal value thereof shall be determined and stated, and the defaulting member shall be entitled to withdraw the same without interest, upon such notice as shall be required of a withdrawing shareholder. Whenever a borrowing member shall be six months in arrears in the payment of his dues, or interest, or premium, the whole loan shall become due at the option of the board of directors, and they may proceed to enforce collection upon securities held by the association. The withdrawal value, at the time of the commencement of the action, of all shares pledged as collateral security for the loan, shall be applied to the payment of the loan, and said shares, from that time, shall be deemed surrendered to the association.

SECTION 638. *Associations may purchase property and borrow money— Profits and losses may be apportioned.*

Sec. 638. Any such association may purchase at any sale, public or private, any real estate upon which it may have a mortgage, judgment, lien, or other incumbrance, or in which it may have an interest; and may sell, convey, lease, or mortgage the same at pleasure to any person or persons, and may borrow money for the purpose of making loans or paying withdrawals. Profits and losses shall be apportioned at least annually, and shall be apportioned to all the shares in each series outstanding at the time of such apportionment, according to the actual value of such shares as distinguished from their withdrawal value.

SECTION 639. *Who may become member—Shares exempt from execution—Stockholders may withdraw upon notice—Withdrawal value of shares; how paid.*

Sec. 639. Any person of the age of majority and of sound mind may become a member of the association by taking one or more shares therein, and subscribing to the by-laws and annexing to his signature his post office address. A minor may hold shares in the name of the parent, guardian, or next friend, as trustee. The shares of stock in any such corporation held by any person, to the value of one thousand dollars, shall be exempt from execution.

Stockholders desiring to withdraw from any association, or to surrender a part or all of their stock, shall have power to do so by giving thirty days' notice, in writing, of such intention to withdraw. On the expiration of such notice, the stockholder so withdrawing shall be entitled to receive the full amount paid in by him or her, together with such proportion of the earnings thereon as the by-laws may provide, or as may have been fixed by the board of directors; *provided*, that no more than one half of the monthly receipts in any one month shall be applied to withdrawals for that month, without the consent of the board of directors, and no shareholder shall be permitted to withdraw whose stock is pledged as security to the association for a loan until such loan is fully paid. Such withdrawals shall be paid in succession, in the order in which the notices are given. All payments on shares, and such portion of profits as the by-laws or board of directors may provide to be paid to withdrawing members, shall be construed as partial payments on the note or other obligation given by the borrower, in the event that the borrower elects and is permitted to discharge his obligation before maturity. Interest shall be payable on the full amount of the loan until paid. For the purposes of taxation, the cancellation value of the mortgage on the first Monday in March of each year (the amount that would be required at that time to cancel said loan if paid off, the shares being surrendered) shall constitute the assessable value of said mortgage.

SECTION 640. *Associations may insure the lives of members and debtors.*

Sec. 640. Such corporations may insure, in some life insurance company incorporated under the laws of this State, the lives of its members and debtors. In case of death of a debtor or member so insured, the amount recovered on the policy must be applied to extinguish the indebtedness, including the premium paid, and the residue, if any, must be paid to the legal representative of the decedent.

SECTION 641. *Secretary must prepare and file annual statement—Two associations may consolidate.*

Sec. 641. The secretary of any such corporation must, at least once in each year during the existence of the corporation, ·prepare a full and explicit statement showing the condition of the financial affairs thereof at twelve o'clock meridian on the first Monday of March of each year, comprising a balance-sheet, statements of receipts and expenditures, profit and loss, and assets and liabilities, which must be audited and verified by two competent persons (not directors), and, as to the value of the assets, be verified by a majority of the directory thereof, elected by the general body of shareholders, and be countersigned by the president and secretary. A copy of such statement must be printed and circulated among the members, and appear immediately after the annual meeting of the corporation, daily at least one week, or weekly at least four weeks, in one or more newspapers published at the place of the principal business of the corporation, and a copy thereof must be filed in the office of the Assessor of the county where such publication is made. Any two or more such corporations may unite and become incorporated in one body, with or without any dissolution or division of the funds of such corporation, or either of them; or any such corporation may transfer its engagements, funds, and property to any other such corporation, upon such terms as may be agreed upon by two thirds of the members of each of such bodies present at general meetings of the members convened for the purpose by notice, stating the object of the meeting, sent through the post office to every member, and by general notice appearing daily at least one week, or weekly at least two weeks, in some newspaper published at the place of the principal business of the corporation; but no such transfer can prejudice any right of any creditor of either corporation.

SECTION 642. *Foreign associations must deposit fifty thousand dollars with State officer for security of members in this State.*

Sec. 642. No mutual building and loan association, or company, association, or corporation organized under the laws of any other State or Territory, to carry on a business of a like character to that authorized by this title, shall be allowed to do business or to sell their stock in this State, without first having deposited with the State Controller or Secretary of State the sum of fifty thousand dollars in money, or in United States bonds, or in municipal bonds of this State, or in mortgages upon real estate located within this State, as a guarantee fund for the protection and indemnity of residents of the State of California with whom such company, association, or corporation shall do business. The fund so deposited shall be paid by the custodian thereof to the residents of California only, and not then until proof of claim, by final judgment, has been filed with the custodian of said fund against such foreign company, association, or corporation. Any of the securities so deposited may be withdrawn at any time upon others, herein provided for, of like amount, being substituted in lieu thereof. Any person or persons who shall be found in this State as agent, or in any other capacity representing such foreign company, association, or corporation which has not complied with the provisions of this section, shall be deemed guilty of a misdemeanor, and upon conviction shall be punished by a fine not exceeding one thousand dollars, or by imprisonment in a county jail for not exceeding twelve months, or by both such fine and imprisonment.

SECTION 643. *Building and Loan Commissioners, their salaries and secretary.*

Sec. 643. All building and loan associations heretofore or hereafter incorporated under the laws of this State, or of any other State or Territory, or those of any foreign country, and doing business in this State, shall be subject to the examination and supervision of a Board of Commissioners of Building and Loan Associations, which board shall consist of two commissioners, each of whom shall be an expert of accounts, and shall be appointed by the Governor, within thirty days after the passage of this title, to hold office for the period of four years, and until their successors are appointed and qualified. The commissioners shall each receive a salary of twenty-four hundred dollars per annum and necessary traveling expenses, not to exceed for the two commissioners and their secretary the sum of seven hundred dollars per annum. Said commissioners are hereby authorized to appoint a secretary, at a salary not to exceed twelve hundred dollars per annum, who shall have power to examine the books and affairs of the associations, the same as the commissioners. All said salaries and traveling expenses shall be audited by the State Controller, and paid in the same manner as the salaries of other state officers. The commissioners shall have their office in San Francisco, which office shall be kept open for business every business day, and during such hours as are commonly observed by the banks of that city as banking hours. They shall procure rooms for their office at a monthly rental not exceeding forty dollars. They may also provide fuel, stationery, printing, and other necessary conveniences connected with their office, not to exceed an aggregate cost of four hundred dollars per annum. All expenses authorized in this section shall be audited and paid in the same manner as the salary of the commissioners. The commissioners, before entering upon the duties of their office, must each execute an official bond in the sum of five thousand dollars, and take the oath of office as prescribed by the Political Code for state officers in general. The secretary appointed by said commissioners shall execute a bond in the sum of two thousand dollars, and take the oath of office as prescribed by said Political Code.

SECTION 644. *Powers and duties of commissioners.*

Sec. 644. The duties of the Commissioners of Building and Loan Associations shall be, to furnish to all corporations legally authorized to transact the business of a building and loan association within this State a license authorizing them to transact the business of a building and loan association for one year from the date of said license; to receive, and place on file in their office, the annual reports required to be made by building and loan associations by this title; to supply each association with blank forms and such statements as the commissioners may require; to make, on or before the first day of October of each year, a tabulated report to the Governor of this State, showing the condition of all institutions examined by them, with such recommendations as they may deem proper, accompanied by a detailed statement, verified by oath, of all moneys received and expended by them since their last report.

The commissioners shall visit, once in every year, and as much oftener as they may deem expedient, every building and loan association doing business in this State. At such visits they shall have free access to the vaults, books, and papers, and shall thoroughly inspect and examine all the affairs of each of said corporations, and make such inquiries as may be necessary to ascertain its condition and ability to fulfill all its engagements, and whether it has complied with the provisions of law governing such associations; they shall preserve, in a permanent form, a full record of their proceedings, including a statement of the condition of each of said corporations, which shall be open to the inspection of the public during their office hours.

To facilitate the examinations of the commissioners as specified in this title, every association shall keep a book of records, written in ink, showing the appraised values of the real estate security held in connection with each loan, and signed in each case by the appraiser, or officer or committee of the association making such estimated value. The commissioners shall have power to order a re-valuation of the securities of any building and loan association when they deem it necessary, and may, for that purpose, appoint local appraisers at the expense of such association, the total expense of such appraisement not to exceed two dollars and fifty cents for each piece of property examined and appraised. Each appraiser shall make a sworn report to the commissioners of the appraised values of all property examined.

Either of the commissioners may summon all trustees, officers, or agents of any such corporation, and such other witnesses as he thinks proper, in relation to the affairs, transactions, and condition of the corporation, and for that purpose may administer oaths; and whoever refuses, without justifiable cause, to appear and testify when thereto required, or obstructs a commissioner in the discharge of his duty, shall be punished by a fine not exceeding one thousand dollars, or by imprisonment not exceeding one year, or by both such fine and imprisonment.

SECTION 645. *Commissioners shall notify Governor and Attorney-General when associations in unsafe condition—Attorney-General shall institute suit—Appoint receiver.*

Sec. 645. If the commissioners, upon examination of any corporation under their supervision, find that such corporation has been violating the provisions of law governing such associations, or is conducting

6—c

its business in an unsafe manner, such as to render its further proceeding hazardous to the public, or to those having funds in its custody, they shall notify the Governor and the Attorney-General of such facts, and the Attorney-General, in his discretion, may apply to the judge of the Superior Court of the county in which such corporation is doing business, to issue an injunction restraining such corporation, in whole or in part, from further proceeding with its business until a hearing can be had. Such judge may, in such application, issue such injunction, and after a full hearing, may dissolve or modify it, or make it perpetual, and may make such orders and decrees according to the course of proceedings in equity, to restrain or prohibit the further prosecution of the business of the corporation, as may be needful in the premises; and may appoint one or more receivers to take possession of its property and effects, subject to such directions as may from time to time be prescribed by the court.

If either of the commissioners, having knowledge of the insolvent condition, or any violation of law, or unsafe practice of any association under their supervision, such as renders, in their opinion, the conduct of its business hazardous to its shareholders or depositors, and shall fail to report the same in writing to the Attorney-General, as required by this title, then such commissioner, on conviction thereof, shall be punished by a fine of not less than five thousand dollars, nor more than ten thousand dollars, or by imprisonment in the county jail not less than one year, nor more than two years, or by both such fine and imprisonment, and his office shall be declared vacant by the Governor, and a successor appointed to fill his unexpired term.

When receivers are so appointed, the secretary of the corporation shall make a schedule of all its property, and its secretary, board of investment, and other officers, transferring its property to the receivers, shall make oath that said schedule sets forth all the property which the corporation owns, or is entitled to. The secretary shall deliver said schedule to the receivers, and a copy thereof to the commissioners, who may at any time examine, under oath, such secretary, board of investment, or other officers, in order to determine whether or not all the property which the corporation owns, or is entitled to, has been transferred to the receivers.

SECTION 646. *Commissioners to make annual inspection of associations—Other examinations.*

Sec. 646. The commissioners, or one of them, shall, at least once in each year, and as much oftener as they may deem expedient, examine the accounts and doings of all such receivers, and shall carefully examine and report upon all accounts and reports of receivers made to the proper court and referred to the commissioners by the court, and, for the purposes of this section, shall have free access to the books and papers relating to the transactions of such receivers, and may examine them under oath relative to such transactions. Upon the certificate, under oath, of any five or more officers, trustees, creditors, shareholders, or depositors of any such corporation, setting forth their interest and the reasons for making such examination, directed to the commissioners, and requesting them to examine such corporation, they shall forthwith make a full investigation of its affairs, in the manner provided. The commissioners, if in their opinion any such corporation, or its officers or trustees, have violated any law in relation to such corporations, shall forthwith report the same, with such remarks as they deem expedient, to the Attorney-General, who shall forthwith institute a prosecution for such violation, in behalf of the people of the State.

SECTION 647. *Expenses of commissioners, how paid.*

Sec. 647. To meet the expenses provided by this title, every building and loan association, or corporation or association doing business on the building and loan plan, shall pay, in advance, to the commissioners, its pro rata amount of such expenses, to be determined by an assessment levied on the shares of each of such associations in force on the thirty-first day of December of each year, according to the par value of such shares. The said commissioners shall levy and collect, in advance, such assessment on the shares of all such associations in force as per report, herein provided for, to be made to said commissioners, of the condition of such associations at the close of business on December thirty-first of each year; *provided, however,* that no association shall pay less than ten dollars per annum, and all associations hereafter organized shall each pay to the commissioners for their licenses not less than one dollar per month for the term expiring December thirty-first succeeding, dating from the time of application for license.

The collection of all moneys assessed, as herein provided, for the annual expenses, or forfeitable as fines for failure to make reports as herein specified, and due from any corporation or association coming within the provisions of this title, may be enforced by action instituted in any court of competent jurisdiction; and all moneys collected or received by the said commissioners under this title, shall be deposited with the State Treasurer, to the credit of a fund to be known and designated as the "building and loan association inspection fund."

SECTION 648. *Associations must procure license before engaging in business—Annual report to commissioners.*

Sec. 648. No association shall transact business in this State without first procuring from the Commissioners of the Building and Loan Associations a certificate of authority or license to do so. To procure such authority it must file with the said commissioners a certified copy of its articles of incorporation, constitution, and by-laws, and all other printed rules and regulations relating to its methods of conducting business, and of all subsequent amendments or changes thereto, and otherwise comply with all requirements of law. No association, after the expiration of the term for which a license has been granted to it by the Commissioners of the Building and Loan Associations, shall continue to transact the business of a building and loan association without first procuring from said commissioners a renewal of such license on the terms provided for in this title; and any corporation violating this provision shall forfeit the sum of ten dollars per day during the continuance of the offense; and any violation of this section by any officer of such association shall be a misdemeanor. The commissioners are authorized and empowered to revoke the license of any association under their supervision, the solvency whereof is imperiled by losses or irregularities; and the commissioners, immediately upon revoking such license, shall report the facts to the Attorney-General, who shall thereupon take such proceedings as are provided by section six hundred and forty-five of this title.

Every building and loan association doing business in this State shall, once in every year, to wit, within thirty days after the expiration of its annual fiscal term, make a report, in writing, to the Commissioners of the Building and Loan Associations, verified by the oath of its president and secretary, showing accurately the financial condition of such association at the close of said term. The report shall be in such form as the commissioners shall prescribe, upon blanks by them furnished for that purpose, and shall specify the following particulars, namely: Name of the corporation, place where located, authorized capital stock, amount of stock paid in, the names of the directors, the amount of capital stock held by each, the amount due to shareholders, the amount and character of all other liabilities, cash on hand, and the number and value of shares in each and every series of stock issued by the association. All money received or disbursed by such association shall be duly accounted for. Any association failing to file the annual report within the time specified herein, shall be subject to a penalty of ten dollars per day for each and every day such report shall be delayed or withheld.

SECTION 709. To be amended to read as follows:

Sec. 709. If a condition precedent requires the performance of an act wrong of itself, or impossible, the instrument containing it is so far void. If it requires the performance of an act not wrong of itself, but otherwise unlawful, the instrument takes effect, and the condition is void. If a condition subsequent requires the performance of an unlawful or impossible act, the instrument takes effect and the condition is void.

SECTION 793. To be amended to read as follows:

Sec. 793. An action for the possession of real property leased or granted, with a right of reëntry, may be maintained at any time in the Superior Court, after the right to reënter has accrued, without the notice prescribed in section seven hundred and ninety-one.

NOTE.—The amendment changes "District Court" to "Superior Court."

SECTION 821. To be amended to read as follows:

Sec. 821. A person to whom any real property, upon which rent has been reserved, is transferred or devised, or who acquires in any manner the title thereto, or the right to collect the rents thereof, or to whom any such rent is transferred, or to whom is assigned the lease wherein such rent is reserved, is entitled, after notice thereof to the tenant or lessee, to the same remedies for the recovery of rent, for non-performance of any of the terms of the lease, or for any waste or cause of forfeiture, as his grantor, devisor, or predecessor might have had.

NOTE.—The amendment requires notice before the tenant is liable to an assignee or transferee (*O'Connor* vs. *Kelly*, 41 Cal. 432), and gives the holder of a Sheriff's certificate the usual remedy to collect rent from a tenant.

SECTION 822. To be amended to read as follows:

Sec. 822. Whatever remedies the lessor of any real property has against his immediate lessee for the breach of any agreement in the lease, or for the recovery of the possession, he has against the assignees, heirs, and personal representatives of the lessee, for any cause of action accruing after the assignment or after the death of said immediate lessee, except where the assignment was made by way of security for a loan, and is not accompanied by possession of the premises, and except that no judgment exceeding the amount of rent due, with interest and costs, shall be entered against the heirs or per· sonal representatives.

NOTE.—The case of *Martel* vs. *Meehan*, 63 Cal. 47, approved in 107 Cal. 112, holds that the personal representatives of a tenant are not subject to the remedies for non-payment of rent which the Code gives to lessors. The proposed amendment will make them subject to such remedies, except that the judgment obtained for rent cannot be trebled.

SECTION 857. To be amended to read as follows:

Sec. 857. Express trusts may be created for any of the following purposes:

1. To sell real property, and apply or dispose of the proceeds in accordance with the instrument creating the trust;

2. To mortgage or lease real property for the benefit of annuitants, legatees, or other beneficiaries, or for the purpose of satisfying any charge thereon;

3. To receive the rents and profits of real property, and pay them to or apply them to the use of any person, whether ascertained at the time of the creation of the trust or not, for himself or for his family, during the life of such person, or for any shorter term, subject to the rules of Title II, Part 1, Division II, of this Code; or,

4. To receive the rents and profits of real property, and to accumulate the same for the purposes and within the limits prescribed by the same title.

NOTE.—The amendment makes Subdivision 2 clearly applicable to beneficiaries other than those entitled under wills, and corrects an erroneous reference in Subdivision 3.

SECTION 970. To be amended to read as follows:

Sec. 970. When two sailing-vessels are approaching each other, so as to involve risk of collision, one of them shall keep out of the way of the other, as follows, namely:

1. A vessel which is running free shall keep out of the way of a vessel which is close-hauled;

2. A vessel which is close-hauled on the port tack shall keep out of the way of a vessel which is close-hauled on the starboard tack;

3. When both are running free, with the wind on different sides, the vessel which has the wind on the port side shall keep out of the way of the other;

4. When both are running free, with the wind on the same side, the vessel which is to the windward shall keep out of the way of the vessel which is to leeward;

5. A vessel which has the wind aft shall keep out of the way of the other vessel.

When two steam-vessels are meeting end on. or nearly end on, so as to involve risk of collision, each shall alter her course to starboard, so that each may pass on the port side of the other; but this provision only applies to cases where vessels are meeting end on, or nearly end on, in such a manner as to involve risk of collision, and does not apply to two vessels which must, if both keep on their respective courses, pass clear of each other; the only cases to which it does apply are when each of the two vessels is end on, or nearly end on, to the other; in other words, to cases in which, by day, each vessel sees the masts of the other in a line, or nearly in a line, with her own; and by night, to cases in which each vessel is in such a position as to see both the side-lights of the other; it does not apply by day to cases in which a vessel sees another ahead crossing her own course; or by night, to cases where the red light of one vessel is opposed to the red light of the other, or where the green light of one vessel is opposed to the green light of the other, or where a red light without a green light, or a green light without a red light, is seen ahead, or where both green and red lights are seen any-where but ahead.

When two steam-vessels are crossing, so as to involve risk of collision, the vessel which has the other on her own starboard side shall keep out of the way of the other.

When a steam-vessel and a sailing-vessel are proceeding in such directions as to involve risk of collision, the steam-vessel shall keep out of the way of the sailing-vessel.

Where, by any of these rules, one of two vessels is to keep out of the way, the other shall keep her course and speed.

Every vessel which is directed by these rules to keep out of the way of another vessel shall, if the circumstances of the case admit, avoid crossing ahead of the other.

Every steam-vessel which is directed by these rules to keep out of the way of another vessel shall, on approaching her, if necessary, slacken her speed or stop or reverse.

Notwithstanding anything contained in these rules, every vessel, over-taking any other, shall keep out of the way of the overtaken vessel.

Every vessel coming up with another vessel from any direction more than two points abaft her beam, that is, in such a position, with reference to the vessel which she is overtaking, that at night she would be unable to see either of that vessel's side-lights, shall be deemed to be an over-taking vessel; and no subsequent alteration of the bearing between the two vessels shall make the overtaking vessel a crossing vessel within the meaning of these rules, or relieve her of the duty of keeping clear of the overtaken vessel until she is finally past and clear.

As by day the overtaking vessel cannot always know with certainty whether she is forward or abaft this direction from the other vessel, she should, if in doubt, assume that she is an overtaking vessel and keep out of the way.

In narrow channels every steam-vessel shall, when it is safe and practicable, keep to that side of the fair-way or mid-channel which lies on the starboard side of such vessel.

Sailing-vessels under way shall keep out of the way of sailing-vessels or boats fishing with nets, or lines, or trawls. This rule shall not give to any vessel or boat engaged in fishing the right of obstructing a fair-way used by vessels other than fishing-vessels or boats.

In obeying and construing these rules due regard shall be had to all dangers of navigation and collision, and to any special circumstances which may render a departure from the above rules necessary in order to avoid immediate danger.

NOTE.—The amendment is a reënactment of the Statutes of the United States upon the subject, inasmuch as it is deemed proper that the Federal and State laws should coincide on this subject.

SECTION 981. To be amended to read as follows:

Sec. 981. Unless otherwise agreed, a product of the mind, to the production of which several persons have jointly contributed, is owned by them in equal proportions.

SECTION 1015. To be amended to read as follows:

Sec. 1015. If a river or stream, navigable or not navigable, carries away, by sudden violence, a considerable and distinguishable part of a bank, and bears it to the opposite bank, or to another part of the same bank, it belongs to the owner of the part carried away, excepting that occupation thereof for one year by the owner of the land to which it has been united, without being reclaimed by the owner of the part carried away, confers title thereto upon the owner of the land to which it has been united.

> NOTE.—The section, as it now stands, leaves the title of the part carried away uncertain, which question the proposed amendment will settle.

SECTION 1057. To be amended to read as follows:

Sec. 1057. A grant may be deposited by the grantor with a third person, to be delivered on performance of a condition, and on such delivery by the depositary it will take effect. While in possession of a third person, and subject to condition, it is called an escrow. A grant deposited by the grantor with a third person, to be delivered upon the death of the grantor, is void, and no estate passes thereunder.

> NOTE.—Under this amendment, the rule will be as contended in the dissenting opinion in *Bury* vs. *Young*, 98 Cal. 446, and as the decision would have been if the court had not felt bound by former adjudications.

SECTION 1096. A new section to be added, to read as follows:

Conveyances by persons whose names are changed.

Sec. 1096. Any person in whom the title of real estate is vested, who shall afterwards, from any cause, have his or her name changed, shall, in any conveyances of real estate so held, set forth the name in which he or she derived title to said real estate.

> NOTE.—The proposed section is the first section of an Act relating to conveyances of real estate, approved March 11, 1874, the remaining two sections of which it is proposed to place in the Political Code.

SECTION 1207. To be amended to read as follows:

Sec. 1207. Any instrument affecting real property, which was, previous to the thirtieth day of January, eighteen hundred and ninety-six, copied into the proper book of record, kept in the office of any County Recorder, shall be deemed to impart, after that date, notice of its contents to subsequent purchasers and incumbrancers, notwithstanding any defect, omission, or informality in the execution of the instrument, or in the certificate of acknowledgment thereof, or the absence of any such certificate; but nothing herein shall be deemed to affect the rights of purchasers or incumbrancers previous to that date. Duly certified copies of the record of any such instrument may be read in evidence, with like effect as copies of an instrument duly acknowledged and recorded, provided it be first shown that the original instrument was genuine.

> NOTE.—The only change made by the proposed amendment is to make it apply to all instruments copied in the proper book of record prior to January 30, 1896, instead of "previous to the thirtieth day of January, eighteen hundred and seventy-three," as it now reads.

SECTION 1214. To be amended to read as follows:

Sec. 1214. Every conveyance of real property, other than a lease for a term not exceeding one year, is void as against any subsequent purchaser or mortgagee of the same property, or any part thereof, without notice, in good faith and for a valuable consideration, whose conveyance or mortgage is first duly recorded, and as against any judgment affecting the title, unless such conveyance shall have been duly recorded prior to the record of a notice of the pendency of the action in which the judgment is rendered.

SECTION 1217. To be amended to read as follows:

Sec. 1217. An unrecorded instrument is valid as between the parties thereto and all other persons, except purchasers and incumbrancers for valuable consideration without notice and in good faith.

SECTION 1238. To be amended to read as follows:

From what may be selected.

Sec. 1238. If the claimant be married, the homestead may be selected from the community property, or the separate property of the husband, or, with the consent of the wife, from her separate property. When the claimant is not married, but is the head of a family within the meaning of section twelve hundred and sixty-one, the homestead may be selected from any of his or her property. When a co-tenant resides upon the property held in common, or upon a specific portion thereof, a homestead may be declared thereon, in the same manner and with the like effect as if the property resided upon were owned in severalty by such co-tenant, except that such declaration shall not prejudice the rights of the other co-tenants, upon partition or otherwise.

> NOTE.—The amendment changes the rule long established in this State, by allowing a valid declaration of homestead to be made by a co-tenant upon the specific portion of the property held in common, upon which he resides.

SECTION 1241. To be amended to read as follows:

Sec. 1241. The homestead is subject to execution or forced sale in satisfaction of judgments obtained:

1. Before the declaration of homestead was filed for record, and which constitute liens upon the premises. But all such judgments must be satisfied, if possible, from other property subject to the lien thereof or belonging to the judgment debtors, or any of them, before the homestead is sold thereunder;

2. On debts secured by mechanics', contractors', sub-contractors', artisans', architects', builders', laborers' (of every class), materialmen's, or vendors' liens upon the premises;

3. On debts secured by mortgages on the premises, executed and acknowledged by the husband and wife, or by an unmarried claimant;

4. On debts secured by mortgages on the premises, executed and recorded before the declaration of homestead was filed for record.

> NOTE.—The effect of the proposed amendment is to compel the satisfaction of any judgment which is a lien upon the homestead to be satisfied out of any other property subject thereto, if possible, before the homestead can be sold.

SECTION 1242. To be amended to read as follows:

Sec. 1242. The homestead of a married person cannot be conveyed or incumbered unless the instrument by which it is conveyed or incumbered is executed and acknowledged by both husband and wife; *provided, however,* that any excess in value of the property described in the homestead declaration over the amount of the homestead exemption may be conveyed or incumbered by the husband alone, where the homestead has not been selected from the wife's separate estate.

> NOTE.—The amendment gives the husband the power of disposition over the excess in the homestead over the exemption, except where a declaration was made upon the wife's separate property.

SECTION 1243. To be amended to read as follows:

Sec. 1243. A homestead can be abandoned only by a declaration of abandonment, or a grant of the whole thereof, or of an undivided interest therein executed and acknowledged:

1. By the husband and wife, if the claimant is married;

2. By the claimant, if unmarried.

> NOTE.—The amendment causes the conveyance of an undivided interest in a homestead to work an abandonment, but allows the conveyance of a specific portion thereof without affecting the homestead on the remainder.

SECTION 1246. To be amended to read as follows:

Sec. 1246. The application must be made upon a verified petition, showing:

1. The fact that an execution has been levied upon the homestead;

2. The name of the claimant;

3. That the value of the homestead exceeds the amount of the homestead exemption, and exceeded such amount when said homestead was declared.

NOTE.—This amendment will prevent the sale of, or interference with, the homestead, by a creditor, unless it exceeds the value of the homestead exemption when the execution is issued, and also exceeded such value when the declaration of homestead was made. The amendment and those proposed to be made *infra* will make the provisions of this Code on the subject of homestead exemption conform to Section 1476 of the Code of Civil Procedure, which provides that no interference in probate shall be made with the homestead, if the value thereof did not exceed the homestead exemption when the declaration was filed. The rule, as laid down in Section 1476 of the Code of Civil Procedure, is deemed preferable to that now existing in the Civil Code in this regard, because it is believed that the policy of the law should encourage the improvement and beautifying of homes, by including any increase in value thereto in the homestead exemption, provided the premises do not exceed in value the homestead exemption at the time of the homestead declaration. ·

SECTION 1251. To be amended to read as follows:

Sec. 1251. They must view the premises, and ascertain and appraise the present value thereof, and also ascertain and appraise the value thereof at the time the same was selected as a homestead, and if its present value exceeds the homestead exemption, and its value exceeded such exemption at the time it was selected, they must determine whether the land claimed can be divided without material injury.

NOTE.—This amendment conforms with that proposed to Section 1246.

SECTION 1253. To be amended to read as follows:

Sec. 1253. If, from the report, it appears to the judge that the present value of the homestead exceeds, and at the time the same was selected exceeded, the homestead exemption, and that the land claimed can be divided without material injury, he must, by an order, direct the appraisers to set off to the claimant so much of the land, including the residence, as will amount in value to the homestead exemption. The appraisers must, within ten days after the making of such order, make to the judge, in writing, a report, which report must show what action they have taken thereunder. Upon the application of the petitioner, upon at least three days' notice to the homestead claimant, the judge shall consider such report and make an order confirming or rejecting the same. If the report is confirmed, the execution may be enforced against the remainder of the land.

SECTION 1254. To be amended to read as follows:

Sec. 1254. If, from the report mentioned in section twelve hundred and fifty-two of this Code, it appears to the judge that the land claimed exceeds in value the amount of the homestead exemption, and exceeded such amount when the homestead was declared, and that it cannot be divided, he must make an order directing its sale under the execution.

SECTIONS 1258 and 1259 to be incorporated in one section, to read as follows:

Sec. 1258. The court must fix the compensation of the appraisers, not to exceed five dollars per day each for the time actually engaged, and the execution creditor must pay the costs of these proceedings in the first instance; but in the cases provided for in sections twelve hundred and fifty-three and twelve hundred and fifty-four, the amount so paid must be added as costs on execution and collected accordingly.

NOTE.—These two sections are proposed to be consolidated to allow a number for the following proposed new section.

SECTION 1259. A new section to be added to read as follows:

Insurance money on homestead protected.

Sec. 1259. Money paid upon a loss under a policy of fire insurance upon any portion of the homestead is entitled, for a period of six months after such payment, to the same protection against legal process and the voluntary disposition of the husband which the law gives to the homestead; and any building constructed or as repaired with the proceeds of such fire insurance shall constitute a part of the homestead in the same manner as if the same had been upon the land when the declaration of homestead was filed.

SECTION 1261. To be amended to read as follows:

Sec. 1261. The phrase "head of a family," as used in this title, includes within its meaning:

1. The husband, when the claimant is a married person;

2. Every person who has residing on the premises with him or her, and under his or her care and maintenance: either, 1. His or her minor child, or minor grandchild, or the minor child of his or her deceased wife or husband; 2. A minor brother or sister, or the minor child of a deceased brother or sister; 3. A father, mother, grandfather, or grandmother; 4. The father, mother, grandfather, or grandmother of a deceased husband or wife; 5. An unmarried sister, or any other of the relatives mentioned in this section, who have attained the age of majority, and are unable to take care of or support themselves; *provided*, that whenever the claimant ceases to be the head of a family, as defined in this section, the amount of the homestead exemption under any declaration of homestead theretofore filed by such person, shall not exceed one thousand dollars.

SECTION 1266. A new section to be added to Chapter II, Title V, Part IV, Division II, to read as follows: •

Alienation of homestead in certain cases.

Sec. 1266. In case of a homestead, if either the husband or wife shall become hopelessly insane, and a guardian of such insane spouse has been duly appointed by a Superior Court, upon application of the husband or wife not insane to the Superior Court of the county in which said homestead is situated, and upon due proof of such insanity and the appointment of a guardian of such insane spouse, the court may make an order permitting the husband or wife not insane to join with such guardian in a sale or mortgage of such homestead or any part, thereof. A notice of the application for such order shall be given by publication of such notice in a newspaper published in the county in which such homestead is situated, if there be a newspaper published therein, once each week for three successive weeks, prior to the hearing of such application, and a copy of such notice shall also be served upon the nearest male relative resident in this State and upon the guardian of such insane husband or wife, at least three weeks prior to such application; and in case there be no such male relative known to the applicant, a copy of such notice shall be served upon the District Attorney of the county in which such homestead is situated; and it is hereby made the duty of such District Attorney, upon being served with a copy of such notice, to appear in court, and see that such application is made in good faith, and that the proceedings thereon are fairly conducted.

SECTION 1267. A new section to be added to Chapter II, Title V, Division I, to read as follows:

Petition for order allowing alienation of homestead.

Sec. 1267. Thirty days before the hearing of any application under the provisions of the foregoing section, the applicant shall present and file in the court in which such application is to be heard a petition for the order mentioned in the preceding section, subscribed and sworn to by the applicant, setting forth the name and age of the insane husband or wife; a description of the premises constituting the homestead; the value of the same; the county in which it is situated; and such facts in addition to the insanity of the husband or wife, and relating to the circumstances or necessities of the applicant and his or her family, as shall demonstrate the necessity of such sale or mortgage.

SECTION 1268. A new section to be added to Chapter II, Title V, Part IV, Division II, to read as follows:

Order allowing alienation of homestead, and effect thereof.

Sec. 1268. If the court shall make the order provided for in section twelve hundred and sixty-six of this Code, the same shall require the proceeds of such sale or the amount received by virtue of the mortgage of said homestead to be paid to the general guardian of the insane spouse, and the order shall be entered upon the minutes of the court, and thereafter, any sale, conveyance, or mortgage made in pursuance of such order shall be as valid and effectual as if the property affected thereby were the absolute property, in fee simple, of the spouse joining in such conveyance or mortgage.

> NOTE.—The three foregoing proposed sections contain the provisions of an Act to enable certain parties therein named to alienate or incumber homesteads, approved March 25, 1874, with the exception that it is proposed to change the scope of the Act so as to require the money realized from a sale or mortgage under the order to be paid to the general guardian of the estate of the insane spouse, who can thereafter disburse the same under the rules of law applicable to the particular case, and make it the duty of the District Attorney of the county where such applications are made to appear, and see that applications therefor are made in good faith, instead of the Public Administrator, as provided in the said Act.

SECTIONS 1266, 1267, 1268, and 1269 to be incorporated in one section, to be Section 1269, Chapter III, Title V, Part IV, Division II, to read as follows:

Mode of selection and effect of filing for record the declaration of homestead.

Sec. 1269.   Any person, other than the head of a family, in the selection of a homestead, must execute and acknowledge, in the same manner as a grant of real property is acknowledged, a "declaration of homestead."   The declaration must contain everything required by the second, third, and fourth subdivisions of section twelve hundred and sixty-three of this Code, and must be recorded in the office of the County Recorder of the county in which the land is situated.   From and after the time the declaration is so filed for record, the land described therein is a homestead.

> NOTE.—The present Sections 1266, 1267, 1268, and 1269 are consolidated in the proposed new Section 1269, so as to allow numbers in the preceding chapter for the proposed sections containing the provisions of the Act in relation to the alienation of homesteads in certain cases.

SECTION 1283.   To be amended to read as follows:

Witness, who is devisee, rights of.

Sec. 1283.   If a witness, to whom any beneficial devise, legacy, or gift, void by the preceding section, is made, would have been entitled to any share of the estate of the testator, in case the will should not be established, he succeeds to so much of the share as would be distributed to him, not exceeding the devise or bequest made to him in the will, and he is entitled to receive the same, on distribution, of the other devisees or legatees named in the will, in proportion to and out of the parts devised or bequeathed to them.

> NOTE.—The change in the section is that the witness, who is a devisee, shall be entitled to receive his proper share of the estate upon distribution.

SECTION 1299. To be amended to read as follows:

Effect of marriage of a man on his will.

Sec. 1299. If, after making a will, the testator marries, and the wife survives the testator, the will is revoked, unless provision has been made for her by written contract, made before or after her marriage, by the testator, or unless she is provided for in the will, or in such way mentioned therein as to show an intention not to make such provision; and no other evidence to rebut the presumption of revocation must be received.

SECTION 1313. To be amended to read as follows:

Restriction on power to devise to charitable uses.

Sec. 1313. No estate, real or personal, shall be bequeathed or devised to any charitable or benevolent society, or corporation, or to any person or persons in trust for charitable uses, except the same be done by will duly executed at least thirty days before the decease of the testator; and if so made, at least thirty days prior to such death, such devise or legacy, and each of them, shall be valid; *provided,* that no such devise or bequests shall collectively exceed one third of the distributable estate of the testator leaving legal heirs, and in such case a pro rata deduction from such devises or bequests shall be made so as to reduce the aggregate thereof to one third of such estate; and all dispositions of property made contrary hereto shall be void, and go to the residuary legatee or devisee, next of kin, or heirs according to law.

NOTE.—The amendment to this section consists in adding the word "distributable" before estate, thereby making it clear that no more than one third of an estate of a testator after the payment of the debts and expenses of administration can be bequeathed to charity.

SECTION 1350. To be amended to read as follows:

Sec. 1350. A devise or legacy given to more than one person vests in them as owners in common, unless a contrary intent appears.

SECTION 1360. To be amended to read as follows:

Sec. 1360. The property of a testator, except as otherwise specially provided in this Code and the Code of Civil Procedure, must be resorted to for the payment of legacies in the following order:

1. The property which is expressly appropriated by the will for the payment of the legacies;
2. Property not disposed of by the will;
3. Property which is devised or bequeathed to a residuary legatee;
4. Property which is not specifically devised or bequeathed.

NOTE.—The amendment consists in the addition of the word "not" before "specifically devised" in Subdivision 4.

SECTION 1361. To be amended to read as follows:

Sec. 1361. Legacies to husband, widow, or kindred of any class are chargeable for debts only after legacies to persons not related to the testator.

SECTION 1384. To be amended to read as follows:

Succession to estates of intestate.

Sec. 1384. The property, both real and personal, of one who dies without disposing of it by will, passes to the heirs of the intestate, subject to the control of the Superior Court, and to the possession of any administrator appointed by that court, for the purposes of administration.

NOTE.—The amendment changes Probate Court to Superior Court.

SECTION 1405. To be amended to read as follows:

Sec. 1405. When succession is not claimed as provided in the preceding section, the Superior Court, on information, must direct the Attorney-General to reduce the property to his or the possession of the State, or to cause the same to be sold, and the same or the proceeds thereof to be deposited in the state treasury for the benefit of such nonresident foreigner, or his legal representative, to be paid to him whenever, within five years after such deposit, he appears and obtains a judgment or order of such Superior Court that he is entitled to succeed thereto.

SECTION 1411. To be amended to read as follows:

Sec. 1411. The appropriation must be for some useful or beneficial purpose, and when the appropriator or his successor in interest ceases to use it for such a purpose for three years the right ceases.

NOTE.—*Smith* vs. *Hawkins,* 110 Cal. 122, decides that five years' non-user is required to work a forfeiture. The amendment places the requisite time of non-user at three years.

SECTION 1572. To be amended to read as follows:

Sec. 1572. Actual fraud, within the meaning of this chapter, consists in any of the following acts committed by a party to the contract, or with his connivance, with intent to deceive another party thereto, or to induce him to enter into the contract:

1. The suggestion, as a fact, of that which is not true, by one who does not believe it to be true;

2. The positive assertion, in a manner not warranted by the information of the person making it, of that which is not true, though he believes it to be true;

3. The suppression of that which is true, by one having knowledge or belief of the fact, and which it is his duty to disclose;

4. A promise made without any intention of performing it; or,

5. Any other act fitted to deceive.

NOTE.—The amendment makes the suppression of that which is true by one having knowledge or belief of the fact fraudulent only when it is his duty to disclose such fact, and conforms the section to the definition of deceit in Section 1710.

SECTION 1917. To be amended to read as follows:

Sec. 1917. Unless there is an express contract in writing, fixing a different rate, interest is payable on all moneys at the rate of six per cent per annum after they become due, on any instrument of writing, except a judgment, and on moneys lent, or due on any settlement of account, from the day on which the balance is ascertained, and on moneys received to the use of another and detained from him. In the computation of interest for a period less than a year, three hundred and sixty days are deemed to constitute a year.

NOTE.—The amendment reduces the rate of legal interest from seven per cent to six per cent per annum.

SECTION 2207. To be amended to read as follows:

Sec. 2207. A carrier of messages by telegraph or telephone must, if it is practicable, transmit every such message immediately upon its receipt. But if this is not practicable, and several messages accumulate upon his hands, he must transmit them in the following order:

1. Messages from public agents of the United States or of this State, on public business;

2. Messages intended in good faith for immediate publication in newspapers, and not for any secret use;

3. Messages giving information relating to the sickness or death of any person;

4. Other messages in the order in which they were received.

SECTION 2208. To be amended to read as follows:

Sec. 2208. A common carrier of messages, otherwise than by telegraph or telephone, must transmit messages in the order in which he receives them, except messages from agents of the United States or of this State, on public business, to which he must always give priority. But he may fix upon certain times for the simultaneous transmission of messages previously received.

SECTION 2310. To be amended to read as follows:

Sec. 2310. A ratification can only be made in the manner that would have been necessary to confer an original authority for the act ratified, or by accepting or retaining the benefit of the act, without inquiry or with a full knowledge of the material facts thereof.

NOTE.—The amendment permits a ratification of an act which can only be authorized in writing where the principal accepts or receives the benefit without inquiry or a full knowledge of the material facts.

7—c

SECTION 2343. To be amended to read as follows:

Sec. 2343. One who assumes to act as an agent is responsible to third persons as a principal for his acts in the course of his agency, in any of the following cases, and in no others:

1. When, with his consent, credit is given to him personally in a transaction;

2. When his acts are wrongful in their nature.

NOTE.—The amendment eliminates from the section the second subdivision thereof, which provides that when an agent enters into a written contract, in the name of his principal, without believing in good faith that he has authority therefor, he is responsible as a principal. There is no doubt of his liability, in the case supposed, for all damages resulting therefrom. To hold him liable as principal in such a case, as has been well said in *Hall* vs. *Crandall*, 29 Cal. 567, is rather to make a new contract for the parties, than to construe the one they have made for themselves.

SECTION 2355. To be amended to read as follows:

Sec. 2355. An agency is terminated, as to every person having notice thereof, by:

1. The expiration of its term;
2. The extinction of its subject;
3. The death of the agent;
4. His renunciation of the agency; or,
5. The incapacity of the agent to act as such.

NOTE.—The amendment changes the word "agency" to "agent" in the fifth subdivision of the section.

SECTION 2356. To be amended to read as follows:

Sec. 2356. Unless the power of an agent is coupled with an interest in the subject of the agency, it is terminated by:

1. Its revocation by the principal, as to every person having notice thereof;
2. The death of the principal;
3. His incapacity to contract.

NOTE.—The amendment terminates the power of an agent, in the cases mentioned, irrespective of the kind of notice thereof. This is the undoubted rule of the common law. (Meecham on Agency, Sec 245.) It is assumed to be in force in California in the decision of *Lowrie* vs. *Salz*, 75 Cal. 349, and in several other cases.

SECTION 2553. To be amended to read as follows:

Sec. 2553. Except in the cases specified in the next four sections, and in the cases of fire, life, accident, and health insurance, a change of interest in any part of a thing insured, unaccompanied by a corresponding change of interest in the insurance, suspends the insurance to an equivalent extent, until the interest in the thing and the interest in the insurance are vested in the same person.

NOTE.—The amendment removes fire insurance policies from the operation of the section, inasmuch as such policies are to be of the standard form provided in the Political Code.

SECTION 2587. To be amended to read as follows:

Sec. 2587. A policy of insurance, other than a policy of fire or marine insurance, must specify:

1. The parties between whom the contract is made;

2. The rate of premium;

3. The property or life insured;

4. The interest of the insured in property insured, if he is not the absolute owner thereof;

5. The risks insured against; and,

6. The period during which the insurance is to continue.

SECTION 2610. To be amended to read as follows:

Sec. 2610. A breach of warranty exonerates an insurer from the time that it occurs; or, where it is broken in its inception, prevents the policy from attaching to the risk.

SECTION 2611. To be amended to read as follows:

Sec. 2611. The violation of a material provision of a policy on the part of either party entitles the other to rescind.

SECTION 2612. To be amended to read as follows:

Sec. 2612. A policy may declare that a violation of a specified provision thereof shall avoid it; otherwise, the breach of an immaterial provision shall not have that effect.

SECTION 2949. A new section to be added to read as follows:

Sale under power in mortgages or trust deeds.

Sec. 2949. Whenever a sale of real property is made under a power of sale contained in a mortgage or deed of trust intended for the security of a debt, such sale shall be subject to redemption by the person who executed the mortgage or deed of trust, or his heirs, executors, administrators, or assigns. Such redemption may be made at any time within six months after the date of the sale by paying or tendering to the purchaser at such sale, or his heirs, executors, administrators, or assigns, the amount paid at such sale, with interest thereon from the date of such sale to the time when the redemption is made, at the rate of one per cent per month. Any person may become a purchaser at a sale under a power of sale mentioned in this chapter.

> NOTE.—The amendment is desirable inasmuch as it has always been the policy of the law to avoid a strict foreclosure of mortgage which can be, and is often had in California, under powers of sale contained in deeds of trust and mortgages.

SECTION 3001. To be amended to read as follows:

Sec. 3001. Before property pledged can be sold, and after performance of the act for which it is security is due, the pledgee must demand performance thereof from the debtor, if the debtor can be found within the State by the exercise of reasonable diligence.

SECTION 3002. To be amended to read as follows:

Sec. 3002. A pledgee must give actual notice to the pledgor of the time and place at which the property pledged will be sold, at least twenty days before the sale, if the pledgor can, by the exercise of reasonable diligence, be found within the State; otherwise, publication of notice of such sale for two weeks in a newspaper published in the county where the property was pledged, and posting the notice in three public places in said county twenty days before the sale, shall be equivalent, when the publication is complete, to actual notice to the pledgor of the time and place at which the property pledged will be sold.

> NOTE.—The amendments to the two preceding sections excuse demand of performance and actual notice to the pledgor of the time and place of sale, when he cannot with reasonable diligence be found within the State, and provide for constructive notice of the time and place of the sale in such cases.

SECTION 3006. To be amended to read as follows:

Sec. 3006. A pledgee cannot sell any evidence of debt pledged to him except the obligations of governments, states, or corporations, but must use ordinary diligence and skill in the collection of the same, when due.

SECTION 3101. To be amended to read as follows:

Sec. 3101. An instrument, otherwise negotiable in form, payable to a person named, but with the words added, "or to his order," or "to bearer," or words equivalent thereto, is in the former case payable to the written order thereon of such person, and in the latter case payable to the bearer.

> NOTE.—This amendment adds "thereon" after "written order" in the section, and is designed to make it clear that the writing affecting a negotiable instrument must be upon the instrument itself.

SECTION 3131. To be amended to read as follows:

Sec. 3131. Presentment of a negotiable instrument for payment, when necessary, must be made as follows, as nearly as by reasonable diligence it is practicable:

1. The instrument must be presented by the holder, or by his agent;

2. The instrument must be presented to the principal debtor, if he can be found at the place where presentment should be made; and if not, then it must be presented to some other person having charge thereof, or employed therein; if the principal debtor cannot be found at the place where presentment should be made, and if no person is found having charge thereof, or employed therein, presentment is excused;

3. An instrument which specifies a place for its payment must be presented there; and if the place specified includes more than one house,

then at the place of residence or business of the principal debtor, if it can be found therein;

4. An instrument which does not specify a place for its payment must be presented at the place of residence or business of the principal debtor, or wherever he may be found, at the option of the presentor;

5. The instrument must be presented upon the day of its maturity, or, if it be payable on demand, it may be presented upon any day. It must be presented within reasonable hours; and if it be payable at a banking-house, within the usual banking hours of the vicinity, but, by the consent of the person to whom it should be presented, it may be presented at any hour of the day;

6. If the principal debtor have no place of business or residence within the State, or if his place of business or residence within the State cannot, with reasonable diligence, be ascertained, presentment for payment is excused.

Note.—The amendment allows the instrument to be presented by an agent of the holder; enacts that if the principal debtor cannot be found at the place of presentment, and no person is found having charge thereof, or employed therein, and if he have no place of business or residence in the State, presentment for payment is excused.

Section 3151. To be amended to read as follows:

Sec. 3151. A notice of the dishonor of a negotiable instrument, if valid in favor of the party giving it, inures to the benefit of the holder thereof, and of all other parties thereto who have given notice of dishonor as provided in the preceding section.

Note.—The present section makes a notice of dishonor inure to the benefit of the parties "whose right tó give the like notice has not then been lost." Under this phraseology the notice, when given by the second indorser to the first indorser, would not inure to the benefit of a sixth indorser who might have succeeded under Section 3150, because his right to notify the first indorser would *then* be lost, because more than one day would have elapsed by reason of the successive notices.

Sections 3400 and 3401 to be repealed.

Note.—Section 3399 fully states the law as to the judicial revision of contracts, and it is deemed expedient to repeal Sections 3400 and 3401, as they tend to hamper the courts in the decision of such cases.

Section 3440. To be amended to read as follows:

Sec. 3440. Every transfer of personal property, other than a thing in action or a ship or cargo at sea or in a foreign port, and every lien thereon, other than a mortgage when allowed by law and a contract of bottomry or respondentia, is conclusively presumed, if made by a person having at the time the possession or control of the property, and not accompanied by an immediate delivery, and followed by an actual and continued change of possession of the things transferred, to be fraudulent and therefore void against those who are his creditors while he remains in possession and the successors in interest of such creditors, and against any persons on whom his estate devolves in trust for the benefit of others than himself, and against purchasers or incumbrancers in good faith subsequent to the transfer; *provided, however,* that the provisions of this section shall not apply to the transfers of wines in the wineries or wine-cellars of the makers or owners thereof, or other persons having possession, care, and control of the same, and the pipes, casks, and tanks in which the said wines are contained, which transfers shall be made in writing, and certified and acknowledged and verified in the same form as provided for chattel mortgages, and which shall be recorded in the book of miscellaneous records in the office of the County Recorder of the county in which the same are situated; *provided, further,* that every transfer of personal property, by husband to wife, and used by them in common, is conclusively presumed to be fraudulent and therefore void under this section, unless at the time of such transfer of such property the same is described in an inventory of the wife's separate property, made and recorded as provided in section one hundred and sixty-five of this Code.

NOTE.—The amendment to this section makes any transfer of personal property by the husband to the wife, used in common by them, void, unless an inventory thereof as the separate property of the wife is at the same time filed, as provided in Section 165.

PROPOSED AMENDMENTS TO THE

CODE OF CIVIL PROCEDURE.

SECTION 11. To be repealed.

NOTE.—All of the provisions of this section are contained in Section 10 of this Code.

SECTION 66. To be amended to read as follows:

Sec. 66. In the County of Los Angeles there shall be elected six judges of the Superior Court; in the County of Alameda there shall be elected four judges of the Superior Court; in the County of Sacramento there shall be elected three judges of the Superior Court; in each of the counties of Fresno, Humboldt, San Joaquin, Santa Clara, Sonoma, San Bernardino, and San Diego, there shall be elected two judges of the Superior Court; and in each of said counties, and in any county, or city and county, other than the City and County of San Francisco, in which there shall be more than one judge of the Superior Court, the judges of such court may hold as many sessions of said court at the same time as there are judges thereof, and shall apportion the business among themselves as equally as may be.

NOTE.—The amendment of this section designates the number of judges in the different counties, as changed by Acts passed subsequent to the enactment of the section.

SECTION 248. A new section to be added to Article X, Chapter II, Title III, Part I, to read as follows:

Fees of jurors in civil cases—how paid.

Sec. 248. The fees of the jury in civil cases shall be paid by the prevailing party at the conclusion of the trial before the jury is discharged, and no judgment shall be entered on the verdict of the jury until such fees are paid. If the prevailing party shall refuse or neglect to pay the jury fees as above provided, the court shall enter an order that the amount of such fees (stating it) shall be paid into court by the prevailing party, and execution may be issued thereon as upon a judgment. If such fees are not paid or collected within five days after the discharge of the jury, the fees of the jury shall be paid by the county in which the action was tried, as in criminal cases. The amount paid by the county must be refunded whenever paid by, or collected from, the prevailing party in the action. It shall be the duty of the District Attorney of the county to attend to the collection, for the benefit of the county, of all jury fees ordered to be paid into court under this section.

NOTE.—The scope of the section is to allow the trial by jury in all proper cases when demanded, irrespective of the question whether the party demanding it is able to advance such fees.

SECTION 269. To be amended to read as follows:

Sec. 269. The judge or judges of any Superior Court in the State may appoint a competent phonographic reporter, or as many such reporters as there are judges, to be known as official reporter or reporters of such court, and to hold office during the pleasure of the judge or judges appointing them. Such reporter, or any of them, where there are two or more, shall, at the request of either party, or of the court, in a civil action or proceeding, and on the order of the court, the District Attorney, or of the attorney for defendant in a criminal action or proceeding, take down, in shorthand, all the testimony, the objections made, the rulings of the court, the exceptions taken, the oral instructions given, and any statement made by counsel, or any other person, and, if directed by the court, or requested by either party, shall, within such reasonable time after the trial of such case as the court may designate, write out the same in plain, legible long-hand or typewriting, and verify and file it with the clerk of the court in which the case was tried.

SECTION 274. To be amended to read as follows:

Sec. 274. The official reporter shall receive for attendance on court and reporting, a monthly salary, payable one half by the State and one half by the county, at the same time and in the same manner as the salaries of the judges of the Superior Court; and for transcription he shall receive fees, payable, in criminal cases, by the county, and in civil cases by the party ordering the same, or, where ordered by the court, by either or both parties, as the court may direct. Said monthly salary shall be as follows: In counties of the first, second, and third classes, one hundred and seventy-five dollars; in counties of the fourth to the twelfth class, both inclusive, one hundred and sixty dollars; in counties of the thirteenth to the twenty-ninth class, both inclusive, one hundred and fifty dollars; in counties of the thirtieth to the thirty-ninth class, both inclusive, one hundred and twenty-five dollars; in counties of the fortieth to the forty-ninth class, both inclusive, seventy-five dollars; in counties of all the remaining classes, fifty dollars. Said fees for transcription shall be ten cents per folio of one hundred words for the original, and five cents per folio of one hundred words for each copy; *provided*, that where the reporter is required to transcribe the whole, or any part, of the testimony during the progress of the trial, he shall be entitled to receive twenty cents per folio for the original and ten cents for each copy. Where there is no regularly appointed official reporter, and the judge temporarily appoints one to report a case, such reporter shall receive ten dollars per day for reporting and the same fees for transcription as are allowed regular reporters, by this section, and in addition his actual traveling expenses where not a resident of the county.

SECTION 335, of Chapter III, Title II, Part II, to be Section 334 of said chapter.

SECTION 335. A new section to be added to read as follows:

Sec. 335. Within six years: All actions of tort, except those hereinafter mentioned.

NOTE.—"The statutes of limitation of the several States apply to actions at law for the infringement of letters-patent." (*Campbell* vs. *Haverhill*, 155 U. S. 610.) There is no Federal statute or section of the Codes which applies to such actions. The object of the foregoing amendment is to supply such an enactment.

SECTION 337. To be amended to read as follows:

Sec. 337. Within four years:

1. An action upon any contract, obligation, or liability, founded upon an instrument in writing;

2. An action against a stockholder of a corporation to enforce a liability created by law.

NOTE.—This amendment, together with the one proposed to Section 359, will make the statute of limitations four years upon an action to recover upon a stockholder's liability, instead of three years after the discovery, by the aggrieved party, of the facts upon which the liability was created.

SECTION 339. To be amended to read as follows:

Sec. 339. Within two years:

1. An action upon a contract, obligation, or liability, not founded upon an instrument in writing;

2. An action against a Sheriff, Coroner, or Constable, upon a liability incurred by the doing of an act in his official capacity, and in virtue of his office, or by the omission of an official duty, including the non-payment of money collected upon an execution; but this subdivision does not apply to an action for an escape;

3. An action to recover damages for the death of one caused by the wrongful act or neglect of another.

NOTE.—The amendment to the last two sections will make the period of limitation four years for actions upon written instruments, whether executed within or without the State.

SECTION 359. To be amended to read as follows:

Sec. 359. The preceding sections of this title do not affect actions against directors or stockholders of a corporation to recover a penalty or forfeiture imposed; but such actions must be brought within three years after the discovery by the aggrieved party of the facts upon which the penalty or forfeiture attached.

SECTION 383. To be amended to read as follows:

Sec. 383. Persons severally liable upon the same obligation or instrument, including the parties to bills of exchange and promissory notes, and sureties on the same or separate instruments, may all or any of them be included in the same action, at the option of the plaintiff; and all or any of them may join as plaintiffs in the same action, concerning or affecting the obligation or instrument upon which they are severally liable.

SECTION 389. To be amended to read as follows:

Sec. 389. The court may determine any controversy between parties before it, when it can be done without prejudice to the rights of others, or by saving their rights; but when a complete determination of the controversy cannot be had without the presence of other parties, the court must then order them to be brought in, and to that end may order amended and supplemental pleadings, or a cross-complaint to be filed, and summons thereon to be issued and served. And when, in an action for the recovery of real or personal property, a person, not a party to the action, but having an interest in the subject thereof, makes application to the court to be made a party, it may order him to be brought in, by the proper amendment.

SECTION 396. To be amended to read as follows:

Sec. 396. If the county in which the action is commenced is not the proper county for the trial thereof, the action may, notwithstanding, be tried therein, unless the defendant, at the time he appears and answers or demurs, files an affidavit of merits, and a notice of motion that the trial be had in the proper county.

> NOTE.—The amendment does away with demands in writing that the trial be had in the proper county, and substitutes therefor a notice of motion.

SECTION 407. To be amended to read as follows:

Sec. 407. The summons must be directed to the defendant, signed by the clerk, and issued under the seal of the court, and must contain:

1. The names of the parties to the action, the court in which it is brought, and the county in which the complaint is filed;

2. A direction that the defendant appear and answer the complaint

within ten days, if the summons is served within the county in which the action is brought; within thirty days, if served elsewhere;

3. A notice that, unless the defendant so appears and answers, the plaintiff will take judgment for any money or damages demanded in the complaint as arising upon contract, and will apply to the court for any other relief demanded in the complaint.

> NOTE.—This amendment will simplify the form of a summons, inasmuch as the summons is served by delivering a copy of the complaint in all cases other than by publication. When publication of the summons is ordered, under the proposed amendment to Section 413, *infra*, the court must order the summons, and a copy of the prayer of the complaint in the action, to be published, which will give the defendant sufficient notice of the nature of the action. ·

SECTION 408. To be amended to read as follows:

Sec. 408. If the summons is returned without being served on any or all of the defendants, or if it has been lost, the clerk, upon the demand of the party causing the issuance of such summons in the first instance, may issue an alias summons in the same form as the original; *provided*, that no such alias summons shall be issued after the expiration of one year from the date of the filing of the pleading on which it is sought to have such alias summons issued.

SECTION 410. To be amended to read as follows:

Sec. 410. The summons may be served by the Sheriff of the county where the defendant is found, or by any other person over the age of eighteen years, not a party to the action. A copy of the complaint or cross-complaint upon which the summons was issued, must be served with the summons upon each of the defendants affected thereby. When the summons is served by the Sheriff, it must be returned, with his certificate of its service and of the service of a copy of the pleading on which such summons was issued, to the office of the clerk from which it was issued. When it is served by any other person, it must be returned to the same place, with an affidavit of such person of its service and of the service of a copy of the pleading on which it was issued.

SECTION 412. To be amended to read as follows:

Sec. 412. Where the person on whom service is to be made resides out of the State; or has departed from the State; or cannot, after due diligence, be found within the State; or conceals himself to avoid the service of summons; or is a foreign corporation having no managing or business agent, cashier, or secretary within the State, and the fact appears by affidavit, or by a verified pleading on file, that a cause of action exists against the defendant in respect to whom the service is to be made, or that he is a necessary or proper party to the action; or when it appears by such affidavit, or by the complaint or other verified pleading on file therein, that it is an action which relates to, or the subject of which is, real or personal property in this State, in which such person defendant, or foreign corporation defendant, has or claims a lien or interest, actual or contingent, therein, or in which the relief demanded consists wholly or in part in excluding such person or foreign corporation from any interest therein, such court or judge may make an order that the service be made by the publication of the summons.

Section 413. To be amended to read as follows:

Sec. 413. The order must direct the publication of the summons and of the prayer of the complaint or cross-complaint on which said summons has been issued, to be made in a newspaper, to be designated as most likely to give notice to the person to be served, and for such length of time as may be deemed reasonable, at least once a week; but publication against a defendant residing out of the State, or absent therefrom, must not be less than two months. In case of publication, where the residence of a non-resident or absent defendant is known, the court or judge must direct a copy of the summons and complaint or cross-complaint on which the summons has been issued to be forthwith deposited in the post office, directed to the person to be served, at his place of residence. When publication is ordered, personal service of a copy of the summons and complaint or cross-complaint, as the case may be, out of the State, is equivalent to publication and deposit in the post office; and in either case the service of the summons is complete at the expiration of the period of publication prescribed by the order directing the publication.

Section 414. To be amended to read as follows:

Sec. 414. When the cause of action stated by the complaint or cross-complaint is against two or more defendants jointly or severally liable on a contract, and the summons is served on one or more, but not on all of them, the plaintiff or cross-complainant, as the case may be, may proceed against the defendants served, in the same manner as if they were the only defendants.

Section 415. To be amended to read as follows:

Sec. 415. Proof of the service of summons and complaint or cross-complaint, as the case may be, must be as follows:

1. If served by the Sheriff, his certificate thereof;
2. If by any other person, his affidavit thereof; or,
3. In case of publication, the affidavit of the printer, or his foreman, or principal clerk, showing the same in accordance with the order therefor; and an affidavit of a deposit of a copy of the summons and complaint or cross-complaint, as the case may be, in the post office, if the same has been deposited; or,

4. The written admission of the defendant.

In case of service otherwise than by publication, the certificate or affidavit must state the time and place of service.

SECTION 416. To be amended to read as follows:

Sec. 416. From the time of the service of the summons and of a copy of the complaint or cross-complaint in a civil action, or of the completion of the publication, when service by publication is ordered, the court is deemed to have acquired jurisdiction of the parties and to have control of all the subsequent proceedings. The voluntary appearance of a defendant is equivalent to personal service of the summons and a copy of the complaint or cross-complaint, as the case may be, upon him.

SECTION 427. To be amended to read as follows:

Sec. 427. The plaintiff may unite several causes of action in the same complaint where they all arise out of:

1. Contracts, express or implied;

2. Claims to recover specific real property, with or without damages for the withholding thereof, or for waste committed thereon, and the rents and profits of the same;

3. Claims to recover specific personal property, with or without damages for the withholding thereof;

4. Claims against a trustee by virtue of a contract, or by operation of law;

5. Injuries to property;

6. Injuries to character and person.

The causes of action so united must all belong to one only of these classes, and must affect all the parties to the action, and not require different places of trial, and must be separately stated.

> NOTE.—The amendment allows all causes of action for injuries to the character and person to be united, being separately stated in the complaint.

SECTION 434. To be amended to read as follows:

Sec. 434. If no objection be taken, either by demurrer or answer, or if a demurrer specifying an objection be overruled for want of prosecution or presentment, the defendant must be deemed to have waived the same, excepting only the objection to the jurisdiction of the court and the objection that the complaint does not state facts sufficient to constitute a cause of action.

> NOTE.—The amendment is that any ground of special demurrer must be deemed waived, although the defendant demurs on that ground, unless he prosecutes his demurrer with due diligence.

SECTION 442. To be amended to read as follows:

Sec. 442. Whenever the defendant seeks affirmative relief against any party, relating to or depending upon the contract or transaction upon which the action is brought, or affecting the property to which the action relates, he may, in addition to his answer, file at the same time, or by permission of the court subsequently, a cross-complaint. New parties may be brought into the action by cross-complaint. The cross-complaint must be served upon the parties affected thereby, and such parties may demur or answer thereto as to the original complaint. Summons may be issued upon a cross-complaint as upon the original complaint.

> Note.—The amendment provides for the issuance of a summons upon a cross-complaint, and also conforms the section to the decision in *Winter* vs. *McMillan*, 87 Cal. 256, by allowing new parties to be brought in by a cross-complaint.

Section 446.   To be amended to read as follows:

Sec. 446.   Every pleading must be subscribed by the party or his attorney; and when the complaint is verified, or when the State, or any officer of the State, in his official capacity, is plaintiff, the answer must be verified, unless an admission of the truth of the complaint might subject the party to a criminal prosecution, or unless an officer of the State, in his official capacity, is defendant.   In all cases of a verification of a pleading, the affidavit of the party must state that the same is true of his own knowledge, except as to the matters which are therein stated on his information or belief, and as to those matters, that he believes it to be true; and where a pleading is verified, it must be by the affidavit of a party, unless the parties are absent from the county where the attorney resides, or from some cause unable to verify it, or the facts are within the knowledge of his attorney, or other person verifying the same.   When the pleading is verified by the attorney, or any other person, except one of the parties, he must set forth in the affidavit the reasons why it is not made by one of the parties, and state therein that the same is true of his own knowledge, or that he believes it to be true.   When a corporation is a party, the verification may be made by any officer thereof.

> Note.—The amendment requires that where the verification is made by a person other than one of the parties, the affidavit must state that the same is true of affiant's own knowledge, or that he believes it to be true.

Section 540.   To be amended to read as follows:

Sec. 540.   The writ must be directed to the Sheriff of any county in which property of such defendant may be, and must require him to attach and safely keep all the property of such defendant within his county, not exempt from execution, or so much thereof as may be sufficient to satisfy the plaintiff's demand, the amount of which must be stated in conformity with the complaint, unless the defendant give him security by the undertaking of at least two sufficient sureties, in an amount sufficient to satisfy such demand, besides costs, or in an amount equal to the value of the property which has been, or is about to be, attached; in which case to take such undertaking. No recovery shall be had against the sureties on such undertaking, neither shall any recovery be had against the Sheriff by reason of any failure to levy the writ on such property, if the court in which the writ of attachment was issued, or the appellate court, shall discharge the same on the ground that it was improperly or irregularly issued, or if the plaintiff fail to recover judgment against the defendant furnishing such undertaking. Several writs may be issued at the same time to the Sheriffs of different counties.

NOTE.—The amendment permits no recovery on the bond if the attachment is afterward dissolved as improperly issued, or if the plaintiff fails to recover judgment against the particular defendant furnishing such bond.

SECTION 542. To be amended to read as follows:

Sec. 542. The Sheriff to whom the writ is directed and delivered must execute the same without delay, if the undertaking mentioned in section five hundred and forty be not given, as follows:

1. Real property, standing upon the records of the county in the name of the defendant, must be attached, by filing with the Recorder of the county a copy of the writ, together with a description of the property attached, and a notice that it is attached; and by leaving a similar copy of the writ, description, and notice with an occupant of the property, if there is one; if not, then by posting the same in a conspicuous place on the property attached;

2. Real property, or an interest therein, belonging to the defendant, and held by any other person, or standing on the records of the county in the name of any other person, must be attached, by filing with the Recorder of the county a copy of the writ, together with a description of the property, and a notice that such real property, and any interest of the defendant therein, held by or standing in the name of such other person (naming him), are attached; and by leaving with the occupant, if any, and with such other person, or his agent, if known and within the county, or at the residence of either, if within the county, a copy of the writ, with a similar description and notice. If there is no occupant of the property, a copy of the writ, together with such description and notice, must be posted in a conspicuous place upon the property. The Recorder must index such attachment when filed, in the names, both of the defendant and of the person by whom the property is held or in whose name it stands on the records;

3. Personal property, capable of manual delivery, must be attached by taking it into custody;

4. Stocks or shares, or interest in stocks or shares, of any corporation or company, must be attached by leaving with the president, or other head of the same, or the secretary, cashier, or other managing agent

thereof, a copy of the writ, and a notice stating that the stock or interest of the defendant is attached. in pursuance of such writ;

5. Debts and credits, and other personal property, not capable of manual delivery, must be attached by leaving with the person owing such debts, or having in his possession, or under his control, such credits and other personal property, or with his agent, a copy of the writ, and a notice that the debts owing by him to the defendant, or the credits and other personal property in his possession, or under his control, belonging to the defendant, are attached in pursuance of such writ; and when a debt due under a judgment is attached, a copy of the writ shall also be filed with the clerk of the court wherein the judgment was rendered, and thereupon the clerk of the Superior Court shall enter in his register the filing of such copy and write upon the face of such judgment, where recorded in his office, the word "attached." When the judgment was rendered in a Justice's Court, a copy of the writ shall be filed with the justice of such court, who shall thereupon enter the fact of such filing in his docket;

6. The interest of a partner in partnership property must be attached by leaving with the person in charge of such property, a copy of the writ and a notice that the interest of the defendant therein is attached in pursuance of such writ.

> NOTE.—The amendment provides for the levy of an attachment or execution in a suit against one partner, upon his interest in partnership property, by the service of notice. It is unfair to the other partners to allow the Sheriff to take possession of any of the partnership assets in a suit affecting one partner alone. The only interest which can be applied to the satisfaction of the judgment obtained in such a case is that of the partner defendant therein, which is a share thereof after the partnership liabilities are settled. The amendment also provides for levy upon a judgment.

SECTION 555.   To be amended to read as follows:

Sec. 555.   Before making such order, the court or judge must require an undertaking on behalf of the defendant, by at least two sureties, residents and freeholders, or householders, in the State, to the effect that in case the writ of attachment be not discharged on motion in the action in which the writ was issued, on the ground that the same was improperly or irregularly issued, or in case the plaintiff recover judgment in the action, defendant will, on demand, re-deliver the attached property so released to the proper officer, to be applied to the payment of the judgment, or, in default thereof, that the defendant and sureties will, on demand, pay to the plaintiff the full value of the property released.   The court or judge making such order may fix the sum for which the undertaking must be executed, and, if necessary, in fixing such sum, to know the value of the property released, the same may be appraised by one or more disinterested persons, to be appointed by the court for that purpose.   The sureties may be required to justify before the court or judge, and the property attached cannot be released from the attachment without their justification, if the same be required.

NOTE.—The present section conditions the liability of the Sheriff on the recovery of judgment by the plaintiff. The proposed amendment adds to this the further condition that the attachment must not be discharged on the ground that the writ was improperly or irregularly issued.

SECTION 581. To be amended to read as follows:

Sec. 581. An action may be dismissed, or a judgment of nonsuit entered, in the following cases:

1. By the plaintiff himself, by written request to the clerk, filed among the papers in the case, at any time before trial, upon payment of costs; *provided*, a counterclaim has not been made, or affirmative relief sought by the cross-complaint or answer of the defendant. If a provisional remedy has been allowed, the undertaking must thereupon be delivered by the clerk to the defendant, who may have his action thereon;

2. By either party upon the written consent of the other;

3. By the court, when the plaintiff fails to appear on the trial, and the defendant appears and asks for the dismissal;

4. By the court, when, upon the trial and before the final submission of the case, the plaintiff abandons it;

5. By the court, upon motion of the defendant, when upon the trial the plaintiff fails to prove a sufficient case for the jury;

6. By the court, when, after verdict or final submission, the party entitled to judgment neglects to demand and have the same entered for more than six months.

The dismissals mentioned in subdivisions one and two hereof, are made by entry in the clerk's register.

The dismissals mentioned in subdivisions three, four, five, and six of this section, shall be made by orders of the court entered upon the minutes thereof, and shall be effective for all purposes when so entered, but the clerk of the court shall note such orders in his register of actions in the case.

7. And no action heretofore or hereafter commenced shall be further prosecuted, and no further proceedings shall be had therein, and all actions heretofore or hereafter commenced shall be dismissed by the court in which the same shall have been commenced, on its own motion, or on motion of any party interested therein, whether named in the complaint as a party or not, unless summons shall have been issued within one year; and all such actions shall be in like manner dismissed, unless the summons shall be served and return thereon made within three years after the commencement of said action. But all such actions may be prosecuted, if appearance has been made by the

defendant or defendants within said three years, in the same manner as if summons had been issued and served.

> NOTE.—The effect of this amendment will be to settle conflicting decisions upon the question whether an action is dismissed before the judgment of dismissal is actually recorded by the clerk. Under the amendment, when a dismissal is filed, the clerk must enter the same in his register, and thereupon the action shall be for all purposes deemed to be dismissed.

SECTION 585.   To be amended to read as follows:

Sec. 585.   Judgment may be had, if the defendant fail to answer the complaint or cross-complaint, as follows:

1. On a cause of action arising upon contract for the recovery of money or damages only, if the defendant has been personally served and no answer has been filed with the clerk of the court within the time specified in the summons, or such further time as may have been granted, the clerk, upon application of the plaintiff, or cross-complainant, must enter the default of the defendant, and immediately thereafter enter judgment for the amount demanded by the complaint or cross-complaint, including the costs, against the defendant, or against one or more of several defendants, in the cases provided for in section four hundred and fourteen;

2. On other causes of action, if the defendant has been personally served and no answer has been filed with the clerk of the court within the time specified in the summons, or such further time as may have been granted, the clerk must enter the default of the defendant; and thereafter the plaintiff or cross-complainant may apply to the court for the relief demanded in the complaint or cross-complaint.   If the taking of an account, or the proof of any fact, is necessary to enable the court to give judgment, or to carry the judgment into effect, the court may take the account or hear the proof; or may, in its discretion, order a reference for that purpose.   And where the action is for the recovery of damages, in whole or in part, the court may order the damages to be assessed by a jury; or if, to determine the amount of damages, the examination of a long account be involved, by a reference as above provided;

3. In actions where the service of a summons was by publication, the plaintiff or cross-complainant, upon the expiration of the time for answering, may, upon proof of the publication, and that no answer has been filed, apply for judgment; and the court must thereupon require proof to be made of the demand mentioned in the complaint or cross-complaint; and if the defendant be not a resident of the State, must require the plaintiff or his agent to be examined on oath respecting any payments that have been made to the plaintiff or cross-complainant, or to any one for his use, on account of such demand, and may render judgment for the amount which he is entitled to recover.

SECTION 632. To be amended to read as follows:

Sec. 632. Upon the trial of a question of fact by the court, its decision must be given within thirty days after the cause is submitted for decision, and, except in cases on appeal to the Superior Court, as a tribunal of final resort, must be in writing, and filed with the clerk.

NOTE.—The amendment makes findings of fact unnecessary in the decision of cases on appeal in the Superior Court.

SECTION 635. A new section to be added to read as follows:

Sec. 635. The court may amend, eliminate from, or add to its decision, or the judgment entered thereon, at any time between the submission of a motion for a new trial and the entry of an order disposing of such motion.

NOTE.—This amendment will allow the court to amend its findings, and the judgment, when, on the argument of the motion for a new trial, it is apparent that a mistake or omission has been made. As the law now is, the court cannot correct such errors, except by granting a new trial.

SECTION 658. To be amended to read as follows:

Sec. 658. When the application is made for a cause mentioned in the first, second, third, and fourth subdivisions of the last section, it must be made upon affidavits; and for any other cause it must be made upon the minutes of the court, as hereinafter provided.

SECTION 659. To be amended to read as follows:

Sec. 659. The party intending to move for a new trial must, within ten days after the verdict of the jury, if the action were tried by a jury, or after notice of the decision of the court or referee, if the action were tried without a jury, file with the clerk, and serve upon the adverse party, a notice of his intention, designating the grounds upon which the motion will be made, and whether the same will be made upon affidavits or the minutes of the court, or both:

1. On affidavits: If the motion is to be made upon affidavits, the moving party must, within ten days after serving the notice, or such further time as the court in which the action is pending, or a judge thereof, may allow, file such affidavits with the clerk, and serve a copy upon the adverse party, who shall have ten days to file counter affidavits, a copy of which must be served upon the moving party;

2. On minutes of court: When the motion is to be made upon the minutes of the court, and the ground of the motion is the insufficiency of the evidence to justify the verdict or other decision, the notice of motion must specify the particulars in which the evidence is alleged to be insufficient; and, if the ground of the motion be errors in law occurring at the trial, and excepted to by the moving party, the notice must specify the particular errors upon which the party will rely. If the

notice does not contain the specifications herein indicated, when the motion is made on the minutes of the court, the motion must be denied.

SECTION 660. To be amended to read as follows:

Sec. 660. The application for a new trial shall be heard at the earliest practicable period after notice of the motion, if the motion is to be heard upon the minutes of the court, and in other cases, after the affidavits are filed, and may be brought to a hearing upon motion of either party. On such hearing reference may be had in all cases to the pleadings and orders of the court on file, and to any depositions and documentary evidence on file, and to any bill of exceptions which may have been settled and filed during the progress of the trial, and to the phonographic reporter's notes, whether the same have been transcribed or not.

SECTION 661. To be amended to read as follows:

Sec. 661. The judgment roll and the affidavits, and such bills of exceptions as may have been settled and filed during the progress of the trial, and the statement of the case to be prepared after the decision of the motion, with a copy of the order, shall constitute the record to be used on appeal from the order granting or refusing a new trial. Such subsequent statement shall be proposed by the party appealing, or intending to appeal, within ten days after notice of the entry of the order, granting or denying a new trial, or such further time as the court in which the action is pending, or a judge thereof, may allow, and the same or a copy thereof shall be served upon the adverse party, who shall have ten days thereafter to prepare amendments thereto, and serve the same, or a copy thereof, upon the party appealing, or intending to appeal. It is the duty of the judge, in settling the statement, to strike out of it all redundant and useless matter, and to make the statement truly represent the case, notwithstanding the assent of the parties to such redundant or useless matter, or to any inaccurate statement. When settled, the statement shall be signed by the judge, with his certificate to the effect that the same is allowed, and it shall then be filed with the clerk.

NOTE.—The four last proposed amendments will require all motions for a new trial, except where made upon affidavits, to be heard upon the minutes of the court. After the disposition of the motion a statement of the case can be settled in the usual way by the party desiring to appeal from the order.

SECTION 671. To be amended to read as follows:

Sec. 671. Immediately after filing the judgment roll, the clerk must make the proper entries of the judgment, under appropriate heads, in the docket kept by him, and from the time the judgment is docketed it becomes a lien upon all the real property of the judgment debtor not exempt from execution in the county, owned by him at the time, or which he may afterwards acquire, until the lien ceases. The lien continues for two years, unless the enforcement of the judgment be stayed on appeal by the execution of a sufficient undertaking, as provided in this Code, in which case the lien of the judgment ceases.

NOTE.—The amendment makes the lien upon real estate of a judgment cease at the end of two years, instead of five years, as by the present section. By Section 674, two years is the limit for a certified transcript of a judgment as filed in any other county, and by Section 900 the filing in the Recorder's office of an abstract of the judgment rendered by a justice of the peace, makes such judgment a lien for only two years. The limit should be the same in all cases, and it is believed that the interest of both creditor and debtor will be best subserved by reducing the time in all cases to two years. The amendment also eliminates the provision that on the filing of a stay bond on appeal, an attachment levied by the respondent is dissolved. The injustice of such a provision is, that where a party has secured his demand by an attachment and recovers judgment, a reversal thereof on appeal on technical grounds, where a stay bond has been filed, leaves him unsecured, if the property attached has been disposed of, pending the appeal.

SECTION 676. A new section to be added to read as follows:

Recording judgment decreeing conveyance equivalent to conveyance.

Sec. 676. Whenever a judgment of a court decrees that a conveyance of real property be made by any person, such judgment, when it becomes final, shall operate as a deed to convey the property therein decreed to be conveyed, without any conveyance being executed by such person. A certified copy of such judgment, when recorded in the office of the County Recorder of the county where the land is situated, shall stand in the place of a deed.

SECTION 691. To be amended to read as follows:

Sec. 691. The Sheriff must execute the writ against the property of the judgment debtor, by levying on a sufficient amount of property, if there be sufficient; collecting or selling the things in action, including judgments in favor of or owned by the judgment debtor, and selling the other property, and paying to the plaintiff, or his attorney, so much of the proceeds as will satisfy the judgment. Any excess in the proceeds over the judgment and accruing costs, must be returned to the judgment debtor, unless otherwise directed by the judgment or order of the court. When there is more property of the judgment debtor than is sufficient to satisfy the judgment and accruing costs within the view of the Sheriff, he must levy only on such part of the property as the judgment debtor may indicate, if the property indicated be amply sufficient to satisfy the judgment and costs.

SECTION 699. To be amended to read as follows:

Sec. 699. When the purchaser of any personal property not capable of manual delivery, or of the interest of a partner in partnership property, pays the purchase money, the officer making the sale must execute and deliver to the purchaser a certificate of sale. Such certificate conveys to the purchaser all the right which the debtor had in such property on the day the execution or attachment was levied.

Note.—This amendment, taken in connection with that proposed to Section 542, provides for the sale on execution of a partner's interest, without interfering with the possession of the property by the partnership.

SECTION 730. A new section to be added to Chapter I, Title X, Part II, to read as follows:

Regulating attorney's fees in foreclosure cases.

Sec. 730. In all cases of foreclosure of a mortgage, the attorney's fee shall be fixed by the court in which the proceeding of foreclosure is had, any stipulation in said mortgage to the contrary, notwithstanding.

Note.—The proposed new section contains the provisions of the Act of March 27, 1874. (Stats. 1873-74, p. 707.)

SECTION 811. A new section to be added to read as follows:

Involuntary dissolution of corporation.

Sec. 811. A corporation may be dissolved, at the suit of the Attorney-General on behalf of the State, for violation of any law of the State under which it was created, or for the non-performance of obligations assumed by it in favor of the State.

Note.—This section provides for the involuntary dissolution of corporations, as indicated in Section 399 of the Civil Code.

SECTION 849. To be amended to read as follows:

Sec. 849. The summons may be served by any Sheriff or Constable of this State, or by any male resident, over the age of eighteen years not a party to the suit. And must be served and returned as provided in title five, part two, of this Code. Or it may be served by publication, and sections four hundred and twelve and four hundred and thirteen, so far as they relate to the publication of summons, are made applicable to justices' courts, the word "justice" being substituted for the word "judge" wherever the latter word occurs.

Note.—The amendment eliminates the useless provision of the section requiring the County Clerk's certificate upon a summons to be served outside of the county in which it is issued, and also allows the summons in such a case to be served by a male resident of the State over the age of eighteen years.

SECTION 868. To be amended to read as follows:

Sec. 868. The writ may be directed to any Sheriff or Constable in the State of California, and must require him to attach and safely keep all the property of the defendant within his county, not exempt from execution, or so much thereof as may be sufficient to satisfy the plaintiff's demand, the amount of which must be stated in conformity with the complaint, unless the defendant give him security, by the undertaking of two sufficient sureties, in an amount sufficient to satisfy such demand, besides costs; in which case, to take such undertaking.

Note.—The amendment allows a writ of attachment to be executed by Constables outside of the county where the justice resides.

Section 939. To be amended to read as follows:

Sec. 939. An appeal may be taken:

1. From a final judgment in an action or special proceeding commenced in the court in which the same is rendered, within six months after the entry of judgment. But an exception to the decision or verdict, on the ground that it is not supported by the evidence, cannot be reviewed on an appeal from the judgment, unless the appeal is taken within sixty days after the rendition of the judgment;

2. From a judgment rendered on an appeal from an inferior court, within ninety days after the entry of such judgment;

3. From an order granting or refusing a new trial; from an order granting or dissolving an injunction; from an order refusing to grant or dissolve an injunction; from an order appointing a receiver; from an order dissolving or refusing to dissolve an attachment; from an order granting or refusing to grant a change of the place of trial; from any special order made after final judgment; from an interlocutory judgment in actions for partition of real property; and from an order confirming, changing, modifying, or setting aside the report, in whole or in part, of the referees in actions for partition of real property in the cases mentioned in section seven hundred and sixty-three of this Code, within sixty days after the order or interlocutory judgment is made and entered in the minutes of the court, or filed with the clerk.

Note.—The amendment allows an appeal from an order appointing a receiver, but under the proposed amendment to Section 943, *infra*, such appeal does not stay the execution of the order, unless a bond be given in an amount to be determined by the court.

Section 943. To be amended to read as follows:

Sec. 943. If the judgment or order appealed from direct the assignment or delivery of documents or personal property, the execution of the judgment or order cannot be stayed by appeal, unless the things required to be assigned or delivered be placed in the custody of such officer or receiver as the court may appoint, or unless an undertaking be entered into on the part of the appellant, with at least two sureties, and in such amount as the court, or a judge thereof, may direct, to the effect that the appellant will obey the order of the appellate court upon the appeal. If the judgment or order appealed from appoint a receiver, the execution of the judgment or order cannot be stayed by appeal, unless a written undertaking be executed on the part of the appellant, with two or more sureties, to the effect that if such judgment or order be affirmed or the appeal dismissed, the appellant will pay all damages which the respondent may sustain by reason of such stay, not exceeding an amount to be fixed by the judge of the court by which the judgment was rendered or order made, which amount must be specified in the undertaking. If the judgment or order appealed from direct the sale of personal property upon the foreclosure of a mortgage thereon, the execution of the judgment or order cannot be stayed on appeal, unless an undertaking be entered into on the part of the appellant, with at least two sureties, in such amount as the court, or the judge thereof, may direct, to the effect that the appellant will, on demand, deliver the mortgaged property to the proper officer if the judgment be affirmed, or in default of such delivery, that the appellant and sureties will, on demand, pay to the proper officer the full value of such property at the date of the appeal.

SECTION 963. To be amended to read as follows:

Sec. 963. An appeal may be taken to the Supreme Court, from a Superior Court, in the following cases:

1. From a final judgment entered in an action or special proceeding commenced in a Superior Court, or brought into a Superior Court from another court;

2. From an order granting or refusing a new trial, or granting or dissolving an injunction, or refusing to grant or dissolve an injunction, or appointing a receiver, or dissolving or refusing to dissolve an attachment, or changing or refusing to change the place of trial, from any special order made after final judgment, and from such interlocutory judgment in actions for partition as determines the rights and interests of the respective parties, and directs partition to be made;

3. From a judgment or order granting or refusing to grant, revoking or refusing to revoke, letters testamentary, or of administration, or of guardianship; or admitting or refusing to admit a will to probate, or against or in favor of the validity of a will, or revoking the probate thereof; or against or in favor of setting apart property, or making an allowance for a widow or child; or against or in favor of directing the partition, sale, or conveyance of real property, or settling an account of an executor, administrator, or guardian; or refusing, allowing, or directing the distribution or partition of an estate, or any part thereof, or the payment of a debt, claim, or legacy, or distributive share; or confirming or refusing to confirm a report of an appraiser or appraisers setting apart a homestead.

SECTION 977. To be amended to read as follows:

Sec. 977. Upon receiving the notice of appeal, and on payment of the fees of the justice or judge, payable on appeal and not included in the judgment, and filing an undertaking as required in the next section, and after settlement or adoption of statement, if any, the justice or judge must, within five days, transmit to the clerk of the Superior Court, if the appeal be on questions of law alone, a certified copy of his docket, the statement as admitted or as settled, the notice of appeal, and the undertaking filed; or, if the appeal be on questions of fact, or both law and fact, a certified copy of his docket, the pleadings, all notices, motions, and all other papers filed in the cause, the notice of appeal, and the undertaking filed; and the justice or judge may be compelled by the Superior Court, by an order entered upon motion, to transmit such papers, and may be fined for neglect or refusal to transmit the same. A certified copy of such order may be served on the justice or judge by the party or his attorney. In the Superior Court, either party may have the benefit of all legal objections made in the Justice's or Police Court.

NOTE.—The amendment will relieve the applicant of the necessity of paying all the costs of the action, as a prerequisite to the hearing of his appeal, including those already charged against him in the judgment, as decided in the case of *Webster* vs. *Hanna*, 102 Cal. 177.

SECTION 978. To be amended to read as follows:

Sec. 978. An appeal from a Justice's or Police Court is not effectual for any purpose unless an undertaking be filed, with two or more sureties, in the sum of one hundred dollars, for the payment of the costs on the appeal, or the undertaking be waived in writing by the adverse party; or, if a stay of proceedings be claimed, in a sum equal to twice the amount of the judgment, including costs, when the judgment is for the payment of money; or twice the value of the property, including costs, when the judgment is for the recovery of specific personal property, and must be conditioned, when the action is for the recovery of money, that the appellant will pay the amount of the judgment appealed from, and all costs, if the appeal be withdrawn or dismissed, or the amount of any judgment and all costs that may be recovered against him in the action in the Superior Court. When the action is for the recovery of, or to enforce or foreclose a lien on, specific personal property, the undertaking must be conditioned that the appellant will pay the judgment and costs appealed from, and obey the order of the court made therein, if the appeal be withdrawn or dismissed, or any judgment and costs that may be recovered against him in said action in the Superior Court, and will obey any order made by the court therein. When the judgment appealed from directs the delivery of the possession of real property, the execution of the same cannot be stayed unless a written undertaking be executed on the part of the appellant, with two or more sureties, to the effect that during the possession of such property by the appellant he will not commit or suffer to be committed any waste thereon, and that if the appeal be dismissed or withdrawn, or the judgment affirmed, or judgment be recovered against him in the action in the Superior Court, he will pay the value of the use and occupation of the property from the time of the appeal until the delivery of possession thereof; or that he will pay any judgment and costs that may be recovered against him in said action in the Superior Court, not exceeding a sum to be fixed by the justice of the court from which the appeal is taken, and which sum must be specified in the undertaking. A deposit of the amount of the judgment, including all costs appealed from, or of the value of the property, including all costs in actions for the recovery of specific personal property, with the justice or judge, is equivalent to the filing of the undertaking, and in such cases the justice or judge must transmit the money to the clerk of the Superior Court, to be by him paid out on the order of the court. The adverse party may except to the sufficiency of the sureties within five days after the filing of the undertaking, and unless they or other sureties justify before the justice or judge, or the County Clerk of the county in which such justice or judge resides, within five days thereafter, upon notice to the adverse party, to the amount stated in their affidavits, the appeal must be regarded as if no such undertaking had been given, and execution may thereafter be issued on the judgment.

> Note.—The amendment allows the justification of sureties upon the appeal bonds mentioned in the section to be made before the County Clerk, and provides that unless they so justify, execution shall be issued on the judgment. It also provides that the undertaking may be waived, by the adverse party, in writing.

Section 980. To be amended to read as follows:

Sec. 980. Upon an appeal heard upon a statement of the case, the Superior Court may review all orders affecting the judgment appealed from, and may set aside, or confirm, or modify any or all of the proceedings subsequent to and dependent upon such judgment, and may, if necessary or proper, order a new trial. When the action is tried anew, on appeal, the trial must be conducted in all respects as other trials in the Superior Court, but unless a judgment is rendered more favorable to appellant than in the court below, the appellant must pay all costs of the trial in the Superior Court. The provisions of this Code as to changing the place of trial, and all the provisions as to trials in the Superior Court, are applicable to trials on appeal in the Superior Court. For a failure to prosecute an appeal, or unnecessary delay in bringing it to a hearing, the Superior Court, after notice, may order the appeal to be dismissed, with costs; and if it appear to such court that the appeal was made solely for delay, it may add to the costs such damages as may be just, not exceeding twenty-five per cent of the judgment appealed from. Judgments rendered in the Superior Court on appeal shall have the same force and effect and may be enforced in the same manner as judgments in actions commenced in the Superior Court.

NOTE.—The amendment puts the costs in the Superior Court upon the appellant, unless the judgment therein rendered is more favorable to him than that appealed from.

SECTION 1015. To be amended to read as follows:

Sec. 1015. When a plaintiff or a defendant, who has appeared, resides out of the State, and has no attorney in the action or proceeding, or when a party has been served with summons and his default for not answering has been entered, the service may be made on the clerk for him. But in all cases where a party has an attorney in the action or proceeding, the service of papers, when required, must be upon the attorney instead of the party, except of subpœnas, of writs, of other process issued in the suit, and of papers to bring him into contempt.

NOTE.—The amendment allows service of notice where necessary to be made upon the clerk, after the entry of the default of the party for not answering.

SECTION 1040. A new section to be added to read as follows:

Printing briefs on appeal—Costs.

Sec. 1040. A party entitled to recover his costs on appeal to the Supreme Court shall be entitled to include in his cost bill the expense of printing the points and authorities on the argument of such appeal, not exceeding fifty dollars in any one case.

SECTION 1161. To be amended to read as follows:

Sec. 1161. A tenant of real property, for a term less than life, is guilty of an unlawful detainer:

1. When he continues in possession, in person or by a subtenant, of the property, or any part thereof, after the expiration of the term for which it is let to him, without the permission of his landlord, or the successor in estate of his landlord, if any there be; but in the case of a tenancy at will, it must first be terminated by notice, as prescribed in the Civil Code;

2. Where he continues in possession, in person or by subtenant, without permission of his landlord, or the successor in estate of his landlord, if any there be, after default in the payment of rent, pursuant to the lease or agreement under which the property is held, and three days' notice, in writing, requiring its payment, stating the amount which is due, or possession of the property, shall have been served upon him, and if there be a subtenant in actual occupation of the premises, also upon such subtenant. Such notice may be served at any time within one year after the rent becomes due. In all cases of tenancy upon agricultural lands, where the tenant has held over and retained possession for more than sixty days after the expiration of his term, without

any demand of possession or notice to quit by the landlord, or the successor in estate of his landlord, if any there be, he shall be deemed to be holding by permission of the landlord, or the successor in estate of his landlord, if any there be, and shall be entitled to hold under the terms of the lease for another full year, and shall not be deemed guilty of an unlawful detainer during said year, and such holding over for the period aforesaid shall be taken and construed as a consent on the part of a tenant to hold for another year;

3. When he continues in possession, in person or by subtenant, after a neglect or failure to perform other conditions or covenants of the lease or agreement under which the property is held, including any covenant not to assign or sublet, than the one for the payment of rent, and three days' notice, in writing, requiring the performance of such conditions or covenants, or the possession of the property, shall have been served upon him, and if there be a subtenant in actual occupation of the premises, also upon such subtenant. Within three days after the service of the notice, the tenant, or any subtenant in actual occupation of the premises, or any mortgagee of the term, or other person interested in its continuance, may perform the conditions or covenants of the lease, or pay the stipulated rent, as the case may be, and thereby save the lease from forfeiture; *provided*, if the covenants and conditions of the lease violated by the lessee cannot afterward be performed, then no notice, as last prescribed herein, need be given to said lessee or his subtenant demanding the performance of the violated covenants or conditions of the lease. A tenant may take proceedings, similar to those prescribed in this chapter, to obtain possession of the premises let to an undertenant, in case of his unlawful detention of the premises underlet to him;

4. Any tenant or subtenant assigning or subletting or committing waste upon the demised premises, contrary to the covenants of his lease, thereby terminates the lease, and the landlord, or his successor in estate, shall, upon service of three days' notice to quit, upon the person or persons in possession, be entitled to restitution of possession of such demised premises under the provisions of this section.

NOTE.—There are two sections numbered 1161, approved on the same day, and the effect of the amendment will be to repeal them, and substitute a more comprehensive one.

SECTION 1166. To be amended to read as follows:

Sec. 1166. The plaintiff, in his complaint, which shall be in writing, must set forth the facts on which he seeks to recover, and describe the premises with reasonable certainty, and may set forth therein any circumstances of fraud, force, or violence, which may have accompanied the alleged forcible entry, or forcible or unlawful detainer, and claim damages therefor. In case the unlawful detainer charged be after default in the payment of rent, the complaint must state the amount of such rent. Upon filing the complaint, a summons must be issued thereon as in other cases, returnable at a day designated therein, which shall not be less than three, nor more thàn five, days from its date, except in cases where the publication of the summons is necessary, in which case the court, or a judge or justice thereof, may order that the summons be made returnable at such time as may be deemed proper, and the summons shall specify the return day so fixed.

NOTE.—The amendment makes the return day not less than three nor more than five days, instead of not less than three nor more than twelve days, as at present.

SECTION 1170. To be amended to read as follows:

Sec. 1170. On or before the day fixed for his appearance, the defendant may appear and answer. He may file a demurrer at the same time with his answer, but not otherwise, and the demurrer shall be disposed of by the court or justice at the trial of the action. If the demurrer is sustained, an immediate amendment of the pleadings shall be allowed. When issue of fact is joined and the case is in a condition to proceed with the trial thereof, such trial shall be had forthwith, if the business of the court or justice will conveniently permit, or at as early a time as may be consistent with the rights of the parties. If a speedy trial will be facilitated by the transfer of the case to another judge or justice of the court, an order may be made transferring such case for trial accordingly.

NOTE.—The amendment is designed to expedite the trial of these cases by providing that a demurrer shall only be filed at the same time with the answer, and disposed of at the trial; for an amendment of pleadings forthwith, if necessary; for the immediate trial, if convenient to the court, and for the transfer of the case, if, thereby, an earlier trial can be had.

SECTION 1209. To be amended to read as follows:

Sec. 1209. The following acts or omissions in respect to a court of justice, or proceedings therein, are contempts of the authority of the court:

1. Disorderly, contemptuous, or insolent behavior toward the judge while holding the court, tending to interrupt the due course of a trial or other judicial proceeding;

2. A breach of the peace, boisterous conduct, or violent disturbance, tending to interrupt the due course of a trial or other judicial proceeding;

3. Misbehavior in office, or other willful neglect or violation of duty, by an attorney, counsel, clerk, sheriff, coroner, or other person appointed or elected to perform a judicial or ministerial service;

4. Deceit or abuse of the process or proceedings of the court by a party to an action or special proceeding;

5. Disobedience of any lawful judgment, order, or process of court;

6. Assuming to be an officer, attorney, counsel of a court, and acting as such, without authority;

7. Rescuing any person or property in the custody of an officer by virtue of an order or process of such court;

8. Unlawfully detaining a witness, or party to an action, while going to, remaining at, or returning from, the court where the action is on the calendar for trial;

9. Any other unlawful interference with the process or proceedings of a court;

10. Disobedience of a subpœna, duly served, or refusing to be sworn or answer as a witness before a court or any officer authorized to issue a subpœna, administer oaths, and take testimony;

11. When summoned as a juror in a court, neglecting to attend or serve as such, or improperly conversing with a party to an action to be tried at such court, or with any other person, in relation to the merits of such action, or receiving a communication from a party or other person in respect to it, without immediately disclosing the same to the court;

12. Disobedience, by an inferior tribunal, magistrate, or officer, of the lawful judgment, order, or process of a Superior Court, or proceeding in an action or special proceeding contrary to law, after such action or special proceeding is removed from the jurisdiction of such inferior tribunal, magistrate, or officer. Disobedience of the lawful orders or process of a judicial officer is also a contempt of the authority of such officer. But no speech or publication reflecting upon, or concerning any court, or any officer thereof, shall be treated or punished as a contempt of such court, unless made in the immediate presence of such court while in session, and in such a manner as to actually interfere with its proceedings.

NOTE.—The amendment is to Subdivision 10 of the section, and is designed, with the amendment proposed to Section 1991, to enable the court to punish as a contempt the non-appearance or refusal of a witness to testify before a notary public in a proper case.

SECTION 1234. A new section to be added to read as follows:

Disposition of unclaimed deposit or dividend.

Sec. 1234. If the applicant be a savings and loan association, or engaged in the business of receiving money on deposit, and there be any unclaimed deposit or dividend in its hands belonging to a person whose whereabouts is unknown to the trustees, directors, or other officers presenting the application, the application shall set forth the name of the person making such deposit or entitled to such dividend, the time when such deposit was made or dividend declared, the residence, if known, of such person at the time of such deposit, the amount of such deposit or dividend, and the fact that the whereabouts of such person is unknown. The same facts shall be stated in the notice of the application given by the clerk. If, at any time before the expiration of the time of publication, any person shall file a claim to such deposit or dividend, the court shall, at the hearing and upon five days' notice to him, hear and determine his claim, and, if such claim be established, order such money to be paid to him. All such deposits or dividends not so claimed, or as to which no claim shall be established, shall, upon order of the court, be paid into the state treasury, accompanied with a copy of the order, which shall set forth the facts hereinbefore in this section required to be stated concerning such deposits or dividends; and, upon production of the State Treasurer's receipt for such payment, the court may proceed to declare the corporation dissolved as in other cases. All unclaimed deposits and dividends so paid into the state treasury shall be received, invested, accounted for, and paid out, in the same manner and by the same officers as is provided by law in the case of escheated estates and in section twelve hundred and seventy-two of this Code.

Section 1278. To be amended to read as follows:

Sec. 1278. Such application must be heard at such time as the court may appoint, and objections may be filed by any person who can, in such objections, show to the court good reason against such change of name. On the hearing, the court may examine on oath any of the petitioners, remonstrants, or other persons, touching the application, and may make such order changing the name or dismissing the application, as to the court may seem right and proper. A certified copy of any order changing the name of a corporation shall be filed with the Secretary of State, and such order shall have no effect until such certified copy thereof is filed with the Secretary of State.

Section 1324. To be amended to read as follows:

Sec. 1324. If, on the hearing, it appears upon the face of the record that the will has been proved, allowed, and admitted to probate in any other of the United States, or in any foreign country, and that it was executed in conformity with the laws of this State, it must be admitted to probate, and have the same force and effect as a will first admitted to probate in this State, and letters testamentary or of administration issued thereon.

Note.—The amendment harmonizes this section with Sections 1276 and 1285 of the Civil Code, which provide that a will made out of the State is not valid unless executed according to the provisions of that Code.

SECTION 1369. To be amended to read as follows:

Sec. 1369. No person is competent, or shall be appointed, to serve as administrator or administratrix who is:

1. Under the age of majority;
2. Not a bona fide resident of the State;
3. Convicted of an infamous crime;
4. Adjudged by the court incompetent to execute the duties of the trust by reason of drunkenness, improvidence, or want of understanding or integrity.

> NOTE.—The amendment adds the words "shall be appointed" to the section, instead of the word "entitled."

SECTION 1379. To be amended to read as follows:

Sec. 1379. Administration may be granted to one or more competent persons, at the written request of the person entitled, filed in the court. The force and effect of such request shall not be affected by the fact that the person entitled may be a non-resident of the State. When the person entitled is a non-resident of the State, affidavits taken *ex parte* before any officer authorized by the laws of this State to take acknowledgments and administer oaths out of this State, may be received as *prima facie* evidence of the identity of the party, if free from suspicion, and the fact is established to the satisfaction of the court.

> NOTE.—The proposed amendment will allow a non-resident person who would be entitled to administer if a bona fide resident of the State, to nominate a competent person for appointment as administrator, with like effect as if he were such resident. .

SECTION 1465. To be amended to read as follows:

Sec. 1465. Upon the return of the inventory, or at any subsequent time during the administration, the court may, on its own motion, or on petition therefor, set apart, for the use of the surviving husband or wife, or in case of his or her death, to the minor children of the decedent, all the property exempt from execution, including the homestead selected, designated, and recorded. If none has been selected, designated, and recorded, the court must select, designate, and set apart, and cause to be recorded, a homestead for the use of the surviving husband or wife and the minor children, or if there be no surviving husband or wife, then for the use of the minor children, in the manner provided in article two of this chapter, out of the common property; or if there be no common property, then out of the real estate belonging to the decedent.

> NOTE.—This amendment will make the section conform, when taken in connection with Section 1468 of this Code, to Section 1265 of the Civil Code, allowing the homestead in all cases to be set apart to the use of the widow or minor children absolutely, if of community property; otherwise, for a limited period.

SECTION 1468. To be amended to read as follows:

Sec. 1468. When property is set apart to the use of the family, in accordance with the provisions of this chapter, if the decedent left a widow or surviving husband and no minor child, such property is the property of the widow or surviving husband. If the decedent left also a minor child or children, the one half of such property shall belong to the widow or surviving husband, and the remainder to the child, or in equal shares to the children if there be more than one; in which cases the property shall constitute a homestead of five thousand dollars if the surviving husband or wife is the head of a family, as defined in the Civil Code; otherwise, of one thousand dollars. If there be no widow or surviving husband, the whole belongs to the minor child or children in equal shares. If the property set apart be a homestead, selected from the separate property of the deceased, either in his lifetime, or by the court after his death, the court can only set it apart for a limited period, to be designated in the order, and the title vests in his heirs or devisees subject to such order.

SECTION 1474. To be amended to read as follows:

Sec. 1474. If the homestead selected by the husband and wife, or either of them, during their coverture, and recorded while both were living, was selected from the community property, it vests, upon the death of the husband or wife, absolutely in the survivor. If the homestead was selected from the separate property of either the husband or the wife, it vests, on the death of the person from whose property it was selected, in his or her heirs or devisees, subject to the power of the Superior Court to assign it for a limited period to the family of the decedent. In any case, it is not subject to the payment of any debt or liability contracted by or existing against the husband and wife, or either of them, previous to or at the time of the death of such husband or wife, except as provided in the Civil Code.

SECTION 1475. To be amended to read as follows:

Sec. 1475. If the homestead selected and recorded prior to the death of the decedent be returned in the inventory appraised at not exceeding five thousand dollars in value, or was previously appraised as provided in the Civil Code, and such appraised value did not exceed that sum, the Superior Court must, by order, set it off to the persons in whom title is vested by the preceding section. If there be subsisting liens or incumbrances on the homestead, the claims secured thereby may be presented and allowed as other claims against the estate; and must be so presented if demand be made therefor as hereinafter provided; if the funds of the estate be adequate to pay all claims against the estate, the claims so secured must be paid out of such funds. If the funds of

9—c

the estate be not sufficient for that purpose, the claims so secured shall be paid proportionately with other claims allowed, and the liens or incumbrances on the homestead shall only be enforced against the homestead for any deficiency remaining after such payment. Any person interested in the homestead may demand that the claims secured by lien or incumbrance thereon, be presented for allowance as other claims against the estate. Such demand must be in writing, and be delivered to the holder of said claim personally, or be inclosed in an envelope addressed to him at his place of residence or business, and deposited in the United States post office, with the postage thereon prepaid, at least thirty days before the expiration of the time specified in the published notice to creditors within which to present claims against the estate. A copy of said published notice must be delivered or mailed with said demand. If demand be made, as in this section provided, and such claim be not presented for allowance, no action shall be maintained thereon. If no demand be made, as in this section provided, the holder of any lien or incumbrance upon the homestead may enforce the same against the property subject thereto, as provided in section fifteen hundred of this Code.

SECTION 1479. A new section to be added to read as follows:

Proceedings on confirmation of report.

Sec. 1479. If the report contains an admeasurement and division of the property, the court shall, in its order confirming the same, set apart the portion allotted as a homestead to the parties entitled, and thereupon the remaining portion of the premises described in the report shall become the property of the estate, free of any homestead claim. If the report contains a finding that the premises exceeded in value, at the time of their selection, the sum of five thousand dollars, and they cannot be divided without material injury, the court shall, in its order confirming the same, decree that the homestead property shall be sold for a sum in cash not less than five thousand dollars and an amount equal to the expenses of the sale.

SECTION 1480. A new section to be added to read as follows:

Proceedings under order of sale.

Sec. 1480. Such order must describe the lands to be sold, and every such sale must be ordered to be made at public auction. If the executor. or administrator neglects or refuses to make the sale under the order, and as directed therein, he may be compelled to sell by order of the court, made on motion of any person interested. After the order of sale is made, all further proceedings for the sale of such property, and for the notice, report, and confirmation thereof, must be in conformity with the provisions of chapter seven, title eleven, part three of this

Code, except that no bid for an amount less than the sums mentioned in the last preceding section shall be received.

SECTION 1481. A new section to be added to read as follows:

Disposition of proceeds of sale.

Sec. 1481. If the sale is confirmed, the proceeds thereof to the amount of five thousand dollars must be paid to the party or parties entitled to the homestead, and the surplus shall belong to the estate. The amount so paid to the party or parties entitled to the homestead shall be exempt from execution for six months thereafter.

SECTION 1485. To be amended to read as follows:

Sec. 1485. The costs of all proceedings in the Superior Court provided for in this chapter must be paid by the estate as expenses of administration.

SECTION 1487. A new section to be added to Article II, Chapter V, Title XI, Part III, to read as follows:

Sec. 1487. In making any order setting apart or assigning property claimed to have been selected and recorded as a homestead prior to the death of the decedent, the court shall ascertain and adjudge the rights therein of the surviving husband or wife, and of all persons claiming under the decedent, and shall, in such order, and in any order made pursuant to this chapter setting apart or assigning property, name the persons to whom the same is set apart or assigned, and their respective estates, or rights and interests therein. Such order shall be conclusive upon the surviving husband or wife, and upon all persons claiming as heirs, legatees, or devisees of the decedent, subject only to be reversed, set aside, or modified upon appeal.

SECTION 1490. To be amended to read as follows:

Sec. 1490. Upon the hearing of a petition for the probate of a will or for letters of administration, the court must, by examining on oath the party applying, or any other person, determine whether the value of the estate exceeds ten thousand dollars or not, and such determination shall be conclusive upon all persons, including creditors of the estate, in so far as the value of the estate affects the time within which claims must be presented against the estate. Every executor or administrator must, immediately after his appointment, cause to be published in some newspaper of the county, if there be one, if not, then in such newspaper as may be designated by the court, a notice to the creditors of the decedent, requiring all persons having claims against him to exhibit them, with the necessary vouchers, to the executor or administrator, at the place of his residence or business, in the county in which the letters testamentary or of administration were granted, to be specified in the notice. Such notice must be published as often as the judge or court shall direct, but not less than once a week for four weeks. The court or judge may also direct additional notice by publication or posting. In case such executor or administrator resigns, or is removed, before the time expressed in the notice, his successor must give notice only for the unexpired time allowed for such presentation.

NOTE.—The amendment provides that the court shall determine the value of the estate, when letters are issued, in so far as that question affects the time within which claims must be presented. It also requires the place at which claims are to be presented to be in the county where the letters are issued.

SECTION 1491.   To be amended to read as follows:

Sec. 1491.   The time expressed in the notice must be ten months after its first publication, if the court determines, under the preceding section, that the value of the estate exceeds ten thousand dollars; otherwise, the time expressed in the notice must be four months after its first publication.

NOTE.—The proposed amendment conforms this section to the change proposed to the preceding section requiring the court to determine the value of the estate for the purpose of fixing beforehand the time within which claims must be presented.

SECTION 1493.   To be amended to read as follows:

Sec. 1493.   All claims against the estates of decedents, whether the same be due, not due, or contingent, must be presented within the time limited in the notice, and any claim not so presented is barred forever; *provided, however*, that when it is made to appear, by the affidavit of the claimant, to the satisfaction of the court, or a judge thereof, that the claimant had no notice as provided in this chapter, by reason of being out of the State, it may be presented at any time before a decree of distribution is entered.

NOTE.—The amendment requires "*all* claims against an estate" to be presented, which is desirable in view of the proposed new section, 1592, which allows actions to be maintained against the estates of deceased persons in all cases except for slander or libel, or for assault and battery. The section as it now stands permits only "claims arising on contracts" to be presented.

SECTION 1496.   To be amended to read as follows:

Sec. 1496.   When a claim, accompanied by the affidavit required in this chapter, is presented to the executor or administrator, he must indorse thereon his allowance or rejection, with the day and date thereof. If he allow the claim, it must be returned to the claimant, who must, within twenty days thereafter, present it to a judge of the Superior Court for his approval, who must in the same manner indorse upon it his allowance or rejection. If the executor or administrator, or the judge, refuse or neglect to indorse such allowance or rejection for ten days after the claim has been presented to him, such refusal or neglect may, at the option of the claimant, be deemed equivalent to a rejection on the tenth day; and if the presentation be made by a notary, the certificate of such notary, under seal, shall be *prima facie* evidence of such presentation and the date thereof. If the claim be presented to the executor or administrator before the expiration of the time limited for the presentation of claims, the same is presented in time, though acted upon by the executor or administrator and by the judge, after the expiration of such time. If the claim be payable in a particular kind of money or currency, it shall, if allowed, be payable only in such money or currency.

> NOTE.—The amendment fixes the time within which the claimant must present his claim to the judge, when he has received it with the approval of the executor or administrator thereon.

SECTION 1561. To be amended to read as follows:

Sec. 1561. When property is directed by the will to be sold, or authority is given in the will to sell property, the executor may sell any property of the estate without order of the court, and at either public or private sale, and with or without notice, as the executor may determine; but the executor must make return of such sales as in other cases; and if directions are given in the will as to the mode of selling, or the particular property to be sold, such directions must be observed. In either case, no title passes unless the sale be confirmed by the court. Whenever the will omits to mention either a child of the testator born after the making of his will, as provided in section thirteen hundred and six of the Civil Code, or omits to provide for any of the children or for the issue of any deceased child of the testator, as provided in section thirteen hundred and seven of the Civil Code, the fact that such child, or any of the children, or the issue of any deceased child, of the testator, are entitled to succeed to the same portion of the testator's real and personal property as in case of intestacy, shall not impair or affect the validity of any sale of property made by authority of such will in accordance with the provisions of this section.

> NOTE.—The amendment renders valid sales under a power in a will, notwithstanding the fact that a pretermitted child, or issue of any deceased child, appears.

SECTION 1582. To be amended to read as follows:

Sec. 1582. Actions for the recovery of any property, real or personal, or for the possession thereof, or to quiet title thereto, and all other actions, whether founded on contract or tort, except as otherwise provided in section fifteen hundred and ninety-two of this Code, may be maintained by and against executors and administrators, in all cases in which the same might have been maintained by or against their respective testators or intestates.

SECTION 1592.   A new section to be added to Chapter VIII, Title XI, Part III, to read as follows:

Survival of right of action.

Sec. 1592.   For wrongs done to the person, character, property, rights, or interests of another, for which an action may be maintained against the wrongdoer, such action may be brought by the person injured, or, after his death, by his executor or administrator, against such wrongdoer, and after the death of such wrongdoer against his executor or administrator, in the same manner and with like effect in all respects as actions founded upon contract; but this section shall not extend to actions for slander or libel, or to actions for assault and battery.

SECTION 1593.   A new section to be added to Chapter VIII, Title XI, Part III, to read as follows:

Executor or administrator may bid at a foreclosure sale.

Sec. 1593.   When a judgment of foreclosure of a mortgage owned by a decedent in his lifetime is rendered in favor of the executor or administrator, such executor or administrator may, on behalf of the estate, purchase the mortgaged property at the foreclosure sale thereunder, but his bid at such sale shall not exceed the amount of the judgment and costs.

SECTION 1598.   To be amended to read as follows:

Sec. 1598.   On the presentation of a verified petition by any person claiming to be entitled to such conveyance from an executor or administrator, setting forth the facts upon which the claim is predicated, the court, or a judge thereof, must appoint a time and place for hearing the petition, and must order notice thereof to be served upon the executor or administrator personally and by posting in three public places in the county not less than twenty-eight days before the time set for the hearing thereof, or to be published at least four successive weeks before such hearing in such newspaper in this State as he may designate.

SECTION 1616.   To be amended to read as follows:

Sec. 1616.   He shall be allowed all necessary expenses in the care, management, and settlement of the estate, including reasonable fees paid to attorneys for conducting the necessary proceedings or suits in court, and for his services such fees as provided in this chapter; but when the decedent, by his will, makes some other provision for the compensation of his executor, that shall be a full compensation for his services, unless, by a written instrument, filed in the court, he renounces all claim for compensation provided by the will.   No executor or administrator, in any estate hereafter commenced, shall be allowed, in his accounts, for fees paid to attorneys under this section, any greater sum in the aggregate, than the highest amount allowable to such executor or administrator in such estate as compensation under section sixteen hundred and eighteen of this Code.

> NOTE.—The amendment will restrict attorney's fees in estates to an amount not exceeding the highest statutory compensation allowable to executors or administrators.

SECTION 1747.   To be amended to read as follows:

Sec. 1747.   The Superior Court of each county, when it appears necessary or convenient, may appoint guardians for the estates of minors who have no guardian legally appointed by will or deed, and who are inhabitants or residents of the county, or who reside without the State and have estate within the county.   Such appointment may be made on the petition of a relative or other person on behalf of the minor, or on the petition of the minor, if fourteen years of age.   Before making such appointment, the court most cause such notice as such court deems reasonable to be given to any person having the care of such minor, and to such relatives of the minor residing in the county as the court may deem proper.

> NOTE.—The amendment deprives the Superior Court of the power to appoint a guardian of the person of the minor in a summary proceeding, leaving the question of whether a parent is entitled to the custody of his minor child to be decided in proceedings under Section 203 of the Civil Code.

SECTION 1870.   To be amended to read as follows:

Sec. 1870.   In conformity with the preceding provisions, evidence may be given, upon a trial, of the following facts:

1. The precise fact in dispute;

2. The act, declaration, or omission of a party, as evidence against such party;

3. An act or declaration of another, in the presence and within the observation of a party, and his conduct in relation thereto;

4. The act or declaration, verbal or written, of a deceased person in respect to the relationship, birth, marriage, or death of any person related by blood or marriage to such deceased person; the act or declaration of a deceased person done or made against his interest in respect to his real property; and also, in criminal actions, the act or declaration

of a dying person, made under a sense of impending death, respecting the cause of his death;

5. After proof of a partnership or agency, the act or declaration of a partner, or agent, of the party, within the scope of the partnership or agency, and during its existence. The same rule applies to the act or declaration of a joint owner, joint debtor, or other person jointly interested with the party;

6. After proof of a conspiracy, the act or declaration of a conspirator against his co-conspirators, and relating to the conspiracy;

7. The act, declaration, or omission forming a part of a transaction, as explained in section eighteen hundred and fifty;

8. The testimony of a witness deceased, or out of the jurisdiction, or unable to testify, given in a former action between the same parties, relating to the same matter;

9. The opinion of a witness respecting the identity or handwriting of a person, when he has knowledge of the person or handwriting; his opinion on a question of science, art, or trade, when he is skilled therein;

10. The opinion of a subscribing witness to a writing, the validity of which is in dispute, respecting the mental sanity of the signer; and the opinion of an acquaintance respecting the mental sanity of a person, the reason for the opinion being given;

11. Common reputation existing previous to the controversy, respecting facts of a public or general interest more than thirty years old, and in cases of pedigree and boundary;

12. Usage to explain the true character of an act, contract, or instrument, where such true character is not otherwise plain; but usage is never admissible, except as an instrument of interpretation;

13. Monuments and inscriptions in public places, as evidence of common reputation; and entries in family bibles, or other family books or charts, engravings on rings, family portraits, and the like, as evidence of pedigree;

14. The contents of a writing, when oral evidence thereof is admissible;

15. Any other facts from which the facts in issue are presumed or are logically inferable;

16. Such facts as serve to show the credibility of a witness, as explained in section eighteen hundred and forty-seven.

NOTE.—The amendment consists in the elimination of the word "intimate" from Subdivision 10 thereof, and allows evidence to be given by an acquaintance respecting the mental sanity of a person, the reason for the opinion being stated. The tendency of the American courts during the last few years has been largely in this direction. (See *Hardy* vs. *Merill*, 56 N. H. 227; and Schouler on Wills, Section 201.)

SECTION 1880. To be amended to read as follows:

Sec. 1880. The following persons cannot be witnesses:

1. Those who are of unsound mind at the time of their production for examination;

2. Children under ten years of age, who appear incapable of receiving just impressions of the facts respecting which they are examined, or of relating them truly;

3. Parties or assignors of parties to an action or proceeding, or persons interested in, or in whose behalf an action or proceeding is prosecuted by complaint or cross-complaint against an executor or administrator upon a claim or demand, or upon a cause of action affecting the title or right of possession of any property which was in the possession of a deceased person at the time of his death, against the estate of a deceased person, as to any matter of fact occurring before the death of such deceased person.

> NOTE.—The scope of the amendment is to prevent any person interested in an estate from testifying as to facts occurring before decedent's death, not only in an action upon a claim (as the section was construed in *Myers* vs. *Reinstein*, 67 Cal. 89), and also in an action against an estate relating to the title to property in decedent's possession at the time of his death. The same policy which closes the mouth of a surviving party to a transaction where a suit is upon a claim against an estate, would prevent his testifying as to facts constituting an alleged trust in property, because the elements of danger of fraud are equal in both cases.

SECTION 1906. To be amended to read as follows:

Sec. 1906. A judicial record of a foreign country may be proved by the attestation of the clerk, with the seal of the court annexed, if there be a clerk and seal, or of the legal keeper of the record, with the seal of his office annexed, if there be a seal, together with a certificate of the chief judge or presiding magistrate, or the certificate of the minister or ambassador, or a consul, vice-consul, or consular agent of the United States in such foreign country, to the effect that the person making the attestation is the clerk of the court, or the legal keeper of the record, and, in either case, that the signature of such person is genuine, and that the attestation is in due form. The signature of the chief judge, or presiding magistrate, must be authenticated by the certificate of the minister or ambassador, or a consul, vice-consul, or consular agent of the United States, in such foreign country.

SECTION 1918. To be amended to read as follows:

Sec. 1918. Other official documents may be proved as follows:

1. Acts of the executive of this State, by the records of the state department of the State; and of the United States, by the records of the state department of the United States, certified by the heads of those departments respectively. They may also be proved by public

documents, printed by the order of the Legislature or Congress, or either house thereof;

2. The proceedings of the Legislature of this State, or of Congress, by the journals of those bodies respectively, or either house thereof, or by published statutes or resolutions, or by copies certified by the clerk, or printed by their order;

3. The acts of the executive, or the proceedings of the Legislature of a sister State, in the same manner;

4. The acts of the executive, or the proceedings of the Legislature of a foreign country, by journals published by their authority, or commonly received in that country as such, or by a copy certified under the seal of the country or sovereign, or by a recognition thereof in some public act of the executive of the United States;

5. Acts of a municipal corporation of this State, or of a board or department thereof, by a copy, certified by the legal keeper thereof, or by a printed book published by the authority of such corporation;

6. Documents of any other class in this State, by the original, or by a copy, certified by the legal keeper thereof;

7. Documents of any other class in a sister State, by the original, or by a copy, certified by the legal keeper thereof, together with the certificate of the Secretary of State, judge of the Supreme, Superior, or County Court, or Mayor of a city of such State, that the copy is duly certified by the officer having the legal custody of the original;

8. Documents of any other class in a foreign country, by the original, or by a copy certified by the legal keeper thereof, with a certificate of the minister or ambassador, or consul, vice-consul, or a consular agent of the United States in such foreign country, to the effect that the document is a valid and subsisting document of such country, and that the person certifying thereto is the legal keeper of such original document; that said certificate is in due form, and that the signature of the legal keeper thereto is genuine;

9. Documents in the departments of the United States government, by the certificate of the legal custodian thereof.

NOTE.—The amendment is of Subdivision 8, of the section, and obviates the necessity of obtaining the seal of the country or sovereign to be attached to a certified copy of such document in a foreign country.

SECTION 1950. To be amended to read as follows:

Sec. 1950. The record of a conveyance of real property, or any other record, a transcript of which is admissible in evidence, must not be removed from the office where it is kept, except upon the order of a court, in cases where the inspection of the record is shown to be essential to the just determination of the cause or proceeding pending, or to a Superior Court held in the same county with such office, when the custodian thereof or his deputy is subpœnaed to appear with such record.

> NOTE.—The amendment will allow records to be used at trials in Superior Courts held in the same county where such records are kept; *provided*, the custodian or his deputy is required to appear with them.

SECTION 1991. To be amended to read as follows:

Sec. 1991. Disobedience to a subpœna, or a refusal to be sworn or to answer as a witness, or to subscribe an affidavit or deposition when required by any officer authorized to administer oaths and take testimony, may be punished as a contempt, by the court in which the proceedings are pending wherein the testimony of the party is desired, and if the witness be a party, his complaint or answer may be stricken out.

> NOTE.—The amendment, taken in connection with that proposed to Subdivision 10 of Section 1209, allows the court to punish, as a contempt, the refusal of a witness to testify before a notary public when duly served with a subpœna.

SECTION 2015. To be amended to read as follows:

Sec. 2015. When an affidavit is taken before a judge or a court in another State, or in a foreign country, the genuineness of the signature of the judge, the existence of the court, and the fact that such judge is a member thereof, must be certified by the clerk of the court, under the seal thereof, or by the superior of such judge under the seal of his office.

SECTION 2016. A new section to be added to Article II, Chapter III, Title III, of Part III, to read as follows:

Testimony in foreign court, when used.

Sec. 2016. The testimony of witnesses taken by a foreign court of record, reduced to writing, and attested by the judge of such court and under the seal of the same, may be used as evidence of the kinship or identity of the parties claiming to be the heirs or legatees of a deceased person in probate proceedings in this State involving the question of such kinship or identity. If such testimony has been given and reduced to writing in a foreign language, an English translation thereof, verified by a person conversant with both languages to be a full, true, and correct translation of such writing, may accompany the same and may be received in evidence with the original.

SECTION 2021. To be amended to read as follows:

Sec. 2021. The testimony of a witness in this State may be taken by deposition in an action at any time after the service of the summons or the appearance of the defendant, and in a special proceeding after an issue of fact has arisen, or when it becomes necessary or expedient to establish a fact by evidence, therein, in the following cases:

1. When the witness is a party to the action or proceeding, or an

officer or member of a corporation which is a party to the action or proceeding, or a person for whose immediate benefit the action or proceeding is prosecuted or defended;

2. When the witness resides out of the county in which his testimony is to be used;

3. When the witness is about to leave the county where the action is to be tried, and will probably continue absent when the testimony is required;

4. When the witness, otherwise liable to attend the trial, is nevertheless too infirm to attend;

5. When the testimony is required upon a motion, or in any other case where the oral examination of the witness is not required;

6. When the witness is the only one who can establish facts or a fact material to the issue; *provided*, that the deposition of such witness shall not be used if his presence can be procured at the time of the trial of the cause.

SECTION 2024. To be amended to read as follows:

Sec. 2024. The deposition of a witness out of this State may be taken upon a commission issued from the court, under the seal of the court, upon an order of the court, or a judge or a justice thereof, on the application of either party, upon five days' previous notice to the other. If the court be a justice's court, the commission shall have attached to it a certificate, under seal by the County Clerk of such county, to the effect that the person issuing the same was an acting justice of the peace at the date of the commission. If issued to any place within the United States, it may be directed to a person agreed upon by the parties, or if they do not agree, to any judge or justice of the peace or commissioner selected by the court or judge or justice issuing it. If issued to any country out of the United States, it may be directed to a minister, ambassador, consul, vice-consul, or consular agent of the United States in such country, or to a judge of any court of record in such country, or to any person agreed upon by the parties.

NOTE.—The amendment allows a commission to be directed to a judge of any court of record in a foreign country.

SECTION 2039. A new section to be added to Article V, Chapter III, Title III, of Part III, to read as follows:

Letters rogatory to foreign courts.

Sec. 2039. Whenever it is made to appear to the court, by affidavit or otherwise, that upon requisition made by a court of record of this State, a court of record of any foreign State or government, or a judge or commissioner thereof, will cause witnesses to be examined and their depositions to be returned to the court making the requisition, letters rogatory, addressed to such foreign court, may be issued, signed by the judge before whom the action or proceeding may be pending, and attested by the clerk, under the seal of the court. Such letters rogatory may be obtained on the application of either party, upon five days' previous notice to the other, or if no one has appeared in opposition to the claim or allegation sought to be proved, and the time within which such appearance should be made has expired, without notice. The question or questions as to which testimony is required shall be concisely stated and form part of such letters rogatory; or written interrogatories, direct and cross, may, upon the request of either party, be prepared and settled, as in the case of a deposition to be taken under a commission, and annexed to the letters, and the examination shall thereupon be had upon such interrogatories and cross-interrogatories only, unless the parties agree that other or additional questions may be put to the witness. In either case, the letters rogatory shall contain a statement that the court, upon requisition made to it by the foreign court, would likewise cause witnesses to be summoned and examined as provided in the next section. The names of the witness or witnesses to be examined may be inserted in the letters; or if the same are unknown and if no objection is made, the requisition may be to summon and examine such witnesses as may be found competent and able to testify to facts material to the question or questions at issue. A deposition taken by such foreign court, judge, or commissioner, certified by the examining court, judge, or commissioner to have been read to and approved and subscribed by the witness, and returned, in a sealed envelope, to the clerk of the court issuing the letters rogatory, may be used upon the trial or other proceeding in the same manner in which a deposition taken upon a commission regularly issued and duly taken might be used.

SECTION 2040. A new section to be added to Article V, Chapter III, Title III, of Part III, to read as follows:

Letters rogatory to the Superior Courts of this State.

Sec. 2040. Whenever it shall appear to the court, by affidavit or otherwise, that upon letters rogatory issued by a court of record of this State, a court of any foreign country will cause to be taken, certified, and returned depositions of witnesses as provided in the preceding section, it shall be the duty of the court, upon similar letters rogatory addressed to the same by such foreign court in any action or proceeding depending therein, to cause witnesses to be examined and their depositions to be certified and returned as hereinafter provided. Such letters rogatory may be filed in the office of the clerk and assigned in the same manner as an original complaint or petition; and upon motion made on behalf of the court making the requisition, or of any party interested in having the same executed, the court shall appoint a commissioner, whose duty it shall be to summon the witness whose testimony is desired, to administer an oath to him, and to take his testimony and reduce the same to writing in the same manner as under a commission issued in an action or proceeding in this State; and his attendance may be compelled and he may be punished for failing to appear, or to answer proper questions propounded to him, in like manner. After the testimony of the witness shall have been reduced to writing and corrected and signed by the witness, the commissioner shall certify the same and return it to the court; and upon motion made for that purpose, the court shall attest the due execution of the requisition and make an order directing the clerk to return the testimony, so certified and attested, to the foreign court. Before returning the testimony, the clerk shall demand payment of all his fees due to him, which shall be the same as for similar services done by him in actions or proceedings commenced in this State, and he shall also require proof, by proper vouchers, that the fee of the commissioner taking the testimony (which shall not exceed the fee properly chargeable by him in the case of depositions taken in an action or proceeding commenced this State) has been paid.

PROPOSED AMENDMENTS TO THE

POLITICAL CODE.

PRELIMINARY PROVISIONS.

SECTION 11. To be repealed.

NOTE.—The provisions of Section 11 are contained in Section 10.

CHAPTER II.

TERRITORIAL JURISDICTION OF THE STATE.

SECTION 35. A new section to be added to read as follows:

Authorizing the Governor to convey land to the United States in certain cases.

Sec. 35. Whenever the United States desires to acquire title to a tract of land, not exceeding ten acres, belonging to the State, and covered by the navigable waters of the United States, within the limits thereof, for the site of lighthouse, beacon, or other aid to navigation, and application is made by a duly authorized agent of the United States, describing the site required for one of the purposes aforesaid, then the Governor of the State is authorized and empowered to convey the title to the United States, and to cede to the said United States jurisdiction over the same, not inconsistent with the provisions hereof. Whenever the United States desires to acquire title to any piece or parcel of land extending from high-water mark out to three hundred yards beyond low-water mark, such land lying contiguous and adjacent to lands of the United States in this State which lie upon tidewaters and are held and occupied or reserved for military purposes or defense, and which is bounded by a line along high-water mark, a line three hundred yards out beyond low-water mark, and lines at right angles to high-water mark at the points where the boundaries of the adjacent lands of the United States touch high-water mark, or any part or parcel of such tract of land, for military purposes, then the Governor of the State is authorized and empowered, upon application made by a duly authorized agent of the United States, to convey the title to the United States, and cede to the United States jurisdiction over the same; *provided*, that the title to each parcel of land hereby granted, released, and ceded to the United States in this latter case, shall be and remain in the United States only so long as the United States shall continue to hold and own the adjacent lands now belonging to the said United States; *and further provided*, that the State shall retain concurrent jurisdiction in all cases, so far that all process, civil or criminal, issuing under the authority of the State may be executed by the proper officers thereof upon any person or persons amenable to the same, within the limits of the land so ceded, in like manner and to like effect as if the title to said land had not been conveyed to the United States.

> NOTE.—The first part of the section contains the provisions of "An Act concerning submarine sites for lighthouses, and other aids to navigation on the coast of this State," approved March 26, 1874. The latter part of the section is a qualified adoption of a recommendation of the honorable Secretary of War of the United States.

CHAPTER II.

SENATORIAL AND ASSEMBLY DISTRICTS.

SECTION 78. A new section to be added to read as follows:

Assembly districts.

Sec. 78. This State is hereby divided into eighty assembly districts, constituted as follows:

1. The Counties of Del Norte and Siskiyou shall constitute the First Assembly District.

2. All that portion of Humboldt County comprising the townships of Orleans, Klamath, Trinidad, Mad River, Union, Eureka, and Bucksport shall constitute the Second Assembly District.

3. All that portion of Humboldt County not included in the Second Assembly District shall constitute the Third Assembly District.

4. The Counties of Tehama and Trinity shall constitute the Fourth Assembly District.

5. The Counties of Shasta and Modoc shall constitute the Fifth Assembly District.

6. The Counties of Lassen, Plumas, and Sierra shall constitute the Sixth Assembly District.

7. The County of Butte shall constitute the Seventh Assembly District.

8. The Counties of Yuba and Sutter shall constitute the Eighth Assembly District.

9. The County of Mendocino shall constitute the Ninth Assembly District.

10. The Counties of Colusa, Lake, and Glenn shall constitute the Tenth Assembly District.

11. The County of Yolo shall constitute the Eleventh Assembly District.

12. The County of Nevada shall constitute the Twelfth Assembly District.

13. The County of Placer shall constitute the Thirteenth Assembly District.

14. The County of El Dorado shall constitute the Fourteenth Assembly District.

15. The County of Amador shall constitute the Fifteenth Assembly District.

16. All that portion of Sonoma County comprising the townships of Analy, Bodega, Mendocino, Ocean, Petaluma, Redwood, Salt Point, and Vallejo shall constitute the Sixteenth Assembly District.

17. All that portion of Sonoma County not included in the Sixteenth Assembly District shall constitute the Seventeenth Assembly District.

18. The County of Napa shall constitute the Eighteenth Assembly District.

19. The County of Solano shall constitute the Nineteenth Assembly District.

20. All that portion of Sacramento City, in Sacramento County, lying north of the center of K Street, of said Sacramento City, shall constitute the Twentieth Assembly District.

21. All that portion of Sacramento City, in Sacramento County, lying south of the center of K Street, of said Sacramento City, shall constitute the Twenty-first Assembly District.

22. All that portion of Sacramento County not included in the Twentieth and Twenty-first Assembly Districts shall constitute the Twenty-second Assembly District.

23. The County of Marin shall constitute the Twenty-third Assembly District.

24. The County of Contra Costa shall constitute the Twenty-fourth Assembly District.

25. All that portion of San Joaquin County comprising the City of Stockton shall constitute the Twenty-fifth Assembly District.

26. All that portion of San Joaquin County not included in the Twenty-fifth Assembly District shall constitute the Twenty-sixth Assembly District.

27. The County of Calaveras shall constitute the Twenty-seventh Assembly District.

28. All that portion of the City and County of San Francisco bounded as follows: Commencing at the point of intersection where the center line of Market Street intersects the Bay of San Francisco, continuing

10—c

thence along the center of the following named streets: Market to Third, Third to Bryant, Bryant to the waters of the Bay of San Francisco; thence along the shore to Market, the place of beginning, shall constitute the Twenty-eighth Assembly District.

29. All that portion of the City and County of San Francisco bounded as follows: Commencing at the intersection of the center of Market and Third streets, continuing thence along the center of the following named streets: Market to Fifth, Fifth to Bryant, Bryant to Third, Third to Market, the place of beginning, shall constitute the Twenty-ninth Assembly District.

30. All that portion of the City and County of San Francisco bounded as follows: Commencing at the intersection of the center of Market and Fifth streets, continuing thence along the center of the following named streets: Market to Seventh, Seventh to Bryant, Bryant to Fifth, Fifth to Market, the place of beginning, shall constitute the Thirtieth Assembly District.

31. All that portion of the City and County of San Francisco bounded as follows: Commencing at the intersection of the center of Market and Seventh streets, continuing thence along the center of the following named streets: Market to Eleventh, Eleventh to intersection of Channel and Bryant, Bryant to Seventh, Seventh to Market, the place of beginning, shall constitute the Thirty-first Assembly District.

32. All that portion of the City and County of San Francisco bounded as follows: Commencing at the point of intersection where the center of Bryant Street intersects the waters of the Bay of San Francisco, continuing thence along the center of the following named streets: Bryant to intersection of Eleventh and Channel, along Eleventh to Harrison, Harrison to Napa, Napa to the waters of the Bay of San Francisco; thence along the shore to Bryant, the place of beginning, shall constitute the Thirty-second Assembly District.

33. All that portion of the City and County of San Francisco bounded as follows: Commencing at the point of intersection of the center of Napa Street and the Bay of San Francisco, continuing thence along the center of the following named streets: Napa to Twentieth, Twentieth to Howard, Howard to Army, Army to Precita Avenue, Precita Avenue to Colusa, Colusa to San Bruno Road or Avenue; thence along San Bruno Road or Avenue to its intersection with the boundary line dividing the counties of San Francisco and San Mateo; thence along said boundary line to the intersection of the waters of the Bay of San Francisco; thence along the shore of said bay to Napa Street, the place of beginning, shall constitute the Thirty-third Assembly District.

34. All that portion of the City and County of San Francisco bounded as follows: Commencing at the point of intersection of the center of Market and Eleventh streets, continuing thence along the center of the

following named streets: Market to Valencia, Valencia to Ridley, Ridley
to Guerrero, Guerrero to Twenty-first, Twenty-first to Howard, Howard
to Twentieth, Twentieth to Harrison, Harrison to Eleventh, Eleventh to
Market, the place of beginning, shall constitute the Thirty-fourth
Assembly District.

35. All that portion of the City and County of San Francisco bounded
as follows : Commencing at the point of intersection of the center of
Howard and Twenty-first streets, continuing thence along the center of
the following named streets: Twenty-first to Church, Church to Army,
Army to Guerrero, Guerrero to Old San José Road, Old San José Road
to Thirtieth, Thirtieth to Mission; thence along Mission Street to Telegraph or the New County Road; thence along said road to the boundary
line dividing the counties of San Francisco and San Mateo; thence
along said boundary line to San Bruno Road or Avenue; thence along
San Bruno Road or Avenue to Colusa, Colusa to Precita Avenue, Precita Avenue to Army, Army to Howard, Howard to Twenty-first, the
place of beginning, shall constitute the Thirty-fifth Assembly District.

36. All that portion of the City and County of San Francisco bounded
as follows: Commencing at the point of intersection of the center of Guerrero and Fourteenth streets, continuing thence along the center of the
following named streets: Fourteenth to South Broderick, South Broderick to Park Road; thence along Park Road to Frederick, Frederick
to First Avenue, First Avenue to J, J to Fourth Avenue, Fourth Avenue
to K, K to the waters of the Pacific Ocean, along the shore of said
ocean to the boundary line dividing the counties of San Mateo and San
Francisco; thence along the said boundary line to New County Road,
along said road to Mission Road, Mission Road to Thirtieth, Thirtieth
to Old San José Road, Old San José Road to Guerrero, Guerrero to
Army, Army to Church, Church to Twenty-first, Twenty-first to Guerrero, Guerrero to Fourteenth, the place of beginning, shall constitute
the Thirty-sixth Assembly District.

37. All that portion of the City and County of San Francisco bounded
as follows: Commencing at the point of intersection of the center of
Market Street and Van Ness Avenue, continuing thence along the center
of the following named streets: Market to Valencia, Valencia to Ridley,
Ridley to Guerrero, Guerrero to Fourteenth, Fourteenth to South
Broderick, South Broderick to Park Road, around Park Road to Frederick, Frederick to First Avenue, First Avenue to J, J to Fourth
Avenue, Fourth Avenue to K, K to the waters of the Pacific Ocean;
thence along the shore of said ocean northerly to Avenue D, Avenue D
to Stanyan, Stanyan to Grove, Grove to Van Ness Avenue, Van Ness
Avenue to Market, the place of beginning, shall constitute the Thirty-
seventh Assembly District.

38. All that portion of the City and County of San Francisco bounded

as follows: Commencing at the intersection of Avenue B and the Pacific Ocean, continuing thence along the center of the following named streets: Avenue B to First Avenue, First Avenue to Turk, Turk to Broderick, Broderick to O'Farrell, O'Farrell to Van Ness Avenue, Van Ness Avenue to Grove, Grove to Stanyan, Stanyan to Avenue D, Avenue D to the Pacific Ocean; thence along the shore to Avenue B, the place of beginning, shall constitute the Thirty-eighth Assembly District.

39. All that portion of the City and County of San Francisco bounded as follows: Commencing at the point of intersection of the center of Sacramento and Hyde streets, continuing thence along the center of the following named streets: Hyde to Sutter, Sutter to Jones, Jones to Market, Market to Van Ness Avenue, Van Ness Avenue to Sacramento, Sacramento to Hyde, the place of beginning, shall constitute the Thirty-ninth Assembly District.

40. All that portion of the City and County of San Francisco bounded as follows: Commencing at the point of intersection of Avenue B and the waters of the Pacific Ocean, continuing thence along the center of the following named streets: Avenue B to First Avenue, First Avenue to Turk, Turk to Broderick, Broderick to O'Farrell, O'Farrell to Van Ness Avenue, Van Ness Avenue to Sacramento, Sacramento to Central Avenue, Central Avenue to California, California to the east line of the City Cemetery; thence northerly in a direct line to the Pacific Ocean; thence along the shore in a southerly and westerly direction to the place of beginning, together with the islands known as the Farallon Islands, shall constitute the Fortieth Assembly District.

41. All that portion of the City and County of San Francisco bounded as follows: Commencing at the intersection of Leavenworth Street with the waters of the Bay of San Francisco, continuing thence along the center of the following named streets: Leavenworth to Broadway, Broadway to Hyde, Hyde to Sacramento, Sacramento to Central Avenue, Central Avenue to California, along California in a direct line to its intersection with the east line of the City Cemetery; thence northerly in a direct line to the waters of the Pacific Ocean; thence along the shore of said ocean and the said bay to Leavenworth, the place of beginning, shall constitute the Forty-first Assembly District.

42. All that portion of the City and County of San Francisco bounded as follows: Commencing at the junction of the center of Market and Mason streets, continuing thence along the center of the following named streets: Mason to Broadway, Broadway to Hyde, Hyde to Sutter, Sutter to Jones, Jones to Market, Market to Mason, the place of beginning, shall constitute the Forty-second Assembly District.

43. All that portion of the City and County of San Francisco bounded as follows: Commencing at the intersection of the center of

Market and Kearny streets, continuing thence along the center of the following named streets: Kearny to Broadway, Broadway to Mason, Mason to Market, Market to Kearny, the place of beginning, shall constitute the Forty-third Assembly District.

44. All that portion of the City and County of San Francisco bounded as follows: Commencing at the point where the center of Kearny Street intersects the Bay of San Francisco, continuing thence along the center of the following named streets: Kearny to Broadway, Broadway to Leavenworth, Leavenworth to the said bay; thence along the shore of said bay to Kearny, the place of beginning, shall constitute the Forty-fourth Assembly District.

45. All that portion of the City and County of San Francisco bounded as follows: Commencing at a point where the center of Market Street intersects the Bay of San Francisco, continuing thence along the center of the following-named streets: Market to Kearny, Kearny to the Bay of San Francisco; thence along the shore of said bay to Market Street, the place of beginning, together with all the waters of the bay of San Francisco, and the islands contained therein, situated within the boundaries of the City and County of San Francisco, shall constitute the Forty-fifth Assembly District.

46. All that portion of the County of Alameda comprising the townships of Murray and Washington, and that certain portion of Eden township within the corporate limits of the town of Haywards and that portion of said Eden township known as Castro Valley election precinct, described as follows, to wit: Commencing at a point where the northerly line of the town of Haywards is intersected by a line known as the dividing line between San Lorenzo and Castro Valley election precincts; thence along said dividing line of said precincts to the middle line of San Lorenzo Creek; thence easterly and northerly along the middle line of said creek to the dividing line of Alameda and Contra Costa counties; thence easterly and southerly along said dividing line of said counties to its point of intersection with the dividing line of Eden and Murray townships aforesaid; thence along said dividing line between Eden and Murray townships to the corner of Eden, Murray, and Washington townships; thence westerly along the line dividing the townships of Washington and Eden to the middle of the mountain road from Haywards; thence northerly along the middle of the said road to the southerly boundary line of the town of Haywards; thence along the boundary line of Haywards and Castro Valley election precincts to the place of beginning, shall constitute the Forty-sixth Assembly District.

47. All that portion of the County of Alameda comprising so much of Eden township as is not included in the Forty-sixth Assembly District, and that portion of Brooklyn township lying outside of the City of

Oakland, and all of Alameda township, shall constitute the Forty-seventh Assembly District.

48. All that portion of the County of Alameda comprising that portion of the City of Oakland bounded as follows: Commencing at a point on the westerly line of the seventh ward, where the same is intersected by Thirteenth Street extended, continuing thence along the center of the following named streets: Thirteenth to Broadway, Broadway to Tenth, Tenth to Jefferson, Jefferson to Twelfth, Twelfth to Adeline, Adeline to the shore line of Oakland Creek, and thence extended to the boundary line of said City of Oakland in said creek; thence along said boundary line in said creek to the intersection of said boundary line with the boundary line between the sixth and seventh wards of said City of Oakland, and thence along said last mentioned boundary line to the place of beginning, shall constitute the Forty-eighth Assembly District.

49. All that portion of the County of Alameda comprising all that portion of the City of Oakland lying west of Adeline Street, and all that portion of the County of Alameda, being a portion of Oakland township, lying outside of said City of Oakland, bounded as follows: Commencing at the intersection of the northern charter line of the City of Oakland with the dividing line between Bay and Temescal election precincts; thence northerly along said dividing line to where it intersects the southerly line of Berkeley election precinct; thence westerly along said line of Berkeley election precinct to the dividing line between Berkeley and West Berkeley election precincts; thence northerly along said dividing line last named to the southerly line of Ocean View election precinct; thence easterly along said last mentioned line to the dividing line between Alameda and Contra Costa counties; thence northwesterly and westerly along said Alameda and Contra Costa boundary line of Alameda County and the City and County of San Francisco; thence southerly along said last named boundary line to the said northern charter line of the City of Oakland; thence easterly along said last named line to the point of beginning, shall constitute the Forty-ninth Assembly District.

50. All that portion of the County of Alameda comprising that portion of the City of Oakland bounded as follows: Commencing at the intersection of the northern boundary line of said city with Adeline Street, continuing thence along the center of the following named streets: Adeline to Twelfth, Twelfth to Jefferson, Jefferson to Tenth, Tenth to Broadway, Broadway to Twentieth or Delger Street, and thence along the continuation of said Twentieth Street to its intersection with the old charter line in the northwesterly arm of Lake Merritt; thence northerly along the old charter line following the meanderings of Cemetery

Creek to the new charter line, or Logan Street, and thence to the place of beginning, shall constitute the Fiftieth Assembly District.

51. All that portion of the County of Alameda comprising all of Oakland township outside the City of Oakland and not included in the Forty-ninth Assembly District, also that portion of Alameda County comprising the annexed district (so called) and lying east of the old charter line of the City of Oakland, as said line follows the center line of Cemetery Creek and into the northwesterly arm of Lake Merritt, north of said charter line as said line extends into the northeasterly arm of Lake Merritt, and north and east of the dividing line between Oakland and Brooklyn townships, including also all that portion of the City of Oakland bounded as follows: Beginning at a point in the north-easterly arm of Lake Merritt where the old charter line is intersected by Twentieth Street extended, thence along the center line of the following named streets: Twentieth to Broadway, Broadway to Thirteenth, Thirteenth to its point of intersection with the line dividing Oakland and Brooklyn townships, thence southerly along said line to its inter-section with the charter line of the City of Oakland, thence easterly along said charter line to its intersection with the said charter line at Park Street, thence northerly along said charter line to Millbury Street; thence along said street and its extension to the boundary line between Oakland and Brooklyn townships; thence southwesterly and westerly along the old charter line to the place of beginning, comprising all the seventh ward and a portion of the fifth ward of the City of Oakland, shall constitute the Fifty-first Assembly District.

52. The County of San Mateo shall constitute the Fifty-second Assembly District.

53. The County of Santa Cruz shall constitute the Fifty-third Assembly District.

54. All that portion of the County of Santa Clara comprising the precincts of Agnews, Campbells, Jefferson, the town of Mountain View, Moreland, the town of Mayfield, the fourth ward of the City of San José, University, Willow Glen, Cupertino, and the town of Santa Clara, shall constitute the Fifty-fourth Assembly District.

55. All that portion of the County of Santa Clara comprising the first, second, and third wards of the City of San José, and the precincts of Hester and Crandalville, shall constitute the Fifty-fifth Assembly District.

56. All that portion of the County of Santa Clara not included in the Fifty-fourth and Fifty-fifth Assembly Districts shall constitute the Fifty-sixth Assembly District.

57. The Counties of Stanislaus and Merced shall constitute the Fifty-seventh Assembly District.

58. The Counties of Tuolumne and Mariposa shall constitute the Fifty-eighth Assembly District.

59. The County of San Benito shall constitute the Fifty-ninth Assembly District.

60. The Counties of Alpine, Inyo, and Mono shall constitute the Sixtieth Assembly District.

61. The County of Monterey shall constitute the Sixty-first Assembly District.

62. The County of Madera shall constitute the Sixty-second Assembly District.

63. The County of Fresno shall constitute the Sixty-third Assembly District.

64. The County of Kings shall constitute the Sixty-fourth Assembly District.

65. The County of Tulare shall constitute the Sixty-fifth Assembly District.

66. The County of Kern shall constitute the Sixty-sixth Assembly District.

67. The County of San Luis Obispo shall constitute the Sixty-seventh Assembly District.

68. The County of Santa Barbara shall constitute the Sixty-eighth Assembly District.

69. The County of Ventura shall constitute the Sixty-ninth Assembly District.

70. All that portion of the County of Los Angeles included in and comprising the following election precincts: Lancaster, Palmdale, Llano, Acton, Elizabeth Lake, La Liebre Esperanza, Fairmount, Langs, Newhall, Los Virgines, Calabassas, San Vicente, National, Electric, Santa Monica, Monte Vista, Cahuenga, Santa Susana, Lankershim, San Fernando, Burbank, Garvanza, Glendale, La Cañada, Tejunga, North Pasadena, Pasadena city precincts numbers one, two, three, four, five, and six, shall constitute the Seventieth Assembly District.

71. All that portion of the County of Los Angeles included in and comprising the following election precincts: Claremont, Lordsburg, Spadra, Pomona city precincts numbers one, two, three, and four, Azusa, Glendora, El Monte, Farmdale, Old Mission, Monrovia, Duarte, Lamanda, Sierra Madre, San Gabriel, Alhambra, Knolls, South Pasadena, Rowland, Covina, Los Nietos, Whittier, and Rivera, shall constitute the Seventy-first Assembly District.

72. All that portion of the County of Los Angeles included in and comprising the following election precincts: San Antonio, Fruitland, Florence, Vernon, Downey, Artesia, Clearwater, Norwalk, Compton, Lugo, Enterprise, Redondo, Long Beach, Cerritas, Wilmington, San

Pedro, Catalina, Chautauqua, Ballona, Centinelli, La Dow, University, and Rosedale, shall constitute the Seventy-second Assembly District.

73. All that portion of the County of Los Angeles included in and comprising the following election precincts: Los Angeles City precincts, numbers one, two, three, four, five, six, seven, eight, nine, ten, eleven, twelve, thirteen, fourteen, fifteen, sixteen, seventeen, and eighteen, shall constitute the Seventy-third Assembly District.

74. All that portion of the County of Los Angeles included in and comprising the following election precincts: Los Angeles City precincts numbers nineteen, twenty, twenty-one, twenty-two, twenty-three, twenty-four, twenty-five, twenty-six, twenty-seven, twenty-eight, twenty-nine, thirty, and thirty-one, shall constitute the Seventy-fourth Assembly District.

75. All that portion of the County of Los Angeles included in and comprising the following election precincts: Los Angeles City precincts numbers thirty-two, thirty-three, thirty-four, thirty-five, thirty-six, thirty-seven, thirty-eight, thirty-nine, forty, forty-one, forty-two, forty-three, forty-four, forty-five, forty-six, and forty-seven, shall constitute the Seventy-fifth Assembly District.

76. The County of Orange shall constitute the Seventy-sixth Assembly District.

77. The County of Riverside shall constitute the Seventy-seventh Assembly District.

78. The County of San Bernardino shall constitute the Seventy-eighth Assembly District.

79. All that portion of San Diego County situated within the corporate limits of the City of San Diego shall constitute the Seventy-ninth Assembly District.

80. All that portion of San Diego County not included in the Seventy-ninth Assembly District shall constitute the Eightieth Assembly District.

At the general election in the year eighteen hundred and ninety-eight, and every two years thereafter, a member of the Assembly shall be elected in each of said hereinbefore constituted assembly districts.

SECTION 79.   A new section to be added to read as follows:

Senatorial districts.

Sec. 79.   This State is hereby divided into forty senatorial districts, constituted as follows:

1. The Counties of Del Norte and Humboldt shall constitute the First Senatorial District.

2. The Counties of Siskiyou, Trinity, Shasta, Modoc, and Lassen shall constitute the Second Senatorial District.

3. The Counties of Plumas, Sierra, and Nevada shall constitute the Third Senatorial District.

4. The Counties of Tehama and Butte shall constitute the Fourth Senatorial District.

5. The Counties of El Dorado and Placer shall constitute the Fifth Senatorial District.

6. The Counties of Yuba, Sutter, and Yolo shall constitute the Sixth Senatorial District.

7. The Counties of Lake and Napa shall constitute the Seventh Senatorial District.

8. The Counties of Mendocino, Colusa, and Glenn shall constitute the Eighth Senatorial District.

9. The County of Solano shall constitute the Ninth Senatorial District.

10. The County of Sonoma shall constitute the Tenth Senatorial District.

11. The Counties of Contra Costa and Marin shall constitute the Eleventh Senatorial District.

12. The Counties of Stanislaus, Merced, Tuolumne, and Mariposa shall constitute the Twelfth Senatorial District.

13. The County of Sacramento shall constitute the Thirteenth Senatorial District.

14. The Counties of Alpine, Amador, Calaveras, and Mono shall constitute the Fourteenth Senatorial District.

15. The County of San Joaquin shall constitute the Fifteenth Senatorial District.

16. The Counties of Fresno and Madera shall constitute the Sixteenth Senatorial District.

17. All that portion of the City and County of San Francisco comprised within the boundaries of the Twenty-eighth and Twenty-ninth Assembly Districts, as fixed and described in the preceding section, shall constitute the Seventeenth Senatorial District.

18. All that portion of the City and County of San Francisco comprised within the boundaries of the Thirtieth and Thirty-second Assembly Districts, as fixed and described in the preceding section, shall constitute the Eighteenth Senatorial District.

19. All that portion of the City and County of San Francisco comprised within the boundaries of the Thirty-third and Thirty-fifth Assembly Districts, as fixed and described in the preceding section, shall constitute the Nineteenth Senatorial District.

20. All that portion of the City and County of San Francisco comprised within the boundaries of the Thirty-fourth and Thirty-sixth Assembly Districts, as fixed and described in the preceding section, shall constitute the Twentieth Senatorial District.

21. All that portion of the City and County of San Francisco comprised within the boundaries of the Thirty-seventh and Thirty-eighth Assembly Districts, as fixed and described in the preceding section, shall constitute the Twenty-first Senatorial District.

22. All that portion of the City and County of San Francisco comprised within the boundaries of the Fortieth and Forty-first Assembly Districts, as fixed and described in the preceding section, shall constitute the Twenty-second Senatorial District.

23. All that portion of the City and County of San Francisco comprised within the boundaries of the Thirty-first and Thirty-ninth Assembly Districts, as fixed and described in the preceding section, shall constitute the Twenty-third Senatorial District.

24. All that portion of the City and County of San Francisco comprised within the boundaries of the Forty-second and Forty-third Assembly Districts, as fixed and described in the preceding section, shall constitute the Twenty-fourth Senatorial District.

25. All that portion of the City and County of San Francisco comprised within the boundaries of the Forty-fourth and Forty-fifth Assembly Districts, as fixed and described in the preceding section, shall constitute the Twenty-fifth Senatorial District.

26. All that portion of the County of Alameda comprised within the boundaries of the Forty-eighth and Forty-ninth Assembly Districts, as fixed and described in the preceding section, shall constitute the Twenty-sixth Senatorial District.

27. All that portion of the County of Alameda comprised within the boundaries of the Fiftieth and Fifty-first Assembly Districts, as fixed and described in the preceding section, shall constitute the Twenty-seventh Senatorial District.

28. All that portion of the County of Alameda comprised within the Forty-sixth and Forty-seventh Assembly Districts, as fixed and described in the preceding section, shall constitute the Twenty-eighth Senatorial District.

29. The Counties of San Mateo and Santa Cruz shall constitute the Twenty-ninth Senatorial District.

30. All that portion of Santa Clara County not included in the Thirty-first Senatorial District shall constitute the Thirtieth Senatorial District.

31. All that portion of Santa Clara County comprising the townships of Redwood, Almaden, Gilroy, and Burnett, and the third ward in the City of San José, and all of the township of San José outside of the City of San José, except the precincts of Berryessa and Orchard, as now constituted, shall constitute the Thirty-first Senatorial District.

32. The Counties of Inyo, Tulare, and Kings shall constitute the Thirty-second Senatorial District.

33. The Counties of San Benito and Monterey shall constitute the Thirty-third Senatorial District.

34. The Counties of San Luis Obispo and Kern shall constitute the Thirty-fourth Senatorial District.

35. The Counties of Santa Barbara and Ventura shall constitute the Thirty-fifth Senatorial District.

36. All that portion of the County of Los Angeles included in and comprising the following townships and election precincts: Antelope, Fairmount, Soledad, Los Angeles, Pasadena, South Pasadena, El Monte, and San Gabriel townships, and all that part of the City of Los Angeles included in and comprising the following election precincts: Numbers one, two, three, four, five, six, seven, eight, nine, ten, eleven, twelve, thirteen, fourteen, fifteen, sixteen, seventeen, and eighteen, shall constitute the Thirty-sixth Senatorial District.

37. All that portion of the County of Los Angeles included in and comprising the following election precincts: All that portion of the City of Los Angeles included in and comprising the following election precincts: Nineteen, twenty, twenty-one, twenty-two, twenty-three, twenty-four, twenty-five, twenty-six, twenty-seven, twenty-eight, twenty-nine, thirty, thirty-one, thirty-two, thirty-three, thirty-four, thirty-five, thirty-six, thirty-seven, thirty-eight, thirty-nine, forty, forty-one, forty-two, forty-three, forty-four, forty-five, forty-six, and forty-seven, shall constitute the Thirty-seventh Senatorial District.

38. All that portion of the County of Los Angeles included in and comprising the following townships: San José, Azusa, Rowland, Los Nietos, San Antonio, Downey, Long Beach, Wilmington, Catalina, Chautauqua, Santa Monica, Calabassas, San Fernando, Compton, Ballona, and Cahuenga, shall constitute the Thirty-eighth Senatorial District.

39. The Counties of San Bernardino, Orange, and Riverside shall constitute the Thirty-ninth Senatorial District.

40. The County of San Diego shall constitute the Fortieth Senatorial District.

At the general election in the year eighteen hundred and ninety-eight there shall be elected twenty Senators from the above named and constituted even-numbered districts, who shall hold office for four years. Twenty Senators shall be elected from said even-numbered districts every four years thereafter. The Senators elected at the general election in the year eighteen hundred and ninety-six in the odd-numbered districts, fixed by the apportionment act of the Legislature, approved March eleventh, eighteen hundred and ninety-one, shall continue in office for four years from and after twelve o'clock noon on the first Monday after the first day of January, eighteen hundred and ninety-seven. At the general election in the year nineteen hundred, twenty Senators shall be elected from the hereinbefore named and constituted odd-numbered districts, who shall hold office for four years. And every four years thereafter twenty Senators shall be elected from said hereinbefore constituted odd-numbered districts.

Neither Boards of Supervisors, municipal authorities, nor any other officer or officers, shall have the power to alter the boundaries of any township, ward, election precinct, or other local subdivision, of any county, city, city and county, or town, so as to change the boundaries of any senatorial or assembly district as constituted and defined herein, or in the preceding section.

CHAPTER III.

CONGRESSIONAL DISTRICTS.

SECTION 80. A new section to be added to read as follows:

Congressional districts.

Sec. 80. For the purpose of electing Representatives in Congress, this State is hereby divided into seven congressional districts, as follows:

1. The Counties of Del Norte, Siskiyou, Modoc, Humboldt, Trinity, Shasta, Lassen, Tehama, Plumas, Sierra, Mendocino, Sonoma, Napa, and Marin shall comprise the First Congressional District.

2. The Counties of Butte, Sutter, Yuba, Nevada, Placer, El Dorado, Amador, Calaveras, Mono, Inyo, Alpine, Tuolumne, Mariposa, San Joaquin, and Sacramento shall comprise the Second Congressional District.

3. The Counties of Colusa, Glenn, Yolo, Lake, Solano, Contra Costa, and Alameda shall comprise the Third Congressional District.

4. All that portion of the City and County of San Francisco bounded as follows: Commencing at a point of intersection of the center of Leavenworth Street and the Bay of San Francisco, continuing thence along the center of the following named streets: Leavenworth to Broadway, Broadway to Hyde, Hyde to Sacramento, Sacramento to Van Ness Avenue, Van Ness Avenue to Market, Market to Eleventh, Eleventh to Harrison, Harrison to junction of Napa and Twentieth; thence along Twentieth to Howard, Howard to Army, Army to Precita Avenue, Precita Avenue to Colusa, Colusa to San Bruno Road or Avenue; thence along San Bruno Road or Avenue to the boundary line dividing the counties of San Mateo and San Francisco; thence along said boundary line to the Bay of San Francisco; thence along the shore of said bay to Leavenworth Street, the place of beginning, with all the islands in the Bay of San Francisco within the boundaries of the City and County of San Francisco, shall comprise the Fourth Congressional District.

5. All that portion of the City and County of San Francisco not

included in the Fourth Congressional District, with the islands known as the Farallon Islands, together with the counties of San Mateo and Santa Clara, shall comprise the Fifth Congressional District.

6. The Counties of Santa Cruz, Monterey, San Luis Obispo, Santa Barbara, Ventura, and Los Angeles shall comprise the Sixth Congressional District.

7. The Counties of Stanislaus, Merced, San Benito, Fresno, Madera, Tulare, Kings, Kern, San Bernardino, Riverside, Orange, and San Diego shall comprise the Seventh Congressional District.

TITLE III.

LEGAL DISTANCES IN THE STATE.

SECTION 150. To be amended to read as follows:

Sec. 150. The legal distance in this State from one place to another is the actual distance from the county seat of the county wherein the first place is located, along the route of the most direct line of public transportation, to the latter place, or place of destination. Where mileage is collected in this State, it shall be computed upon this basis.

SECTIONS 151, 152, 153, 154, 155, 156, 157, 158, 159, 160, 161, 162, 163, 164, 165, 166, 167, 168, 169, 170, 171, 172, 173, 174, 175, 176, 177, 178, 179, 180, 181, 182, 183, 184, 185, 186, 187, 188, 189, 190, 191, 192, 193, 194, 195, 196, 197, 198, 199, 200, 201, 202, and 203 to be repealed.

NOTE.—The end sought to be attained by these sections will be better subserved by the elastic general provisions of Section 150.

ARTICLE II.

MEETING AND ORGANIZATION OF THE LEGISLATURE.

SECTION 237. To be amended to read as follows:

Sec. 237. The Secretary of the Senate, the Clerk of the Assembly, the Minute Clerk, and the Sergeant-at-Arms of each house, shall, at the next succeeding session of the Legislature, perform the duties of their office until their successors are elected and qualified; and the employment of all other officers and employés of any session shall terminate with the termination of the session at which they were appointed.

NOTE.—See note to Section 263.

ARTICLE III.

NUMBER, DESIGNATION, ELECTION, AND APPOINTMENT OF OFFICERS AND
EMPLOYÉS OF THE LEGISLATURE.

SECTION 245. To be amended to read as follows:

Sec. 245. The officers and employés of the Senate shall consist of a President, President pro tem., a Secretary, three Assistant Secretaries (who shall be appointed by the Secretary, by and with the advice and consent of the Senate), one Sergeant-at-Arms, one Assistant Sergeant-at-Arms, one Bookkeeper for the Sergeant-at-Arms (who shall be appointed by the Sergeant-at-Arms, by and with the advice and consent of the Senate), one Minute Clerk, two Assistant Minute Clerks, one Journal Clerk, one Assistant Journal Clerk, one Engrossing and Enrolling Clerk, one Assistant Engrossing and Enrolling Clerk (to be elected when the Engrossing and Enrolling Clerk is elected), two Assistant Engrossing and Enrolling Clerks (to be elected on the thirtieth day of the session), a Chaplain, one Postmistress, one Assistant Postmistress, one Mail Carrier (who shall be Mailing and Folding Clerk), one Page to the President of the Senate, four Pages, four Porters (one of whom shall have charge of the cloak-room), four Watchmen, three Gatekeepers, one Doorkeeper, one Messenger to the Printer, one History Clerk, one Bill Clerk, one Assistant Bill Clerk, ten committee clerks, five skilled stenographers (who shall be at the service of the Senate and its committees, and under the supervision of the Secretary of the Senate), ten committee messengers (who shall be committee sergeants-at-arms); and no other officers, employés, or attachés, excepting that the Secretary may employ, at any time, temporary employés, with the consent of four fifths of the members elected to the Senate.

NOTE.—See note to Section 268.

SECTION 246. To be amended to read as follows:

Sec. 246. The officers and employés of the Assembly shall consist of a Speaker, Speaker pro tem., one Chief Clerk, three Assistant Clerks (who shall be appointed by the Chief Clerk, by and with advice and consent of the Assembly), one Sergeant-at-Arms, one Assistant Sergeant-at-Arms, one Bookkeeper to the Sergeant-at-Arms (who shall be appointed by the Sergeant-at-Arms, by and with the advice and consent of the Assembly), one Minute Clerk, three Assistant Minute Clerks, one Journal Clerk, one Assistant Journal Clerk, one Engrossing and Enrolling Clerk, one Assistant Engrossing and Enrolling Clerk (to be elected when the Engrossing and Enrolling Clerk is elected), two Assistant Engrossing and Enrolling Clerks (to be elected on the thirtieth day of each session), a Chaplain, one Postmistress, one Assistant Postmistress, one Mail Carrier (who shall be Mailing and Folding Clerk), one Page to the Speaker, six Pages, four Porters (one of whom shall have charge of the cloak-room), four Watchmen, four Gatekeepers, one Messenger to the Printer, one History Clerk, one Bill Clerk, two Assistant Bill Clerks, twelve committee clerks, six skilled stenographers (who shall be at the service of the Assembly and its committees, and under the supervision of the Clerk), twelve committee messengers (who shall be committee sergeants-at-arms); and no other officers, employés, or attachés are to be employed, excepting that the Clerk may employ, at any time, temporary employés, with the consent of four fifths of the members elected to the Assembly.

NOTE.—See note to Section 268.

ARTICLE V.

COMPENSATION OF MEMBERS, OFFICERS, AND EMPLOYÉS OF THE LEGISLATURE.

SECTION 268.   To be amended to read as follows:

Sec. 268.   There shall be paid to the officers and employés of the Senate the following salaries: To the Secretary, Sergeant-at-Arms, Minute Clerk, Journal Clerk, Engrossing and Enrolling Clerk, each eight dollars per day; to Assistant Secretaries, Assistant Clerks, Assistant Sergeants-at-Arms, Bookkeepers to the Sergeant-at-Arms, one History Clerk, each six dollars per day; to the Chaplain and stenographers, each five dollars per day; to the Bill Clerks, Committee Clerks (except that one Clerk of the Judiciary Committee, and one Clerk of the Finance Committee shall receive each, six dollars per day), Postmistress, Assistant Postmistress, each four dollars per day; to the Mail Carrier, Committee Messengers, Porters, Watchmen, Gatekeepers, Doorkeepers, Messenger to the Printer, each three dollars per day; to each Page, two dollars and fifty cents per day.

There must be paid to the officers and employés of the Assembly the following salaries: To the Chief Clerk, Sergeant-at-Arms, Minute Clerk, Journal Clerk, Engrossing and Enrolling Clerk, each eight dollars per day; to the History Clerk, the Assistant Clerk, Assistant Sergeants-at-Arms, Bookkeepers to Sergeant-at-Arms, Assistant Minute Clerks, Assistant Journal Clerks, Assistant Engrossing and Enrolling Clerks, each six dollars per day; to the Chaplain and stenographers, each five dollars per day; to the Committee Clerks (except that the Clerk of the Ways and Means Committee and of the Appropriation Committee of the Assembly shall receive six dollars per day), Bill Clerks, Postmistress, Assistant Postmistress, each four dollars per day; to the Mail Carrier, Committee Messengers, Porters, Watchmen, Gatekeepers, Messenger to the Printer, each three dollars per day; to each Page, two dollars and fifty cents per day.

And no officer or employé of the Senate or Assembly, whose per diem is not hereinbefore fixed, shall receive a per diem exceeding the sum of five dollars.

NOTE.—A special committee appointed at the last session of the Legislature prepared and reported the above sections as herein reported. The bill passed both houses, but failed of enactment because of certain objections by the Governor. The Governor referred the bill to this Commission for such changes as have been made in Section 237, in which amended form we now present it without recommendation.

ARTICLE XI.

SECTION 329. To be amended to read as follows:

Sec. 329. The repeal of any law creating a criminal offense, or providing for the punishment thereof, does not constitute a bar to the indictment or information and punishment of an act already committed in violation of the law so repealed, unless the intention to bar such indictment or information and punishment is expressly declared in the repealing act.

NOTE.—The amendment consists in inserting the words, "or providing for the punishment thereof," after the word offense in the first line.

ARTICLE XII.

PUBLIC REPORTS.

SECTION 333. To be amended to read as follows:

Sec. 333. The Governor shall, upon receipt of such reports, transmit the same to the Superintendent of State Printing, who shall print the whole or such part of such reports, and such number of such whole or part, as he may deem necessary and proper; *provided*, that if he does not print the whole of such report, or the number of copies of such report requested by the person, board, or officer making such report, he shall notify such person, board, or officer, in writing, of the part of such report which he does not intend to print, and if he intends printing a less number of copies than requested, of what number he intends printing. Such person, board, or officer, if dissatisfied with such decision, shall immediately appeal to the State Board of Examiners, who shall consider the question, and determine if the whole of such report should be printed, or how much, and how many copies. They shall thereupon notify the Superintendent of State Printing of such decision, and he shall comply therewith. The Superintendent of State Printing must print such reports before the first Monday in December next after the receipt thereof, except the report of the State Controller, which shall be printed before the fifteenth day of January after the receipt thereof;

11—c

provided, that in no case shall a less number of copies of such reports be printed than is necessary to furnish at least ten copies to the officers, boards, commissions, trustees, regents, or directors making such report.

SECTION 334.   To be repealed.

> NOTE.—The provisions of this section are incorporated in Section 333, which section has been amended to harmonize with Section 531 of this Code.

ARTICLE I.

CLASSIFICATION, NUMBER, AND DESIGNATION OF EXECUTIVE OFFICERS.

SECTION 343.   To be amended to read as follows:

Sec. 343.   Civil executive officers in this State are such as are provided for in, or designated as such by, the constitution, or by any act of the Legislature.

> NOTE.—This amendment is suggested because there appears no good reason why all civil executive officers should be enumerated in this section, and to prevent the constant amendment of this section by additions to or withdrawals from our civil service.

ARTICLE II.

THE MODE OF ELECTION OR APPOINTMENT AND TERM OF OFFICE OF CIVIL EXECUTIVE OFFICERS.

SECTION 349.   To be amended to read as follows:

Sec. 349.   The Superintendent of State Printing shall be elected at the same time and place and in the same manner as the Governor of the State, and his term of office and qualifications shall also be the same.

> NOTE.—Amended to conform to Section 530 of this Code.

SECTION 352.   To be amended to read as follows:

Sec. 352.   The State Board of Equalization shall consist of five members, as follows:

1. The Controller, who is ex officio a member of said board;

2. One member to be elected from the first district, comprising the City and County of San Francisco;

3. One member to be elected from the second district, comprising the Counties of Contra Costa, Alameda, San Joaquin, Calaveras, Amador, El Dorado, Sacramento, Placer, Nevada, Alpine, and Tuolumne;

4. One member to be elected from the third district, comprising the Counties of Marin, Sonoma, Napa, Lake, Solano, Yolo, Sutter, Yuba, Sierra, Butte, Plumas, Lassen, Tehama, Colusa, Glenn, Mendocino, Humboldt, Trinity, Shasta, Siskiyou, Modoc, and Del Norte;

5. One member from the fourth district, comprising the Counties of

San Diego, Los Angeles, Orange, San Bernardino, Riverside, Santa Barbara, Ventura, San Luis Obispo, Tulare, Kings, Monterey, San Benito, Fresno, Madera, Kern, Merced, Mariposa, Stanislaus, Santa Clara, Santa Cruz, San Mateo, Mono and Inyo.

Their term of office shall be four years, commencing on the first Monday after the first day of January following their election.

Note.—This amendment was made that the section might conform to Section 9, Article XIII, of the Constitution, and on its face correctly express the number of members of the Board of Equalization.

SECTION 354. To be amended to read as follows:

Sec. 354. The normal schools at San José, at Los Angeles, and at Chico, and any normal school established by the Legislature of the State of California, after the first day of January, eighteen hundred and ninety-seven, shall be known as state normal schools, and shall each have a board of trustees, constituted as follows: The Governor and Superintendent of Public Instruction shall be ex officio members of each board, and the president of each school shall be ex officio a member of the local board of the school with which he is connected. There shall also be four other members of the local board for each normal school, whose terms of office shall be four years and who shall be appointed by the Governor. It shall be the duty of the Governor, on or before the first day of July, eighteen hundred and ninety-seven, to appoint four trustees as members of each of the local boards, one to serve for one year, one for two years, one for three years, and one for four years, and thereafter to fill vacancies in such board, the terms of service thereafter to be for four years, and to begin July first of each fourth year.

SECTION 361. To be repealed.

Note.—The board of health provided for by this section, and Sections 3042 to 3049, has been dispensed with and superseded by a board of health provided for in the charter of the city. Approved February 7, 1893. (See Stats. 1893, pp. 545, 598.)

SECTION 364. To be amended to read as follows:

Sec. 364. The Board of Examiners shall consist of the Governor, the Secretary of State, the Attorney-General, or in his absence the Assistant Attorney-General. The secretary of the board shall be ex officio member of the board, to act only when but one other member of the board is present.

Note.—The amendment consists in providing for the qualifications of the Assistant Attorney-General, as provided for in Section 472.

SECTION 367. To be amended to read as follows:

Sec. 367. The Board of State Prison Directors are appointed and hold their offices as prescribed in the constitution and the special statute creating the board.

SECTION 368. To be amended to read as follows:

Sec. 368. The following executive officers are appointed by the Governor with the consent of the Senate:

1. The trustees of the state burying-ground; the trustees of the asylum for the deaf, dumb, and blind; the trustees of the California home for the care and training of feeble-minded children; harbor commissioners for the Bay of San Diego; a board of state harbor commissioners for the Bay of San Francisco; members of the state board of health; directors of the insane asylum at Stockton; the insurance commissioner; the port wardens; directors of the state prisons; trustees of the state reform school for juvenile offenders; the regents of the state university. These officers hold their office for the term of four years, except the directors of the state prisons, whose term shall be ten years;

2. The fish commissioners, the pilot commissioners, the pilots for each harbor where there is not a board of pilot commissioners. These officers hold office during the Governor's pleasure.

> NOTE.—The amendment consists in dropping from the list such offices as have been abolished, and including such offices as have been provided for by later enactment. The term of trustees of state burying-ground is extended to four years.

SECTION 369. To be repealed, as its purpose is served by the preceding section.

ARTICLE V.

OF THE SECRETARY OF STATE.

SECTION 408. To be amended to read as follows:

Sec. 408. In addition to the duties prescribed by the constitution, it is the duty of the Secretary of State:

1. To attend at every session of the Legislature, for the purpose of receiving bills and resolutions thereof, and to perform such other duties as may be devolved upon him by resolution of the two houses, or either of them;

2. To keep a register of and attest the official acts of the Governor;

3. To affix the great seal, with his attestation, to commissions, pardons, and other public instruments to which the official signature of the Governor is required;

4. To record, in proper books, all conveyances made to the State, and all articles of incorporation filed in his office; and to file in his office all documents required or directed by law to be filed therein, upon receipt of the fees allowed by law for such filing;

5. To receive, and record in proper books, the official bonds of all the officers whose bonds are fixed by part three of this Code, and then deliver the originals to the State Treasurer;

6. To record, in a proper book, all changes of names certified to him by the County Clerks, in the manner in which such record is now made;

7. To take and file in his office receipts for all books distributed by him, and to direct the County Clerk of each county to do the same;

8. To certify to the Governor the names of those persons who have received at any election the highest number of votes for any office, the incumbent of which is commissioned by the Governor;

9. To furnish, on demand, to any person paying the fees therefor, a certified copy of all or any part of any law record, or other instrument, filed, deposited, or recorded in his office;

10. To notify, in writing, the District Attorney of the proper county of the failure of any officer in his county to file in his office his sworn statement of fees received by such officer;

11. To present to the Legislature, at the commencement of each session thereof, a full account of all purchases made and expenses incurred by him in furnishing fuel, lights, and stationery;

12. To keep a fee-book, in which must be entered all fees, commissions, and compensation of whatever nature or kind by him earned, collected, or charged, with the date, name of payer, paid or not paid, and the nature of the service in each case, which book must be verified annually by his affidavit entered therein;

13. To file in his office descriptions of seals in use by the different state officers, and furnish such officers with new seals whenever required.

14. To discharge the duties of member of the State Board of Examiners, State Capitol Commissioner, State Sealer of Weights and Measures, and all other duties required of him by law;

15. To report to the Governor, at the time prescribed in section three hundred and thirty-two of this Code, a detailed account of all his official actions since his previous reports, and accompanying the report with a detailed statement, under oath, of the manner in which all appropriations for his office have been expended;

16. He must distribute of the bound volumes of the decisions of the Supreme Court as soon as he receives them:

(1) To each State, one copy;

(2) To the library of Congress, the State library, and the Supreme Court library, two copies each;

(3) To each department of this State, and to each of the United States district judges for this State, justices of the Supreme Court, and judges of the Superior Courts, one copy;

(4) To each District Attorney and County Clerk, one copy;

(5) To the reporter of the decisions, ten copies.

SECTION 415.   To be repealed.

NOTE.—No further necessity exists in this State for a Spanish edition of our Statutes, while Article IV, Section 24, of the Constitution, provides that the laws shall be published in no other than the English language.

SECTION 416. To be amended to read as follows:

Sec. 416. The Secretary of State, for services performed in his office, must charge and collect the following fees:

For filing a certified copy of original or amended articles of incorporation of any railroad, telegraph, or telephone company, twenty dollars;

For filing a certified copy of original or amended articles of incorporation of any company not hereinbefore in this section mentioned, five dollars;

For filing a certified copy of any certificate of the increase or decrease of the capital stock of a corporation, ten dollars;

For filing a certified copy of any certificate creating or increasing the funded indebtedness of any corporation, ten dollars;

For filing any document relative to a corporation, directed or required by law to be filed, not hereinbefore in this section mentioned, five dollars;

For furnishing a copy of any document on file in his office, fifteen cents per folio;

For certifying a copy of any document on file in his office, five cents per folio;

For affixing the great seal of the State, two dollars;

For recording any official bond, five dollars;

For each commission or passport, signed by the Governor and attested by the Secretary of State, except pardons, military commissions, and extradition papers, five dollars;

For each patent for land issued by the Governor, if for one hundred and sixty acres or less, one dollar; and for each additional one hundred and sixty acres or fractional part thereof, one dollar;

For filing trademark, three dollars;

For filing and recording notice of appointment of agent, five dollars;

For filing map and profile of the final location of any railroad, five dollars;

For filing certified copy of official oath of notary public, one dollar;

For recording miscellaneous documents or papers, twenty-five cents per folio;

For searching records and archives of the State, one dollar;

For filing certified copy of an order of the Superior Court changing the name of a corporation, three dollars.

No member of the Legislature or state officer shall be charged for any search relative to matters appertaining to the duties of their offices; nor shall they be charged any fee for a certified copy of any law or resolution passed by the Legislature relative to their official duties.

All fees collected by the Secretary of the State must, at the end of each month, be paid into the state treasury, and shall constitute the state library fund.

ARTICLE X.

REGISTER OF THE STATE LAND OFFICE.

SECTION 501. To be amended to read as follows:

Sec. 501. The register must charge and collect fees as follows: For each certificate of purchase, duplicate, or patent, three dollars; for certifying a contested case to Superior Court, three dollars; for copies of papers in his office, ten cents per folio, and fifty cents for the certificate with the seal attached; and such other fees as may be allowed by law. All fees received by the register must be disposed of as provided in title eight of part three of this Code.

NOTE.—The amendment consists of substituting the word "superior" for "district" in designating the court in the above section.

ARTICLE XII.

SUPERINTENDENT OF STATE PRINTING.

SECTION 526. To be amended to read as follows:

Sec. 526. It is the duty of the Superintendent of State Printing:

1. To print the laws; the journals of the Legislature; reports of state officers; public documents ordered to be printed by the Legislature, Supreme Court, state university, state normal schools, state asylums, state reform schools, state prisons, all state officers, boards, bureaus, commissions, and trustees; the bills, resolutions, and other job printing which may be ordered by either of the two houses of the Legislature, and all other public printing for the State, unless otherwise expressly ordered by law;

2. To publish, prefixed to each volume of the laws, the names and place of residence of the Governor, and other executive officers of the State, Lieutenant-Governor, Senators, and Representatives in the Legislature, the presiding officers of the Senate and Assembly, and of commissioners of the State of California residing out of the State, and in office at the time of such publication;

3. To perform the duties required by the provisions of article twelve, chapter two, title one, part three, of this Code, and such other 'duties as are imposed upon him by law;

4. He shall keep in his office, open to public inspection, a time-book, containing the name of every employé connected with the state printing office, the time employed, the rate of wages, and amount paid; and he shall certify, under oath, to the correctness of all claims for services rendered and materials furnished, which certificate shall be attached to and presented with each claim that shall be presented to the Board of

Examiners for allowance, and no such claim shall be certified or allowed unless it is fully itemized;

5. He shall file, in the office of the Secretary of State, all proposals, bids, contracts, bonds, and other papers appertaining to the awarding of contracts now in his possession, or which may hereafter come into his possession, retaining in his office copies of the same; and the Secretary of State shall promptly furnish the State Board of Examiners, for their use, certified copies of all such papers;

6. All printing required by any of the state departments, institutions, boards, or any state officer, for the State, the order for the same shall be made out upon a printed blank, with voucher attached, to be furnished by the Superintendent of State Printing, and forwarded to the office of said Superintendent, who shall enter, upon a book kept in his office for that purpose, a transcript of said order; and shall return with the work, when completed, to the person ordering the same, the original order, with a duplicate voucher attached; said voucher to be signed by the person receiving the work, and returned to the Superintendent of State Printing, and both original and duplicate orders shall be kept on file in his office, and shall be a sufficient voucher for said work. The Superintendent of State Printing shall enter upon a book, to be kept for such purpose, the name, quantity, and weight of paper used for each order printed. He shall also certify, under oath, that the items constituting the claim attached were incurred in the manner and on the dates shown in said bills, and that the materials described in the annexed account were of the quality, kind, and weight required, and that the services named in the annexed account were actually rendered, and the money is to be paid, as therein mentioned, and solely for the benefit of the State; and no claim arising under any contract shall be allowed or paid unless accompanied by such certificate. He shall also retain and file in his office one copy or sample of each blank, circular, pamphlet, book, legislative bill, file, or report, or any other work emanating from the state printing office, excepting blank books, of which he shall file only sample sheets. Said copies or samples shall bear a uniform number and date with the voucher, and shall be preserved one year. Copy for all printing, except job work, must be furnished to the Superintendent of State Printing, typewritten, or written legibly, on paper, legal cap or letter size, except in cases of tables or diagrams which cannot be confined to above-mentioned size; and written on one side only. The Superintendent of State Printing is hereby authorized to reject all copy not conforming to the above requirements;

7. No printing for the Senate, or any committee of the same, shall be executed except upon an official order of the secretary, and no order for any printing shall be made by that officer unless the same is ordered by a majority vote of the Senate. All printing done for the

Senate shall be delivered to the sergeant-at-arms of that body, whose duty it shall be to distribute one third of the copies of any document printed to the members of the Senate, and two thirds to the sergeant-at-arms of the Assembly, who shall receipt therefor, for distribution to the members thereof. There shall be printed such number of copies of all bills, resolutions, and reports for the Senate as shall be ordered by that body;

8. No printing for the Assembly, or any committee of the same, shall be executed except upon an official order of the chief clerk, and no order for any printing shall be made by that officer unless the same is ordered by a majority vote of the Assembly. All printing done for the Assembly shall be delivered to the sergeant-at-arms of that body, whose duty it shall be to distribute two thirds of the copies of any document printed to the members of the Assembly, and one third to the sergeant-at-arms of the Senate, who shall receipt therefor, for distribution to the members thereof. There shall be printed such number of copies of all bills, resolutions, and reports for the Assembly as shall be ordered by that body;

9. The receipts of the respective sergeants-at-arms of the Senate and Assembly shall be a sufficient voucher to the Superintendent of State Printing for all work done for either house.

SECTION 527. To be amended to read as follows:

Sec. 527. Whenever any message or document, in book form, is ordered printed by either house, four hundred and eighty copies thereof, in addition to the number ordered, must be struck off and retained in sheets, and bound with the journals of the house ordering the same, as an appendix. Of bills ordered printed, when the number is not fixed in the order, there must be printed five hundred copies.

NOTE.—The number of bills and other legislative documents in both of the above sections has been increased, as two hundred and forty copies have proven totally inadequate for several years, and the practice has been for each house, by resolution, to fix the number at five hundred at the beginning of each session.

SECTION 528. To be amended to read as follows:

Sec. 528. There must be printed, and bound in law sheep, of the laws of each session of the Legislature such number of volumes as in the judgment of the Superintendent of State Printing will be required by the Secretary of State for sale or distribution under the law, not exceeding three thousand five hundred copies, to be deposited with the Secretary of State, who, after retaining a sufficient number of said volumes for distribution in accordance with the provisions of section four hundred and nine of this Code, shall deposit one hundred copies with the state library; the remaining copies to be sold at a price to be fixed by the State Board of Examiners, not to exceed three dollars per bound volume for single copies; and when ten or more copies are desired by any citizen at one time, then there shall be a discount of ten per cent from said established price; *provided,* that any such citizen purchasing ten or more copies shall agree with and file an affidavit with the Secretary of State, certifying that such copies have not been purchased for resale in lots of more than five copies, nor at a greater price than the maximum price fixed by the State Board of Examiners for their sale by the State. Stereotype plates shall be made, and whenever the Secretary of State has less than fifty copies on hand, the Superintendent of State Printing shall print from said plates and bind in law sheep such number of copies as shall be ordered by the Secretary of State, and deliver the same to the Secretary of State, to be sold by him as herein provided; the moneys thus received to be paid into the state treasury at the end of each month, and to be added to and constitute part of the fund for the support of the state printing office.

Whenever any bill, joint or concurrent resolution is passed to enrollment, by either the Senate or Assembly, the committee on enrollment of the house in which the bill, joint or concurrent resolution originated, shall transmit the same without delay to the Superintendent of State Printing, who shall receipt for all such bills and resolutions, and proceed at once to have the same printed, in the order in which received, and in the measure prescribed by law for statutes. So soon as printed, one copy, with the proper blanks for the signatures of the officers whose duty it is to sign enrolled bills, shall be printed on bond paper, which, together with the engrossed bill, shall be sent to the committee on enrollment of the house in which the bill originated. Said committee shall compare such copy with the engrossed bill, and, if it is found to be correct, shall present it to the proper officers for their signatures. When such officials shall have signed their names thereon, as required by law, it shall be an enrolled bill, and shall be transmitted to the Governor for his approval. If the same is signed by the Governor and becomes a law, the printed law shall go then to the Secretary of State and become the official record. Whenever a law is signed by the Governor, official notice shall be forwarded, in writing, to the Superintendent of State Printing, informing him of the fact. Upon the receipt of said official notice, the Superintendent of State Printing shall cause to be printed, for the use of the Legislature, five hundred copies of said law, joint or concurrent resolution, to be distributed one third to the Senate and two thirds to the Assembly, the sergeants-at-arms of the respective houses to receipt to the Superintendent of State Printing for the same, whose receipt shall be a proper voucher for the work. The Superintendent of State Printing shall also cause to be printed of all laws, as fast as signed by the Governor, five hundred copies, the same to be immediately distributed to the County Clerks of the various counties of the State, for the use of that official and the Superior Judges of his county. He shall also cause to be printed the requisite number of sheets to make the number of the copies of the statutes required by law to be printed, and one composition of type shall answer the purpose of printing the three editions. Of the journals and appendices of the Senate and Assembly, there must be printed four hundred and eighty copies, in one volume or more, as may be required by the size thereof. The Superintendent of State Printing shall have the laws, journals of Senate and Assembly, and the appendices thereto, properly indexed and bound, the laws in full law sheep binding, and the journals and appendices in half law sheep binding, marble sides, and deliver the same to the Secretary of State for distribution as soon as practical after the final adjournment of the Legislature; the receipt of the Secretary of State shall be his voucher therefor.

SECTION 529. To amended to read as follows:

Sec. 529. Printing must be done as follows: The laws, journals, messages, and other documents in book form, must be printed solid, with long primer type, on good white paper; each page, except of the laws, must be thirty-three ems wide and fifty-eight ems long, including title, blank line under it, and foot line; of the laws the same length, and twenty-nine ems wide, exclusive of marginal notes, which notes must be printed in nonpareil type, seven ems wide. Figure work, and rule and figure work, in messages, reports, and other documents in book form, must be on pages corresponding in size with the journals, if it can be brought in by using type not smaller than nonpareil; if not, it must be executed in a form to fold and bind with the volume. Bills, and other work of a similar character, must be printed with long primer type, on plain white paper, commencing the heading one fourth of the length of the sheet from its top, and be forty-six ems wide and seventy-three ems long, including running head, blank line under it, and foot line, and between each printed line there must be a white line corresponding with the body of the type, and each line must be numbered. Blanks must be printed in such form, and on such paper, and with such sized type, as the officers ordering them may direct, subject to the approval of the Superintendent of State Printing. The laws must be printed without chapter headings, and without blank lines, with the exception of one head line, one foot line, two lines between the last section of an act and the title of the next act. When there is not space enough between the last section of an act to print the title and enacting clause, and one line of the following act, upon the same page, such title may be printed upon the following page. The journals must be printed without blank lines, with the exception of one head line, one foot line, and two lines between the journal of one day and

that of the following day. In printing the ayes and noes, the word
"ayes" and the word "noes" must be run in with the names.

> Note.—The amendment consists in changing the words "white plain cap paper"
> to read "plain white paper," and in providing that the form and style of certain
> printing shall be "subject to the approval of the Superintendent of State Print-
> ing." This last to prevent unreasonable and very expensive requisitions for print-
> ing from captious officials.

SECTION 531. To be amended to read as follows:

Sec. 531. The duties of the Superintendent of State Printing shall
be as follows: He shall have the entire charge and superintendence of
the state printing and binding. He shall take charge of, and be
responsible on. his bond for, all manuscripts and other matter which
may be placed in his hands to be printed, bound, engraved, or litho-
graphed, and shall cause the same to be promptly executed. He shall
purchase all supplies and materials for the state printing office, in such
manner as he shall deem most advantageous to the State. He shall
receive from the Senate or Assembly all matter ordered by either house
to be printed and bound, or either printed or bound, and shall keep a
record of the same, and of the order in which it may be received; and
when the work shall have been executed, he shall deliver the finished
sheets or volumes to the sergeant-at-arms of the Senate or Assembly, or
of any department authorized to receive them, whose receipt therefor
shall be a sufficient voucher to the said Superintendent of State Printing
for their delivery. He shall receive, and promptly execute, all orders
for printing or binding required to be done for the various state officers;
provided, that the said Superintendent of State Printing shall have
discretionary authority to revise, reduce, or decline to execute any order,
or part of any order, which, in his judgment, is unnecessary or unwar-
ranted by law, and which will tend to unnecessarily consume the
appropriation for support of the state printing office; *and provided
further*, that in the event that any state officer, board, commission, or
institution shall consider the decision of the said Superintendent of
State Printing unfair, he may refer the matter to the State Board of
Examiners, which board shall determine the matter. He shall employ
such compositors, pressmen, and assistants as the exigency of the work
from time to time requires, and may at any time discharge such
employés; *provided*, that at no time shall he pay said compositors,
pressmen, or assistants a higher rate of wages than is paid by those
employing printers in Sacramento for like work. He shall at no time
employ more compositors or assistants than the absolute necessities of
the state printing may demand, and he shall not permit any other
than state work to be done in the state printing office. The Superintendent of State Printing shall make a biennial report, in writing, to
the Governor, embracing a record of the complete transactions of his

office for the two preceding fiscal years, which report shall show, in detail, all the items of expense attending the state printing and all the expenses of the office, including repairs and the purchase of materials of all kinds. Said report shall also state the number of reams and various kinds of paper delivered to him, and the amount and quality remaining on hand, which report shall be printed, biennially, for the use of the Legislature.

SECTION 534. To be amended to read as follows:

Sec. 534. The annual salary of the Superintendent of State Printing shall be three thousand dollars. He may appoint a Deputy Superintendent of State Printing, who shall receive a salary of two thousand four hundred dollars per annum.

NOTE.—The amendment consists in eliminating surplus provision of the original section, and in providing for the appointment of a deputy, which official shall take the place of, exercise the same authority, perform the same services, and receive the same salary as the present chief clerk or bookkeeper in the superintendent's office.

SECTIONS 535 and 536. To be repealed.

NOTE.—The above sections are obsolete, and have no proper application to the state printing office as now conducted.

SECTION 537. To be amended to read as follows:

Sec. 537. The State Treasurer is hereby authorized, when the general fund is exhausted, to advance the money on the Controller's warrants, drawn for wages and salaries of the employés in the state printing office, out of any public fund in the treasury, which warrants shall be his vouchers until there is money in the general fund to cancel them; *provided,* that this section shall not apply to any fund against which there are any warrants then due, or to become due, or so as to keep claimants out of their just demands.

NOTE.—The amendment consists in omitting the last sentence of the original section, as the same has now no proper application.

ARTICLE XIII.

SEALER OF WEIGHTS AND MEASURES.

SECTIONS 561, 562, 563, 564, 565, 566, and 567, as they now exist, to be transferred from Article XIV and made to constitute Article XIII, and renumbered, as follows: Section 561 to be renumbered 548; Section 562 to be renumbered 549; Section 563 to be renumbered 550; Section 564 to be renumbered 551; Section 565 to be renumbered 552; Section 566 to be renumbered 553; Section 567 to be renumbered 554.

SECTIONS 548, 549, 550, 551, 552, 553, and 554 to be repealed.

NOTE.—The office of State Geologist has fallen into disuse, and was practically abolished by Act of March 27, 1874. (Stats. 1873–74, page 694.)

We recommend that Article XIV, as reconstructed, shall read as follows:

ARTICLE XIV.

BOARD OF BANK COMMISSIONERS.

SECTION 555. A new section to be added to read as follows:

Board of Bank Commissioners.

Sec. 555. The State Board of Bank Commissioners shall continue to exist, and its present members shall hold office until the expiration of the term for which they were appointed, and until their successors are appointed and qualified. Upon the expiration of the term of each of the incumbents, the Governor shall appoint a person to the office of Bank Commissioner for the term of four years and until his successor is appointed and qualified. No two commissioners appointed shall be residents of the same section of the State. No appointee shall have official connection with, or be in the employ of, any savings bank, bank, or banking company, or of any person, partnership, association, or corporation engaged in the business of banking or publicly receiving money or credits on deposit, nor shall they, during their term of office, hold or be interested, directly or indirectly, in the stock, business, or other property of such person, partnership, association, or corporation. Before entering upon the duties of his office, each appointee shall execute an official bond in the sum of twenty thousand dollars, and take the oath of office as prescribed by the Political Code for state officers. The State Board of Bank Commissioners shall have their office in the City of San Francisco.

SECTION 556. A new section to be added to read as follows:

Duties of Bank Commissioners, to license.

Sec. 556. The duties of the Bank Commissioners shall be, to prepare and furnish to every savings bank, commercial bank, and banking company, or person or persons engaged in the business of banking or of publicly receiving money or credits on deposit, or to any other corporation incorporated under the laws of this State, or of any other State or Territory, or foreign country, doing a banking business in this State, applying therefor, a license in the form to be prescribed by them, authorizing such person, firm, association, or corporation, to transact the business of a savings bank, bank, or banking company, or to publicly receive money or credits on deposit, until the first day of July next thereafter; to receive and place on file in their office the reports required to be made by any person, or persons, engaged in the banking business or publicly receiving money or credits on deposit, or by savings banks, banks, or banking corporations or associations; to prepare and furnish, on demand, to all persons, firms, partnerships, corporations, or associations required to make and return statements or reports to said Bank Commissioners by the provisions of this article, blank forms for such statements or reports as may by law be required of them; to make, on or before the first day of October in each year, a report to the Governor of this State, containing a tabular statement and synopsis of the several reports which have been filed in their office since their last report, and any other proceedings had or done by them under this article, showing generally the condition of the several savings, commercial, and other banking corporations, or institutions of this·State, and the condition of the affairs of any person, or persons, or partnerships engaged in the business of publicly receiving money or credits on deposit, and such other matters as in their opinion may be of interest to the public, with a detailed statement, verified by their oaths, of all moneys and fees of office received by them during the same period.

SECTION 557.   A new section to be added to read as follows:

Duties of commissioners as to examination of financial condition.

Sec. 557.   It shall be the duty of one or more of the Bank Commissioners, as designated by the commissioners, once in each year, and as often as in their judgment may be deemed necessary, without previous notice, to visit and make, personally, a full examination of the business and affairs of each and every person, partnership, association, or corporation, mentioned in section five hundred and fifty-six of this Code; to inspect all books, papers, notes, bonds, or evidences of debt of such persons, partnerships, associations, or corporations, and all securities; to ascertain the financial condition of every such person, partnership, association, or corporation, its solvency, its ability to fulfill its obligations, and, if in their opinion, it is deemed necessary for any purpose, to report its condition to the Attorney-General and the Governor as soon as practicable after such examination.   Such commissioner or commissioners must examine, under oath, any person or persons, and the members, officers, directors, trustees, servants, and employés of any association, partnership, or corporation engaged in the banking business, or publicly receiving money or credits on deposit, and any and all persons who, they believe, have knowledge in relation to the affairs and condition of the business of any such person, or persons, association, partnership, or corporation, and administer such oath personally; and whoever shall neglect or refuse, after demand and notice thereof, and without justifiable cause, to appear, or testify under oath, before the said commissioners in the discharge of their duties, shall be deemed guilty of a misdemeanor, and upon conviction thereof shall be punished by a fine of not less than one thousand dollars, or by imprisonment in the county jail for not less than ninety days, or by both such fine and imprisonment.

SECTION 558. A new section to be added to read as follows:

Not to transact business without license.

Sec. 558. No person, partnership, association, or corporation, shall use the name or transact the business of a savings bank, bank, or banking association or corporation, or of publicly receiving money or credits on deposit, without the license provided for in section five hundred and fifty-six of this Code; and any person, partnership, association, or corporation, violating this provision, shall forfeit to the State of California the sum of one hundred dollars per day during the continuance of the offense; and any person who enters upon, engages in, or carries on, or in any manner attends to the business or management of a savings bank, bank, or banking association, or corporation, or the business of publicly receiving money or credits on deposit, without such license, whether as manager, principal, agent, officer, employé, or otherwise, shall forfeit to the State of California the sum of one hundred dollars for every day he so enters upon, engages in, carries on, or attends to such business; and in addition to the forfeiture herein provided for, any violation of this section by any person, partnership, association, or corporation, is also hereby declared to be a misdemeanor, and on conviction thereof such person, partnership, association, or corporation, shall be punished by a fine of not less than five hundred dollars, or by imprisonment in the county jail for not less than thirty days, or by both such fine and imprisonment.

SECTION 559. A new section to be added to read as follows:

Report of financial condition to be filed with commissioners.

Sec. 559. Every person, partnership, association, or corporation, mentioned in section five hundred and fifty-six of this Code, including banks in liquidation or insolvency, shall, on or before the first day of April of each year, file with the Board of Bank Commissioners a report, in writing, verified by the oath of a person, or the members of the partnership, conducting a banking business, or publicly receiving money or credits on deposit, or by the president and secretary, or cashier, or the two principal officers of the association or corporation; *provided*, that the statement of an association or corporation shall be further verified by a majority of the board of directors of such banking association or corporation as to the correctness of the statement made by the principal officers, and as to the value of the assets therein set forth. Such report shall show the actual financial condition of the person, partnership, association, or corporation, at twelve o'clock meridian, of the first Monday in March, by stating:

1. The amount of capital, or capital stock, and the number of shares into which it is divided;

2. The name of the person, partnership, association, or corporation, and the names of the directors or trustees, and the number of shares of stock held by each; .

3. The total amount actually paid, in money, by the stockholders for capital stock, and the total amount of reserve fund;

4. The total amount due to depositors;

5. The total amount and character of any and all other liabilities, of such person, partnership, association, or corporation;

6. The amount at which the lot and building or buildings occupied by the bank or institution, for. the transaction of its regular business, stand debited on its books, together with the market value of all other real estate held, whether acquired in the settlement of loans or otherwise; the amount at which it stands debited on the books of such person, partnership, association, or corporation; in what county situated, and in what name the title is vested, if not in the name of such person, partnership, association, or corporation;

7. The amount loaned on real estate, specifying the amount secured on real estate in each county separately; also, specifying the name of the person in whose name the property is held in trust or as security, in case it is held in any other name than that of the banker or banking institution, and in case the instrument creating the trust or security does not disclose the name of such banker or banking institution;

8. The amount invested in bonds, designating each particular class, and the amount thereof;

9. The amount loaned on stocks and bonds, designating each particular class, and the amount thereof;

10. The amount of money loaned on other security, with a particular designation of each class and kind of security, and the amount loaned on each;

11. The actual amount of money on hand or deposited in any other bank or place, with the name of the place where deposited, and the amount in each place;

12. Any other property held, or any amount of money loaned, deposited, invested, or placed, not · otherwise herein enumerated, with the place where situate, and the value of such property, and the amounts so loaned, deposited, or placed;

13. The character of business, if any, conducted in connection with the receiving of money or credits on deposit, and the amount of such money or credits used in the conduct of the business.

12—c

The oaths of the persons and officers to the statements above required shall state that they, and each of them, have a personal knowledge of the matters therein contained, and that they believe every allegation, statement, matter, and thing therein contained to be true; and any willfully false statement in the premises shall be perjury, and shall be punished as such. The reports as provided for by this section shall, by the Commissioners, be required from each and every person, partnership, association, or corporation herein mentioned, at least twice in each year in addition to the statement required to be made as to the financial condition on the first Monday in March, and at such times as they may designate. The report shall show the actual financial condition of the person, partnership, association, or corporation, making the report, up to the close of any past day to be by the commissioners designated; and such report shall be transmitted to the commissioners by the person, partnership, association, or corporation, within fifteen days after the receipt from them of a request or requisition therefor. Any person, partnership, association, or corporation, mentioned in section five hundred and fifty-six of this Code, failing to furnish to the Bank Commissioners any report by them required under the provisions of this article, within the time herein specified, shall forfeit the sum of one hundred dollars per day during the time of such default. No savings bank shall receive the license in this article provided for, unless fifty per cent of its loans shall be secured by first mortgage, or other prior lien, on real estate situate within this State. Such loans, at the date when made, hereafter, are not to exceed fifty per cent of the market value of the security, except when made for the purpose of facilitating the sale of property owned by the association, or corporation; and it shall be unlawful for any savings or loan society, or savings bank, to purchase, invest, or loan its capital, or the money of its depositors, in mining shares or stocks. No savings bank shall receive the license in this article provided for, if, after the first day of July, eighteen hundred and ninety-seven, the charter of incorporation of such savings bank shall provide for conducting a savings bank and a commercial bank, under the same management or directory, or in the same place of business. All reports required to be made to the Bank Commissioners by the provisions of this Code shall be filed and kept on file by the Bank Commissioners in their office, and shall be open to the inspection of the public during the office hours of such Commission; *provided*, that a copy of the report required to be made by each person, partnership, association, or corporation, of the condition of the business of such person, partnership, association, or corporation, at twelve o'clock, noon, of the first Monday in March, of each year, shall be forwarded by the commissioners by the fifteenth day of April of each year, to the Assessor of the county in which the business of such person, partnership, association, or corporation, is transacted or located.

Section 560. A new section to be added to read as follows:

Conduct of affairs when in involuntary liquidation.

Sec. 560. If the Bank Commissioners, on examination of the affairs of any person, partnership, association, or corporation mentioned in section five hundred and fifty-six of this Code, shall find that any such person, partnership, association, or corporation has been guilty of violating its charter or the laws of this State, or is conducting business in an unsafe manner, they shall, by an order addressed to the person, partnership, association, or corporation so offending, direct discontinuance of such illegal and unsafe practice, and a conformity with the requirements of the law and its charter. And if such person, partnership, association, or corporation shall refuse or neglect to conform with such requirements before the expiration of the time in the order specified, or if it shall appear to said commissioners and they shall unanimously decide that it is unsafe for any such person, partnership, association, or corporation to continue to transact business, it shall be the duty of the commissioners immediately to take such control of the business of such person, partnership, association, or corporation, and all the property and effects thereof, as may be necessary to prevent waste or diversion of assets, and to hold possession of the same until the order of court hereinafter mentioned, and to immediately notify the Governor and the Attorney-General of their action; and it is hereby made the duty of the Attorney-General, upon receiving such notification, to immediately commence suit in the proper court against such person, partnership, association, or corporation, and all the directors or trustees thereof, to enjoin and prohibit them from the transaction of any further business. If upon the hearing of the case the court shall find that such person, partnership, association, or corporation is solvent, and may safely continue business, it shall dismiss the action and order that the person, partnership, association, or corporation be restored to the possession of the property; but if the court shall find that it is unsafe for such person, partnership, association, or corporation to continue business, or that such person, partnership, association, or corporation is insolvent, said court shall by its decree order such person, partnership, association, or corporation into involuntary liquidation, and shall issue the injunction applied for and shall cause the same to be served according to law, and shall order the commissioners to surrender the property of the person, partnership, association, or corporation in their possession to a receiver appointed by the court for the purpose of liquidation in such proceeding, under the orders and direction of the court. The issuance of the injunction hereinbefore provided for shall, by operation of law, dissolve any and all attachments levied upon any property of such person, partnership, association, or corporation within one month next preceding the date of the notification by the commissioners to the Governor and the Attorney-General as provided for in this section; and no attachment or execution shall, after the issuance of such injunction and during the process of liquidation, be levied upon any property of such person, partnership, association, or corporation, nor shall any lien be created thereon. If a receiver be appointed, before surrendering to him the property of the person, partnership, association, or corporation for purposes of liquidation, the person named as receiver shall execute to the people of the State of California, an undertaking, with sufficient sureties, in an amount to be fixed by the court, that he will well and truly perform all the duties devolving on him by reason of such receivership, and that he will faithfully discharge the duty of receiver in the proceeding, and obey the orders of the court therein. Every receiver appointed under the provisions of this section shall make report of the condition of the affairs under his charge to the Bank Commissioners in the same manner as the solvent banks mentioned in this article are, by law, required to do, and, in addition thereto, shall state the amount of dividends paid, debts collected, and the money realized on property sold, if any, since the previous report. The Bank Commissioners shall have the power, and it is hereby made their duty, to examine the condition of the affairs of every such person, partnership, association, or corporation in liquidation, in the same manner as in case of solvent banks, businesses, and institutions, and they shall have a general supervision of the affairs of such person, partnership, association, or corporation in liquidation. They shall have the power to limit the number of employés necessary to close up the business of any such person, partnership, association, or corporation in liquidation, and also to limit the salaries of the same, and shall do all in their power to make such liquidation as economical and as expeditious as the interests of the creditors, depositors, and stockholders will admit. If any officer or employé of any association or corporation solvent, insolvent, or in liquidation, or if any other person, shall refuse to comply with the provisions of this section, or disregard or refuse to obey the directions of said Bank Commissioners, given in accordance with the provisions of this article, such person, officer, or employé shall be punished by a fine not exceeding five thousand dollars, or by imprisonment in the county jail not exceeding one year, or by both such fine and imprisonment. When the receiver herein provided for shall have been appointed and qualified, the duties of the Attorney-General shall end, and the court may, in its discretion, on application of the Bank Commissioners or of the receiver, appoint an attorney to act further in the proceeding. All salaries and expense of conducting such affairs in liquidation, shall be paid from the business in liquidation, on approval by the Bank Commissioners and on order of the court made therein.

SECTION 561. To be amended to read as follows:

Conduct of affairs when in voluntary liquidation.

Sec. 561. Whenever any person, partnership, association, or corporation mentioned in section five hundred and fifty-six of this Code shall determine to go into voluntary liquidation, before taking any further step to that end, he or they shall notify the Bank Commissioners by written notice of such determination, and such notice shall be accompanied by a full and complete statement of their financial condition as required in section five hundred and fifty-nine of this Code. If the Bank Commissioners, on examination of the affairs of the person, partnership, association, or corporation, deem it safe and in the interest of creditors that the person, partnership, or officers or directors of the association or corporation should conduct the business thereof in liquidation, they shall grant permission to do so, and shall file a copy of the permission given, together with the notice and statement served upon them by the person, partnership, association, or corporation desiring to go into voluntary liquidation, in the Superior Court of the county in which the business of such party is located. Such proceeding in the Superior Court shall be entitled, "In the matter of the voluntary liquidation of ———."

If it shall appear to the court, at any time after the filing of the notice, statement, and permission herein provided for, and during the liquidation, from the petition of one or more of the Bank Commissioners, or any interested party, that the person or member or members of the partnership, or the directors or trustees, or other officers or employés of any association or corporation, have been guilty of fraud, malversation, or criminal negligence, or that any of them are not the proper persons to be entrusted with the closing of the affairs and business of such person, partnership, association, or corporation, in the interest of the depositors, creditors, or stockholders thereof, the said court shall cause to be issued and served upon said person, persons, officers, directors, trustees, or employés, or any of them, an order to show cause why they, or any or all of them, should not be removed from office, or from all participation in the closing of such business and affairs, which order shall briefly recite the grounds of the application, and shall be returned at a time to be fixed by the court; and if, upon the hearing, the court shall find that such person, persons, officers, directors, trustees, or employés, or any of them, ought to be removed from office, or from further participation in the closing of such business and affairs, it shall enter its order of removal accordingly, which order shall be final in the premises; and the court shall, by an order entered in the proceeding, appoint a successor for any officer so removed; and the court shall also have power in like manner to fill all vacancies occurring in the board, and to appoint directors or trustees in their place, when, from any cause, there are no directors or trustees, or not sufficient number thereof to constitute a quorum for the transaction of the business; or when, from any cause, there are no directors or trustees, the court may order an election by the members or stockholders of such association or corporation, to be held according to law.

Subject to this right of removal and appointment, all persons, partnerships, associations, or corporations engaged in or conducting a banking business, or publicly receiving moneys or credits on deposit, when permitted to go into voluntary liquidation, shall be permitted to continue the management of the affairs of such person, partnership, association, or corporation, during the process of liquidation, under the direction of the Bank Commissioners, but not otherwise.

The affairs of every person, partnership, association, or corporation mentioned in this article, which may hereafter be permitted to go into liquidation, shall be closed, and the business thereof settled, within three years from the time it shall enter into liquidation, unless at the expiration of such time it shall obtain the consent, in writing, from a majority of the Board of Bank Commissioners, to continue in liquidation for the period of one year longer.

Every person, partnership, association, or corporation mentioned herein, that hereafter goes into liquidation, shall make report of the condition of its affairs to the Bank Commissioners in the same manner as the solvent banks mentioned in this article; and in addition thereto shall make a monthly statement of the financial condition up to the close of business on the last day of each calendar month, and forward the same, addressed to the Bank Commissioners, at their office, in the City of San Francisco. Such monthly statement shall show the amount of dividends paid, debts collected, and the amounts realized on property sold, if any, during the month covered by such report.

The Bank Commissioners have the power, and it is hereby made their duty, to examine the condition of the affairs of every person, partnership, association, or corporation in process of voluntary liquidation, in the same manner as in the case of solvent banks, and they shall have a direct supervision of the affairs of any such person, partnership, association, or corporation while in process of voluntary liquidation, and the further power to limit the number of employés thereof, and to fix the salaries of the same. And they shall do all in their power to make such liquidation as economical and as expeditious as the interests of depositors, creditors, and stockholders will admit.

If the officers or employés of any association, or corporation, or any person whose affairs are in process of voluntary liquidation, shall refuse to comply with the provisions of this article, or shall disregard or refuse to obey the directions of said Bank Commissioners, given in accordance with the provisions of this article, such person, officer, or employé shall be deemed guilty of a misdemeanor, and shall be punished by a fine not exceeding five thousand dollars, or by imprisonment in the county jail not exceeding one year, or by both such fine and imprisonment.

SECTION 562. To be amended to read as follows:

Capital and reserve fund required.

Sec. 562. No person or partnership engaged in the business of banking or of publicly receiving money or credits on deposit, shall receive a license, as in this article provided, to transact such business, or publicly receive money or credits on deposit, unless such person or partnership shall have a bona fide cash capital of ten thousand dollars, which shall not be reduced during the continuance of such business. And of the annual net profits of such business, at least fifty per centum shall go into a reserve fund, which reserve fund shall not be diminished or reduced without the written consent of the Bank Commissioners. No savings bank, commercial bank, bank, or banking corporation, shall hereafter be incorporated in this State to conduct a savings bank and a commercial bank, or a savings bank and any other banking business, under the same directory or management, or at the same place of business where such commercial or other banking business is conducted, or to conduct a banking business in a city or town of five thousand inhabitants or under, with a capital stock of less than twenty-five thousand dollars, or in a city or town of over five thousand, and not exceeding ten thousand inhabitants, with a capital stock of less than fifty thousand dollars, or in a city or town of over ten thousand, and not exceeding twenty-five thousand inhabitants, with a capital stock of less than one hundred thousand dollars, or in a city or town of over twenty-five thousand inhabitants, with a capital stock of less than two hundred thousand dollars. Before the Secretary of State issues to any corporation that proposes to do a banking business, his certificate of the filing of the articles of incorporation, there must be filed in his office the affidavit of the persons named in said articles as the first directors of the corporation, that all the capital stock has been actually and in good faith subscribed, and at least fifty per centum thereof paid, in lawful money of the United States, to a person in such affidavit named, for the benefit of the corporation. The remainder of the capital stock must be paid in within two years after said banking corporation receives from the Commissioners its first license to transact business, and if not so paid, no further license shall be issued to it.

The directors of any savings bank, bank, or banking corporation having a capital stock, may semi-annually declare a dividend of so much of the net profits of the stockholders as they shall judge expedient; but every such corporation shall, before the declaration of such dividend, carry at least one tenth part of the net profits of the stockholders, for the preceding half year, to its surplus or reserve fund, until the same shall amount to twenty-five per centum of its paid-up capital stock. But the whole, or any part, of such surplus or reserve fund, if held as the exclusive property of stockholders, may at any time be converted into paid-up capital stock, in which event such surplus or reserve fund shall be restored in the manner above provided, until it amounts to twenty-five per centum of the aggregate paid-up capital stock. A larger surplus or reserve fund may be created, and nothing herein contained shall be construed as prohibitory thereof. No license shall be issued to any savings bank violating the provisions of this section.

SECTION 563. To be amended to read as follows:

Use of words or terms denoting or implying a banking business.

Sec. 563. The use of the word "bank," or any other word or terms denoting or implying the conduct of the business of banking, or the use of the word "savings," alone or in connection with other words, denoting or implying the conduct of the business of a savings institution, or a savings and loan society, is hereby prohibited to all persons, firms, associations, companies, or corporations other than those subject to the supervision of the Bank Commissioners, or required by this article to report to them; and no license, as in this article provided, shall be issued by the commissioners to any corporation or other institution or concern, that does not receive money from the public as deposits in the manner customary with commercial or savings banks. Any person, firm, association, company, or corporation, not subject to the supervision of the Bank Commissioners, or not required by this article to report to them, making use of terms or adopting or employing forms or methods or practices of business implying conduct of a bank, savings bank, or savings and loan society, as by means of signs, advertisements, letterheads, billheads, blank notes, blank receipts, certificates, checks, circulars, or any written or printed, or partly written and partly printed, paper whatever, having thereon any artificial or corporate name or other word or words indicating that such business is the business of a bank, savings bank, or savings or loan society, shall forfeit for each day the offense is continued the sum of one hundred dollars, to be recovered as provided in this article.

SECTION 564. To be amended to read as follows:

Sec. 564. Whenever any of the officers, directors, agents, or employés of any commercial bank, or banking corporation, shall make a loan of such commercial bank, or banking corporation, of any sum of money for which such officer, director, agent, or employé shall give to such commercial bank, or banking corporation, a promissory note or other obligation for the payment of such loan, such promissory note or obligation shall be approved by a majority of the members of the board of directory of such bank, who are not directly or indirectly interested in said loan, and such approval shall be indorsed upon such note or obligation executed to the commercial bank, or banking corporation. And no officer, director, agent, or employé of any commercial bank, or banking corporation, shall make any overdraft in his own behalf, or by his indorsement of the note or obligation of another person, unless such indorsement be approved by a majority of the board of directory, such approval to be indorsed upon the note or obligation executed to such commercial bank, or banking corporation. The Bank Commissioners shall, upon information that the provisions of this section have been violated by any officer, director, agent, or employé of any commercial bank, or banking corporation, by petition, apply to the Superior Court of the county in which such commercial bank, or banking corporation, is located, asking for the removal of such officer, director, agent, or employé from the office held by such person in such commercial bank, or banking corporation, or as a director thereof; and if it appear to the court that this section has been violated by such officer, director, agent, or employé, he shall be so removed and shall be ineligible to hold office as an officer or director of such corporation thereafter.

SECTION 565. To be amended to read as follows:

Requirement as to publication of statements.

Sec. 565. Every person, partnership, association, or corporation, doing business under a license from the Board of Bank Commissioners, shall, in the months of March and September of every year, publish, in at least one newspaper published in the county in which the principal place of business of such person, partnership, association, or corporation is situated, and shall also file for record, prior to such publication, in the Recorder's office of such county, a statement, verified by the person or partnership conducting such business, and in case of an association or corporation, by its president or manager, and by its secretary or cashier, and by a majority of the members of the board of directors or trustees of such association or corporation, of the amount of capital stock actually paid into such association or corporation, and the amount of the capital so paid in that is actually and continually used in such business; *provided*, that nothing shall be deemed capital actually paid in, except money bona fide paid into and used in the business, or money bona fide paid into the treasury of any association or corporation, and under no circumstances shall the promissory note, check, or other obligation of any director or stockholder of any association or corporation, or of any person conducting such business, or of the member or members of any partnership transacting such business, be treated, computed, or in any manner considered as a part of such actually paid-in capital. The statement herein required to be published and verified shall show the actual condition and value of all the assets and liabilities of such business, and where the same are situated. The Recorder of every county in this State shall keep two sets of well-bound books for the recording of the sworn statements herein provided for; one of which sets of books shall be labeled "Statements of Banking Capital," and the other "Statements of Banking Assets"; and said Recorder shall, upon the payment of his fees for the same, by the person, partnership, or institution making such statement, record, separately, said sworn statements in their proper book, and shall keep a separate index of each of said sets of books. The statement herein required need not be acknowledged in order to be recorded, as herein provided, or to be used as evidence before any court in this State, and the original statement shall always remain and be kept on file in the office of said Recorder. The Recorder of every county in this State shall receive, for recording any of the sworn statements herein provided for, to be paid by the party making such statement, for every folio, twenty-five cents, and for noting on any such sworn statement the time when, and the place where, recorded, twenty-five cents, and for a certified copy of such sworn statements, twenty-five cents per folio. No person, partnership, association, or corporation doing business under a license from the Board of Bank Commissioners, shall advertise in any manner or publish a statement of the capital stock authorized or subscribed, unless he advertise and publish in connection therewith the amount of capital actually paid up. Any person, or member of a partnership, officer, manager, agent, or director of an association, or corporation, doing business under a license from the Board of Bank Commissioners, advertising in any manner or publishing a statement of the capital stock of such business or banking corporation, authorized or subscribed, without the statement in connection therewith of the amount of stock actually paid up in cash, and every person, or member of a partnership, officer, manager, or director of an association, or corporation, who shall fail to advertise or publish a statement of the capital stock of such business or banking corporation, and of the assets and liabilities thereof, as herein provided, shall be guilty of a misdemeanor, and shall be punishable by fine not exceeding five thousand dollars, or by imprisonment in the county jail not exceeding one year, or by both such fine and imprisonment.

NOTE.—This section embraces in substance the provisions of an Act concerning corporations and persons engaged in the business of banking, approved April 1, 1876, and the repeal of such Act is therefore recommended. (Banking Act, found on page 81, Deering's Civil Code.)

SECTION 566.   To be amended to read as follows:

Action for collection of penalties and forfeitures.

Sec. 566.   All penalties and forfeitures provided for in this article for the failure to act as herein provided, or for action hereby prohibited, shall be recovered of the party offending by civil action in the Superior Court of the county in which the business of the person, partnership, association, or corporation is located in relation to which the act was done or as to which the failure to act has occurred.   On request of the Bank Commissioners, such action shall be commenced by the District Attorney of such county, and shall be conducted to final judgment by such District Attorney as civil actions for the recovery of money are conducted; *provided*, that in every case but one action shall be brought for all forfeitures or penalties made or incurred by any person or officer of an association or corporation prior to the bringing of such action, and for this purpose all causes of action existing against any person or party, for penalties and forfeitures incurred under this article, may be united in one suit, but each distinct cause of action shall be separately stated.

SECTION 567.   To be amended to read as follows:

Salaries of Bank Commissioners.

Sec. 567.   The Bank Commissioners shall each receive a salary of three thousand six hundred dollars per annum, and necessary traveling expenses, not to exceed, for the three commissioners, the sum of three thousand dollars per annum, to be audited by the State Controller and paid by the State Treasurer, in the same manner as the salaries and expenses of other state officers.   No person, while holding any other office, or engaged in business of any kind requiring his personal attention between the hours of nine A. M. and four P. M., shall serve as Bank Commissioner.

SECTION 568.   To be amended to read as follows:

Salaries and expenses.

Sec. 568.   The Bank Commissioners shall have power to appoint a secretary, at a salary of two hundred dollars per month.   The said commissioners shall keep their office open for business from nine o'clock A. M. until four o'clock P. M., every day, except non-judicial days.   They shall procure rooms necessary for their offices, at a rent not to exceed seventy-five dollars per month.   They may also provide stationery, fuel, and other conveniences necessary for the transaction of their duties, not exceeding in the aggregate the sum of five hundred dollars per annum. All expenditures authorized in this section shall be audited and paid in the same manner as the salary of the commissioners.

SECTION 569.   To be amended to read as follows:

Bank Commissioners' Fund.

Sec. 569.   To pay the salaries and all other necessary expenses of the commissioners, as provided for by this article, every person, partnership, association, or corporation, receiving a license, shall pay annually, in advance, to the commissioners, in gold coin, its share of the amount required to pay such salaries and expenses; the share to be paid by any person, partnership, association, or corporation to be determined by the proportion which its deposits bear to the aggregate deposits of all such persons, partnerships, associations, or corporations receiving licenses, as shown by the latest reports of such persons, partnerships, associations, or corporations to the commissioners.   Said commissioners shall, upon demand made therefor, and without charge, furnish to every person, partnership, association, or corporation mentioned in this article, copies of papers, statements, and reports filed in their office, and may, as provided by this article, recover any and all moneys payable to them by any person, partnership, association, or corporation, herein mentioned; and all moneys collected or received by such Bank Commissioners, or either of them, under or by virtue of the provisions of this article, shall be by them delivered to the treasurer of this State, who shall pay the same into a fund which is hereby created, and which shall be known as the "Bank Commissioners' Fund."   And the unexpended balance of all moneys heretofore paid into the state treasury by said Bank Commissioners shall be transferred to said fund and become a part thereof.

NOTE.—This article, "Board of Bank Commissioners," Section 555 to Section 569 inclusive, is constructed on the Bank Commissioners Act as amended in 1895. It is sought to make definite the authority of the Bank Commissioners in protecting the interests of creditors and stockholders, and provides for the closing up of the affairs of persons or corporations doing a banking business, by the Commissioners, when they determine the business of such institution to be unsafe,through the local court, but under such a general supervision by the Bank Commissioners that any waste or dissipation of funds or assets may be brought immediately to the attention of the court. It provides that in case of voluntary liquidation persons or corporations closing up their affairs will be under the direct control and supervision of the Bank Commissioners; that savings banks cannot be merged in commercial banks ; that officers and directors cannot make loans unless the note or obligation to the corporation is approved by a majority of the directory ᴀ and overdrafts are prohibited. The provisions of the Act of April 1, 1876, concerning persons and corporations engaged in the business of banking, have been embodied in this article, and we would recommend the repeal of that Act as being of no further necessity. The Act of March 29, 1878, to protect stockholders and persons dealing with corporations of this State, has been, in substance, embodied in a new section of the Penal Code. The previous sections constituting Article XIV, being Sections 561 to 567, have been transferred to and constitute Article XIII hereof.

SECTIONS 577, 578, 579, 580, 581, 582, 583, and 584 to be repealed.

NOTE.—The office of Inspector of Gas Meters and the system of inspection provided for in the foregoing sections is in conflict with Article XI, Section 14, of the Constitution.

SECTION 611. To be amended to read as follows:

Statement, what to contain—Publication and filing.

Sec. 611. The statement mentioned in the preceding section must exhibit the financial condition and the affairs of every such corporation, person, firm, or association on the first Monday in March of each and every year and for the year then next preceding, and must be filed with the Insurance Commissioner, as follows:

1. If made by a person or corporation organized under the laws of this State, such statement must be filed with the Insurance Commissioner on or before the twentieth day of March of each year;

2. If made by a person or corporation organized under the laws of any other of the States or Territories of the United States, such statement must be filed with the Insurance Commissioner on or before the first day of April of each year;

3. If made by a person or corporation organized under the laws of any country foreign to the United States, such statement must be filed with the Insurance Commissioner on or before the twentieth day of April of each year.

The statement herein mentioned, when adjusted by the Insurance Commissioner, must be published by such corporation, person, firm, or association, daily, for the period of one week, in some newspaper published in the city where the principal office of such corporation, person, firm, or association is located.

NOTE.—The change is to fix time of filing statement to meet changes in the revenue laws.

SECTION 612. To be amended to read as follows:

Statement, what to show.

Sec. 612. Such statement, if made by a fire, marine, or inland insurance company, fidelity, steam-boiler, plate-glass, or title insurance company, or by companies organized under section four hundred and twenty of the Civil Code, must show:

First—The amount of the capital, or capital stock, specifying:

1. The number of shares into which such capital stock is divided;

2. The par value of each share of such capital stock;

3. The number of shares of such capital stock held by subscribers or purchasers thereof;

4. The amount of cash actually paid into the treasury of the association, or corporation.

Second—The property or assets held by the company, specifying:

1. The value of real estate held by such company;

2. The amount of cash on hand and deposited in banks to the credit of the company, specifying the same;

3. The amount of cash in the hands of agents, and in course of transmission;

4. The amount of loans secured by bonds and mortgages constituting the first lien on real estate, on which there is less than one year's interest due or owing;

5. The amount of loans on which interest has not been paid within one year previous to such statement;

6. The amount due the company on which judgments have been obtained;

7. The amount of stocks of this State, of the United States, or of any incorporated city of this State, and of any other stock owned by the company, specifying the amount, number of shares, and par and market value of each kind of stocks;

8. The amount of stocks held as collateral security for loans, with the amount loaned on each kind of stock, its par value and market value;

9. The amount of interest due and unpaid;

10. The amount of all other loans made by the company, specifying the same;

11. The amount of premium notes on hand on which policies are issued;

12. All other property belonging to the company, specifying the same.

Third—The liabilities of such company, specifying:

1. The amount of losses due and unpaid;

2. The amount of claims for losses resisted by the company;

3. The amount of losses in process of adjustment, or in suspense, including all reported or supposed losses;

4. The amount of dividends declared, due, and remaining unpaid;

5. The amount of dividends declared, but not due;

6. The amount of money borrowed and security given for the payment thereof;

7. Gross premiums (without any deductions) received and receivable upon all unexpired fire risks running one year or less from date of policy, reinsurance thereon at fifty per cent;

8. Gross premiums (without any deductions) received and receivable upon all unexpired fire risks running more than one year from date of policy, reinsurance thereon pro rata;

9. Gross premiums (without any deductions) received and receivable upon all unexpired marine and inland navigation risks, except time risks, reinsurance thereon at one hundred per cent;

10. Gross premiums (without any deductions) received and receivable on marine time risks, reinsurance thereon at fifty per cent;

11. Amount reclaimable by the insured on perpetual fire insurance policies, being ninety-five per cent of the premiums or deposit received;

12. Reinsurance fund and all other liabilities, except capital, under the life insurance or any other special department;

13. Unused balances of bills and notes taken in advance for premiums on open marine and inland policies, or otherwise, returnable on settlement;

14. Principal unpaid on scrip or certificates of profits, which have been authorized or ordered to be redeemed;

15. Amount of all other liabilities of the company, specifying the same;

Fourth—The income of the company during the preceding year, specifying:

1. The amount of cash premiums received;

2. The amount of notes received for premiums;

3. The amount of interest money received, specifying the same;

4. The amount of income received from all other sources, specifying the same.

Fifth—The expenditures of the preceding year, specifying:

1. The amount of losses paid;

2. The amount of dividends paid;

3. The amount of expenses paid, including commissions and fees to agents and officers of the company;

4. The amount paid for taxes;

5. The amount of all other payments and expenditures;

Sixth—1. The amount of risks written during the year;

2. The amount of risks expired during the year;

3. The amount of risks written during the year in the State of California;

4. The amount of premiums thereon.

> NOTE.—The amendment requires the statement to be made by fidelity, steam-boiler, plate-glass, and title insurance companies, and adds the specifications 1, 2, 3, and 4, first subdivision. This is done to meet the requirements of the revenue laws and to facilitate the work of the Assessor.

SECTION 613. To be amended to read as follows:

Statement by life, health, and accident companies.

Sec. 613. Such statement, if made by life, health, accident, or assessment life companies, must show:

First—The amount of capital, or capital stock, of the company, specifying:

1. The number of shares into which such capital stock is divided;

2. The par value of each share of such capital stock;

3. The number of shares of such capital stock held by subscribers or purchasers thereof;

4. The amount of cash actually paid into the treasury of the association or corporation.

Second—The property or assets held by the company, specifying:

1. The value of the real estate held by the company;

2. The amount of cash on hand and deposited in banks to the credit of the company, specifying the same;

3. The amount of loans secured by bonds and mortgages on real estate, specifying the same;

4. Amount of loans secured by pledge of bonds, stocks, or other marketable securities as collateral, specifying the same;

5. Cash market value of all stocks and bonds owned by the company, specifying the same;

6. Interest due the company and unpaid;

7. Interest accrued but not due;

8. Premium notes and loans in any form taken in payment of premiums on policies now in force;

9. Gross amount of premiums in process of collection and transmission on policies in force;

10. Gross amount of deferred premiums;

11. All other assets, specifying the same;

Third—Liabilities. 1. Claims for death losses and matured endowments, due and unpaid;

2. Claims for death losses and matured endowments in process of adjustment, or adjusted and not due;

3. Claims resisted by the company;

4. Amount due and unpaid on annuity claims;

5. Trust fund on deposit, or net present value of all the outstanding policies, computed according to the American experience tables of mortality, with four and one-half per cent interest;

6. Additional trust fund on deposit, or net present value of extra and special risks, including those on impaired lives;

7. Amount of all unpaid dividends of surplus percentages, bonuses, and other description of profits to policy-holders, and interest thereon;

8. Amount of any other liability to policy-holders or annuitants, not included above;

9. Amount of dividends unpaid to stockholders;

10. Amount of national, state, and other taxes due;

11. All other liabilities, specifying the same.

Fourth—Income. 1. Cash received for premiums on new policies during the year;

2. Cash received for renewal of premiums during the year;

3. Cash received for purchase of annuities;

4. Cash received for all other premiums;

5. Cash received for interest on loans, specifying the same;

6. Rents received;

7. Cash received from all other sources, specifying the same;

8. Gross amount of notes taken on account of new premiums;

9. Gross amount of notes taken on account of renewal premiums.

Fifth—Expenditures.   1. Cash paid for losses;

2. Cash paid to annuitants;

3. Cash paid for lapsed, surrendered, and purchased policies;

4. Cash paid for dividends to policy-holders;

5. Cash paid for dividends to stockholders;

6. Cash paid for reinsurances;

7. Commission paid to agents;

8. Salaries and other compensation of officers and employés, except agents and medical examiners;

9. Medical examiners' fees and salaries;

10. Cash paid for taxes;

11. Cash paid for rents;

12. Cash paid for commuting commissions;

13. All other cash payments;

Sixth—Balance-sheet of premium note account.

Seventh—Balance-sheet of all the business of the company.

Eighth—1. Total amount of insurance effected during the year on new policies;

2. Total amount of insurance effected during the year in the State of California;

3. Premiums received during the year on risks written in the State of California.

NOTE.—As amended, assessment, life, and accident companies are added to those required to make this statement; also, specifications 1, 2, 3, and 4, as in preceding section, and for the same purpose.

SECTION 625.   To be amended to read as follows:

Insurance Commissioner to furnish Assessor with certain information.

Sec. 625.   The Insurance Commissioner must, within five days after the filing in his office of any of the statements required to be therein filed by the provisions of section six hundred and eleven of this Code, furnish a copy of such statement to the Assessor of the county in which the principal office of the person or corporation doing the business of insurance and filing such statement is situated, and when so requested by any Assessor, the Insurance Commissioner shall furnish such Assessor all of the data concerning premiums collected by such person or corporation and all other necessary information in relation to the business of such person or corporation as will assist the Assessor in the performance of the duties of his office.

SECTION 635. A new section to be added to read as follows:

Uniform policy of fire insurance.

Sec. 635. The Insurance Commissioner shall prepare and file in his office, on or before the first day of June, eighteen hundred and ninety-seven, a printed form, in blank, of a contract or policy of fire insurance, together with such agreement, provisions, or conditions as may be indorsed thereon, or added thereto, and form a part of such contract or policy; and such form, when so filed, shall be known and designated as the "California standard fire insurance policy," and such form shall, as near as can be made applicable, conform to the New York standard fire insurance policy, so called and known. Immediately after filing said form of policy in the office of said Insurance Commissioner, he shall have five hundred copies of the same printed, and mail a copy of the same to each company doing a fire insurance business in this State.

NOTE.—This section is to be taken in connection with the proposed Section 431 of the Civil Code.

ARTICLE XVIII.

BOARD OF EXAMINERS.

SECTION 680. To be amended to read as follows:

Sec. 680. Whenever and as often as there is in the state treasury the sum of ten thousand dollars as the proceeds of the sale of state school lands, the board must invest the same in bonds of the State of California, or in the county or consolidated city and county bonds of this State, or in the bonds of the cities of the State of California, or in the bonds of the United States; the investments to be made in such manner and on such terms as the board shall deem for the best interests of the state school fund; *provided*, that no bonds of any county, or city and county, or city shall be purchased of which the debt, debts, or liabilities at the time exceed fifteen per cent of the assessed value of the taxable property of said county, city and county, or city.

NOTE.—Amended by dropping the designation "civil funded bonds." the meaning of which is obscure, and enlarging the scope of investment to include city bonds.

SECTION 686. A new section to be added, to read as follows:

To prescribe a uniform system of accounts.

Sec. 686. A uniform system of books of account, blanks, payrolls, reports, accounts, and records shall be adopted by all officers, boards, commissions, trustees, and institutions supported by state funds, or money appropriated by the State, and chargeable with accounting for their expenditures to the State Board of Examiners. The State Board of Examiners shall prescribe and prepare a form of such books of account, reports, payrolls, vouchers, blanks, records, and forms as shall be necessary to effect such uniformity, and shall supply a copy thereof to the boards, officers, commissions, trustees, or institutions which are to use the same, and thereafter such boards, officers, commissions, trustees, or institutions shall use the same, and no other.

ARTICLE XIX.

POWERS AND DUTIES OF OTHER EXECUTIVE OFFICERS.

SECTION 695. To be amended to read as follows:

Sec. 695. The secretary of the State Board of Health is ex officio vaccine agent. His powers and duties as such are prescribed by sections twenty-nine hundred and ninety-three and twenty-nine hundred and ninety-four of this Code.

SECTION 696. To be repealed to conform to the amendment of Section 368 and repeal of Sections 2949 to 2969.

ARTICLE I.

CLERK OF THE SUPREME COURT.

SECTION 749. To be amended to read as follows:

Sec. 749. The Clerk of the Supreme Court is elected at the same time, and in the same manner, as the Governor is elected, and holds his office for the same term.

> NOTE.—Amended to conform to the requirements of Section 20, Article XX, of the Constitution, relating to the time of commencement of term.

ARTICLE II.

REPORTER OF THE SUPREME COURT.

SECTION 767. To be amended to read as follows:

Sec. 767. The justices of the Supreme Court shall appoint a reporter of the decisions of the Supreme Court, who shall hold his office and be removable at their pleasure.

> NOTE.—Amended to conform to the provisions of Article VI, Section 21, of the Constitution.

ARTICLE I.

DISQUALIFICATIONS.

SECTION 841. To be amended to read as follows:

Sec. 841. No person is capable of holding a civil office, who, at the time of his election or appointment, is not of the age of twenty-one years, and a citizen of this State. Women over the age of twenty-one years, who are citizens of the United States, and of this State, shall be eligible to all educational offices within this State, except those from which they are excluded by the constitution.

NOTE.—The amendment consists in adding to the section as it originally existed the provisions of the Act of March 12, 1874 (Stats. 1873–74, page 356).

ARTICLE II.

RESTRICTIONS UPON THE RESIDENCE OF OFFICERS.

SECTION 852. To be amended to read as follows:

Sec. 852. The following officers must reside at and keep their offices in the City of Sacramento: The Governor, Secretary of State, Controller, State Treasurer, Attorney-General, Surveyor-General, Superintendent of State Printing, Superintendent of Public Instruction, and the Adjutant-General.

ARTICLE III.

POWERS OF DEPUTIES.

SECTION 865. To be amended to read as follows:

Sec. 865. In all cases not otherwise provided for, each deputy, or in case there be no deputy, then the chief clerk, possesses the powers and may perform the duties attached by law to the office of his principal.

ARTICLE X.

RESIGNATIONS, VACANCIES, AND THE MODE OF SUPPLYING THEM.

SECTION 1001. To be amended to read as follows:

Sec. 1001. A vacancy in the office of either the Secretary of State, Controller, Treasurer, Attorney-General, Surveyor-General, Clerk of the Supreme Court, Superintendent of Public Instruction, or Superintendent of State Printing, must be filled by a person appointed by the Governor, who shall hold his office for the balance of the unexpired term.

NOTE.—The amendment consists in providing for filling a vacancy in the offices of Superintendent of State Printing and Superintendent of Public Instruction.

CHAPTER I.

ARTICLE II.

ELECTION PROCLAMATION.

SECTION 1054. To be amended to read as follows:

Sec. 1054. Such proclamation must contain:

1. A statement of the time of election and of the offices to be filled;

2. Whenever the Legislature, at its session preceding any general election, shall have proposed any amendments to the constitution of this State, or any other question for submission to the qualified electors of this State, the Governor shall include such proposed amendments or other question in such proclamation, numbering them, respectively, in the order of their adoption by the Legislature, and giving them the additional designation of the number given them by the Legislature. In such proclamation, after such proposed amendments or other question has been set forth, the same shall be restated by number, including number given by the Legislature, in manner and form as the same shall appear upon the ballot. Such form shall be substantially as follows, the proper numbers to be inserted: "Amendment Number ——, being (Senate or Assembly) Constitutional Amendment No. ——. (Then a short statement or syllabus of the purposes or object of the amendment is to be inserted in brackets.) For the Amendment?" The words "Yes" and "No" are then to be inserted in manner and form as provided in section eleven hundred and ninety-seven of this Code;

3. An offer of a reward in the following form: "I do hereby offer a reward of one hundred dollars for the arrest and conviction of any and every person violating any of the provisions of title four, part one of the Penal Code, such rewards to be paid until the total amount hereafter expended for the purpose reaches the sum of ten thousand dollars."

SECTION 1055. To be amended to read as follows:

Sec. 1055. The Board of Supervisors, upon the receipt of such proclamation, must, in case of general or special elections, cause a copy of the same to be published in some newspaper printed in the county, if any, and to be posted at each place of election at least ten days before the election; and in case of special elections to fill a vacancy in the office of State Senator or member of Assembly, the Board of Supervisors, upon receipt of such proclamation, may, in their discretion, cause a copy of the same to be published or posted as hereinbefore provided, except that such publication or posting need not be made for a longer period than five days before such election.

NOTE.—Amended by changing the word "may" to "must."

CHAPTER III.

REGISTRATION OF ELECTORS.

SECTION 1083.   To be amended to read as follows:

Sec. 1083.   Every male citizen of the United States, every male person who shall have acquired the right of citizenship under or by virtue of the treaty of Queretaro, and every male naturalized citizen thereof, who shall have become such ninety days prior to any election, of the age of twenty-one years, who shall have been a resident of the State one year next preceding the election, and of the county in which he claims his vote ninety days, and in the election precinct thirty days, and whose name shall be enrolled on the great register of such county, as provided for in section ten hundred and ninety-four of this Code, shall be a qualified elector at any and all elections held within the county, city and county, city, town, or district within which such elector resides.

NOTE.—Amended to prevent conflict with Section 1094.

CHAPTER V.

BOARD OF ELECTION.

SECTION 1144.   To be amended to read as follows:

Sec. 1144.   If the Board of Supervisors fail to appoint the board of election, or all the members of said board fail to attend at the hour set for the opening of the polls on election day, the electors of the precinct present at that hour may appoint or elect the board.   If part only of the board of election are present at the hour of opening the polls, any two members so present, of opposite political faith, shall proceed to fill the vacancies on the board; *provided*, that in each case the partisan qualifications required by section eleven hundred and forty-two of this Code be present in any person elected to fill any such vacancies.

SECTION 1145.   To be amended to read as follows:

Sec. 1145.   The inspector who for the time is in charge of the ballot-box and receiving the ballots, is chairman of the board, and may:

1. Administer all oaths required in the progress of an election;

2. Appoint judges and clerks, if, during the progress of an election, any judge or clerk ceases to act.

NOTE.—Amended to meet the requirements of Section 1142, which provides for two inspectors.

CHAPTER VII.

POLL LISTS.

SECTION 1174. To be amended to read as follows:

Sec. 1174. A poll list shall be kept by the clerks of election as provided for in section twelve hundred and twenty-nine, and shall be substantially of the following form:

POLL LIST.

Of the election held in the precinct of ———, in the County of ———, on the ——— day of ———, eighteen hundred and ———. A and B inspectors, C and D judges, G and H ballot clerks, and J and K tally clerks, of said election, were respectively sworn (or affirmed), as required by law, previous to their entering on the duties of their respective offices.

Number and Names of Electors Voting.

No.	Name.	No.	Name.
1	--------------------	4	--------------------
2	--------------------	5	--------------------
3	--------------------	6	--------------------

We hereby certify that the number of electors voting at this election in this precinct amounts to (here write out in full the proper number).

The County Clerk of each county shall furnish to the board of election, at each precinct, a tally sheet, to be kept as provided for in section twelve hundred and fifty-eight. Such tally list or sheet shall be printed upon a good quality of paper, and be entitled "Election return and tally list of votes polled at the general election held in ——— ward, precinct ———, County of ———, State of California, on the ——— day of ———, 18—." At the extreme left of the sheet shall be a column headed "Title of office," and in this column, immediately preceding the name of any candidate for an office, shall be printed the title of his office, or in case of officers elected from minor political divisions of a county, space shall be left for writing the title of his office. In the case of constitutional amendments or other question to be voted upon, the name "Constitutional Amendment" or other proper descriptive title shall be printed. Immediately to the right of this column shall be another column, at the head of which shall be printed "Names of candidates and parties to which candidates belong." In this column shall be printed the names of all persons to be voted for by the electors of the precinct to which the tally sheet is sent; such names in such column to follow the title of his office as printed in the first-mentioned column. In this second column, and following their title, shall be printed the name or title of the proposed constitutional amendment or other question to be voted upon. The names of all the candidates for the same office shall be printed in the column immediately succeeding each other and in exactly the same order and arrangement as they appear upon the official ballot, and blank spaces shall follow each set of offices, in which to write the names of persons voted for whose names are not printed upon the ballot. In this second column, and immediately following the name of the candidate, shall be printed his party name or political designation, as the same appears upon the ballot. Immediately following this second column, in a narrow third column, each line upon which the name of a candidate has been printed and the blank lines shall be numbered numerically, commencing at one and continuing to the end of the sheet. Continuing thence to the extreme right of the sheet, perpendicular lines shall be drawn, at a distance of not more than one half inch apart, parallel with the before-mentioned columns. At the head of each of the columns so formed shall be printed figures, commencing with five in the first, ten in the second, and thus increasing in arithmetical progression to the right of the sheet, where, in another column, shall be printed the figures one, two, three, and so on to the end of the sheet, such figures to correspond with the figures in the third column hereinbefore provided for, leaving room, on the extreme right of the sheet, to write, in figures, the total vote in that precinct for each officer voted for and each proposed constitutional amendment or other question voted upon. Attached to this sheet, or being part of the tally list, shall be printed a form under the general heading first hereinabove provided for. Under this shall be printed a sub-heading, reading "We hereby certify that," and immediately following, on the extreme left of the sheet, shall be printed the names of all of the candidates to be voted for by the electors of the precinct to which the sheet is sent; *provided*, that the names of officers to be voted for in districts less than a county, except members of the Legislature, need not be printed, space being left for writing the names of such officers. The names of candidates shall be printed on this part of the tally sheet in the same order as they appear upon the first part thereof, and upon the ballot; *provided*, that they shall not be preceded by the title of the office for which they are a candidate, nor followed by their party or political designation. Immediately to the right

of and following the name of each candidate shall be printed the word
"received," after which shall be left a blank space for writing out in full
the number of votes cast at such election for such candidate. Immediately following this blank space shall, in each case, be printed the words
"votes for ————," the blank to be. filled by printing the title of the
office for which the person is a candidate; after which, on the right of
the sheet, the line will be completed by printing the words "and that."
Where proposed constitutional amendments or other questions have
been voted upon, the name or title of such proposed amendment or other
question shall be printed upon the extreme left of the sheet and under
the names of the candidates for office. The name or title of each of
such proposed amendments or other question shall be printed once, followed on the right by the word "Yes," and immediately under it on the
next line such names or title shall be repeated, followed on the right by
the word "No," after which the line shall be completed as above provided in case of candidates for office. At the end of and completing the
sheet shall be printed the following certificate, to be signed by the board
of election and the clerks thereof:

"Witness our hands this ———— day of ————, 189—.

———— } Clerks
———— } of
———— } Election.

———— Inspector. }
———— Inspector. } Board
———— Judge. } of
———— Judge. } Election."

CHAPTER VIII.

ELECTION BALLOTS.

SECTION 1192. To be amended to read as follows:

Sec. 1192. Certificates of nomination required to be filed with the
Secretary of State shall be filed not less than sixty days before the day
fixed by law for the election of the persons in nomination, when the
nomination is made by a convention; and not less than forty days
before the day of election, when the nomination is made by electors, as
provided in section eleven hundred and eighty-eight of this Code
Certificates of nomination required to be filed with County Clerks,
or with the clerk or secretary of the legislative body of any city or town,
shall be filed not less than thirty days before the day of election, when
the nomination is made by a convention; and not less than twenty days
before the day of election, when the nomination is made by electors.
Should a vacancy in the list of nominees of a convention occur, such
vacancy may be filled by the convention upon being reconvened, or if the
power to fill vacancies has been delegated to a committee, such committee
may, upon the occurrence of such vacancy, proceed to fill the same; *pro-*

vided, that such vacancy be filled and certificate of nomination thereof be filed with the proper officer not less than thirty days before the day of election. The chairman and secretary of the convention or of such committee shall thereupon make and file with the proper officer a certificate setting forth the cause of the vacancy, the name of the person nominated, the office for which he was nominated, the name of the person for whom the new nominee is to be substituted, the fact that the committee was authorized to fill vacancies, and such further information and affidavit by the chairman and secretary as is required to be given in an original certificate of nomination. When a certificate to fill any vacancy shall be filed with the Secretary of State, he shall, in certifying the nomination to the various County Clerks, insert the name of the person who has been thus nominated to fill a vacancy in the place of that of the original nominee. Any person whose name has been presented as a candidate, may, at least five days before the making of the publication of the nominations prescribed in this section, cause his name to be withdrawn from nomination, by filing, in the office where his original certificate of nomination is required by this Code to be filed, his request therefor, in writing, signed by him and acknowledged before the County Clerk of the county in which he resides; and no name so withdrawn shall be printed on the ballot. Whenever any certificate of nomination is presented for filing to any officer authorized to file the same, such officer shall forthwith, upon receipt of the same and before filing, examine the same, and if there is any defect, omission, or reason why the same should not be filed, such officer shall then and there forthwith designate, in writing, the defect, omission, or reason why such certificate cannot be filed, and return the said certificate to the person presenting the same, with such written designation of defect, omission, or reason for not filing the same; and after the filing of any certificate of nomination, no officer required by law to transmit any nomination, or to make up or print any ballot, shall fail or omit to transmit such nomination, or omit to print the name of any nominee or candidate named in any certificate of nomination which has been filed; and unless a certificate of nomination is returned as herein required, the officer to whom the same is properly presented shall file the same as soon as he shall receive and examine the same as herein required, and must file it . as of the day it is presented.

NOTE.—Amended by permitting nominations to be filed at any time prior to sixty days before an election, the minimum time being increased to sixty days. The minimum time for filing nominations upon petition has been increased to forty days, prior to which no limit has been fixed. The manner of filling vacancies by the convention is made more certain, while committees are given until thirty days before an election to fill vacancies. The chairman and secretary of the committee are required to verify their certificate of nomination.

SECTION 1193. To be amended to read as follows:

Sec. 1193. Thirty days before an election to fill any office, the Secretary of State shall certify to the chairman of the state central committee or other governing body of each political party which has filed nominations in his office, and to each candidate nominated under the provisions of section eleven hundred and eighty-eight of this Code, all nominations filed in his office, in the same manner and form as he is hereinafter required to certify the same to the County Clerks. Twenty-five days before an election he shall also certify all nominations to the County Clerk of each county within which any of the electors may by law vote for candidates for such office, the name of each person nominated for such office, and each proposed constitutional amendment or other proposition to be voted upon, arranged in ballot form, as such form is provided for in section eleven hundred and ninety-seven of this Code.

SECTION 1194. To be amended to read as follows:

Sec. 1194. At least fifteen days before an election to fill any public office, the County Clerk of each county shall cause a sample ballot to be sent to the chairman of the county committee of each organized political party of such county, containing the nominations to office as certified to him by the Secretary of State, and also all those filed with the County Clerk, together with other questions to be voted upon. In all counties where a new registration shall take place preceding the next ensuing election, the County Clerk shall cause the name of each voter, as enrolled, to be addressed upon an envelope, and also the number of the residence of said voter, or the correct post office address of said voter, as the same is written on said register, and which name and address shall be written on the envelope at the time that each voter is duly registered thereon. All of said envelopes shall be securely kept by the said County Clerk, and ten days before election to fill any public office he shall cause to be folded and placed in said envelope, for mailing, a copy of so much of the election proclamation as contains the constitutional amendments or other questions to be voted upon, which copy has been supplied to him by the Secretary of State under the provisions of section eleven hundred and ninety-five hereof, and a sample ballot containing the nominations to office certified to him by the Secretary of State, and also all those filed with the County Clerk, each of which shall be inclosed in said envelope, and cause the same to be mailed in the United States post office as printed matter, for delivery to each of said voters. The mailing of all such envelopes shall commence at least ten days before the time of election to fill any public office, as aforesaid, and continue so that all of said envelopes containing said sample ballots shall have been mailed at least three whole days before the day of election to fill any public office, as above provided. If a new registration does not take place in any county preceding the next ensuing election, the County Clerk shall cause envelopes to be addressed to each voter, together with the number of the residence of said voter, or correct post office address, as the same appears upon the register corrected at that time, as the law provides, and cause to be inclosed therein the copy of the proposed constitutional amendments or other question, and sample ballot, as aforesaid, and cause the same to be mailed in the manner and within the time as above provided. The clerk or the secretary of the legislative body of any incorporated city or town, with whom the names of any candidates have been filed, shall mail, in the United States post office, envelopes addressed to each voter, together with the sample ballots inclosed therein, the list of nominations filed with him in the same manner as the lists of nominations mailed by the County Clerk, as provided in this section.

SECTION 1195. To be amended to read as follows:

Sec. 1195. Whenever a proposed constitutional amendment or other question is to be submitted to the people of the State for the popular vote, the Superintendent of State Printing shall, at the same time that he prints the Governor's proclamation provided for in section ten hundred and fifty-four, print of that part of the proclamation relating to such amendments or other questions, as many copies as twice the total number of votes cast at the general election next preceding. Such copies of such proposed amendments or other question shall be printed from the same composition of type as was used in printing that part of the election proclamation, upon plain white paper of light weight and convenient size for mailing. He shall, at least thirty days before the succeeding general election at which such amendments or other questions are to be voted upon, deliver such copies to the Secretary of State, who shall immediately distribute the same to the various County Clerks for distribution as provided for in section eleven hundred and ninety-four. The Secretary of State, in making such distribution, shall send to each County Clerk a number not less than one and one half times as many copies as there were votes cast in said county at the last general election held therein.

SECTION 1197. To be amended to read as follows:

Sec. 1197. All ballots printed by County Clerks, other than the separate ballots containing the names of candidates for city and county offices, printed by the County Clerks of consolidated cities and counties, shall be headed "general ticket"; and all ballots printed by County Clerks of consolidated cities and counties, containing the names of candidates for city and county offices, and also all tickets printed by the clerk or secretary of a legislative body of any incorporated city or town, shall be headed "municipal ticket." Under the heading of all general tickets the respective number of the congressional, senatorial, and assembly districts in which each ticket is to be voted shall be printed. At the head of the column or columns in which the names of candidates for presidential electors are printed shall be printed the following direction to voters: "To vote for electors of one party, mark a cross in the square at the right of the party name." Immediately following this shall be printed the title of their office and a direction to mark once, as "Electors of President and Vice-President ——— mark once." At the head of the columns in which the names of candidates for other offices are printed shall be printed the following direction to voters: "To vote for a person, stamp cross (X) in square at right of name of political party or designation following his name." Each group of names of candidates for any one office, except presidential elector, provision for which has hereinbefore been made, shall be immediately preceded by the title of the office at the extreme left of the column, followed on the extreme right of the column by a direction to the voter specifying the number of persons to be voted for for that office, thus "Governor ——— vote for one."

Where proposed amendments to the constitution or other questions are to be voted upon, the statement and description thereof shall be printed upon the ballot in manner and form as provided for in section ten hundred and fifty-four of this Code, opposite which shall be printed the words "Yes" and "No" on separate lines. Such statement shall be immediately preceded by the following direction to voters: "To vote on the following questions, stamp a cross (X) in the square at the right of 'Yes' or 'No' in each case." All municipal tickets containing the names of candidates for ward or district offices, in addition to such direction to voters, shall have the number of the ward or district in which such ticket is to be voted printed thereon. All municipal tickets shall be printed upon paper of a different tint from that of the general ticket. On each ballot a perforated line shall extend from top to bottom, one half inch from the right-hand side of such ballot, and upon the half inch strip thus formed there shall be no printing, except the number of the ballot, which shall be upon the back of such strip, in such position that it shall appear on the outside when the ballot is folded. The number on each ballot shall be the same as that on the corresponding stub, and the ballots and stubs shall be numbered consecutively in each county. All ballots shall be eighteen inches in length and four and one half inches in width, and as many times such width as shall be necessary to contain the names of all candidates nominated. Where the names of candidates are printed in separate columns, such columns shall be separated by heavy rules; and on all ballots the names of candidates shall each be separated by a rule extending to the extreme right of the column, and each group of names of candidates for any office shall be separated, by a heavy ruled line extending to the extreme right of the column, from the names of the candidates for the next and succeeding office printed upon the ticket.

All ballots shall be printed in plain roman type, and shall contain the name of every candidate whose nomination for any office specified in the ballot has been certified to and filed according to the provisions of this Code, and no other name; and there shall be added to all the names of candidates for each office, where such officer is to be elected from a section or district comprising more than one county, the name of the county from which he was nominated, followed by their party or political designation or designations, as far to the right of the column as possible, leaving room for the square or space hereinafter provided for, as

---

W. M. CUTTER, of Yuba.._Independent. Silver. Republican.

The names of the candidates for each office shall be arranged, under the designation of the office, in alphabetical order, according to surname, except that the names of candidates for the office of elector for President and Vice-President shall be arranged in groups as presented in the several certificates of nomination, and there shall be printed at the head of each group of electors so nominated the name of the candidates of the party they represent for President and Vice-President, followed by the political principle or party represented by said electors, after which, on the extreme right of the column, shall be a space or square, in one of which the voter must stamp a cross (X) signifying his intention to vote for the group of electors immediately following, as

---

McKinley and Hobart_____Republican.

---

in great primer title type or the like. There shall be left at the end of the list of candidates for each office as many blank spaces as there are persons to be elected to such office, in which the voter may insert the name of any person not printed upon the ballot, for whom he desires to vote as candidate for such office; and the names and blank spaces on the whole ticket shall be consecutively numbered, the figures being placed on the left-hand side of such names and blank spaces. There shall be a margin on the right-hand side of the names of all candidates, except presidential electors, provision for which is hereinabove made, at least one half an inch wide, along the left-hand edge of which margin a line shall be drawn forming squares, so that the voter may clearly indicate in the way to be hereinafter pointed out, the candidate or candidates for whom he wishes to cast his ballot.

SECTION 1200. To be amended to read as follows:

Sec. 1200. Whenever it shall appear by affidavit that an error or omission has occurred in the publication of the name or description of the candidates nominated for office, or in the printing of the ballots, the Superior Court of the county, or the judge thereof, shall, upon application by any elector, by order, require the County Clerk or Secretary of State to correct such error, or to show cause why such error should not be corrected.

CHAPTER IX.

VOTING AND CHALLENGES.

SECTION 1239. To be amended to read as follows:

Sec. 1239. The board of election, in determining the place of residence of any person, must be governed by the following rules, as far as they are applicable:

1. That place must be considered and held to be the residence of a person, in which his habitation is fixed, and to which, whenever he is absent, he has the intention of returning;

2. A person must not be held to have gained or lost residence by reason of his presence or absence from a place while employed in the service of the United States, or of this State, nor while engaged in navigation, nor while a student at any institution of learning, nor while kept in an almshouse, asylum, or prison;

3. A person must not be considered to have lost his residence who leaves his home to go into another State, or precinct in this State, for temporary purposes merely, with the intention of returning;

4. A person must not be considered to have gained a residence in any precinct into which he comes for temporary purposes merely, without the intention of making such precinct his home;

5. If a person remove to another State with the intention of making it his residence, he loses his residence in this State;

6. If a person remove to another State with the intention of remaining there for an indefinite time, and as a place of present residence, he loses his residence in this State, notwithstanding he entertains an intention of returning at some future period;

7. The place where a man's family resides must be held to be his residence; but if it be a place of temporary establishment for his family, or for transient objects, it is otherwise;

8. If a man have a family fixed in one place, and he does business in

another, the former must be considered his place of residence; but any man having a family, and who has taken up his abode with the intention of remaining, and whose family does not so reside with him, must be regarded as a resident where he has so taken up his abode;

9. The mere intention to acquire a new residence, without the fact of removal, avails nothing; neither does the fact of removal, without the intention.

NOTE.—The amendment consists in striking out Subdivision 3, which was held unconstitutional in *Russell* vs. *McDowell*, 83 Cal. 80.

CHAPTER X.

CANVASSING AND RETURNING THE VOTES.

SECTION 1253.   To be amended to read as follows:

Sec. 1253.   In the City and County of San Francisco, at the closing of the polls, the inspector must administer to the additional members of the board of canvassers the oath prescribed in section eleven hundred and forty-eight, and likewise to two clerks appointed by such additional members.

SECTION 1254.   To be amended to read as follows:

Sec. 1254.   The canvass must be commenced by taking out of the box the ballots, unopened (except so far as to ascertain whether each ballot is single), and counting the same to ascertain whether the number of ballots corresponds with the number of names on the list of voters kept by the clerks.   If two or more separate ballots are found so folded together as to present the appearance of a single ballot, they must be laid aside until the count of the ballots is completed; then, if upon comparison of the count with the number of names of electors on the lists which have been kept by the clerks, it appears that the two ballots thus folded together were cast by one elector, they must be rejected. The inspector must then replace the ballots in the box, and then proceed to take out of the box the ballots, unopened, one at a time, numbering them on the backs in numerical order, commencing with number one, and writing with ink the initials of his own name upon the back of each ballot as taken out.   He shall pass each ballot, as soon as thus indorsed, to the additional inspector, who must, in like manner, write thereon the initials of his own name, so that each ballot can be subsequently identified by either or both such inspectors.

SECTION 1255.   To be amended to read as follows:

Sec. 1255.   The ballots must be immediately replaced in the box, and if the ballots in the box exceed in number the names on the lists, one of the judges must publicly, and without looking in the box, draw out therefrom singly, and destroy, unopened, a number of ballots equal to such excess; and the board of election must make a record, upon the poll list, of the number of ballots so drawn and destroyed, and the numbers appearing on the backs of the ballots so drawn must likewise be recorded.

SECTION 1257. To be amended to read as follows:

Sec. 1257. After the lists are thus signed, the board must proceed to open the ballots, and count and ascertain the number of votes cast for each person voted for. At all elections where a general ticket and a municipal ticket are used, the canvass of the general ticket shall be completed before the canvass of the municipal ticket is commenced. All the ballots must be taken out of the ballot-box, one at a time, and opened by one of the members of the board, and the name of each person marked in the ballots as voted for shall be distinctly read in connection with the office for which he is a candidate. As the ballots are counted and an official record, as hereinbefore mentioned, made, they must be strung upon a string by one of the judges. All ballots rejected for illegality must have the cause of such rejection indorsed upon the ballot, and such indorsement must be signed by a majority of the election board. All such rejected ballots shall be immediately strung upon a string by one of the judges.

NOTE.—The amendment goes only to form and not to substance.

SECTION 1258. To be amended to read as follows:

Sec. 1258. Each clerk must keep the number of votes cast for each candidate or proposition to be voted on by tallies, as they are read aloud. Such tallies must be made with pen and ink, and immediately upon the completion of the tallies, which must follow the name of the candidate or statement of the proposition on the tally sheet, the clerks who respectively complete the same must draw one heavy line in ink from the last tally mark to the end of the line in which such tallies terminate, and also write at the end of each line the initials of the person making the last tally in such line.

SECTION 1259. To be amended to read as follows:

Sec. 1259. The ballots when strung on a string must not thereafter be examined by any person, but must, as soon as all are counted, be carefully sealed in a strong envelope, each member of the board writing his name across the seal.

SECTION 1260. To be amended to read as follows:

Sec. 1260. As soon as all the votes are counted and the ballots sealed up, the tally sheets must be completed by writing in ink, at full length, opposite the name of each candidate as it appears on the second part of

14—c

said sheet, the number of votes cast for such candidate, and such list must be signed by the members of the board and attested by the clerks, substantially in the form required by section eleven hundred and seventy-four hereof.

SECTION 1261. To be amended to read as follows:

Sec. 1261. The board must, before it adjourns, inclose in a cover, and seal up and direct to the County Clerk, the copy of the register upon which one of the judges marked the word "voted" as the ballots were received, all certificates of registration received by it, one of the lists of the persons challenged, one copy of the list of voters, and one of the tally lists and list attached thereto. The board shall also, at the completion of their other duties, post, in a conspicuous place at the entrance to the polls, a statement containing the name of each candidate and the name or title of each question voted on, together with the number of votes cast for such candidate or for or against such question. Such statement shall remain so posted for ten days; and to tear down, destroy, or deface the same within that time shall constitute a misdemeanor, and be punishable as such.

CHAPTER XI.

CANVASS OF RETURNS—DECLARATION OF RESULT—COMMISSIONS AND CERTIFICATES OF ELECTION.

SECTION 1281. To be amended to read as follows:

Sec. 1281. The canvass must be made in public, and by opening the returns and estimating the vote of such county or township for each person voted for, and for and against each proposed constitutional amendment or other question voted upon at such election, and declaring the result thereof.

SECTION 1282. To be amended to read as follows:

Sec. 1282. The clerk of the board must, as soon as the result is declared, enter on the records of such board a statement of such result, which statement must show:

1. The whole number of votes cast in the county;

2. The names of the persons voted for, as they appeared upon the ballot, and the proposed constitutional amendments and other questions voted upon;

3. The office to fill which each person was voted for;

4. The number of votes given at each precinct to each of such persons, and for and against each of such proposed constitutional amendments or other questions voted upon;

5. The number of votes given in the county to each of such persons, and for and against each of such proposed constitutional amendments or other questions voted upon.

As soon as said statement is entered upon the records of the Board of Supervisors, the clerk must make a certified abstract of said statement, seal up such abstract, indorse it "election returns," and without delay transmit the same to the Secretary of State.

SECTION 1283. To be amended to read as follows:

Sec. 1283. The board must declare elected the person having the highest number of votes given for each office to be filled by the votes of a single county or subdivision thereof, except to the person elected judge of the Superior Court.

SECTION 1284. To be amended to read as follows:

Sec. 1284. The County Clerk must immediately make out and deliver to such person (except to the person elected judge of the Superior Court) a certificate of election, signed by him, and authenticated with the seal of the Superior Court.

SECTION 1285. To be amended to read as follows:

Sec. 1285. When there are officers, other than those to be filled by the electors of the entire State, Representatives in Congress, members of the State Board of Equalization, and Railroad Commissioners, voted for, who are chosen by the electors of a district composed of two or more counties, each of the County Clerks of the counties composing such district, immediately after making out the statement specified in section twelve hundred and eighty-two, must make a certified abstract of so much thereof as relates to the election of such officer.

SECTION 1287. To be amended to read as follows:

Sec. 1287. The County Clerk to whom the election returns of a district are made, must, as soon as the returns from all the counties in the district have been received, open in public such returns, and from them and the statement of the vote for such officers in his own county:

1. Make a statement of the vote of the district for such officers, and file the same, together with the returns, in his office;

2. Immediately transmit a certified copy of such statement to the Secretary of State;

3. Make out and deliver, or transmit by mail, to the persons elected a certificate of election (unless it is by law otherwise provided).

SECTION 1288. To be amended to read as follows:

Sec. 1288. Whenever in any case the name of any candidate for an office appears more than once upon the ballot, all votes cast for him shall be counted for him by the various precinct election boards, upon the tally sheet, in manner and form as his name appears upon the ballot and tally sheet, and be so returned by the board of election. When the Board of Supervisors of the county wherein the election was held meet to canvass the returns as provided for in section twelve hundred and seventy-eight, in the case of all officers voted for by the electors of that county only, or a minor political division thereof, except judges of the Superior Court, they shall add together all votes cast for any such candidate for any one office, no matter what political party or political principle, or number of such parties or principles, he may represent. In cases provided for in section twelve hundred and eighty-five, the various Boards of Supervisors canvassing the votes shall certify the same to the County Clerk of the proper county, as provided for in section twelve hundred and eighty-six, and such County Clerk shall so add together all votes cast for such officer as aforesaid. In the case of officers to be voted for by the entire State, and Representative in Congress, member of State Board of Equalization, Railroad Commissioner, and judge of the Superior Court, the various Boards of Supervisors shall certify the vote to the Secretary of State, as provided for in section twelve hundred and eighty-two, and the Secretary of State, in estimating and 'certifying the returns, shall add together all votes cast for any such candidate for any one office, no matter what political party or principle, or number thereof, he may represent. In all cases herein provided for, identity of name shall be considered identity of person, and the vote for any candidate, after having been so added together, shall constitute his entire or total vote, and shall determine the question of his election.

SECTION 1289. To be amended to read as follows:

Sec. 1289. Whenever the name of any candidate appears more than once upon the ballot for any one office, followed by different political or party designations, and a voter stamps a cross in all of the squares following such name, the intention of the voter shall be respected and the vote counted as one for such candidate.

> NOTE.—Sections 1288 and 1289, as they originally read, are, since the amendment of Section 1282, no longer required. The amended sections are designed to meet the contingencies which so forcibly presented themselves during the presidential election of 1896.

SECTION 1290. To be amended to read as follows:

Sec. 1290. On the fortieth day after the election, or as soon as the returns have been received from all the counties of the State, if received within that time, the Secretary of State must compare and estimate the vote for offices, proposed constitutional amendments or other questions, to be voted upon by the electors of the entire State, and make out and file in his office a statement thereof, and transmit a copy of such statement to the Governor, and certify to said official, except as otherwise herein provided for, the name of each person who received the highest number of votes for each office; *provided*, that when an election has been held for member of Congress, member of Board of Equalization, Railroad Commissioner, or judge of the Superior Court, the Secretary of State must, as soon as all the returns have been received from the county or district in which such officers are voted for, compare and estimate the vote, and make out and file in his office a statement thereof, and transmit a copy of such statement to the Governor, and certify to such officer the name of the person who received the highest number of votes for each office.

SECTION 1291. To be amended to read as follows:

Sec. 1291. Upon receipt of such copy, the Governor must issue commissions to the persons who from it appear to have received the highest number of votes for offices, except that of Governor or Lieutenant-Governor, or electors of President or Vice-President, to be filled at such election, and declare the result of the election upon proposed constitutional amendments or other questions voted upon, and file such declaration with the Secretary of State.

CHAPTER XII.

ELECTION FOR ELECTORS OF PRESIDENT AND VICE-PRESIDENT.

SECTIONS 1308 and 1309. To be repealed.

NOTE.—The purpose of these sections is accomplished by Section 1282.

SECTION 1313. To be repealed.

NOTE.—The purpose of this section is served by Section 1290.

SECTION 1314. To be amended to read as follows:

Sec. 1314. The Governor must, upon the receipt of the statement and certificate required by section twelve hundred and ninety of this Code, transmit to each of the persons elected as an elector of President and Vice-President, a certificate of election, and on or before the day of their meeting deliver to the electors a list of the names of electors, and must do all other things required of him in the premises by any act of Congress in force at the time.

SECTIONS 1344 and 1345. To be repealed.

NOTE.—The purpose of these sections is served by Section 1282, as amended.

CHAPTER XIII.

ARTICLE II.

ELECTION FOR REPRESENTATIVES.

SECTION 1346. To be repealed.

NOTE.—It is a repetition of Section 1290, as amended.

SECTION 1347. To be amended to read as follows:

Sec. 1347. The Governor must, upon the receipt of the statement and certificate required by section twelve hundred and ninety hereof, transmit to each of the persons elected as Representative to Congress, a certificate of his election, sealed with the great seal and attested by the Secretary of State.

Chapter XIV of Part III, Title II, containing Sections 1357, 1358, 1359, 1360, 1361, 1362, 1363, 1364, and 1365, are to be superseded by a new primary elections law, which the Commission now has in course of preparation. Several systems of primary elections are to be proposed to the Legislature at its approaching session, and it is the design of this Commission to withhold its recommendation until it has examined such measures.

CHAPTER II.

STATE NORMAL SCHOOLS.

SECTION 1487. To be amended to read as follows:

Sec. 1487. The state normal schools have for their objects the education of teachers for the public schools of this State.

SECTION 1488. To be amended to read as follows:

Sec. 1488. The state normal schools shall be under the management and control of boards of trustees, constituted as provided in section three hundred and fifty-four of this Code.

SECTION 1489. To be amended to read as follows:

Sec. 1489. The powers and duties of each board of trustees are as follows:

1. To elect a secretary, who shall receive such salary, not to exceed one hundred and fifty dollars per annum, as may be allowed by the board;

2. To prescribe rules for their government and the government of the school;

3. To prescribe rules for the report of officers and teachers of the school, and for visiting other schools and institutions;

4. To provide for the purchase of school apparatus, furniture, stationery, and text-books for the use of pupils;

5. To establish and maintain model and training schools of the kindergarten, primary, and grammar grades, and require the students of the normal schools to teach and instruct classes therein;

6. To elect necessary teachers, upon their nomination by the president, fix their salaries, and prescribe their duties; *provided*, that after the principal teachers have served successfully and acceptably for a term of two years, their appointment thereafter shall be made for a term of four years at least, unless removed for cause as hereinafter specified;

7. To control and expend all moneys appropriated for the support and maintenance of the school, and all moneys received for tuition or donations;

8. To cause a record of all their proceedings to be kept, which shall be open to public inspection at the school;

9. To keep, open to public inspection, an account of receipts and expenditures;

10. To annually report to the Governor a statement of their transactions, and of all matters pertaining to the school;

11. To transmit with such report a copy of the president's annual report;

12. To revoke any diploma by them granted, on receiving satisfactory evidence that the holder thereof is addicted to drunkenness, is guilty of gross immorality, or is reputedly dishonest in his dealings; *provided*, that such person shall have at least thirty days' previous notice of such contemplated action, and shall, if he asks it, be heard in his own defense.

SECTION 1490. To be amended to read as follows:

Sec. 1490. Each board of trustees must hold two regular meetings in each year, and may hold special meetings at the call of the secretary, when directed by the chairman.

SECTION 1491. To be amended to read as follows:

Sec. 1491. · The time and place of regular meetings must be fixed by the by-laws of the board. The secretary must give written notice of the time and place of special meetings to each member of the board. Each member shall be allowed his expenses in attending the meetings of the board, the bills to be audited the same as any bills for the maintenance of the school.

SECTION 1492. To be amended to read as follows:

Sec. 1492. There shall be a joint board of normal school trustees, to be composed of the members of the local boards of the several state normal schools. This board shall meet on the second Friday of April of each year, alternately at the different state normal schools. The first meeting after the passage of this act shall be at Los Angeles; the second meeting at Chico, and the third at San José. Thereafter the places of meeting shall be in the order named above. A special meeting may be called by the Governor for the transaction of any urgent business affecting the welfare of any or all of the state normal schools. It shall be the duty of this joint board:

1. To fill a vacancy in the presidency of any of the state normal schools, and to fix the salaries of the presidents of the several normal schools;

2. To sit as a board of arbitration in matters concerning the management of each state normal school that may need adjustment;

3. To dismiss a teacher from either of the state normal schools for good and sufficient cause after having been elected as designated under section fourteen hundred and eighty-nine of this Code;

4. To prescribe a series of text-books for use in the state normal schools;

5. To prescribe a uniform course of study, and time and standard for graduation from the state normal schools;

6. To prescribe a uniform standard of admission for students entering the normal schools;

7. The joint board shall also have the power to pass any general regulations that may be applied to all of the state normal schools, thus affecting their well-being;

8. Members in attending the meetings of the joint board shall receive mileage while in actual attendance upon the meeting, the same to be paid out of any appropriation made by the Legislature for that purpose;

9. The Superintendent of Public Instruction shall be the secretary of the joint board. The secretary shall keep a full record of all proceedings of the joint meetings of the trustees, and shall notify the secretary of each board of trustees of any changes made in the course of study or the text-books to be adopted.

SECTION 1497. To be amended to read as follows:

Sec. 1497. Every person making application for admission as a pupil to the normal school must, at the time of making such application, file with the president of the school a declaration that he enters the school to fit himself for teaching, and that it is his intention to engage in teaching in the public schools of this State, or in the State or Territory where the applicant resides.

SECTION 1501. To be amended to read as follows:

Sec. 1501. The president of each state normal school must make a detailed annual report to the board of trustees, with a catalogue of the pupils, and such other particulars as the board may require or he may think useful.

SECTION 1503. To be amended to read as follows:

Sec. 1503. First—The board of trustees of each state normal school, upon the recommendation of the faculty, may issue to those pupils who worthily complete the full course of study and training prescribed, diplomas of graduation, either from the normal department, the kindergarten department, or both;

Second—Said diploma from the normal department shall entitle the holder thereof to a grammar grade certificate from any City, City and County, or County Board of Education in the State. One from the kindergarten department shall entitle the holder to teach in any kindergarten in the State;

Third—Whenever any City, City and County, or County Board of Education shall present to the State Board of Education a recommendation showing that the holder of a normal school diploma from the normal department has had a successful experience of two years in the public schools of this State, subsequent to the granting of such diploma, the State Board of Education shall grant to the holder thereof a document signed by the president and secretary of the state board, showing such fact. The said diploma accompanied by said document of the state board attached thereto, shall become a permanent certificate of qualification to teach in any primary or grammar school of this State, valid until such time as said diploma may be revoked, as provided in subdivision thirteen of section fourteen hundred and eighty-nine of this Code;

Fourth—Upon presentation of the diploma and document referred to in section fifteen hundred and three, subdivision third thereof, to any City, City and County, or County Superintendent of Schools, said superintendent shall record the name of the holder thereof in a book provided for that purpose in his office, and the holder shall henceforth be absolved from the requirements of subdivision first of section sixteen hundred and ninety-six of this Code:

Fifth—Said diploma of graduation from any normal school in this State, when accompanied by a certificate granted by the faculty of the state university, showing that the holder thereof, subsequent to receiving said diploma, has successfully completed the prescribed course in the pedagogical department of the state university, shall entitle the holder to a high school certificate authorizing the holder to teach in any primary or grammar school, and in any high school in this State, except in those in which the holder would be required to teach languages other than English.

SECTION 1504. To be repealed.

SECTION 1505. To be amended to read as follows:

Sec. 1505. The Superintendent of Public Instruction must visit each school from time to time, inquire into its condition and management, enforce the rules and regulations made by the board, require such report as he deem proper from the teachers of the school, and exercise a general supervision over the same.

SECTION 1506. To be repealed.

SECTION 1507. To be amended to read as follows:

Sec. 1507. Each order upon the Controller of State by the board of trustees of the state normal school must be signed by the chairman of the local board and countersigned by the secretary. Upon presentation of the order aforesaid, the Controller of State must draw his warrant upon the State Treasurer in favor of the board of trustees, for any moneys, or any part thereof, appropriated and set apart for the support of the normal school, and the State Treasurer must pay such warrants upon presentation.

CHAPTER III.

ARTICLE I.

STATE BOARD OF EDUCATION.

SECTION 1517. To be amended to read as follows:

Sec. 1517. The State Board of Education consists of the Governor, the Superintendent of Public Instruction, the Principals of the State Normal Schools, the President of the University of California, and the Professor of Pedagogy therein.

NOTE.—Changed to conform to Article IX, Constitution, as amended in 1894.

SECTION 1520. To be amended to read as follows:

Sec. 1520. The board shall meet at the call of secretary, and at least twice in each year.

NOTE.—Changed to improve expression.

SECTION 1521. To be amended to read as follows:

Sec. 1521. The powers and duties of the board are as follows:

First—To adopt rules and regulations, not inconsistent with the laws of this State, for its own government, and for the government of the public schools and district school libraries.

Second—To grant life diplomas of two grades, valid throughout the State, as follows:

1. High School: authorizing the holder to teach in any primary, grammar, or high school in the State;

2. Grammar School: authorizing the holder to teach in any primary or grammar school in the State.

Third—High school life diplomas may be issued only to such persons as have held for three years, and who still hold, a valid high school certificate, and who shall furnish satisfactory evidence of having had a successful experience in teaching of not less than eighty months, twenty-four of which must have been in the University of California, a California state normal school, or a high school established under the laws of California.

Fourth—Grammar school life diplomas may be issued only to such persons as have held for three years, and who still hold, a valid grammar school certificate, or a certificate or diploma of California which is the equivalent of a grammar school certificate, and who shall furnish satisfactory evidence of having had a successful experience in teaching of not less than eighty (80) months, twenty-four of which must have been in the public schools of California. Every application for a life diploma must be accompanied to the State Board of Education by a certified copy of a resolution adopted by at least a four-fifths vote of all the members composing a City or County Board of Education, recommending that the diploma be granted, and also by an affidavit of the applicant, specifically setting forth the places in which, and the dates between which, said applicant has taught. The application must also be accompanied by a fee of two dollars, for the purpose of defraying the expense of issuing the diploma.

Fifth—To revoke or suspend, for immoral or unprofessional conduct, or for evident unfitness for teaching, diplomas, or other certificates of qualification to teach, heretofore issued, or that may hereafter be issued; and to adopt such rules for the revocation of diplomas as they may deem expedient or necessary.

Sixth—To have done by the Superintendent of State Printing, or other officer having the management of the state printing, any printing required by it; *provided*, that all orders for printing shall first be approved by the State Board of Examiners.

Seventh—To adopt and use, in authentication of its acts, an official seal.

Eighth—To keep a record of its proceedings.

NOTE.—The amendment consists principally in dispensing with educational diplomas, in the second subdivision, and in dropping subdivision ninth, which provided for an educational journal. This was done at the unanimous request of the State Board of Education.

SECTION 1525. A new section to be added to read as follows:

No discrimination against women teachers.

Sec. 1525. Women employed as teachers in the public schools of this State shall in all cases receive the same compensation as is allowed men teachers for like services when holding the same grade certificates.

NOTE.—This creates a new section for the purpose of embodying the substance of the statute on this subject into the Code.

ARTICLE II.

SUPERINTENDENT OF PUBLIC INSTRUCTION.

SECTION 1532. To be amended to read as follows:

Sec. 1532. It is the duty of the Superintendent of Public Instruction:

First—To superintend the schools of this State.

Second—To report to the Governor, on or before the fifteenth day of September preceding each regular session of the Legislature, a statement of the condition of the state normal schools and other educational institutions supported by the State, and of the public schools.

Third—To accompany his report with tabular statements showing the number of census children in the State; the number attending public schools, and the average attendance; the number attending private schools; the amount of state school fund apportioned, and the sources from which derived; the amount raised by county and district taxes, or from other sources of revenue, for school purposes; and the amount expended for salaries of teachers, for building school-houses, for district school libraries, and for incidental expenses.

Fourth—To apportion the state school fund; and to furnish an abstract of such apportionment to the State Controller, the State Board of Examiners, and to the County Auditors, County Treasurers, and County Superintendents of Schools of the several counties of the State.

Fifth—To draw his order on the Controller in favor of each County Treasurer for school moneys apportioned to the county.

Sixth—To prepare, have printed, and furnish all officers charged with the administration of the laws relating to the public schools, and to teachers, such blank forms and books as may be necessary to the discharge of their duties, including blank teachers' certificates to be used by County Boards of Education.

Seventh—To have the laws relating to the public schools printed in pamphlet form, and to supply school officers and school libraries with one copy each.

Eighth—To visit the several orphan asylums to which State appropriations are made, and examine into the course of instruction therein.

Ninth—To visit the schools in the different counties, and inquire into their condition; and the actual traveling expenses thus incurred (*provided*, that they do not exceed fifteen hundred dollars per annum) shall be allowed, audited, and paid out of the general fund in the same manner as other claims are audited and paid.

Tenth—To authenticate with his official seal all drafts or orders drawn by him, and all papers and writings issued from his office.

Eleventh—To have bound, at the state bindery, all valuable school reports, journals, and documents in his office, or hereafter received by him.

Twelfth—To report to the Controller, on or before the tenth day of July of each year, the total number of children in the State between the ages of five and seventeen years, as shown by the latest reports of the County Superintendents on file in his office.

Thirteenth—To deliver over, at the expiration of his term of office, on demand, to his successor, all property, books, documents, maps, records, reports, and other papers belonging to his office, or which may have been received by him for the use of his office.

> NOTE.—The amendment is in the third and fourth subdivisions, "census children" being substituted for "school children."

ARTICLE III.

SCHOOL SUPERINTENDENTS.

SECTION 1543. To be amended to read as follows:

Sec. 1543. It is the duty of the County Superintendent of Schools of each county:

First—To superintend the schools of his county.

Second—1. To apportion the school moneys to each school district, as provided in section eighteen hundred and fifty-eight of this Code, at least four times a year. For this purpose he may require of the County Auditor a report of the amount of all school moneys on hand to the credit of the several school funds of the county not already apportioned; and it is hereby made the duty of the Auditor to furnish such report when so required; and whenever an excess of money has accumulated to the credit of a school district by reason of a large census roll and a small attendance, beyond a reasonable amount necessary to maintain a school for eight months in such district for the year, the Superintendent of Schools shall place said excess of money to the credit of the unapportioned school funds of the county, and shall apportion the same as other school funds are apportioned.

2. If in any school district there has been an average daily attendance of only five, or a number of pupils less than five, during the whole school year, the County Superintendent of Schools shall at once suspend the

district, and report the fact to the Board of Supervisors at their next meeting. The Board of Supervisors, upon receiving such report from the Superintendent, shall declare the district lapsed, and shall attach the territory thereof to one or more of the adjoining school districts in such manner as may be by them deemed most convenient for the residents of said lapsed district.

3. When any district has been declared lapsed, the Board of Supervisors shall sell or otherwise dispose of the property thereto belonging, and shall place the proceeds of such sale to the credit of the district. Thereupon, the County Superintendent of Schools shall determine all outstanding indebtedness of said lapsed district, and shall draw his requisition upon the County Auditor in payment thereof. Any balance of moneys remaining to the credit of said lapsed district shall be transferred by the Superintendent to the unapportioned school funds of the county, and shall be apportioned as other school funds are apportioned. Should there not be sufficient funds to the credit of the lapsed district to liquidate all the outstanding indebtedness thereof, the Superintendent shall draw his requisition upon the County Auditor pro rata for the several claims.

Third—On the order of the Board of School Trustees, or Board of Education of any city or town having a Board of Education, to draw his requisition upon the County Auditor for all necessary expenses against the school fund of any district. The requisitions must be drawn in the order in which the orders therefor are filed in his office. Each requisition must specify the purpose for which it is drawn, but no requisition shall be drawn unless the money is in the fund to pay it, and no requisition shall be drawn upon the order of the Board of School Trustees or Board of Education against the funds of any district except the teachers' salaries, unless such order is accompanied by an itemized bill showing the separate items, and the price of each, in payment for which the order is drawn; nor shall any requisition for teachers' salaries be drawn unless the order shall state the monthly salary of teacher, and name the months for which such salary is due. Upon the receipt of such requisition the Auditor shall draw his warrant upon the County Treasurer in favor of the parties for the amount stated in such requisition.

Fourth—To keep, open to the inspection of the public, a register of requisitions, showing the fund upon which the requisitions have been drawn, the number thereof, in whose favor, and for what purpose they were drawn, and also a receipt from the person to whom the requisition was delivered.

Fifth—To visit and examine each school in his county at least once in each year. For every school not so visited the Board of Supervisors must, on proof thereof, deduct ten dollars from his salary.

Sixth—To preside over teachers' institutes held in his county, and to secure the attendance thereat of lecturers competent to instruct in the art of teaching, and to report to the County Board of Education the names of all teachers in the county who fail to attend regularly the sessions of the institute; to enforce the course of study, the use of text-books, and the rules and regulations for the examination of teachers prescribed by the proper authority.

Seventh—He shall have power to issue, if he deem it proper to do so, temporary certificates, valid for a period not to exceed six months, upon credentials upon which the county boards are empowered to grant certificates without examination, as specified in section seventeen hundred and seventy-five; *provided*, that no person shall be entitled to receive such temporary certificate more than once in the same county.

Eighth—To distribute all laws, reports, circulars, instructions, and blanks which he may receive for the use of school officers.

Ninth—To keep in his office the reports of the Superintendent of Public Instruction.

Tenth—To keep a record of his official acts, and of all the proceedings of the County Board of Education, including a record of the standing, in each study, of all applicants examined, which shall be open to the inspection of any applicant or his authorized agent.

Eleventh—Except in incorporated cities having Boards of Education, to pass upon and approve or reject, all plans for school-houses. To enable him to do so, all Boards of Trustees, before adopting any plans for school buildings, must submit the same to the County Superintendent of Schools for his approval.

Twelfth—To appoint trustees to fill all vacancies, to hold until the first day of July succeeding such appointment; when new districts are organized, to appoint trustees for the same, who shall hold office until the first day of July next succeeding their appointment. In case of the failure of the trustees to employ a janitor, as provided in section sixteen hundred and seventeen, subdivision seventh, of this Code, he shall appoint a janitor, who shall be paid out of the school fund of the district. Should the Board of School Trustees of any district fail or refuse to issue an order for the compensation of such service, the County Superintendent of Schools is hereby authorized to issue, without such order, his requisition upon the county school fund apportioned to such district.

Thirteenth—To make reports, when directed by the Superintendent of Public Instruction, showing such matters relating to the public schools in his county as may be required of him.

Fourteenth—To preserve carefully all reports of school officers and teachers, and, at the close of his official term, deliver to his successor all records, books, documents, and papers belonging to the office, taking a receipt for the same, which will be filed in the office of the County Clerk.

Fifteenth—The County Superintendent of Schools shall, unless otherwise provided by law, in the month of May, fix the grade of each school for the succeeding school year, and a record thereof shall be made in a book to be kept by the County Superintendent of Schools in his office for this purpose.   And no teacher holding a certificate below the grade of said school shall be employed to teach the same.

> NOTE.—The amendment of the first, eleventh, and twelfth subdivisions consists only in an effort to improve their construction. Subdivision seven is amended to fix definitely the life of a temporary certificate. The amendment of subdivision fifteen was made so that the grade of a school might be known before the beginning of the school year, and be a guide to the proper selection of a teacher.

SECTION 1545.   To be amended to read as follows:

Sec. 1545.   If the trustees of any school district refuse or neglect to engage a teacher for a period of six months, it shall be the duty of the County Superintendent of Schools to appoint a teacher, fix his salary, and draw his requisition upon the County Auditor, who shall draw his warrant upon the fund of such district for the expenses incurred.

> NOTE.—Changed in the interest of the children. By this change the County Superintendent of Schools has power to force or compel a six months' school, provided the district has funds.

SECTION 1549.   To be amended to read as follows:

Sec. 1549.   Each County Superintendent of Schools may appoint a deputy, but no salary payable out of the school fund must be allowed such deputy.

> NOTE.—Changed to improve the expression.

SECTION 1551.   To be amended to read as follows:

Sec. 1551.   Every County Superintendent of Schools, and Superintendent of City and County Schools, in this State, must, on or before the first day in July of each year, report to the Superintendent of Public Instruction, and to the Board of Supervisors of his county, the number of children therein between the ages of five and seventeen years, as appears by the latest returns of the census marshals on file in his office. It shall be the duty of every County Superintendent of Schools to inquire and ascertain whether the boundaries of the school districts in his county are definitely and plainly described in the records of the Board of Supervisors, and to keep in his office a full and correct transcript of such boundaries.   In case the boundaries of the districts are conflicting or incorrectly described, he shall report such fact to the Board of Supervisors, and the Board of Supervisors shall immediately take such steps as are necessary to change, harmonize, and clearly define them.   The County Superintendent of Schools, if he deem it necessary for the guidance of school census marshals, may order the description of the district boundaries printed in pamphlet form, and pay for the same out of the county school fund.

NOTE.—Changed to improve the expression. The change includes San Francisco, having a "Superintendent of City and County Schools."

SECTION 1552. To be amended to read as follows:

Sec. 1552. Each County Superintendent of Schools shall receive his actual and necessary traveling expenses, said expenses to be allowed by the Board of Supervisors, and to be paid out of the county general fund; *provided*, that this amount shall not exceed ten dollars per district per annum.

NOTE.—Changed to improve the expression.

SECTION 1553. To be amended to read as follows:

Sec. 1553. No County Superintendent of Schools who receives an annual salary of fifteen hundred dollars or more must follow the profession of teaching, or any other vocation that can conflict with his duties as Superintendent; but those receiving less than fifteen hundred dollars per annum may teach in the public schools of this State.

NOTE.—Changed to be specific in its application.

ARTICLE IV.

TEACHERS' INSTITUTES.

SECTION 1560. To be amended to read as follows:

Sec. 1560. The County Superintendent of Schools of every county in which there are twenty or more school districts, and of every city and county in the State, must hold at least one teachers' institute in each year; and every teacher employed in a public school in the county must attend such institute and participate in its proceedings; *provided*, that cities employing seventy or more teachers may have a separate institute, to meet at least once a year, the sessions to be of not less than three, nor more than five, days; *and provided further*, that teachers attending such city institute shall not be required to attend the county institute. The expenses of such city institutes, not exceeding two hundred dollars annually, shall be paid from the special school funds of said city.

NOTE.—Changed to improve the expression.

SECTION 1561. To be amended to read as follows:

Sec. 1561. In any county in which there are less than twenty school districts, the County Superintendent of Schools may, in his discretion, hold an institute. When directed by the County Board of Education,

15—c

he shall hold an institute, not oftener than once each year, at such time and place as the board may direct.

NOTE.—Changed to improve the expression.

SECTION 1564. To be amended to read as follows:

Sec. 1564. The County Superintendent of Schools must keep an accurate account of the actual expenses of said institute, with vouchers for the same, and draw his requisition upon the County Auditor, who shall draw his warrant on the unapportioned county school fund to pay said amount; *provided*, that such amount must not exceed two hundred dollars for any one year.

NOTE.—Changed to improve the expression.

SECTION 1565. To be amended to read as follows:

Sec. 1565. Except for a temporary certificate, every applicant for a teacher's certificate, or for the renewal of a certificate, upon presenting his application, shall pay to the County Superintendent of Schools a fee of two dollars, to be by him immediately deposited with the County Treasurer, to the credit of a fund to be known as the teachers' institute and library fund. All funds so credited shall be drawn out only upon the requisition of the County Superintendent of Schools upon the County Auditor, who shall draw his warrant in payment of the services of instructors in the county teachers' institute; *provided*, they be not teachers in the public schools of the county in which such institute is held; and for the purchase of books for a library for the use of the teachers of the county. At least fifty per cent of the teachers' institute and library fund shall be expended for books. The County Superintendent of Schools shall take charge of the teachers' library, prepare a catalogue of its contents, and keep a correct record of books taken therefrom and returned thereto.

NOTE.—Changed in order that there shall be a fee required for every certificate issued by either City or County Boards of Education. The following: "and except as provided in subdivision second of Section 1503 of the Political Code," is dropped from the section as it now stands.

ARTICLE V.

SCHOOL DISTRICTS.

SECTION 1577. To be amended to read as follows:

Sec. 1577. First—No new school district shall be formed at any other time than between the first day of November and the tenth day of February, nor at that time, unless the parents or guardians of at least fifteen census children, residents of such proposed new district, and residing at a greater distance than two miles by a traveled road from the public school-house in the district in which said parents or guardians reside, present a petition to the County Superintendent of Schools, setting forth the boundaries of the new district asked for; *provided*, that the provision requiring that the petitioners shall reside a distance of more than two miles by a traveled road from the said public school-house may be dispensed with when the petition shall be signed by the parents or guardians of fifty or more census children, residents of a district containing more than three hundred census children.

Second—The boundaries of a school district, except as provided in section fifteen hundred and fifty-one of the Political Code, shall be changed only between the first day of November and the tenth day of February in any year, and then only when at least ten heads of families residing in the districts affected by the proposed change of boundaries shall present to the County Superintendent of Schools a petition setting forth the changes of boundaries desired, and the reasons for the same; *provided*, that two or more districts lying contiguous may at any time be united to constitute but one district, whenever a petition, signed by a majority of the heads of families residing in each of said districts, shall be presented to the County Superintendent of Schools.

Third—Joint districts (that is, districts lying partly in one county and partly in another) may be formed at any time between the first day of December and the fifth day of April in any year, whenever a petition signed by the parents or guardians of at least fifteen census children, residents of such proposed joint district, and residing at a greater distance than two miles by a traveled road from any public school-house, shall be presented to the County Superintendent of Schools of each county affected by the proposed formation of the joint district; *and provided further*, that the provision requiring that the petitioners shall reside a distance of more than two miles by a traveled road from any public school-house may be dispensed with, when the petition shall be signed by the parents or guardians of fifty or more census children, residents of districts any one of which contains more than three hundred census children. All the provisions relative to the formation of joint districts shall be by concurrent action of the County Superintendent of Schools and the Board of Supervisors of each county affected.

Fourth—The children residing in any newly formed district in any district whose boundaries have been changed, or in any joint district, shall be permitted to attend the school in the district or districts from which the newly formed district was constituted until the first day of July next succeeding the formation or change.

Fifth—Whenever a district shall be united with a municipality, or with another district, all funds belonging to said district shall be transferred, by requisition of the County Superintendent of Schools of the county, upon the County Auditor, to the municipality or district with which said district is united.

Note.—Changed in order that all districts may be complete and organized by the 1st of March, thus enabling the Assessors to list district property. This will furnish the basis for taxation, and will enable new districts to provide buildings, etc., without delay.
Other changes are to improve the general expression.

SECTION 1578. To be amended to read as follows:

Sec. 1578. After giving due notice to all parties interested, by sending notice by registered mail to each of the trustees of any school district that may be affected by the proposed change, or by causing notices to be posted in three public places in each district affected, one of which shall be at the door of the school-house of said district, for at least one week, the County Superintendent of Schools must transmit the petition to the Board of Supervisors, with his approval or disapproval. If he approves the petition, he may note such changes in the boundaries as he may think desirable.

Note.—Changed to improve the expression.

SECTION 1581. To be amended to read as follows:

Sec. 1581. After the making of an order by the Board of Supervisors creating a new district, the school must be opened therein not later than the first Monday of October following the date of said order; otherwise said order shall be null and void.

Note.—Changed in order to be definite as to what year is meant.

SECTION 1583. To be amended to read as follows:

Sec. 1583. Whenever a district lies partly in one county and partly in another, the County Superintendent of Schools must apportion to such district such proportion of the school money to which such district is entitled, as the number of school census children residing in that portion of the district situated in his county bears to the whole number of school census children in the whole district. The text-books to be used, and the rules governing the school, in such district, shall be those adopted by the Board of Education of the county in which the school-house in said joint district is located. The trustees and teachers of joint districts shall make to the County Superintendent of Schools of each county in which the district is located, the reports which other trustees and teachers are required to make, and also the number of pupils attending the school from each county. The teacher in such joint district shall not be required to hold a certificate in both counties.

Note.—Changed to improve the expression.

ARTICLE VI.

ELECTIONS FOR SCHOOL TRUSTEES.

SECTION 1599. To be amended to read as follows:

Sec. 1599. The voting must be by ballot (without reference to the general election law in regard to nominations, form of ballot, or manner of voting).

NOTE.—Changed to improve the section. We think it unnecessary to retain the last three (3) lines as they now appear in the section.

SECTION 1600. To be amended to read as follows:

Sec. 1600. Any person offering to vote may be challenged by any elector of the district, and the judges of election must thereupon administer to the person challenged an oath, in substance as follows: "You do swear that you are a citizen of the United States, that you are twenty-one years of age, that you have resided in this State one year, in this county ninety days, and in this school district thirty days next preceding this election, and that your name appears on the great register of this county as an elector of this precinct, and that you have not before voted this day." If he takes the oath prescribed in this section, his vote must be received, otherwise his vote must be rejected.

NOTE.—Changed to comply with Section 1083 of the Political Code, relating to "qualifications of electors."

ARTICLE VII.

BOARDS OF SCHOOL DISTRICTS, AND CITY BOARDS OF EDUCATION.

SECTION 1615. To be amended to read as follows:

Sec. 1615. First—When a new district is organized, such of the trustees of the old district as reside within the boundaries of the new shall be trustees of the new district until the expiration of the time for which they were elected.

Second—When joint districts are formed, three trustees shall be elected at the June election next succeeding the formation thereof, to hold office for one, two, and three years respectively, from the first day of July next succeeding their election. The terms of the trustees in the districts uniting to form the joint district shall expire on the formation of said joint district, and the County Superintendent of Schools of the county in which lies the district having the greater number of census children shall appoint two trustees, and the County Superintendent of Schools of the county in which the other district lies shall appoint one trustee, to hold office until the first day of July next succeeding the formation of the joint district.

Section 1617. To be amended to read as follows:

Sec. 1617. The powers and duties of trustees of school districts, and of Boards of Education in cities, are as follows:

First—To prescribe and enforce rules, not inconsistent with law or those prescribed by the State Board of Education, for their own government and government of schools, and to transact their business at regular or special meetings called for such purpose, notice of which shall be given each member.

Second—To manage and control the school property within their districts, and to pay all moneys collected by them, from any source whatever, for school purposes, into the county treasury, to be placed to the credit of the special fund of their districts.

Third—To purchase text-books of the State series for the use of pupils whose parents are unable to purchase them; school furniture, including organs and pianos, and apparatus and such other things as may be necessary for the use of schools; *provided*, that, except in incorporated cities having Boards of Education, they purchase such books and apparatus only as have been adopted by the County Board of Education.

Fourth—To rent, furnish, repair, and insure the school property of their respective districts.

Fifth—When directed by a vote of their district, to build school-houses, or to purchase or sell school-lots, and to make, in the name of the district, conveyances on all property so purchased or sold.

Sixth—To employ the teachers, and except in incorporated cities having Boards of Education, immediately notify the County Superintendent of Schools, in writing, of such employment, naming the grade of certificate held by the teachers employed; also to employ janitors and other employés of the schools; to fix and order paid their compensation, unless the same be otherwise prescribed by law; *provided*, that no Board of Trustees shall enter into any contract with such employés to extend beyond the thirtieth day of June next ensuing; *and provided further*, that Boards of Trustees may elect teachers in the month of June for the succeeding school year.

Seventh—To suspend and expel pupils for misconduct.

Eighth—To exclude from schools children under six years of age; *provided*, that in cities and towns in which the kindergarten has been adopted, or may hereafter be adopted, as a part of the public primary schools, children may be admitted to such kindergarten classes at the age of four years.

Ninth—To enforce in schools the course of study and the use of text-books prescribed and adopted by the proper authority.

Tenth—To appoint district librarians, and enforce the rules prescribed for the government of district libraries.

Eleventh—To exclude from school and school libraries all books, publications, or papers of a sectarian, partisan, or denominational character.

Twelfth—To furnish books for the children of parents unable to purchase them; the books so furnished to belong to the school district, and to be kept in the district school library when not in use.

Thirteenth—To keep a register, open to the inspection of the public, of all children applying for admission and entitled to be admitted into the public schools, and to notify the parents or guardians of such children when vacancies occur, and receive such children into the schools in the order in which they are registered.

Fourteenth—To permit children from other districts to attend the schools of their district only upon the consent of the trustees of the district in which such children reside; *provided,* that should the trustees of the district in which children whose parents or guardians desire them to attend in other districts reside, refuse to grant their consent, the parents or guardians of such children may appeal to the County Superintendent of Schools, and his decision shall be final.

Fifteenth—On or before the first day of April in each year, to appoint a school census marshal, and notify the County Superintendent of Schools thereof; *provided,* that in any city, or city and county, the appointment of all school census marshals shall be subject to the approval of the County Superintendent of Schools.

Sixteenth—To make an annual report, on or before the first day of July, to the County Superintendent of Schools, in the manner and form, and on the blanks, prescribed by the Superintendent of Public Instruction.

Seventeenth—To make a report, whenever required, directly to the Superintendent of Public Instruction, of the text-books used in their schools.

Eighteenth—To visit every school in their district at least once in each term, and examine carefully into its management, condition, and wants. This clause to apply to each and every member of the Board of Trustees.

Nineteenth—Boards of Trustees may, and upon a petition signed by a majority of the heads of families resident in the district, as shown by the last preceding school census, must, call meetings of the qualified electors of the district for determining or changing the location of the school-house, or for consultation in regard to any litigation in which the district may be engaged, or be likely to become engaged, or in regard to any affairs of the district. Such meetings shall be called by posting three notices in public places, one of which shall be in a conspicuous place on the school-house, for not less than ten days previous to the time for which the meeting shall be called, which notices shall specify the purposes for which said meeting shall be called; and no other business shall be transacted at such meetings. District meetings shall be organized by choosing a chairman from the electors present, and the district clerk shall be clerk of the meeting, and shall enter the minutes thereof on the records of the district. A meeting so called shall be competent to instruct the Board of Trustees:

1. In regard to the location or change of location of the school-house, or the use of the same for other than school purposes; *provided*, that in no case shall the school-house be used for purposes which necessitate the removal of any school desks or other school furniture;

2. In regard to the sale and purchase of school sites;

3. In regard to prosecuting, settling, or compromising any litigation in which the district may be engaged, and may vote money from the county fund of the district, not exceeding one hundred dollars in any one year, for any of these purposes. All funds raised by the sale of school property may be disposed of by direction of a district meeting. District meetings may be adjourned from time to time, as found necessary, and all votes instructing the Board of Trustees shall be taken by ballot. The Board of Trustees shall in all cases be bound by the instructions of the district meeting in regard to the subjects mentioned in this subdivision of this section; *provided*, that the vote in favor of changing the location of the school-house shall be two thirds of all electors voting at said meeting upon the proposition to change the location.

> NOTE.—The fifth and sixth subdivisions are combined, while in the sixth as amended, the Board of Trustees are empowered to elect teachers in June for the succeeding school year, which will do much to avert the evil of changing teachers, who have heretofore sought new positions, pending the delay in organizing the new board in July. In the fifteenth, the approval of census marshals is taken from the city superintendent and given to the county superintendent, as the latter is charged with the apportionment of school moneys to cities.

SECTION 1621. To be amended to read as follows:

Sec. 1621. The Boards of School Trustees and City Boards of Education must use the school moneys received from state and county apportionments exclusively for the support of schools for that school year, until at least an eight months' school has been maintained. If at the end of any year, during which an eight months' school has been maintained, there is an unexpended balance, it may be used for the payment of claims outstanding against the district, or it may be used for the year succeeding. Any balance remaining on hand at the end of any school year in which school has not been maintained eight months may be re-apportioned by the County Superintendent of Schools, as other moneys are apportioned; *provided*, that if a district has been prevented from maintaining a school for eight months in any year in consequence of fire, flood, prevailing epidemic, or other cause which may, upon investigation by the County Superintendent of Schools of the county, be determined to be a good and sufficient one, said balance shall not be re-apportioned.

NOTE.—Changed "shall" to "may" in the interest of very weak districts. A district may close at end of four or five months because of no funds. In July following, an apportionment is made (belonging to the year ending June 30 preceding.) It is not right to deprive the district of this apportionment. The present recommendations aim to prevent it.

SECTION 1622. To be amended to read as follows:

Sec. 1622. Boards of School Trustees and City Boards of Education may use the school moneys received from state and county apportionments during the school year for any of the purposes authorized by this chapter; but a sum equal to the amount received from the state apportionment, and at least sixty (60) per cent of the county apportionment, exclusive of the library fund, must be used exclusively for the payment of teachers of primary and grammar grade schools.

NOTE.—This change is calculated to prevent trustees from using money in excess of a reasonable amount, for purposes other than the actual maintenance of the school. The children will receive the direct benefit to which they are entitled if this recommendation prevails.

SECTION 1623. To be amended to read as follows:

Sec. 1623. Boards of Trustees and City Boards of Education are liable as such, and in the name of the district, for any judgment against the district for salary due any teacher on contract, and for all debts contracted under the provisions of this chapter, and they must pay such judgment or liabilities out of the school moneys to the credit of such district; *provided*, that the contracts mentioned in this section are not in excess of the school moneys accruing to the district for the school year for which the contracts are made, otherwise the district shall not be held liable.

NOTE.—Changed to be consistent with Section 1617.

ARTICLE VIII.

DISTRICT CENSUS MARSHALS.

SECTION 1635. To be amended to read as follows:

Sec. 1635. Whenever a district is formed lying partly in two adjoining counties, the census marshal must report to each County Superintendent of Schools the number of children in each county.

NOTE.—Changed to improve the expression.

SECTION 1639. To be amended to read as follows:

Sec. 1639. The compensation of census marshal must be audited and paid as other claims upon the school fund of the district are audited and paid; *provided,* such compensation shall not exceed six dollars per day for time actually and necessarily employed; *and provided further,* that in no case shall the compensation be computed at a per capita sum; nor shall any order for such compensation be drawn by the trustees of any district, or by any Board of Education, until they shall have been notified by the County, City, or City and County Superintendent of Schools that the report of the census marshal has been approved by him.   In case the report should not be approved by the County, City, or City and County Superintendent of Schools, the census marshal shall not be entitled to receive any compensation.

NOTE.—Changed to improve and complete the expression and intent.

ARTICLE IX.

CLERKS OF SCHOOL DISTRICTS.

SECTION 1650.   To be amended to read as follows:

Sec. 1650.   It is the duty of the clerk:

First—To call meetings of the board at the request of two members, and to act as clerk of the board, and keep a record of its proceedings, and an accurate account of the receipts and expenditures of school moneys.

Second—To keep his records and accounts open to the inspection of the electors of the district, in suitable books provided by the Board of School Trustees for that purpose.

Third—To perform such other duties as may be prescribed by the board.

NOTE.—Subdivision third is stricken out to correspond with the amendment to Section 1521, and subdivision fourth renumbered third.

ARTICLE X.

SCHOOLS.

SECTION 1663.   To be amended to read as follows:

Sec. 1663.   1. All schools, unless otherwise provided by law, must be divided into primary and grammar grades, and the first five years, exclusive of the kindergarten classes, shall constitute the primary grades.   The County Board of Education must, except in incorporated cities having Boards of Education, on or before the first day of July, prescribe the course of study in each grade for the ensuing year.

2. Except in incorporated cities having Boards of Education, the County Board of Education shall provide for issuing certificates of promotion to such pupils as are prepared to take up the work of a higher grade.   It shall also provide for conferring diplomas of graduation on

those who have satisfactorily completed the course of study provided for the schools of the county.

3. The County Board of Education may amend and change, subject to section sixteen hundred and sixty-five, either of the above courses of study, whenever necessary.

NOTE.—Changed in order that there shall be uniformity in the several counties of the State as to the number of years in the primary grades.

SECTION 1672. To be amended to read as follows:

Sec. 1672. No publication of a sectarian, partisan, or denominational character must be used or distributed in any school, or be made a part of any school library; nor must any sectarian or denominational doctrine be taught therein. Any school district, town, or city, the officers of which knowingly allow any schools to be taught in violation of these provisions, forfeits all right to any state or county apportionment of school moneys; and upon satisfactory evidence of such violation, the County Superintendent of Schools or the Superintendent of Public Instruction must withhold both state and county apportionments.

NOTE.—Changed because the County Superintendent of Schools is the officer who apportions the school moneys to districts. San Francisco is the only city, or city and county, that could be reached by the Superintendent of Public Instruction in case of violation of this provision.

SECTION 1674. A new section to be added to read as follows:

Sec. 1674. In schools of more than one teacher, the Board of School Trustees, or City Board of Education, must designate one of the teachers as the principal of the school, who shall have general supervision of the entire school.

NOTE.—This is a new section and aims to fix authority and responsibility. Its enactment into law will settle many differences, and will strengthen many schools. It is a good measure.

ARTICLE XII.

TEACHERS.

SECTION 1696. To be amended to read as follows:

Sec. 1696. Every teacher in the public schools must:

First—Before assuming charge of a school, file his or her certificate with the County Superintendent of Schools; *provided*, that when any teacher so employed is the holder of a California state normal school diploma, accompanied by the certificate of the State Board of Education, as provided in subdivision third of section fifteen hundred and three of the Political Code, an educational or a life diploma of California, upon presentation thereof to the Superintendent, he shall record the name of said holder in a book provided for that purpose in his office, and the holder of said diploma shall thereupon be absolved from the provisions of this subdivision.

Second—Before taking charge of a school, and one week before closing a term of school, notify the County Superintendent of Schools of such fact, naming the day of opening or closing. Boards of Education, and Boards of School Trustees, must in every case give to the teacher a notice of at least two weeks of their intention to close the term of school under their charge. No County Superintendent of Schools shall draw any requisition for the last month's salary of any teacher until said teacher has filed with him the notice required by this subdivision.

Third—Enforce the course of study, the use of the legally authorized text-books, and the rules and regulations prescribed for schools.

Fourth—Hold pupils to a strict account for their conduct on the way to or from school, on the playgrounds, or during recess; suspend for good cause any pupil from the school, and report such suspension to the Board of School Trustees or City Board of Education for review. If such action is not sustained by them, the teacher may appeal to the County Superintendent, whose decision shall be final.

Fifth—Keep a state school register, in which shall be left, at the close of the term, a report showing program of recitations, classification, and grading of all pupils who have attended school at any time during the school year. The County Superintendent of Schools shall in no case draw a requisition in favor of the teacher until the teacher has filed with him a certificate from the clerk of the Board of School Trustees to the effect that the provisions of this subdivision have been complied with.

Sixth—Make an annual report to the County Superintendent of Schools, at the time and in the manner and on the blanks prescribed by the Superintendent of Public Instruction. Any teacher who shall end any school term before the close of the school year, shall make a report to the County Superintendent of Schools immediately after the close of such term; and any teacher who may be teaching any school at the end of the school year, shall, in his or her annual report, include all statistics for the entire school year, notwithstanding any previous report for a part of the year. The County Superintendent of Schools shall in no case draw a requisition for the salary of any teacher for the last month of the school term, until the report required by this subdivision has been filed, and by him approved.

Seventh—Make such other reports as may be required by the Superintendent of Public Instruction, County Superintendent of Schools, Board of School Trustees, or City Board of Education.

Eighth—Issue to pupils on removing from the district transfers, signed by the teacher, showing the grade of such pupil, and his standing in studies.

> NOTE.—Changes in subdivisions first to seventh, inclusive, to improve the expression. Subdivision eighth is a new subdivision. Its aim is to save the time of the pupil by having him furnished with a certificate of standing upon his removal from a school district.

SECTION 1697. To be amended to read as follows:

Sec. 1697. A school month is construed and taken to be twenty school days, or four weeks of five school days each, including legal holidays.

> NOTE.—Changed in order to settle the question of legal holidays occurring during a school month.

SECTION 1698. To be amended to read as follows:

Sec. 1698. In case of the dismissal of any teacher before the expiration of any oral or written contract entered into between such teacher and a Board of Trustees, for alleged unfitness or incompetence, or violation of rules, the teacher may appeal to the County Superintendent of Schools, and if said Superintendent decides that the removal was made without good cause, the teacher so removed must be reinstated, and shall be entitled to compensation for the time lost during the pending of the appeal.

> NOTE.—Changed to improve the expression.

SECTION 1699. To be amended to read as follows:

Sec. 1699. First—Any teacher whose salary is withheld may appeal to the Superintendent of Public Instruction, who shall thereupon require the County Superintendent of Schools to investigate the matter, and present the facts thereof to him. The judgment of the Superintendent of Public Instruction shall be final; and upon receiving it, the County Superintendent of Schools, if the judgment is in favor of the teacher, shall, in case the trustees refuse to issue an order for said withheld salary, issue his requisition in favor of said teacher.

Second—Should any teacher employed by a Board of School Trustees for a specified time leave the school before the expiration of such time, without the consent of the trustees in writing, said teacher shall be deemed guilty of unprofessional conduct, and the Board of Education of the county is authorized, upon receiving notice of such fact, to suspend the certificate of such teacher for the period of one year. Should said teacher be the holder of an educational or a life diploma, the County Superintendent of Schools shall report the delinquency of the teacher to the State Board of Education, who are thereupon authorized to suspend said diploma for the period of one year.

> NOTE.—Changed to improve the expression.

SECTION 1701. To be amended to read as follows:

Sec. 1701. No requisition for a warrant shall be drawn in favor of any teacher, unless such teacher is the holder of a proper certificate in force for the full time for which the requisition is drawn, nor unless he was employed by the Board of Trustees, or the City Board of Education, or by the County Superintendent of Schools, as provided in section ten hundred and forty-five.

NOTE.—Changed to improve the expression.

ARTICLE XIII.

DISTRICT LIBRARIES.

SECTION 1712. To be amended to read as follows:

Sec. 1712. First—The Board of School Trustees, and the City Board of Education in any city, must expend the library fund, together with such moneys as may be added thereto by donation, in the purchase of school apparatus and books for a school library, including books for supplementary work; and no warrant shall be drawn by the County Superintendent of Schools upon the order of any Board of Trustees against the library fund of any district, unless such order is accompanied by an itemized bill, showing the books and apparatus, and the price of each, in payment of which the order is drawn, and unless such books and apparatus have been adopted by the County, or City, or City and County Board of Education, all orders of the Boards of Trustees and Boards of Education for books or apparatus must in every case be submitted to the Superintendent of Schools of the county, or city, or city and county respectively, for his approval, before said books or apparatus shall be purchased.

Second—The trustees of each district shall cause each book now in their district school library, or that may hereafter be placed in said library, to be stamped on the fly-leaf, on the title-page, and on each one hundredth page of the book, with the words, "Department of Public Instruction, State of California, ——— County, ——— District Library," and the County Superintendent of Schools is hereby authorized and instructed to procure such stamp for each district in his county, and to pay for the same out of the county school fund of such district.

NOTE.—Changed to improve the expression.

SECTION 1713. To be amended to read as follows:

Sec. 1713. The library fund shall consist of not less than three, nor more than ten, per cent of the county school fund (the rate to be determined by the County Superintendent of Schools) annually apportioned to the districts; *provided*, that in cities or school districts having five

hundred or more census children, there shall be apportioned a sum not
to exceed seventy-five dollars for every one thousand census children or
fraction thereof of five hundred or more.

NOTE.—Changed the word "five" to "three," because in many districts three per
cent is enough for library purposes. Changed the conditions in large districts and
in cities, because such districts and cities do not need more than seventy-five
dollars for library purposes for every one thousand census children or fraction
thereof not less than five hundred.

SECTION 1714 is stricken out, as Section 1713 as recommended covers
the entire subject.

ARTICLE XVIII.

COUNTY SCHOOL TAX.

SECTION 1817. To be amended to read as follows:

Sec. 1817. The County Superintendent of Schools of each county
having a population of less than two hundred thousand inhabitants,
must, on or before the first regular meeting of the Board of Supervisors,
in September in each year, furnish the Supervisors and Auditor,
respectively, an estimate, in writing, of the minimum amount of county
school fund needed for the ensuing year. This amount he must com-
pute as follows:

First—He must ascertain, in the manner provided for in subdivisions
one and two of section eighteen hundred and fifty-eight, the total number of teachers for the county.

Second—He must calculate the amount required to be raised at five
hundred dollars per teacher. From this amount he must deduct the
total amount of state apportionment, and the remainder shall be the
minimum amount of county school fund needed for the ensuing year;
provided, that if this amount is less than sufficient to raise a sum equal
to six dollars for each census child in the county, then the minimum
amount shall be such a sum as will be equal to six dollars for each
census child in the county.

NOTE.—Changed to improve the expression.

SECTION 1818. To be amended to read as follows:

Sec. 1818. The Board of Supervisors of each county having less than
one hundred thousand inhabitants must, annually, at the time of levying other county taxes, levy a tax to be known as the county school
tax, the maximum rate of which must not exceed fifty cents on each
one hundred dollars of taxable property in the county, nor the minimum rate be less than sufficient to raise a minimum amount reported
by the County Superintendent of Schools in accordance with the provisions of the preceding section. The Supervisors must determine the

minimum rate of the county school tax, as follows: They must deduct fifteen per cent from the equalized value of the last general assessment roll, and the amount required to be raised, divided by the remainder of the assessment roll, is the rate to be levied; but if any fraction of a cent occur, it must be taken as a full cent on each one hundred dollars.

NOTE.—Changed to improve the expression.

ARTICLE XX.

GENERAL PROVISIONS RELATIVE TO SCHOOL FUNDS AND TAXES.

SECTION 1858. To be amended to read as follows:

Sec. 1858. All state school moneys apportioned by the Superintendent of Public Instruction must be apportioned to the several counties in proportion to the number of school census children, as shown by the returns of the school census marshals of the preceding school year; *provided*, that Indian children whose parents are on government reservations, or are living in the tribal relation, and Mongolian children not native born, shall not be included in the apportionment list. The County Superintendent of Schools in each county must apportion all state and county school moneys, as follows:

First—He must ascertain the number of teachers each district is entitled to by calculating one teacher for every seventy school census children, or fraction thereof, not less than twenty school census children, as shown by the next preceding school census; *provided*, that all children in any asylum and not attending the public schools, of whom the authorities of said asylum are the guardians, shall not be included in making the estimate of the number of teachers to which the district in which the asylum is located is entitled.

Second—He must ascertain the total number of teachers for the county, by adding together the number of teachers assigned to the several districts.

Third—Five hundred dollars shall be apportioned to each district for every teacher assigned to it; *provided*, that to districts having ten, and less than twenty, school census children, shall be apportioned four hundred dollars; *provided further*, that to districts having over seventy school census children and a fraction of less than twenty, there shall be apportioned twenty dollars for each census child in said fraction.

Fourth—All school money remaining on hand after apportioning to the districts the moneys provided for in subdivision three of this section, must be apportioned to the several districts in proportion to the average daily attendance in each district during the preceding school year. Census children, wherever mentioned in this chapter, shall be construed to mean those between the ages of five and seventeen years.

Fifth—Whenever in any school year, prior to the receipt by the counties, cities, or cities and counties of this State, of their state, county, or city school fund, the school districts or cities shall not have sufficient money to their credit to pay the lawful demands against them, the County, City, or City and County Superintendent of Schools shall give the Treasurer of said county, city, or city and county, an estimate of the amount of school money that will next be paid into the county, city, or city and county treasury, stating the amount to be apportioned to each district. Upon the receipt of such estimate it shall be the duty of the Treasurer of said county, city, or city and county, to transfer from any fund not immediately needed to pay claims against it, to the proper school fund, an amount not to exceed ninety per cent of the amount estimated by the Superintendent, and he shall immediately notify the Superintendent of the amount so transferred. The funds so transferred to the school fund shall be re-transferred by the Treasurer to the fund from which they were taken, from the first money paid into the school fund after the transfer.

NOTE.—Changed to improve the expression.

ARTICLE XXI.

MISCELLANEOUS PROVISIONS RELATING TO PUBLIC SCHOOLS.

SECTION 1869. To be amended to read as follows:

Sec. 1869. Any State, County, or City and County Superintendent of Schools, any State, County, or City and County Board of Education, who shall issue a certificate or diploma, except as provided for in this title, shall be guilty of a misdemeanor.

NOTE.—Changed to improve the expression.

SECTION 1874. To be amended to read as follows:

Sec. 1874. In the adoption of text-books, all County, City, and City and County Boards of Education shall be governed by the following rules:

First—Any books hereafter adopted as a part of a uniform series of text-books must be continued in use for not less than four years.

Second—No change of text-books must be made at any other time than in the months of April, May, or June of the year in which the change is made, and no changes shall be made to take effect till the beginning of the school term commencing after the thirtieth day of June of that year; and no books, other than those published by the State, shall be adopted by the Board of Education of any county, city, city and county, or be used as text-books in any of the public schools of this State, in the subjects of reading, orthography, English grammar,

16—c

arithmetic, geography, United States history, physiology, and civil government.

Third—At least sixty days' notice of any proposed change in text-books must be given by publication in a newspaper of general circulation, published in the county, if there be one, in which such change is to be made. If there be no newspaper published in the county, then such publication shall be made in any newspaper having a general circulation in the county. A copy of the newspaper containing such publication, with such notice marked, must, immediately after the first publication thereof, be by the secretary of the board transmitted to the State Board of Education, and the same, when received, must be filed by the secretary of said state board. Said notice shall state what text-books it is proposed to change; that sealed bids or proposals will be received by the board for furnishing books to replace them; the place where and the day and hour when all bids or proposals will be opened, and that the board reserves the right to reject any and all bids or proposals. Said notice shall be published in such newspaper as often as the same shall be issued after the first publication thereof.

Fourth—At the time and place specified in said notice, the Board shall meet and publicly open and read all of the bids or proposals which have been received by them, and shall make their awards thereon within ten days thereafter.

Fifth—Said bids or proposals must be accompanied by sample copies of the books proposed to be furnished, together with a statement of the wholesale and retail price at which the publisher agrees to furnish each book within the county, or at San Francisco, during the full time for which said books are to be adopted.

Sixth—If no satisfactory bids or proposals are received, then the books already in use may continue in use until changed, as herein provided.

Seventh—The publisher or publishers whose proposals shall be accepted, must enter into a written contract with the Board of Education making the award, and shall give a good and sufficient bond in a reasonable sum, to be fixed by the Board of Education, for the faithful performance thereof. Publishers of books already in use may bid under the provisions of this section as well as others, and such bids, if satisfactory, may be accepted by the board.

Eighth—High schools shall be exempt from the provisions of this section.

Ninth—Nothing in this section shall conflict with any provision of law relating to the state series of text-books; nor shall anything be construed to permit the adoption of any text-books upon any subject covered by the state series of books.

NOTE.—The word "April" is introduced in order to give a longer time during which a change in books may be made.

SECTION 1875. To be amended to read as follows:

Sec. 1875. If any city or district refuse or neglect to use the books that may be prescribed, or use any other text-books in any of the prescribed studies, the County Superintendent of Schools must withhold from such city, town, or district, twenty-five per cent of all state school moneys to which it may be entitled, until it comply; and any moneys so withheld must be apportioned by the Superintendent at the next apportionment of state school money, in the same manner as other school moneys in the treasury.

NOTE.—The expression "Superintendent of Public Instruction" is changed to "County Superintendent of Schools," because it is the County Superintendent of Schools who apportions school moneys to school districts—San Francisco is the only exception in the State. The Superintendent of Public Instruction apportions state school money to the County of San Francisco as to other counties. There is no apportionment by the school officers of San Francisco County.

TITLE IV.

NATIONAL GUARD.

CHAPTER I.

ENROLLED MILITIA.

SECTION 1895. To be amended to read as follows:

Sec. 1895. Every able-bodied male citizen of this State, except Mongolians and Indians, between the ages of eighteen and forty-five years, not exempt by law, is subject to military duty. But no alien is obliged to serve or bear arms against the State to which his allegiance is due.

SECTION 1897. To be amended to read as follows:

Sec. 1897. The County Assessor of each county in this State must, at the same time in each year when he prepares a roll containing the taxable inhabitants of his district or county, enroll all the inhabitants thereof subject to military duty, which roll must be sworn to by him, and delivered to the clerk of the Board of Supervisors at the same time he delivers the assessment roll. In the City and County of San Francisco the Tax Collector must perform the duties by this section imposed upon Assessors.

SECTION 1898. To be amended to read as follows:

Sec. 1898. If any Assessor, or the Tax Collector of the City and County of San Francisco, neglects or refuses to perform any of the duties required of him by this chapter, he is subject to the same liabilities as are provided by law for a neglect or refusal to perform any of the duties required of him in the assessment of taxes, and, in addition, forfeits not less than three hundred, nor more than one thousand, dollars, to be sued for in the name of the people of the State, by the District Attorney of the respective counties, and when recovered to be paid into the military fund of the State. If the clerk of the Board of Equalization neglects or refuses to make and deliver to the brigadier-general of the brigade to which his county belongs the duplicate of the military assessment roll, as directed in this chapter, he forfeits not less than three hundred, nor more than five hundred, dollars, to be sued for, recovered, and disposed of in the same manner.

SECTION 1900. To be amended to read as follows:

Sec. 1900. The clerk of the Board of Supervisors must deliver to the brigadier-general of the brigade to which his county belongs a duplicate of such roll, certified by him, within ten days after the Board of Equalization have completed their corrections.

CHAPTER II.

ARTICLE I.

GENERAL PROVISIONS RELATING TO THE NATIONAL GUARD.

SECTION 1912. To be amended to read as follows:

Sec. 1912. The organized uniformed militia of the State of California are known as the National Guard of California. This force shall not exceed sixty-nine companies, of which sixty companies shall be cavalry, artillery, or infantry, as the board of location may direct, and five divisions of the naval battalion, and the other four companies shall be distributed to such arms of the service as the board of location may direct. The National Guard must be located throughout the State with reference to the military wants thereof, means of concentration, and other military requirements. The word "division," as used in this title in connection with the naval battalion, shall have the same meaning and effect as "company" when used in connection with the infantry.

SECTION 1918. To be amended to read as follows:

Sec. 1918. The commander-in-chief, by and with the advice and consent of the Senate, must appoint one major-general, and for each brigade of the National Guard of California, one brigadier-general, who must be citizens of the United States and of the State, and have served at least four years as officers in the National Guard of California; and the brigadier-generals must be residents of the localities within the brigades for which they are appointed. They take rank according to the date assigned them in their commissions, and hold their office until their successors are appointed and qualified.

Section 1919. To be amended to read as follows:

Sec. 1919. All staff officers shall be citizens of the State of California.

Section 1924. To be amended to read as follows:

Sec. 1924. All commissioned officers of regiments, battalions, troops, batteries, and companies of the National Guard must take rank according to the date assigned them by their commissions; and when two of the same grade are of the same date their rank must be determined by length of previous military service in the State; and if of equal service, then by lot. Officers of regiments, battalions, troops, batteries, and companies of the National Guard, in all cases, are of superior rank to officers of the enrolled militia of the same grade, irrespective of the date of their commissions.

Section 1936. To be amended to read as follows:

Sec. 1936. All officers, musicians, and privates of the National Guard who comply with all military duties, as provided in this chapter, are entitled to the following privileges and exemptions, viz.: exemption from road tax, and head tax of every description except the poll tax provided for in article thirteen, section twelve, of the Constitution, exemption from jury duty, and service on any *posse comitatus*. All officers, non-commissioned officers, musicians, and privates, who have faithfully served in the military service of this State for the space of seven consecutive years, and received the certificate of the adjutant-general certifying the same, are thereafter exempted from further military and jury duty, except in time of war. And the adjutant-general must issue such certificate of exemption when it appears that the party applying is entitled to the same.

Note.—Amended to conform to the requirements of the Constitution, Article XIII, Section 12.

Section 1945. To be amended to read as follows:

Sec. 1945. The State shall provide a bronze service medal, with a bronze bar attached thereto, for ten years' active service; for fifteen years' active service, a silver bar shall be attached; and for twenty years' active service, a gold bar shall be attached to the same medal. There shall be no other or different medals for service. Such medals shall be prepared and issued by the adjutant-general, upon application of the party entitled thereto, and upon proof of such service from the records of the National Guard.

Note.—The amendment consists in adding the last sentence, taken from Section 2101, which can now be repealed.

ARTICLE II.

COMPANIES AND THE DISTRIBUTION OF ARMS.

SECTION 1955.   To be amended to read as follows:

Sec. 1955.   1. If such company has been organized and the officers elected in accordance with the provisions of law, orders, and regulations, the company must be listed in the office of the adjutant-general as a company of the National Guard, and the officers elected, if commissioned, hold office for the term of four years; *provided,* that in case of a vacancy occurring in any office during the term thereof the officer elected to fill such vacancy shall hold for the unexpired term;

2. All commissioned officers of the National Guard shall be commissioned by the Governor, but he may refuse to issue a commission to any officer elected or appointed, if, in his opinion, the person elected or appointed is in any way unqualified or unworthy to be an officer in the National Guard;

3. The Secretary of State shall make no charge for issuing a military commission.

> NOTE.—The amendments consist in adding subdivision three, the same being Section 26 of the Act of April 15, 1880. (See amendments to Codes, 1880, page 57.) Also, increasing the terms of office, and providing for filling vacancies.

SECTION 1962.   To be amended to read as follows:

Sec. 1962.   The companies, troops, and batteries of the National Guard shall be composed of officers and men as follows:

1. Each company of infantry shall have not less than fifty, nor more than one hundred and three, officers, non-commissioned officers, and privates, which must include one commissioned officer, and may include one captain, one first lieutenant, one second lieutenant, one first sergeant, one quartermaster-sergeant, four sergeants, eight corporals, and two musicians;

2. Each troop of cavalry shall have not less than fifty, nor more than one hundred and three, officers, non-commissioned officers, and privates, which must include one commissioned officer, and may include one captain, two first lieutenants, one second lieutenant, one first sergeant, one quartermaster-sergeant, four sergeants, eight corporals, two trumpeters, two farriers, and one saddler;

3. Each foot battery shall have not less than fifty, nor more than one hundred and three, officers, non-commissioned officers, and privates, which must include one commissioned officer, and may include one captain, one first lieutenant, one second lieutenant, one first sergeant, one quartermaster-sergeant, four sergeants, eight corporals, and two trumpeters;

4. Each field battery shall have not less than sixty-one, nor more than one hundred and forty-nine, officers, non-commissioned officers, and privates, which must include one commissioned officer, and may include one captain, two first lieutenants, one second lieutenant, one first sergeant, one quartermaster-sergeant, six sergeants, eight corporals, two trumpeters, two farriers, and one saddler;

5. The line officers of the naval battalion shall be a commander and a lieutenant-commander, and each division shall consist of one lieutenant, one lieutenant junior grade, two ensigns, and not less than sixty, nor more than one hundred, petty officers and men;

6. The numerical strength, rank, titles, and insignia of rank of the companies, troops, and batteries, and their officers and men, of the National Guard, shall conform to the laws, rules, and regulations of the United States army and navy, so far as the same may be effectively applicable; and upon changes being made in the said laws, rules, and regulations of the United States army and navy, the commander-in-chief of the National Guard shall cause the same changes to be made in the National Guard to correspond thereto so far as they may be effectively applicable as aforesaid;

7. Each company, troop, battery, or division naval militia, may have not to exceed ten honorary members, who shall pay fifty dollars per annum each into the company, troop, battery, or naval division treasury, and shall thereupon be entitled to all the exemptions to which men on the active list are entitled, and shall not be required to drill or perform any military duty by reason of such membership;

8. The staff officers of the naval battalion shall consist of one adjutant, one ordnance officer, one paymaster, one engineer officer, and one surgeon, each with the rank of lieutenant junior grade; also, one assistant surgeon and one assistant ordnance officer, each with the rank of ensign. All such officers shall be appointed and commissioned as staff officers upon the staff of a colonel commanding a regiment in the National Guard are appointed and commissioned;

9. The organization of the naval militia shall conform generally to the provisions of the laws of the United States; and the system of discipline and exercise shall conform, as nearly as may be, to that of the navy of the United States as it now is, or may hereafter be, prescribed by Congress. When not otherwise provided for, the government of the naval militia shall be controlled by the provisions of the Political Code relating to the National Guard of California, and the Governor shall have power to alter, divide, annex, consolidate, or disband the same, whenever, in his judgment, the efficiency of the State forces will thereby be increased, and he shall have power to make such rules and regulations as may be deemed proper for the use, government, and instruction of the naval militia; but such rules and regulations shall

conform as nearly as practicable to those governing the United States navy;

10. The duty of the naval militia required by law, or any part of it, may be performed afloat in United States vessels. Officers and men of the naval militia mustered temporarily into the service of the United States for instruction and drill, and receiving compensation therefor from the United States, shall not, during the same term, be entitled to compensation from the State;

11. The Governor is authorized to apply to the President of the United States for the detail of commissioned and petty officers of the navy, to act as inspectors and instructors in the art of naval warfare;

12. The naval militia battalion and divisions shall receive the same allowance from the State as infantry battalions and companies.

> NOTE.—Subdivision 5 changed considerably; 6 and 7 but slightly; Subdivisions 8, 9, 10, 11, and 12, being the essential provisions of an Act of the Legislature approved March 1, 1893. (Stats. 1893, page 62), are added.

SECTION 1965. To be amended to read as follows:

Sec. 1965. The commanding officer of each troop, battery, company, naval division, or signal corps must give such bonds and security as may be required by the adjutant-general to secure the State and the company from loss on account of misuse or misapplication of any State property or funds. Said bond must be with two or more good and sufficient sureties conditioned upon his faithful performance of all duties, and accounting for all property and moneys, both State and company funds, of which the commander, as ex officio treasurer, shall be the custodian.

SECTION 1966. To be amended to read as follows:

Sec. 1966. Such bonds being to his satisfaction, and on receiving duplicate receipts from such officer, the adjutant-general must make the issue.

SECTION 1970. To be amended to read as follows:

Sec. 1970. There must be an annual inspection and muster of the National Guard between January first and June thirtieth, each year, by brigade, regiment, battalion, or company, as may be deemed advisable by the commander-in-chief; and the commanding officer of each company must make out and certify the necessary muster rolls, showing the names and number of the members of the company, the officers in the order of their rank, and the privates in alphabetical order, and also a list of the ordnance, ordnance stores, clothing, and other property of the State, in the possession of the company. He must transmit, through the proper military channels, one copy of the roll and list attached to each superior headquarters.

SECTION 1974. To be amended to read as follows:

Sec. 1974.   1. Every elected or staff officer of the National Guard must, upon his appointment or reappointment, election or reëlection, to any office in the National Guard, appear before an examining board for examination as to his qualifications for the office to which he has been appointed or reappointed, elected or reëlected; *provided*, that the provisions of this section do not apply to surgeons, judges-advocate, chaplains, or the staff of the commander-in-chief;

2. Such boards shall consist of three officers for each brigade, three officers for the naval battalion, and three officers for the division staff. All of such boards to be designated by the commander-in-chief, and to be removable at his pleasure;

3. The officer duly appointed to preside at any election shall, immediately after declaring the result of such election, notify the officer or officers elected that they must appear before the examining board for examination, when notified by that board;

4. If the officer elected or reëlected, and duly notified, does not appear before the said examining board when summoned by them, he shall be deemed to have declined his commission, and there shall be another election ordered. The filing of a proper certificate of said board with the officer ordering the election, that the officer has failed to pass an examination, or declined to appear before the board when notified, shall be deemed sufficient for ordering a new election.

SECTION 1976. To be amended to read as follows:

Sec. 1976.   Application or propositions for membership in any troop, battery, naval division, or company of the National Guard shall be made only at a regular weekly meeting or assemblage of such organization; and the names of such applicants shall be posted in a conspicuous place in its headquarters or armory, until the next succeeding regular weekly meeting or assemblage of such organization, at which time, and not before, such applicants may be balloted for.

SECTION 1981. To be amended to read as follows:

Sec. 1981.   Each brigadier-general commanding a brigade, with the consent of the commander-in-chief, may muster in and attach to it a hospital and ambulance corps, consisting of not to exceed twelve men for each regiment in his brigade.   Such corps shall have such commissioned and non-commissioned officers as the commander-in-chief shall prescribe, and shall report directly to the brigade commander, who shall appoint such non-commissioned officers as may be prescribed. When for drill, or in the performance of duty, any expense shall be incurred by any such corps, such expense shall be paid by the State; *provided*, that the same shall have been first authorized by the commanding officer of the brigade, afterward approved by such commanding officer and superior officers, as provided by law in the case of other commands. ·

ARTICLE III.

REGIMENTS AND BATTALIONS.

SECTION 1982. To be amended to read as follows:

Sec. 1982. A regiment of the National Guard consists of not less than eight, nor more than twelve, companies. Each regiment shall be divided into battalions.

SECTION 1984. To be amended to read as follows:

Sec. 1984. The field officers of a regiment are one colonel, one lieu-tenant-colonel, and one major for each battalion. The field officer of a battalion is one major. No person shall be eligible for election as a field officer unless he shall have served at least two years in the National Guard of this State.

SECTION 1990. To be amended to read as follows:

Sec. 1990. The staff of a colonel commanding a regiment consists of one surgeon, with rank of major; one adjutant, with rank of captain; one assistant surgeon for each battalion, with rank of captain; one chaplain, with rank of captain; one battalion adjutant for each battalion, one quartermaster (who shall also act as paymaster), one commissary, one inspector of rifle practice (who shall be ordnance officer), each with the rank of first lieutenant; one sergeant-major, one principal musician, one quartermaster-sergeant, one commissary sergeant, one hospital steward, two color sergeants, one battalion sergeant-major for each battalion, one drum major. All of whom shall be appointed by, and hold office at the pleasure of, the colonel, or until their successors are appointed and qualified.

The staff of a major commanding an unattached battalion consists of one adjutant, with the rank of first lieutenant; one assistant surgeon, with the rank of captain; one commissary (who shall also be quartermaster), one inspector of rifle practice (who shall also be ordnance officer), each with the rank of second lieutenant; one sergeant-major, one commissary sergeant (who shall also be quartermaster-sergeant), one hospital steward, and two color sergeants. All of whom shall be appointed by such commanding officer, and hold office at his pleasure, or until their successors are appointed and qualified.

ARTICLE IV.

DIVISIONS AND BRIGADES.

SECTION 2008. A new section to be added to Article IV to read as follows:

Duties of inspectors of rifle practice.

Sec. 2008. It shall be the duty of the inspector-general of rifle practice to exercise general supervision over the rifle practice of the National Guard; to inspect, or cause to be inspected, from time to time, all ranges and practice grounds, and see that the prescribed regulations for rifle practice are carried out by the National Guard, and that the proper returns thereof are made out; to report direct to general headquarters, from time to time, the improvement in marksmanship among the uniformed forces, together with all other matters pertaining to his duties. Commanders of brigades, regiments, and companies shall furnish to the inspector-general of rifle practice such information as he shall require in regard to the rifle practice of their commands, and as to the number and condition of all targets or other military property of the State issued to their respective commands for use in rifle practice; and if, at the conclusion of his inspection of any armory, range, or practice ground, he shall find any property appertaining to rifle practice, which ought to be kept therein, missing, injured, unfit for use, or deficient in any respect, or that such range or practice ground is dangerous, he shall forthwith report the facts in respect thereto to general headquarters. He may, from time to time, examine the officers upon the theory and practice of marksmanship, and upon the system of instruction of rifle practice. It shall be his duty to attend, as far as practicable, all general competitions in marksmanship among the National Guard, and see that such competitions are conducted with fairness and according to prescribed regulations. He shall make an annual report to general headquarters, in which he shall state the result of all competitions in marksmanship, with the names of the winners, together with such suggestions as he may see fit. The brigade inspectors of rifle practice shall have supervision of all matters appertaining to rifle practice within the limits of their respective brigades, under the direction of the brigade commander, as above prescribed for the inspector-general of rifle practice. They shall report to such inspector-general of rifle practice, whenever required by him, the condition of rifle practice in their respective brigades, and what practice of that description has been carried on during any period, and shall also, at his request, report to him upon any matter relating to rifle practice which may require examination within their respective brigades. They shall attend the competition for any prizes that may be offered by the State to the command to which they are attached, or that may be arranged between any of the companies of their brigades, and see that the same are conducted with fairness and according to the prescribed regulations for such competitive matches, and report to the inspector-general of rifle practice the result of such competitions, with the names of the winners, together with such suggestions as they may see fit to make. Regimental and battalion inspectors of rifle practice shall have supervision of all matters appertaining to rifle practice within the limits of their respective regiments or battalions, as prescribed for the brigade inspector of rifle practice. They shall report to said brigade inspector of their respective brigades, the condition of · rifle practice in their respective regiments or battalions, and what practice has been carried on during any period, and shall also, at his request, report to him upon any matter relating to rifle practice which may require examination within their respective regiments or battalions. They shall attend the competitions for any prize that may be offered, or that may be arranged between any of the companies of their respective regiments or battalions, and see that the same are conducted with fairness and according to the prescribed regulations for such competitive matches, and report to the brigade inspector of rifle practice the result of all such competitions, with the names of the winners, together with such suggestions as they may see fit.

NOTE.—The above section contains the provisions of an Act of the Legislature approved March 30, 1878. (Stats. 1878, page 758.)

SECTION 2009. A new section to be added to this Code, to be known as Section 2009, and to read as follows:

Sanitary corps.

Sec. 2009. 1. The medical department of the National Guard of California is hereby organized into a sanitary corps, which shall consist of one surgeon-general, with the rank of colonel, who shall be the executive head of the corps, and such number of commissioned officers, non-commissioned officers, and privates as may be required to furnish an efficient service for the organized strength of the National Guard.

2. The commissioned strength of the sanitary corps shall be determined by the organization of the National Guard, to wit: To each organized division one chief surgeon, with the rank of colonel; to each organized brigade, one chief surgeon, with the rank of lieutenant-colonel; to each organized regiment, one surgeon, with the rank of major; and a surgeon, with the rank of captain, for each battalion.

3. The appointment of the commissioned officers of the sanitary corps shall be made by the commander-in-chief, as hereinafter provided.

4. The commander-in-chief is hereby authorized to transfer enlisted men of the National Guard to the sanitary corps, or cause to be enlisted for the same as many hospital sergeants, hospital corporals, and

privates as the service may require, who may be mounted, and permanently attached to the sanitary corps, under such regulations as the commander-in-chief may prescribe.

5. No person shall receive the appointment of surgeon unless he is a graduate of a medical school and unless he shall have been examined and approved by a medical board, consisting of not less than three surgeons, designated by the commander-in-chief, upon the recommendation of the surgeon-general.

6. No person shall be transferred to or enlisted into the sanitary corps unless he shall have passed a satisfactory examination, as to his qualifications, before a board of medical officers, to be appointed by the commander-in-chief, upon the recommendation of the surgeon-general.

7. Assignments of commissioned and non-commissioned officers and privates of the sanitary corps shall be made, and their duties prescribed, by the commander-in-chief, upon the recommendation of the surgeon-general.

8. Privates of the sanitary corps shall do duty as cooks, nurses, and attendants in hospitals, and as stretcher-bearers and ambulance-drivers and attendants in the field, and such other duties as may be required of them by proper authority.

9. The pay and emoluments of members of the sanitary corps shall be the same as provided by law for the pay of troops of the National Guard.

10. The sanitary corps shall be equipped and uniformed the same as the same department in the United States army. The funds to be expended by this department shall be expended by the authority of the commander-in-chief, upon the recommendation of the surgeon-general.

ARTICLE V.

PARADES AND DRILLS.

Section 2018. To be amended to read as follows:

Sec. 2018. The National Guard of California must parade in each year as follows:

1. On the fourth of July;

2. For target practice at such times as may be designated by the commander-in-chief, and at least once in each year;

3. These parades shall be made by brigade, regiment, battalion, or company, as may be deemed most advisable by the commander-in-chief, who shall issue orders to the National Guard to carry out the provisions of this section.

SECTION 2022. To be amended to read as follows:

Sec. 2022. The commander-in-chief may annually order an encampment for discipline and drill, either by division, brigade, regiment, battalion, or unattached company, and all troops assembled and encamped, under orders of the commander-in-chief, for not less than seven days, shall receive a sum equal to one dollar and twenty-five cents per day for each officer and man regularly on duty in such camp; *provided*, that the aggregate for each company of such last mentioned allowance of one dollar and twenty-five cents per day shall not exceed the sum of four hundred dollars per company; all officers and men shall receive, in addition to the above allowance, the actual fare to and from the place of encampment; *and provided further*, that when the division or a brigade is regularly assembled and encamped for discipline and drill for not less than seven days, then, in addition to the above allowance, the major-general, brigadier-general, the members of the staff of the commander-in-chief, and each staff officer on the general staff, shall receive from the State the sum of one dollar and twenty-five cents per day while regularly on duty in such camp; *and provided further*, that in any camp held in pursuance of orders from the commander-in-chief, all mounted officers and enlisted men shall receive the sum of two dollars per day for each horse necessarily used by them at such encampment; *and provided further*, that by all officers and enlisted men of companies of the naval battalion such services may be performed afloat. Aforesaid allowances shall be paid only when appropriations are made sufficient for that purpose.

CHAPTER IV.

COURTS-MARTIAL AND OF INQUIRY.

SECTON 2076. To be amended to read as follows:

Sec. 2076. The following officers may appoint courts-martial:

1. The commander-in-chief, for the trial of general officers, retired officers, and all officers of the staff of the commander-in-chief;

2. The major-general, for the trial of all staff officers of the division and brigades, and of field officers of regiments and battalions;

3. The brigadier-general, for the trial of officers and soldiers in their respective brigades;

4. The commanding officers of regiments and unattached battalions, for the trial of all enlisted men in their respective commands. For the trial of enlisted men of regiments or battalions, the commanding officer thereof may, at any time, appoint a summary court-martial, to consist of one officer whose rank is not below that of captain. For the trial of enlisted men of unattached companies, troops, or batteries, the brigade

commander may, at any time, appoint a summary court-martial, to consist of a first lieutenant of such company, troop, or battery;

5. The officer appointing said court shall fix the day on which it shall convene, and when convened the court may adjourn from time to time, as shall become necessary for the transaction of business; but the whole session of the court, from the day on which it shall convene until its dissolution, shall not exceed three weeks, and in case any vacancy shall happen in the court, or a new court shall be required, the officer ordering the court, or his successor in command, may fill such vacancy, or order a new court;

6. The officer constituting such court shall, before he enters on his duties as such, take the following oath: "I, ——, do swear (or affirm) that I will well and truly try and determine, according to evidence, all matters between the people of the State of California and any person or persons who may come before the summary court-martial to which I have been appointed. And such oath shall be taken by him before a justice of the peace of the county in which he resides, or a field officer, and it shall be the duty of such justice of the peace or field officer to administer the oath without fee or reward;

7. Such court shall direct a non-commissioned officer, or other fit person or persons, to be by him designated, to summon all delinquents and parties accused to appear before the court, at a time and place to be by him appointed, which service shall be personal or by leaving such summons at the residences of such delinquents and parties accused;

8. Such non-commissioned officer, or other person or persons so designated, shall make the like returns and with like effect as commissioned and non-commissioned officers are authorized and required to make in cases of warning to a company or regimental parade, and shall be subject to the like penalties for neglect of duty;

9. The court shall be conducted in the same manner as summary courts-martial are in the service of the United States, and shall have the trial of all offenses, delinquencies, and deficiencies that occur in the regiment or battalion for which it shall have been appointed, and also of any that occur in the separate companies, troops, or batteries; and the said court shall have power to impose and direct to be levied all the fines or penalties to which enlisted men are declared to be subject by the provisions of this chapter;

10. The proceedings and sentence of any such court shall, without delay, be delivered to the officer ordering the court, who shall approve or disapprove the same within thirty days thereafter, and shall give notice of his approval or disapproval to the president thereof; and from the' sentence of any such court imposing a fine or penalty for any offense, delinquency, or deficiency, an appeal, if made within twenty days after the fine or penalty was made known to the person fined, shall be

allowed to the officer ordering the court, or to his successor in command, and he may remit or mitigate such penalty or fine.

SECTION 2084.　To be amended to read as follows:

Sec. 2084.　Every Sheriff and Constable must serve all orders, subpœnas, or process delivered to him for that purpose by any member of a court-martial or court of inquiry.

CHAPTER V.

THE BOARD OF MILITARY AUDITORS.

SECTION 2094.　To be amended to read as follows:

Sec. 2094.　There must be audited and allowed by the board of military auditors, and paid out of the appropriation for military purposes, upon the warrant of the State Controller, to the commanding officer of each infantry or artillery company of the National Guard, the sum of one hundred dollars per month; to the commanding officer of each light battery having not less than four guns, with which they regularly drill and parade, and to the commanding officer of each troop of cavalry, the sum of two hundred dollars per month; and to the commanding officer of each division of the naval battalion, the sum of one hundred dollars per month; the sum so paid to be used for armory rent, care of arms, and proper incidental expenses of the company.　There must also be audited, allowed, and paid, out of the same appropriations, to the commanding officer of each regiment or battalion, the sum of six dollars per month for each company in his command, for clerical expenses, stationery, printing, and postage; and if the regiment or battalion has more than four companies, and has attached to it an organized and uniformed band of not less than twenty people, the additional sum of thirty-five dollars per month for such band; to the major-general, six hundred dollars per annum; to the brigadier-general of each brigade, four dollars per month for each company in his brigade, and to each company, a sum necessary for uniforms, and to keep the same in repair, not to exceed one hundred and fifty dollars per annum; and to the adjutant-general, four thousand dollars per annum, to be expended by him in promoting rifle practice.　There shall also be paid, from the military appropriations of the State, a sum not exceeding five hundred dollars for the first year of its existence, to the brigadier-general for a hospital and ambulance corps in their respective brigades, which sum shall be expended in the purchasing of proper supplies, equipments, and medicines for such corps, and thereafter to such corps there shall be paid a sum, for the same purpose, of not exceeding five hundred dollars per annum.

SECTION 2099. To be amended to read as follows:

Sec. 2099. The annual sum of two hundred and fifty dollars may be audited by the board, and paid out of the appropriation for military purposes, to each company of the National Guard of fifty members or over, and an amount in proportion to every company of less than fifty members. The amount so audited and allowed must be paid to the commanding officers of such companies for the use thereof.

SECTION 2101. To be repealed.

NOTE.—The provisions of this section, in an amended form, are contained in Section 1945 of this Code.

SECTION 2105. To be amended to read as follows:

Sec. 2105. There must be audited and allowed by the board of military auditors, and paid out of the appropriations for military purposes, to the commanding officer of each signal corps in the National Guard, the sum of twenty-five dollars per month for each ten enlisted members of said corps, the sum so paid to be used for armory rent, care of arms, and proper incidental expenses of the signal corps. Demand shall be made and presented in the same manner as for the expenses of a company.

Chapter I of Part III, Title V, Article I, containing Sections 2136, 2137, 2138, 2139, 2140, 2150, 2151, 2152, 2153, 2154, 2155, 2165, 2166, 2167, 2168, 2169, 2179, 2180, 2181, 2182, 2183, 2193, 2194, 2195, 2196, 2197, 2198, 2199, 2200, 2210, 2211, 2212, 2213, 2214, 2215, 2216, 2217, 2218, 2219, 2220, 2221, and 2222, is to be revised and entirely rewritten. The Commissioners have in preparation a measure to occupy this chapter, designed to apply to all the asylums for the insane in this State, providing for their harmonious and uniform management and control. This proposed enactment will be submitted to the Legislature at the commencement of its session.

CHAPTER II.

INSTITUTION FOR THE DEAF AND THE BLIND.

ARTICLE I.

GENERAL PROVISIONS.

SECTION 2237. To be amended to read as follows:

Sec. 2237. The institution for the deaf and the blind, located at Berkeley, Alameda County, is a part of the school system of the State, except that it shall derive no revenue from the public school fund, and has for its object the education of the deaf and the blind who, by

17—c

reason of their infirmity, cannot be taught in the public schools. It shall be known and designated as the Institution for the Deaf and the Blind.

SECTION 2238. To be amended to read as follows:

Sec. 2238. Every deaf or blind child, of suitable age and mental capacity for instruction, and whose parents or guardians are actual residents of the State, is entitled to education and maintenance, except clothing, in this institution, free of charge.

SECTION 2239. To be amended to read as follows:

Sec. 2239. Any such deaf or blind child, whose parents or guardians are not residents of the State, is entitled to the benefits of the institution upon paying to the treasurer thereof three hundred dollars for each academic year, to be paid semi-annually in advance. If the parents or guardians of any pupil in the institution shall be unable to clothe such child, the parent or guardian may testify to such inability before the judge of the Superior Court of the county wherein he or she is resident, and if said judge is satisfied that the parent or guardian is not able to provide suitable clothing for the child, he shall issue a certificate to that effect; and upon presentation of such certificate, it shall be the duty of the directors of said institution to clothe the child, the expenses to be paid out of the appropriation made for the support of the institution.

SECTION 2240. To be repealed.

NOTE.—The provisions of this section are incorporated in the preceding section.

SECTION 2242. To be repealed.

NOTE.—The office of State Geologist has ceased to exist, and this section has been inoperative.

SECTION 2243. To be amended to read as follows:

Sec. 2243. The salaries mentioned in this chapter must be paid monthly out of the moneys appropriated for the support of the institution.

SECTION 2244. To be amended to read as follows:

Sec. 2244. The official bonds required by the provisions of this chapter must be approved by the board, and filed and recorded in the office of the Secretary of State.

ARTICLE II.

BOARD OF DIRECTORS.

SECTION 2255. To be amended to read as follows:

Sec. 2255. The powers and duties of the board are as follows:

1. To make by-laws, not inconsistent with the laws of the State, for their own government, and the government of the institution;

2. To elect a principal, and to discharge him whenever, in their opinion, the interests of the institution require it;

3. To elect a treasurer, who shall not be a member of the board of directors;

4. To elect a physician for the institution for a term of two years, who shall not be a member of the board of directors;

5. To fix the compensation of teachers and employés;

6. To make diligent inquiry into the departments of labor and expense, the condition of the institution, and its prosperity;

7. To receive gifts or bequests of money or property for the benefit of the institution, and to invest or expend the same according to the wishes of the donor.   All official acts performed by them shall be in the name of the "Institution for the Education of the Deaf and the Blind," and by that name they may make loans, and maintain action to enforce the payment thereof;

8. To hold stated meetings at the institution at least once in every three months;

9. To keep a record of their proceedings;

10. To report to the Governor a statement of the receipts and expenditures, the condition of the institution, and of such other matters touching the duties of the board as they deem advisable;

11. To provide in the institution rooms and board for the principal and his family.

ARTICLE III.

PRINCIPAL TEACHER.

SECTION 2267. To be amended to read as follows:

Sec. 2267. The principal must have had not less than three years' experience in the art of teaching the deaf.

SECTION 2268. To be amended to read as follows:

Sec. 2268. He is the chief executive officer of the institution, with powers and duties as follows:

1. To superintend the grounds, buildings, and property of the institution;

2. With the consent of the board of directors, to fix the number of, and appoint and remove, the teachers and employés;

3. To prescribe and enforce the performance of the duties of teachers and employés;

4. To control the pupils, and to prescribe and enforce a system of instruction;

5. To live at the institution;

6. To keep a record of his official acts in the manner prescribed in the by-laws;

7. To estimate quarterly, in advance, the expenses of the institution, and report such estimates to the board of directors;

8. To make up his annual accounts to the first of July in each year, and as soon thereafter as possible report a statement thereof, and of the condition of the institution, to the board of directors;

ARTICLE IV.

TREASURER.

SECTION 2280. To be amended to read as follows:

Sec. 2280. It is the duty of the treasurer:

1. To act as secretary of the board of directors;

2. To keep the accounts of the board, the receipts, expenditures, assets, and liabilities of the institution;

3. To report quarterly to the board a statement, under oath, of the expenditures and receipts of the preceding quarter;

4. To perform such other duties as may be required of him by the by-laws or the board of directors.

SECTION 2327. To be amended to read as follows:

Sec. 2327. The control and management of the University of California, and the state normal schools, are provided for in title three of part three of this Code.

NOTE.—The amendment consists in changing the word "school" to "schools."

SECTION 2328. To be amended to read as follows:

Sec. 2328. The control and management of the state prisons is provided for in "An act to regulate and govern the state prisons of California," approved March nineteenth, eighteen hundred and eighty-nine, and acts amendatory thereof and supplemental thereto.

CHAPTER II.

HIGHWAYS.

ARTICLE I.

ENUMERATION OF HIGHWAYS.

SECTION 2618. To be amended to read as follows:

Sec. 2618. In all counties of this State public highways are roads, streets, alleys, lanes, courts, places, trails, and bridges, laid out or erected as such by the public, or if laid out and erected by others, dedicated or abandoned to the public, or made such in actions for the partition of real property; *provided*, that no route of travel used by one or more persons, over the lands of another, shall hereafter become a public road or byway by use, unless so declared by the Board of Supervisors, or by dedication by the owner of the land affected.

SECTION 2621. To be repealed.

NOTE.—The provisions of this section are contained in Sections 2618 and 2623.

SECTION 2623. To be amended to read as follows:

Sec. 2623. Any road laid out by the Board of Supervisors, as provided in this chapter, or used and worked as therein provided, shall not be vacated or cease to be a highway until so ordered by said board, and each county shall be deemed to have acquired title to any road opened over any land in conformity to any order made by its Board of Supervisors, pursuant to this chapter, after one year shall have elapsed from the time of making the order opening the road; *provided*, no contest shall have previously been entered.

NOTE.—The amendment consists in the addition of the proviso.

ARTICLE II.

RULES AND RESTRICTIONS RESPECTING THE USE OF HIGHWAYS.

SECTION 2633. To be amended to read as follows:

Sec. 2633. Any owner or occupant of land adjoining a highway not less than three rods wide may plant deciduous trees in and along said highway on the side contiguous to his land. They must be set in regular rows, at a distance of at least twenty feet from each other, and not more than six feet from the boundary of the highway. If the highway is more than eighty feet wide, the row must not be less than six, nor more than twelve, feet from the boundary of the highway. Whoever willfully injures any of them is liable to the owner or to the occupant for the damage which is thereby sustained; *provided*, if, in the judgment of the Board of Supervisors, the whole width of such road is needed for use for highway purposes, the whole thereof may be so used.

> NOTE.—The word "deciduous" is inserted before "trees" to prevent the planting of evergreens, which shade the road in winter, when not needed, and prevent the drying of the road in wet weather.

ARTICLE III.

POWERS AND DUTIES OF HIGHWAY OFFICERS.

SECTION 2643.   To be amended to read as follows:

Sec. 2643.   The Boards of Supervisors of the several counties of the State shall have general supervision over the roads within their respective counties.   They must, by proper order:

1. Cause to be surveyed, viewed, laid out, recorded, opened, and worked, such highways as are necessary to public convenience, as in this chapter provided;

2. Cause to be recorded as highways all highways which have become such by usage, dedication, or abandonment to the public, or by any other means provided by law, and to prepare and record proper deeds and titles thereto;

3. Abolish or abandon such as are not necessary;

4. Acquire the right of way over private property for the use of public highways, and for that purpose require the District Attorney to institute proceedings under title seven, part three, of the Code of Civil Procedure, and to pay therefor from the general road fund, or the district road fund of the county;

5. Levy a property tax for road purposes;

6. Cause to be erected and maintained, at the intersections and crossings of highways, guide-posts, properly inscribed;

7. Cause the road tax collected each year to be apportioned to the several road districts entitled thereto, and kept by the County Treasurer in separate funds;

8. Audit all claims on the funds set apart for highway purposes, and specify the fund or funds from which the whole or any part of any claim or claims must be paid;

9. In their discretion, they may provide for the establishment of gates on the public highways in certain cases, to avoid the necessity of building road fences, and prescribe rules and regulations for closing the same, and penalties for violating said rules; *provided*, that the expense for the erection and maintenance of such gates shall in all cases be borne by the party or parties for whose immediate benefit the same shall be ordered;

10. For the purpose of watering roads in any part of the county, the

Board of Supervisors may erect and maintain waterworks, and for such purpose may purchase or lease real or personal property.. The costs for such waterworks, and the watering of said roads, may be charged to the general county fund, the general road fund, or the district fund of the district or districts benefited;

11. Whenever it shall be determined that any grading, graveling, macadamizing, ditching, sprinkling, or other work upon highways, is necessary, and is to be done, and where the estimated cost of such work amounts to three hundred dollars, the Board of Supervisors must, by proper order, direct the County Surveyor to make definite surveys of the proposed work, and to prepare profiles and cross-sections thereof, and to submit the same, with the estimate of the amount or amounts of work to be done, and the cost thereof, and with specifications therefor. Said report shall be prepared in duplicate, one copy to be filed in the Surveyor's office, and the other to be filed with the clerk of the Board of Supervisors. The board, upon receipt of such report, must advertise for bids for the performance of the work specified. Such advertisement for bids must be published for two weeks in two newspapers, one published at the county seat and the other at a point nearest the proposed work. Such advertisement must be in the following form:

"Office of the Clerk of the Board of Supervisors,
———— County, ———— ————, 189—.

"Sealed bids will be received by the clerk of the Board of Supervisors of ———— County, at his office, until ———— o'clock, — M., ———— ————, 189—, for ———— ————, on ————, in ———— District, in ———— County.

"Specifications for this work are on file in the office of the said board, to which bidders are hereby referred.
                                        "———— ————,

"Clerk of the Board of Supervisors of the County of ————."

And such advertisement must also be posted, for at least two weeks prior to the opening of the bids for the proposed work, in three conspicuous places in the district or districts in which the proposed work lies, and one at the site of the proposed work. Bids must be inclosed in a sealed envelope, addressed to the clerk of the Board of Supervisors, and must be indorsed, "Bids for ————," and must be delivered to said clerk prior to the hour specified in the advertisement. The board shall publicly open and read such bids as may be submitted, and must award the contract for the work to the lowest bidder; unless it shall appear to the board that the bids are too high, and the work can be done more cheaply by day labor, in which case the bids must be rejected, and the work ordered done by the road commissioner or commissioners in whose district or districts the work may be situated. In case the work shall be let to contract, monthly or quarterly payments may be made thereon, upon the receipt of a certified estimate by the County Surveyor of the amount of work done during the preceding month or quarter, to the extent of seventy-five per cent of the value of said work, the remaining twenty-five per cent being due on the completion of the work. The services of the surveyor in making such partial estimates must be paid for by the contractor. Upon the completion of the work, the County Surveyor must examine the same, and, if completed in accordance with the specifications therefor, he must submit to the Board of Supervisors a certificate, over his signature and official seal, to the effect that such work by the contractor therefor has been completed in accordance with the specifications therefor, and recommending its acceptance. The Board of Supervisors shall thereupon audit the same, and direct its payment out of the proper fund or funds.

SECTION 2645. To be amended to read as follows:

Sec. 2645. Road commissioners, under the direction and supervision and pursuant to orders of the Board of the Supervisors, must:

1. Take charge of the highways within their respective districts, and shall employ all men, teams, watering-carts, and all help necessary to do the work in their respective districts, when the same is not let by contract; *provided*, that no road commissioner shall be interested, directly or indirectly, in any contract work done, or material supplied, upon the highways in the county of which he is an officer;

2. Keep them clear from obstructions, and in good repair, and destroy, or cause to be destroyed, at least once a year, all thistles, Mexican cockleburs, of any kind, and all noxious weeds, growing or being on any portion of the public highways or public roads in their respective districts;

3. Cause banks to be graded, bridges and causeways to be made when necessary, keep the same in good repair, and renew them when destroyed.

NOTE.—Amended by adding the proviso to subdivision one.

ARTICLE IV.

HIGHWAY TAXES.

SECTION 2652. To be amended to read as follows:

Sec. 2652. The Board of Supervisors may, annually, at any regular meeting held between the first days of January and March of each year, levy on each male person over twenty-one and under fifty-five years of age found in each road district during the time for the collection of road poll taxes for that year, excepting all persons who were honorably discharged from service in the army or navy of the United States at any time within the first day of April in the year of our Lord eighteen hundred and sixty-one, and the first day of September in the year of our Lord eighteen hundred and sixty-five, an annual road poll tax not exceeding three dollars; and from every such person not above excepted, in a road district, who has not paid the same in some other district, must be collected the amount of road poll tax so levied. Said road poll tax shall be collected by the County Assessor in the same manner that state poll taxes are collected, and all remedies given by law for the collection of state poll taxes shall apply to and be in force for the collection of road poll taxes. Road poll tax receipts, in blank, signed and numbered in the same manner that other poll tax receipts are signed and numbered, shall be delivered by the Auditor of the county to said County Assessor on or before the first Monday of March of each year; and said Assessor shall be charged with the amount of such road poll tax receipts delivered to him, and be credited with those returned, and shall settle with the Auditor, and pay over the amounts collected, in the manner provided by section thirty-eight hundred and fifty-three of this Code. Such road poll tax so collected shall be applied to and constitute a part of the district road fund of the district from which it was collected.

SECTION 2654. To be amended to read as follows:

Sec. 2654. The annual property tax for road purposes must be levied by the Board of Supervisors, at their session when the tax is by them levied for county purposes. This property road tax, when levied, must be annually assessed and collected by the same officers and in the same manner as other state and county taxes are levied, assessed, and collected, and turned over to the County Treasurer.

ARTICLE V.

PERFORMANCE OF HIGHWAY LABOR AND COMMUTATION.

SECTION 2671. To be amended to read as follows:

Sec. 2671. Corporations, or other employers of persons, in any road district subject to the road tax, are chargeable for the road poll tax assessed against their employés to the extent of any credit in their hands not exceeding such tax; *provided*, the Assessor shall first give notice to such employer, or the managing agent of such corporation; and from the time of such notice the amount of any credit in his hands, or that shall thereafter accrue, sufficient to satisfy said tax, shall be paid to the Assessor, whose receipt shall be evidence in bar of the prosecution of any action by the employé against the principal for the recovery of the same.

ARTICLE VI.

LAYING OUT, ALTERING, AND DISCONTINUING ROADS.

SECTION 2681. To be amended to read as follows:

Sec. 2681. Any ten or more resident freeholders of a section which may be benefited by the construction of a new road, the correction, or alteration, or the discontinuance and abandonment of an existing road, may petition the Board or Boards of Supervisors of the county or counties in which the proposed or existing road, in whole or in part, lies, in the form herein provided. In case the petition relate to a section situated in more than one county, copies of the petition must be presented to the Board of Supervisors of each county.

SECTION 2683. To be amended to read as follows:

Sec. 2683. The petition must be accompanied by a good and sufficient bond, to be approved by the Board of Supervisors, in double the amount of the probable cost of surveying, viewing, and estimating the exact nature and cost of the matter petitioned for, and conditioned that in case the petition be not granted the bondsmen will pay all costs of surveying, viewing, and estimating the nature of the matters petitioned for, and further providing that in no case shall any costs incurred become a charge against the county, or payable out of any county funds.

SECTION 2684. To be amended to read as follows:

Sec. 2684. Upon filing such petition and bond, the Board of Supervisors may, if they deem it advisable, appoint three viewers, one of whom must be the County Surveyor, one the County Assessor, and a distinterested freeholder of the county, not resident in the district affected, to view and survey any proposed alteration of an old, or opening of a new, road, and submit to the board an estimate of the change, alteration, or opening, together with the probable cost thereof, including the purchase of the right of way, and their views of the necessity thereof.

SECTION 2685. To be amended to read as follows:

Sec. 2685. The road viewers must be sworn to discharge their duties faithfully, must view and lay out the proposed alterations or new road over the lightest grades and most direct alignments which the nature and topography of the country will permit; they must notify the resident owners, or agent of the owners, of the lands affected by the matter petitioned for. A majority number of the viewers, providing one shall be the County Surveyor, shall be competent to act in all matters pertaining to their duties mentioned in this chapter. The Board of Supervisors, in making the order appointing viewers, may, in their discretion, direct said viewers to first view the proposed road, and if, in the opinion of the viewers, the road is impracticable or unnecessary, the said viewers shall discontinue further proceedings in the matter, and report accordingly.

SECTION 2687. To be amended to read as follows:

Sec. 2687. The viewers must be paid as follows: The Assessor must be paid his actual expenses whilst in the discharge of his duty. The Surveyor shall receive ten dollars per day, and if the services of assistants, chainmen, and laborers be necessary, the Surveyor must present a sworn bill of the cost of their services and actual expenses, which must be paid as herein provided. The third member of the board of viewers shall be paid three dollars per day for the time occupied in the discharge of his duties. These payments, in case the petition be not granted, must be paid by the signers of the bond accompanying the petition, and shall in no way become due or be paid from highway funds. In case the petition be favorably acted upon, these expenses must be paid from such highway fund or funds, as the Board of Supervisors shall direct.

SECTION 2691. To be amended to read as follows:

Sec. 2691. All awards by agreement, determined by the board or the proper court, must be paid out of the road fund of the district, except that which may be paid by interested parties, on the order of the Board of Supervisors, and except also that whenever it appears to the Board of Supervisors that any road district would be unreasonably burdened by the payment of such awards and expenses, the Board of Supervisors, by a two-thirds vote, may cause a portion of such awards and expenses to be paid from the general road fund; *provided, however,* that not to exceed ten per cent of the general road fund shall be devoted to such purposes in any one fiscal year. If the road lies in more than one district, the Board of Supervisors must proportionately divide the awards and other costs between said districts; *provided, however,* that when money is paid out by any interested person, the same may be given to the credit of either fund, at the discretion of the board.

SECTION 2692. To be amended to read as follows:

Sec. 2692. Private or by-roads may be opened, laid out, or altered for the convenience of one or more residents or freeholders of any road district, in the same manner as public roads are opened, laid out, or altered, except that only one petitioner shall be necessary, who must be either a resident or a freeholder in said road district; and the Board of Supervisors may, for like cause, order the same to be viewed, opened, laid out, or altered, the person for whose benefit the said road is required paying the damages awarded to land-owners, and keeping the same in repair; *provided*, that the petitioners must accompany the petition with a bond mentioned in section twenty-six hundred and eighty-three, conditioned as provided in said section, and with a further condition that the bondsmen will pay to the person over whose land said road is sought to be opened his necessary costs and disbursements in contesting the opening of such road, in case the petition be not granted and the road finally not opened.

ARTICLE VII.

ERECTION AND MAINTENANCE OF BRIDGES.

SECTION 2715. To be amended to read as follows:

Sec. 2715. If the road commissioner of any road district, chargeable with the repair of a bridge, fails to make the needed repairs, after being informed that a bridge is impassable or unsafe, and is requested to make the same by two or more freeholders of the district in which it is situate, or the two districts which it unites, the freeholders may represent the fact to the Board of Supervisors, who, upon being satisfied that the bridge is unsafe, must cause the same to be repaired.

SECTION 2716. To be amended to read as follows:

Sec. 2716. The Board of Supervisors of each county must hold special meetings on the third Monday in July and the third Monday in January, for the consideration of highway matters and interests. At these meetings each Supervisor, as ex officio road commissioner, must submit, in writing, a report upon the expenditures made and work performed in his district during the previous six months. Such report must show:

1. The mileage of permanently located and improved roadway, and by what method, and from what material constructed;

2. The number, location, and character of permanent bridges, culverts, and drains constructed;

3. The character and extent of water supply developed for road-sprinkling, and the mileage of sprinkled road, with the total and per mile cost;

4. The character, condition, and number of all road machinery and tools owned by the county or district, and used in his district;

5. Recommendations as to the highways, and the management of his district for the ensuing six months, and the scope of work contemplated;

6. In the case of retiring commissioners, he shall make a report to and through his successor.

ARTICLE VIII.

OBSTRUCTION AND INJURIES TO HIGHWAYS.

SECTION 2731. To be amended to read as follows:

Sec. 2731. If any highway duly laid out or erected is encroached upon, by fences, buildings, or otherwise, the road commissioner of the district must, in writing, require the encroachment to be removed from the highway.

NOTE.—Amended by requiring that notice "must" be given, and always in writing.

SECTION 2734. To be amended to read as follows:

Sec. 2734. If the encroachment be denied, and the owner, occupant, or person controlling the matter or thing charged with being an encroachment, refuses either to remove or permit the removal thereof, the Board of Supervisors must direct the District Attorney to institute an action to abate the same as a nuisance; and if he recovers judgment, he may, in addition to having the same abated, recover ten dollars for every day such nuisance remained after notice, and also his costs in said action.

NOTE.—Amended by dropping the words "road overseer" and providing that the Board of Supervisors must require the District Attorney to commence the action.

SECTION 2735. To be amended to read as follows:

Sec. 2735. If the encroachment is not denied, but is not removed for five days after the notice is complete, the road commissioner must remove the same at the expense of the owner, occupant, or person controlling the same, and recover his costs and expenses, together with the penalty provided for in the preceding section.

NOTE.—"Road overseer" changed to "road commissioner," and the word "may" to "must."

SECTION 2737. To be amended to read as follows:

Sec. 2737. Whoever obstructs or injures any highway, or diverts any watercourse thereon, or drains water from his land upon any highway, to the injury thereof, by means of ditches or dams, is liable to a penalty of ten dollars for each day such obstruction or injury remains, and must be punished as provided in section five hundred and eighty-eight of the Penal Code. Any person, persons, or corporation who shall be storing or distributing water for any purpose, and shall permit the water to overflow, or saturate by seepage, any highway, to the injury thereof, shall, upon notification of the road commissioner of the district where such overflow or seepage occurs, repair the damages occasioned by such overflow or seepage; and should such repair not be made within ten days by such person, persons, or corporation, said road commissioner may make such repairs and recover the expense thereof from such person, persons, or corporation, in an action at law. All persons excavating irrigation, mining, or drainage ditches across public highways are required to permanently bridge said ditches at such crossings, and upon neglect to do so, the road commissioner for that road district shall construct the same, and recover the cost of constructing, of such persons, by action, as provided in this section. And whoever willfully injures any public bridge is hereby declared to be guilty of a misdemeanor, and is also liable for actual damages for such injury, to be recovered by the county in a civil action; *provided*, that every person who knowingly allows the carcass of any dead animal (which animal belongs to him at the time of its death) to be put or to remain within one hundred feet of any street, alley, public highway, or road in common use, and every person who puts the carcass of any dead animal within one hundred feet of any street, alley, highway, or road in common use, or who shall deposit on any highway any refuse or waste, is guilty of a misdemeanor.

> Note.—The amendment consists in limiting the time within which certain repairs shall be made to ten days, requiring ditches or cuts across highways to be permanently bridged, and in substituting the words "road commissioner" for "road overseer." The word "shall" was also changed to "may," to conform to the decision of the court in *County of Fresno* vs. *Canal Co.*, 68 Cal. 359.

Sections 2949, 2950, 2952, 2953, 2954, 2955, 2956, 2957, 2958, 2959, 2960, 2961, 2962, 2963, 2964, 2965, 2966, 2968, and 2969, relating to immigration, to be repealed.

Section 2993. To be amended to read as follows:

Sec. 2993. The secretary of the State Board of Health is ex officio vaccine agent. He must obtain a supply of the genuine vaccine matter, and preserve the same for the use and benefit of the citizens of the State.

> Note.—Amended by consolidating the offices of secretary of State Board of Health and State vaccine agent.

CHAPTER X.

HOURS OF LABOR.

Section 3246. A new section to be added to read as follows:

Regulating hours of labor.

Sec. 3246. Any contractor who employs any laborer to work, or permits any laborer to work, more than eight hours in any twenty-four hours of time, upon any work done, performed, or contracted to be done or performed, for the state, or for any county, city and county, town, or city, therein, shall not maintain an action in the courts of this State upon the contract under which the work was performed; nor any action in anywise relating to, or affecting, such contract. It shall be the duty of all officers, state, county, and municipal, to refuse to pay any contractor for work performed or materials furnished, if he shall have been guilty of a violation of any of the provisions of this section. All mechanics, workingmen, and laborers employed by any contractor, as aforesaid, shall receive not less than the prevailing rate of wates in the respective trades or callings in which such mechanics, workingmen, and laborers are employed in said locality. None but citizens of the United States, or persons who have declared their intention to become such, shall be employed by any such contractor upon any of the contracts hereinabove mentioned.

SECTION 3247. A new section to be added to read as follows:

Preference to be given to California products.

Sec. 3247. Any person, committee, board, officer, or any other person, charged with the purchase, or permitted or authorized to purchase, supplies, goods, wares, merchandise, manufactures, or produce, for the use of the State, or of any of its institutions or officers, or for the use of any county or consolidated city and county, or city, or town, shall always, price, fitness, and quality equal, prefer such supplies, goods, wares, merchandise, manufactures, or produce as has been grown, manufactured, or produced in this State, and shall next prefer such as has been partially so manufactured, grown, or produced in this State. All state, county, city and county, city, or town officers, all boards, commissions, or other persons, charged with advertising for any such supplies, shall state in their advertisement that such preferences will be made. In any such advertisement no bid shall be asked for any article of a specific brand or mark when such requirement would prevent proper competition on the part of dealers in other articles of equal value, utility, or merit.

SECTION 3248. A new section to be added to read as follows:

Convict-made goods to be branded or labeled.

Sec. 3248. All goods, wares, and merchandise made by convict labor in any penitentiary, prison, reformatory, or other establishment in which convict labor is employed, shall, before being sold, or exposed for sale, be branded, labeled, or marked as hereinafter provided, and shall not be exposed for sale in any place within this State without such brand, label, or mark. The brand, label, or mark hereby required shall contain at the head or top thereof the words "convict made," followed by the year and name of the penitentiary, prison, reformatory, or other establishment in which it was made, in plain English lettering, of the style and size known as great primer roman condensed capitals. The brand or mark shall, in all cases where the nature of an article will permit, bo placed upon the same, and only where such branding or marking is impossible shall a label be used, and where a label is used it shall be in the form of a paper tag, which shall be attached by wire to each article, where the nature of the article will permit, and placed securely upon the box, crate, or other covering in which such goods, wares, or merchandise may be packed, shipped, or exposed for sale. Said brand, mark, or label shall be placed upon the outside of and upon the most conspicuous part of the finished article and its box, crate, or covering. It shall be the duty of the Commissioner of the Bureau of Labor Statistics, and the District Attorneys of the several counties, to enforce the provisions of this section, and of section —— of the Penal Code, and when, upon complaint or otherwise, the Commissioner of the Bureau of Labor Statistics has reason to believe that this section is being violated, he shall advise the District Attorney of the county wherein such alleged violation has occurred of that fact, giving the information in support of his conclusions, and such District Attorney shall at once institute the proper legal proceedings to compel compliance with this section. It shall be lawful for any person, persons, or corporation to furnish evidence as to the violations upon the part of any person, persons, or corporation, and upon the conviction of any such person, persons, or corporation one half of the fine provided for by section —— of the Penal Code, which shall be secured, shall be paid, upon certificate by the District Attorney, to the Commissioner of the Bureau of Labor Statistics, who shall use such money in investigating and securing information in regard to the violation of this section and in paying the expenses of such conviction.

SECTION 3249. A new section to be added to read as follows:

License not to discriminate against California products.

Sec. 3249. No license shall hereafter be imposed upon any person soliciting orders for the sale of any article or articles manufactured or produced in this State which, under the constitution or laws of the United States, cannot be legally imposed upon a person or persons soliciting orders in this State for the sale of a similar article in a like manner, made or produced in any of the states of the United States. This section shall, in no manner, affect the right or power of counties or municipalities to impose licenses upon persons conducting regular places of business therein.

We recommend that all of Chapter XV, Title VII, being inoperative under the Constitution (Sec. 12, Art. XI), be replaced by the following state license tax:

CHAPTER XV.

LICENSES.

ARTICLE I.

CORPORATION LICENSE TAX.

Sec. 3350. Upon all corporations doing business for profit in this State, and having a capital stock of not more than one hundred thousand dollars, other than corporations organized under the laws of this State exclusively for the purpose of distributing water to their stockholders and members, and corporations organized under the laws of this State exclusively for the purpose of mining in this State, there is assessed an annual license tax of one hundred dollars, to be paid to the Treasurer of the county in which such corporation or association has its office or principal place of business; such license to be paid on or before the first day of June of each and every year, and if not so paid upon the first day of June in any year, all acts of such corporations so delinquent shall be null and of no effect, and such corporations shall not further transact business in this State.

Sec. 3351. Upon all corporations doing business for profit in this State, and having a capital stock of more than one hundred thousand dollars, other than corporations organized under the laws of this State exclusively for the purpose of distributing water to their stockholders and members, and corporations organized under the laws of this State exclusively for the purpose of mining in this State, there is assessed an annual license tax of two hundred dollars, to be paid to the Treasurer of the county in which such corporation or association has its office or principal place of business; such license to be paid on or before the first day of June of each and every year, and if not so paid upon the first day of June in any year, all acts of such corporations so delinquent shall be null and of no effect, and such corporations shall not further transact business in this State.

ARTICLE II.

STATE EXCISE LICENSE TAX.

Sec. 3360. No person, firm, co-partnership, association, or corporation shall, after the first day of May, eighteen hundred and ninety-seven, sell or give away, or engage in the traffic in, spirituous, malt, or vinous liquor, to be drunk on the premises where sold or otherwise dispensed, without first having paid to the State of California, as herein

18—c

provided, an excise license tax of three hundred dollars, and procured therefor an excise license tax certificate and posted the same in a conspicuous place on the premises or place where such spirituous, malt, or vinous liquor is thereby permitted to be sold or otherwise dispensed for the time mentioned in such certificate; *provided,* that no state excise license tax shall be required to permit the giving away of malt or vinous liquors upon the premises where the same are manufactured. No excise license tax certificate, issued or procured hereunder, shall be authority for any person to sell or otherwise dispense, or to engage in the traffic in, spirituous, malt, or vinous liquor in more than one place of business.

Sec. 3361. No license shall hereafter be granted or permission given by any county, city and county, city, or town, or the authority thereof, to any person, partnership, association, or corporation, to sell or traffic in spirituous, malt, or vinous liquors, to be drunk on the premises where sold, unless the petition or application for such license or permit be accompanied by a certificate of the County Treasurer of the county in which is located the place where such sale or traffic in spirituous, malt, or vinous liquors is to be conducted, certifying that the applicant or petitioner is a holder of a state excise license tax certificate good for a period not shorter than that for which a license is sought from such local authority, or has deposited in such county treasury the sum of three hundred dollars for the purpose of paying the state excise license tax herein provided, and that said deposit was accompanied by a state excise license tax certificate issued by the Auditor of the county, which is to be delivered to the applicant or petitioner for such license upon the issuing of the license petitioned for by such local authority. Every license granted or permission given by any county, city and county, city, or town, in violation of the provisions of this article, shall be absolutely void.

Sec. 3362. When the application or petition for a license to sell or traffic in spirituous, malt, or vinous liquors, to be drunk upon the premises where sold, has been acted upon by the authorities of a county, city and county, city, or town, authorized to grant such license, the clerk of such authorities shall certify the action taken by the authorities on such application for a license, to the Treasurer and Auditor of the county, and should the action of such local authorities be a refusal to grant any license to such applicant for the sale or traffic in such liquors to be drunk on the premises where sold or otherwise dispensed, any sum deposited by such applicant with the County Treasurer, in anticipation of the granting of a license to him by such local authorities, shall be returned to him. If the action of such local authorities be to grant such license to such applicant, then the County Treasurer shall retain the sum deposited and deliver to the applicant the state excise license tax certificate deposited with him as provided by the next preceding section.

Sec. 3363. Any person, partnership, association, or corporation, required to take out a state license as in this chapter provided, who fails, neglects, or refuses to take out such license, or who carries on or attempts to carry on any business for the carrying on of which a license is required by this chapter, without first procuring such license, and every person, officer, director, or employé of any person, partnership, association, or corporation who carries on or attempts to carry on the business of such person, partnership, association, or corporation, without such license having been first taken out as authority therefor, shall be deemed guilty of a misdemeanor, and on conviction thereof shall be punished by a fine not less than five hundred dollars, or by imprisonment in the county jail not less than six months, or by both such fine and imprisonment. Any judgment that a defendant pay a fine, may also direct that he be imprisoned until the fine be satisfied, in the proportion of one day's imprisonment for every two dollars of the fine.

Sec. 3364. The Treasurer of each county shall, on the first day of August in each year, pay to the State Treasurer, at Sacramento, through the State Controller, as by law provided in other cases, all moneys collected up to that date in payment of corporation license tax, and of state excise license tax, and the State Controller and the State Treasurer are hereby required to receipt therefor to the County Treasurer so paying the amount held by him.

Sec. 3365. All moneys received by the County Treasurer as corporation license tax and as state excise license tax, shall be held by such Treasurer in a separate fund, to the credit of the State of California, and such fund shall be known as "The State License Tax Fund." He shall keep a ledger account showing all certificates for payment of license tax issued to him by the Auditor, all certificates returned by him for any reason, and the amount of moneys received as corporation license tax and as state excise license tax, and he shall certify to the State Controller, on the first day of each month, the amount of such license tax held by him.

Sec. 3366. It is hereby made the duty of each County Auditor to affix his official seal to, and sign, all certificates of payment of corporation tax, or of state excise license tax, and deliver them to the County Treasurer when requested so to do, and to charge him therewith in a book to be kept for such purpose. He shall also keep in his office the stubs of all certificates by him delivered to the County Treasurer, and his account shall show all state excise license tax certificates delivered by him and all such certificates returned to him.

Sec. 3367. The State Controller shall have printed suitable certificates of payment of the state excise license and corporation license tax, and shall furnish such certificates to the Auditors of the several counties of the State for the purposes herein provided. Such certificates shall be made in book form, with a stub attached, which stub shall be firmly bound in said book, and shall show in detail all facts stated in the certificate, particularly the county in which the tax is paid, the person, partnership, association, or corporation to whom the license is issued, the place where the business is located for which such license is granted, described by street number or other accurate description. It is hereby made the duty of every County Auditor in this State, to receive such excise license tax and corporation license tax books, and to fill out such license tax certificates when informed by the County Treasurer of his county that the sum required to pay such license tax has been deposited with him for the said license tax. And when such license tax certificate is issued by the Auditor to the Treasurer, the Treasurer shall receipt for the same upon the stub from which such license tax certificate was taken. It is made the duty of every County Treasurer to receive the excise license tax herein provided for, and to notify the Auditor that the sum necessary to pay the license tax has been deposited with him; to accept from said Auditor the state excise license tax and corporation license tax certificates, and receipt for the same to the Auditor, on the stub; and when an excise license tax certificate is to be returned for failure of the local authorities to grant the license petitioned for, the Treasurer shall indorse upon the face thereof, "Returned for failure of the authorities to grant license," sign his name thereto, and return the same so indorsed and signed to the County Auditor. The County Auditor shall certify to the State Controller, upon the first day of each month, all corporation license tax and all excise license tax certificates issued by him during the preceding month, and a statement of all excise license tax certificates that have been returned to him by the Treasurer on account of the action of the local authorities in refusing to grant the license. All license tax certificates, when issued by the Controller, shall be properly numbered, and charged to the County Auditor to whom they are sent, and such Auditor shall receipt for the same. The Controller shall open a proper account with each County Auditor in the State, wherein shall be shown all state excise license tax and corporation tax certificates issued, the amounts collected therefor, to whom each is issued, and the location of the place of business where the traffic in liquor is carried on, described by street number or other accurate description, and the principal place of business of the corporation paying such license.

Note.—It is the intention to provide a part of the revenue of the State from the licensing of liquor without diminishing or affecting the rights of counties, cities or towns to control that matter, as provided by Section 11, Article XI, of the Constitution, and without entering into the domain of local government as indicated by the general tendency of our laws. It is, however, a question that has been brought home to the taxpayers of the country that very much of the burden of taxes required for the maintenance of State prisons, asylums, and industrial schools, and for the care of paupers, indigents, and inebriates, is the result of the liquor traffic, and that the entire license imposed upon the traffic never finds its way into the channels tending to relieve the taxpayer at large, but is applied to the maintenance of streets, local improvements, and the expenses of the government of cities and towns without in any way tending to relieve the burden imposed upon outlying taxable property by reason of the existence of this traffic. While not intending to harass the traffic where it is the intention or wish of the authorities to grant licenses for its sale and distribution, and with no desire to enter the local domain for the purpose of legislating for or against the traffic, it is sought to provide that, if the license is to be granted, some portion of the amount paid shall be applied directly under the law to the discharge of the burden incurred by reason of such licensing.

TITLE VIII.

PROPERTY OF THE STATE.

SECTION 3547. To be amended to read as follows:

Sec. 3547. Upon receipt of the delinquent list the District Attorney must add thereto a notice that if the amount due is not paid in fifty days after the date thereof, he will commence suit to foreclose the interest of the purchasers in the lands, and must publish the list and notice once a week for five weeks, being five publications, in a daily or weekly newspaper published in the county, or if there is no newspaper published therein then he must post copies of the same in at least five public places in the county. He shall also file a copy of such notice with the County Treasurer, and shall notify him of the amount of costs incurred, and from time to time, as fast as additional costs are incurred, he shall notify him of the character and amount thereof.

> NOTE.—The amendment provides for notice to the Treasurer of all costs incurred, which will enable that official to include the same in any settlement he may make with the delinquent.

SECTION 3549. To be amended to read as follows:

Sec. 3549. Service of the summons must be made upon the defendant personally where such service can be had. Where personal service cannot be had the District Attorney must apply to the court, as provided for in section four hundred and twelve of the Code of Civil Procedure, for an order for the publication of such summons, and after such order has been obtained, the District Attorney must make service thereof by publication by publishing the same in some newspaper published in the county once a week for five weeks, being five publications, or if no newspaper is published in the county, then by posting one copy of the summons for four weeks at the court-house door of the county, and two copies in public places in the township where the land is situated.

> NOTE.—The amendment makes definite the publication necessary and provides directly for the order of publication of summons necessary to the validity of the judgment, which order in a large number of cases heretofore brought has not been applied for or obtained.

SECTION 3553. To be amended to read as follows:

Sec. 3553. The fees and costs for the publications, proceedings, and services provided for herein shall be as follows:

1. For printing delinquent list and notice, where such list contains not more than ten names, the publisher shall be paid five dollars per name; where such list contains more than ten and less than twenty names, he shall be paid four dollars per name; and where the notice contains twenty or more names, he shall be paid three dollars per name;

2. For publication of each summons, twenty dollars;

3. The County Recorder shall be paid twenty-five cents for filing each judgment, and twenty-five cents for issuing his certificate of such filing;

4. The District Attorney shall receive ten dollars for each suit brought.

If the District Attorney cannot procure the publication in this article provided for, for the sum above provided for, he shall report the same to the State Board of Examiners, who are authorized to make a contract for such publication, and pay therefor such sum as may be necessary.

> NOTE.—By establishing definite fees, the exorbitant charges heretofore made in many instances are sought to be avoided.

SECTION 3554. To be amended to read as follows:

Sec. 3554. In all cases where the title of purchasers of land from the State has been foreclosed, or attempted to be foreclosed, or that may hereafter be foreclosed, for non-payment of interest, said purchasers, their executors, administrators, or successors in interest, shall have twelve months after said foreclosures are or have been completed, within which to redeem such land by paying to the County Treasurer, for the benefit of the fund, or parties entitled thereto, all delinquent interest, and interest that would have accrued in case there would have been no foreclosure, also, all costs of foreclosure, to be paid to the fund, or the parties who paid said costs. When said payments are made, and indorsed on the certificate of purchase, specifying the amount paid as interest and for costs, and duly reported to the register of the land office, the annulments shall be canceled by said officer, and the rights of the purchasers shall thereby be fully restored.

> NOTE.—Section 3554, as it now exists, is dropped, and the Act of March 7, 1881 (Stats. 1881, page 65), is substituted.

SECTION 3555. To be amended to read as follows:

Sec. 3555. Upon the rendition of a judgment foreclosing the interest of the purchaser, or of his assigns, in the land, and annulling the certificate of purchase, judgment for costs must be entered against the defendant; but if execution issued thereon is returned not satisfied, the judgment and costs must be paid from the principal or interest paid by the purchaser, and if such payments so made by him are not sufficient in amount to pay such costs, the balance thereof shall be paid from the general fund of the State.

> NOTE.—The fund for the payment of foreclosure proceedings is increased from the amount paid at the time of the original entry, to include all sums paid by the delinquent. In case this sum should prove insufficient the creditor is then given recourse to the general fund, thus insuring the payment of his claim.

SECTION 3557. A new section to be added to read as follows:

Failure to pay works forfeiture.

Sec. 3557. Any person who hereafter enters or purchases any of the public lands of this State, or who contracts for the purchase thereof, or who has a certificate of purchase therefor issued to him, who shall, for the period of three years, fail to make the payments thereon required by law, shall forfeit all his right, title, and interest in and to said land, and shall forfeit all sums paid on account of the principal or interest of the purchase price thereof. At the expiration of three years from the time when any such sum became due, and which shall not have been paid, the register of the land office shall cancel the entry of such person upon his books, and thereafter such land shall be subject to reëntry and sale.

> NOTE.—This section is designed to dispense with the present vexatious and expensive method of foreclosing the claims of delinquent purchasers.

TITLE IX.

REVENUE.

CHAPTER I.

PROPERTY LIABLE TO TAXATION.

SECTION 3608. To be amended to read as follows:

Sec. 3608. Each person, firm, or corporation owning or having in his or its possession any shares of capital stock of any corporation, association, or joint-stock company, shall be assessed therefor. If the corporation, association, or joint-stock company has its principal place of business in this State, the assessable value of each share of its stock shall be ascertained by taking from the value of its entire capital stock the value of all the property assessed to such corporation, association, or joint-stock company, and dividing the remainder by the entire number of shares into which its capital stock is divided. The owner or holder of the capital stock in corporations, associations, or joint-stock companies, organized and existing under the laws of this State or of the United States, and whose principal place of business is situated within this State, shall be assessed for such capital stock in the county, city and county, city, or town where such principal place of business in this State is located, and not elsewhere. The owner or holder of capital stock in corporations, associations, or joint-stock companies, organized under the laws of this State, and whose principal place of business is not within this State, must be individually assessed for such stock in the county in which said owner or holder of stock resides. The owner of shares of stock, to be entitled to the deduction provided for in this section, must produce to the County Assessor a certificate of the assessment of the property of the corporation, association, or joint-stock company, when such property is situated in a county other than that in which the stock is assessable.

NOTE.—This section should be repealed, if not amended as herein suggested. The statement made by the first sentence is a species of subtle reasoning which, while it is true, has no relation to and cannot be made the basis for a law, as declared in the second sentence of this section. It is true that to assess all the property of a corporation, and also its shares of stock, at their market value, without deducting from the value of such shares the value of the corporate property assessed, would be double taxation, but it does not follow because that is so that no assessment should be made of the shares of stock of corporations, if they have any value over and above that given to them by the tangible property owned by the corporation. It has been uniformly held in the case of water companies which supply cities that the property of such companies subject to taxation includes their real estate, personal property, and their franchises, and that the true measure of the value of the franchises is the market value of all of the stock of the corporation, less the value of its real estate and all other property except the franchise. Therefore, the true method of assessment is to assess all tangible property of a corporation to such corporation, and the value of the franchise, which may be fluctuating, dependent upon the earnings of the corporation, to the capital stock as a whole.

Corporations may be assessed either by assessing their corporate property, including their franchises, or by assessing their capital stock, or by assessing a part of their corporate property, and the remainder of the taxable value to be assessed against them upon their capital stock. Since such capital stock has no value, except as the representative, in whole or in part, of such corporative property, the taxation of the whole of such stock and property at the same time would be double taxation ; therefore, either a part of one and a part of the other may be assessed and taxed at the same time, provided that the total valuation assessed and taxed against such corporation and the holders of its capital stock shall in all cases equal the value of its capital stock, including its corporate and other franchises. This section, as now in the Code, is in violation of the Constitution (Section 1, Article XIII), which provides that stock is property. It is also in violation of the spirit of our laws, for by it is prevented the payment of their just taxes by national banks ; the statutes of the United States requiring as follows : "Nothing therein shall prevent the assessment of shares of stock to their owners under State law," subject to two restrictions : (1) "Taxation shall not be greater than is assessed upon the money capital in the hands of individual citizens of the State, and shares of stock of non-residents of the State shall be taxed in the city and town where the bank is situated, but not elsewhere." The United States laws provide that the real property of national banks shall be assessed to the corporation, and stock to the stockholders, under the restrictions above mentioned.

In the amendment presented we have sought to overcome all obstacles apparent in the present revenue laws to the equitable assessment of all corporations and of the property of individuals.

The present Section 3608, as it now stands, and the deduction of credits, or solvent credits, make it impossible to assess national banks. Of the deduction of credits we speak in Section 3641. We present an amendment to Section 3608, which we think provides fully, as far as the same may be done under our present Constitution, for the assessment of the property and stock of corporations, including national banks.

SECTION 3609. A new section to be added to read as follows:

Sec. 3609. Every association or corporation organized under the laws of any other State, or of any country foreign to the United States, and doing business in this State, as a bank, banking association, or banking corporation, shall be assessed and taxed as are like associations or corporations existing under the laws of this State.

SECTION 3610. A new section to be added to read as follows:

Sec. 3610. Every association or corporation, other than banking associations or banking corporations, existing under the laws of other States, or of countries foreign to the United States, doing business in this State, shall be assessed on the full number of shares of the capital stock of such association or corporation. For the purpose of assessment and taxation in this State, the value of the capital stock of such association or corporation shall be determined by the gross receipts or earnings of such association or corporation on the business transacted in this State for the year next preceding the first Monday in March, the basis of value being the value of a franchise held by a like association or corporation existing under the laws of this State, and making like earnings. The tax levied on the corporation's capital stock, on the assessment herein provided, shall be paid by such corporation as personal property taxes are paid in the county where the principal place of business of such association or corporation is located.

CHAPTER II.

DEFINITIONS OF TERMS.

Sec. 3617. Whenever the terms mentioned in this section are employed in this Code, they are employed in the sense hereinafter affixed to them, to wit:

First—The term " property " includes moneys, credits, bonds, stocks, dues, franchises, and all other matters and things, real, personal, and mixed, capable of private ownership.

Second—The term "real estate" includes:

1. The possession of, claim to, ownership of, or right to the possession of, land;

2. All mines, minerals, and quarries in and under the land;

3. All timber belonging to individuals, partnerships, associations, or corporations, growing or being on the lands of the United States, and all rights and privileges appertaining thereto, and interests therein;

4. A mortgage, deed of trust, contract, or other obligation by which a debt is secured, wherein land is pledged for the payment or discharge thereof, shall, for the purposes of assessment and taxation, be deemed and treated as an interest in the land so pledged;

5. Improvements.

Third—The term "improvements" includes:

1. All buildings, fences, and other structures, except telegraph and telephone lines, erected upon, built, made, or placed in, or affixed to, the land;

2. All fruit trees, nut-bearing trees, and ornamental trees and vines not of natural growth; but fruit and nut-bearing trees, while under four years of age from the time of planting in orchard form, and grape-vines, while under three years of age from the time of planting in vineyard form, are exempt from taxation.

Fourth—The term "personal property" includes everything which is capable of private ownership, not included within the meaning of the terms "real estate" and "improvements."

Fifth—The terms "value," "actual value," "full value," and "full cash value" mean the amount at which property would be taken in payment of a just debt due from a solvent debtor.

Sixth—The term "credits" means all debts not secured by mortgage, deed of trust, or other lien on real or personal property, due or owing to the person, firm, corporation, or association assessed.

Seventh—The term "debts" means all liabilities of whatsoever kind, which are unsecured by deed of trust, mortgage, or other lien on real or personal property, due or owing to any person, firm, corporation, or association, and subject to be assessed in this State as credits to any person, firm, corporation, or association; but credits, claims, rights, and demands due, owing, or accruing to any person, for or on account of money deposited with savings and loan institutions or corporations, shall, for the purposes of taxation, be deemed and treated as a part of, and as represented in, the property of such institution or corporation, and shall, when the property of such institution or corporation is assessed and taxed, be deemed thereby assessed and taxed, and, to avoid double taxation, shall not be assessed or taxed to such person owning or claiming them.

Eighth—A ferry-boat is a vessel traversing across any of the waters of the State, between two points, employed for the transfer of passengers or freight, authorized or permitted by law so to do, and also any boat employed as a part of the system of a railroad for the transfer of passengers or freight, and plying between two points.

NOTES.—Under "Second—2" two subjects, mines and timber, were treated, and it has accordingly been again subdivided.

Under "Third—2" young fruit trees and vines are made exempt from taxation in the new Section, instead of being treated as not being improvements, as in the old section. They are, in fact, improvements, but are exempted from taxation by Section 12¾, Article XIII, Constitution.

Under "Fourth," "capable" is substituted for "subject," to make the language conform exactly to Section 1, Article XIII, Constitution.

Under "Fifth," other equivalents of value and full cash value, which are used in the Constitution and statutes, are inserted.

Under "Sixth," material changes are made. It is "credits," not merely "solvent credits," that are taxable by Section 1, Article XIII, Constitution.

A corresponding change is made in the section requiring the assessed to make a statement or return to the Assessor. The purpose of this change is to leave no discretion to the assessed as to what credits he will return. If he be instructed to return solvent credits, a discretion is left to him as to what credits are solvent; but if the requirement of the statute be that he shall return all credits, then his duty is made simple, and purely ministerial, and he can hardly make a mistake. The value of these credits will depend upon the degree of their solvency, and will vary, according to their character, from the amount represented on their face to nothing. But the Assessor, and not the assessed, is made by law the judge of the assessable value; that is to say, of the degree of solvency of credits.

Under "Seventh," the definition of "debts" has been changed so as to make it the exact opposite of "credits." The rule allowing a deduction of debts due bona fide residents of this State from credits is abrogated in this revision, and, therefore, the only purpose of considering debts in making assessment under the theory here adopted, is to secure a check upon the credits returned. The credits returned by all the creditors ought to equal the debts returned by all the debtors.

In the old text it was stated, the deposits in savings banks should be deemed an interest in the property of the bank. On this theory they ought to be taxed. This phraseology has been so changed as to cause them to be deemed a part of the property of the bank, and thus taxable as such only.

"Eighth" is a part of Section 3643 in the old text, brought here among the other definitions. The language of this definition as it stood in Section 3643 contained so many limiting terms as to render it subject to be almost entirely construed away. These have been omitted so as to leave it general, and of more practical value.

In the following arrangement it is sought to put each subject under the proper head with reference to the subject treated, without regard to the position now held as to number of section:

CHAPTER III.

ARTICLE I.

ASSESSMENT OF PROPERTY.

SECTION 3620.   New section.

Sec. 3620.   All taxable property shall be assessed at its full cash value.

NOTE.—Taken from Section 3627.

SECTION 3621.   New section.

Sec. 3621.   Every mortgage, deed of trust, contract, or other obligation by which a debt is secured, shall, for the purposes of assessment and taxation, be deemed, and shall be, assessed at its full face value; *provided*, that reduction therefrom may be made of any payment or payments made thereon by the debtor prior to the first Monday in March, at twelve o'clock meridian, if notice of such payment, in writing, shall have been filed with the Assessor, by the mortgagee, or other person owning such security, prior to the assessment thereof.

NOTE.—Taken from Section 3627—constructed to provide that no reduction from face value shall be made except on notice of payment.

Sec. 3622.   All lawful money of the United States has value equal to, and shall be assessed at, the actual amount thereof.

Sec. 3623.   Land, and the improvements thereon, shall be separately assessed. Cultivated and uncultivated land, of the same quality, and similarly situated, shall be assessed at the same value. Land shall be assessed in parcels, or subdivisions, not exceeding six hundred and forty acres each; lands which have been sectionized by the United States government shall be assessed, by accurate description, by sections, or fractions of sections; and lands which have not been so sectionized, or which do not conform to the boundaries of regular government subdivisions, shall be assessed in tracts containing not more than six hundred and forty acres, and shall be described by accurate description by metes and bounds. Lands sold by the State, for which no patent has been issued, shall be assessed the same as other lands, but the owner shall be entitled to a reduction from such assessed valuation in the amount due the State as principal upon the purchase price. A mortgage, deed of trust, contract, or other obligation by which a debt is secured, shall, for the purposes of assessment and taxation, be deemed and treated as an interest in the property affected thereby. Except as to railroads, and other quasi-public corporations, in case of debts so secured, the value of the property affected by such mortgage, deed of trust, contract, or other obligation, less the value of such security, shall be assessed and taxed to the owner of the property, and the value of such security shall be assessed and taxed to the owner thereof, in the county, city, or district in which the property affected thereby is situated. The taxes so levied shall be a lien upon the property and security, and may be paid by either party to such security; if paid by the owner of the security, the tax so levied upon the property affected thereby shall become a part of the debt so secured. If the owner of the property shall pay the tax so levied on such security, it shall constitute a payment thereon, and, to the extent of such payment, a full discharge thereof. If any such security or indebtedness shall be paid by any such debtor or debtors after assessment, and before the tax thereon shall have been levied and become payable, the amount of such levy may likewise be retained by such debtor or debtors, and shall be computed according to the tax levy for the preceding year; unless the new levy shall already have been made; in which case such amount shall be computed and retained according to such new levy. And every contract by which a debtor is obliged to pay any tax or assessment on money loaned, or on any mortgage, deed of trust, or other lien, shall, as to any interest specified therein, and as to such tax or assessment, be null and void.

Sec. 3624. All personal property consigned for sale to any person within this State, from any place outside of this State, must be assessed and taxed in like manner as other property.

Sec. 3625. Where ferries connect more than one county, the wharves, storehouses, and all stationary property belonging to or connected with such ferries, must be assessed, and the taxes paid, in the county where located. The value of the franchise, and watercraft, and of all toll bridges connecting more than one county, must be assessed in equal proportions in the counties connected by such ferries, or toll bridges. All vessels, except ferry-boats, which may be registered, of every class which are by law required to be registered, must be assessed, and the taxes thereon paid, only in the county, or city and county, where the same are registered, enrolled, or licensed. Vessels registered, licensed, or enrolled out of, and plying in whole or in part in the waters of this State, must be assessed in this State, in the county, or city and county, in which the owner or part owner thereof resides; and all boats and small craft not required to be registered must be assessed in the county, or city and county, in which the owner or part owner thereof resides; *provided*, that all vessels, boats, and craft required to be assessed in the county, or city and county, where the owner or part owner thereof resides, shall be assessed in each such county, or city and county, to the extent, but only to the extent, of the value of the interest of such owner or part owner therein.

Sec. 3626. The right to collect compensation for all water appropriated or held by any person, co-partnership, or corporation, for sale, rental, or distribution, for the use of which compensation is collected of any county, city and county, city, or town, or the inhabitants thereof, shall be assessed as a franchise. Water ditches constructed for mining, manufacturing, or irrigating purposes must be assessed and described the same as real estate, by the Assessor of the county, at a rate per mile for such portion of such property as lies within his county.

Sec. 3627. All telegraph and telephone lines shall be described in the same manner as real estate is described, but assessed as personal property, by the Assessor of the county, at a rate per mile for such portion of such property as lies within his county. The box, transmitters, and appliances of all telephone lines installed in buildings, or places of any kind, for which compensation is collected, shall be assessed as hereinafter provided. The right to collect toll by wagon and turnpike roads shall be assessed as a franchise at a rate per mile for such portion of such property as lies in the county.

Sec. 3628. The franchise, roadway, roadbed, rails, and rolling-stock of all railroads operated in more than one county in this State, shall be assessed by the State Board of Equalization, as hereinafter provided for. Other franchises, if granted by the authorities of a county, city, or city and county, must be assessed in the county, city, or city and county within which they were granted; if granted by any other authority, they must be assessed in the county in which the corporations, firms, or persons owning or holding them have their principal place of business. All corporations doing business in this State, both those organized under the laws of this State, and those organized under the laws of other states and of foreign countries, shall pay to the Treasurer of the county in which its principal office or place of business is located, such annual state license tax as may be required by law. A state license tax for the sale and traffic in spirituous and malt liquors shall be paid by all persons, firms, or corporations before engaging in such sale or traffic, in the county in which they intend to carry on such sale and traffic.

SECTION 3629. To be repealed.

NOTE.—Its provisions as amended to meet this theory are found in Section 3641 hereof

SECTION 3630. The text is new.

Sec. 3630. Each county and each city and county of the State shall form an assessment district, and shall be divided into subdivisions, as follows:

First—Supervisor districts, which shall be subdivided into road districts;

Second—Said road districts, which shall be subdivided into school districts;

Third—Said school districts, which shall be subdivided into districts of valuation of real estate;

Fourth—Said districts of valuation of real estate.

Maps shall be prepared by the County Surveyor of each county, under direction of the County Assessor of such county, as follows:

First—An outline map of the county, showing, in outlines in different colors, the supervisor districts, road districts, school districts, and districts of valuation of real estate;

Second—An outline map of each supervisor district, showing, in outlines in different colors, each road district, school district, and district of valuation of real estate;

Third—An outline map of each road district, showing, in outlines in different colors, each school district, and district of valuation of real estate;

Fourth—An outline map of each school district, showing, in different colors, each district of valuation of real estate;

Fifth—A map of each district of valuation of real estate, showing all property held by different owners, cultivated and uncultivated, that is of the same quality or general character, and which shall be assessed at the same value.

Land lying in more than one of the foregoing districts, and divided by the boundaries of such districts, owned by the same owner, shall be so divided, described, and assessed as to make the assessment complete as to each district. Each map shall show by number, or other designation, the county and district, or districts, delineated thereon, as follows:

County of_____
Supervisor District No. _____
_____Road District (or Road District No. __)
_____ _____School District.
District of Valuation of Real Estate No. ____

The foregoing map shall be made in duplicate, and one thereof shall be filed in the office of the County Assessor, and the other in the office of the State Board of Equalization, at, or before, the completion of the assessment.

In a county in which is situated an incorporated city, or town, a map

of such city, or town, shall be made under direction of the County
Assessor of such county, by the city engineer, or surveyor of the city or
town, to be delineated as follows:

First—An outline map showing the boundaries of the city, or town,
and all its subdivisions into blocks, lots, streets, and other ways and
places:

Second—A map showing the outline, in different colors, of each
"block" or "tract" of district of valuation of real estate, if such district
contains more than one block or tract.

Districts of valuation may be subdivided as convenience may suggest,
showing the subdivision of property, city or town blocks or lots; *provided*, that all maps of a district of valuation shall be kept together,
and so numbered, or designated, as to show the valuation district,
school, road, and supervisor district, or ward, town, or city.

The county and district maps hereby required shall be paid for from
the county general fund of each county, and the bills therefor shall be
presented to, and passed upon and allowed by, the Board of Supervisors
of such county, in like manner as other county charges. The maps of
cities and towns hereby required shall be paid for out of the general
funds of such cities and towns, and the bills therefor shall be presented,
passed upon, and allowed in like manner as are other claims and
charges against the said general funds of such cities and towns presented,
passed upon, and allowed.

The State Board of Equalization shall provide the forms for such
maps and plat books, and shall require such maps and plat books to be
uniform throughout the State, to be indexed to show owners' names, to
give ample data for accurate description for all purposes of assessment
and taxation, show improvements, and assessed valuation of each
separate holding, and of each several quality of land therein, and the
acreage, and the kinds of trees and vines thereon.

Sec. 3631. All property must be assessed in the county, or city and
county, city, town, township, and district where the same is situated,
in the name of the person, firm, association, or corporation who owns it,
or in whose name such property stands upon the records of the county.

Sec. 3632. When a person is assessed as agent, trustee, bailee,
guardian, executor, or administrator, his representative designation
must be added to his name, and the assessment entered on a separate
line from his individual assessment.

Sec. 3633. The undistributed or unpartitioned property of deceased
persons may be assessed to the heirs, guardians, executors, or administrators; and a payment of taxes made by either binds all parties in
interest for their equal proportions.

Sec. 3634. Money and property in litigation, in possession of a County Treasurer, of a court, County Clerk, or receiver, must be assessed to such treasurer, clerk, receiver, or the judge of such court, and the taxes thereon to be paid under direction of the court.

Sec. 3635. Any property discovered by the Assessor to have escaped assessment for the last preceding year, if such property is in the ownership or under the control of the same person who owned or controlled it for such preceding year, may be assessed at double its value.

Sec. 3636. Any property willfully concealed, removed, transferred, or misrepresented by the owner, or agent thereof, to evade taxation, upon discovery, must be assessed at not exceeding ten times its value, and the assessment so made must not be reduced by the Board of Supervisors.

Sec. 3637. Lands once described on the assessment book need not be described a second time; but any person claiming the same, and desiring to be assessed therefor, may have his name inserted with that of the person to whom such land is assessed.

NOTE.—The foregoing sections, 3631 to 3637, are subjects in the present law placed here for order.

ARTICLE II.

DUTIES OF ASSESSORS.

Sec. 3640. The Assessor, or his deputies, must, before the first Monday in June of each year, in each of the counties, and cities and counties, visit each house and place of business in their districts, and enroll in a field enrollment book, in such form as may be required by the State Board of Equalization, all male persons residing in said county over eighteen years of age and under sixty years of age on the first Monday in March of that year. On such field enrollment book shall be stated whether the person enrolled is liable to a state poll tax, a road poll tax, or military duty; give the number of the poll tax receipt, and the amount paid, if poll taxes are collected; where his residence is, post office address, giving street and number, if any; occupation; by whom employed; whether the owner of real estate; the State or country of nativity; whether naturalized or not, and any reason that may be given why poll tax was not paid. From such enrollment books the military roll, as required by section eighteen hundred and ninety-seven, and the roll of poll-tax payers, required by section thirty-eight hundred and fifty-seven, shall be made. Personal property unsecured by real estate must be assessed and taxes collected at the time of enrollment of persons for poll taxes; receipts must be issued for personal property tax from a stub-book, having the stubs numbered the same as the receipt; such

19—c

stub-books shall have a line for the name of the person assessed, the amount of the assessment, the rate collected, and lines for the items assessed for collection, the total amount, the date of collection, and the name of the deputy making the collection. Such blank personal-tax receipt books shall be furnished for such purpose by the Auditor, and all unused receipts must be turned in by the Assessor with his settlement for personal property taxes on the first Monday in August of each year. The Assessor, or his deputy, shall also note on the assessment statement, against each tract of land or lot assessed, the condition of surface of such tract or lot of land assessed, the condition of surface of each tract, using the words level, rolling, broken, hilly, or rocky; also, the quality of soil, using the words fruit, grain, timber, pasture, or rocks; also, whether it is wet, dry, semi-moist, or has water-rights; also, the kind and value of improvements located on each tract or lot. .

Sec. 3641. The County Assessor must, between the first Monday in March and the first Monday in July of each year, ascertain the names of all taxable inhabitants, and all the property in his county subject to taxation, except such as is required to be assessed by the State Board of Equalization, and must assess such property to the persons by whom it was owned or claimed, or in whose possession or control it was, at twelve o'clock meridian on the first Monday in March next preceding; but no mistake in the name of the owner, or supposed owner, of real property shall render the assessment thereof invalid. He must exact from each person a statement, under oath, setting forth specifically all the real and personal property owned by such person, or in his possession, or under his control, at twelve o'clock meridian on the first Monday in March. Such statement shall be in writing, showing separately:

1. All property belonging to, claimed by, or in the possession or under the control or management of such person;

2. All property belonging to, claimed by, or in the possession or under the control or management of any firm of which such person is a member;

3. All property belonging to, claimed by, or in the possession or under the control or management of any corporation of which such person is president, secretary, cashier, or managing agent;

4. The county in which such property is situated, or in which it is liable to taxation, and (if liable to taxation in the county in which the statement is made) also the city, town, township, school district, road district, or other revenue districts in which it is situated;

5. An accurate description of all lands, in parcels or subdivisions not exceeding six hundred and forty acres each, describing the same by sections and subdivisions of sections in case of all tracts of land which have been sectionized by the United States government; improvements, per-

sonal property, including all vessels, steamers, and other watercraft; and all taxable state, county, city, or other municipal or public bonds, and the taxable bonds of any person, firm, or corporation, and all deposits of money, gold-dust, or other valuables, and the names of the persons with whom such deposits are made, and the places in which they may be found; all mortgages, deeds of trust, contracts, and other obligations by which a debt is secured, and the property in the county affected thereby;

6. All credits, unsecured by deed of trust, mortgage, or other lien on real or personal property, due or owing to such person, or any firm of which he is a member, or due or owing to any corporation of which he is president, secretary, cashier, or managing agent; all credits shall be itemized so as to show the face amount of each thereof, and the name and place of residence of the debtor owing the same. All debts unsecured by trust deed, mortgage, or other lien on real or personal property, due or owing by the person, firm, or corporation making such statement, to any person, firm, association, or corporation subject to be assessed therefor in this State as credits; all such debts shall be itemized so as to show the face amount thereof, and the name and place of residence of the creditor to whom the same are due.

All firms, persons, associations, or corporations, conducting or operating any works or lines for the purpose of supplying any county, city and county, city, or town, or the inhabitants thereof, with gas, water, electric light, heat, or power, telegraph or telephone lines, or street-car lines, or other business, under a franchise granted by such county, city and county, city, or town, or by the State, shall, in addition to the statement of its property, file with the Assessor, on or before the first day of April of each year, a statement of its gross receipts for the year next preceding the first Monday in March; also, the amount of its operating expenses; also, a copy or copies of any and all statements and showings made by such corporation to any court, board, council, commission, or public body since the first Monday of March in the year next preceding, as the basis for the fixing by such court, board, council, commission, or other public body, of rates, freights, fares, or other charges by or compensation to such corporation, firm, association, or person; also, the amount of expenditures for betterments, extensions, and permanent improvements; the amount expended for repairs and maintenance; the amount of bonded indebtedness; if a corporation, the amount of dividends declared and paid, and whether in cash or stock, or other form; the amount of capital stock; the amount of capital stock paid up, if any, or the amount of capital stock subscribed, and the amount assessed thereon and paid; if a person or firm, the amount of money invested, net income, or profit. The statement made by a corporation shall be made and verified by the president and secretary thereof, if residents of the county, or if the principal office of the corporation be located in the county. If they do not reside in the county, or if the principal office be not in the county, the statement shall be made and verified by the managing agent, or other person in possession or control of the property. Whenever one member of a firm has made a statement showing the property of the firm, another member of the firm need not include such property in the statement made by him. But his statement must show the name of the person who made the statement in which such property is included. The Assessor may fill out the statement herein required to be made, at the time he presents it, or he may deliver it to the person and require him, within an appointed time, to return the same to him, properly filled out. If any person, after demand made by the Assessor, neglects or refuses to give, under oath, the statement herein provided for, or to comply with the other requirements of this title, the Assessor must note the refusal on the assessment book, opposite his name, and must make an estimate of the value of the property of such person; and the value so fixed by the Assessor must not be reduced by the Board of Supervisors; but nothing herein shall be construed as abridging the power of the Assessor to compel the making of the statement herein required, as provided in section thirty-six hundred and sixty. The Board of Supervisors of each county shall furnish the Assessor with "blank forms" of the statements herein provided for, to which shall be affixed the following affidavit, to be made and subscribed by the person making the statement:

"I, ———, do swear that I am a resident of the county of (naming it); that the above list contains a full and correct statement of all property subject to taxation which I, or any firm of which I am a member, or any corporation, association, or company of which I am president, cashier, secretary, or managing agent, owned, claimed, possessed, or controlled, at twelve o'clock meridian on the first Monday in March last, and which is not already assessed this year, and that I have not, in any manner whatsoever, transferred or disposed of any property, or placed any property out of said county, or my possession, for the purpose of avoiding any assessment upon the same, or of making this statement; and that the debts therein stated as owing by me are the only debts owing by me to any person, firm, association, or corporation, subject to assessment thereon, in this State, as credits."

The affidavit to a statement on behalf of a firm, or corporation, must state the principal place of business of the firm, or corporation, and in other respects must conform substantially to the preceding form.

NOTE.—From Subdivision 6 of Section 3641 is omitted the provision for deducting debts due bona fide residents of this State from solvent credits. The reason for this omission is that the provision is a discrimination in favor of moneyed capital, other than that invested in national banks, and makes it impossible, with the provision in existence, to assess national banks in this State. This is made so by Section 5219, Revised Statutes U. S., as construed in the case of *Miller* vs. *Heil-*

bron, 58 Cal. 133, and *The Bank of Commerce* vs. *New York City*, 2 Blatchford, 620. The United States Statutes provide that national banks may be assessed under State law in the manner following: The real estate of the association must be assessed to the association, the shares of stock in the association must be assessed to the owner or holder of such shares. The Legislature may direct the manner and place of taxing all the shares of national banking associations within the State, subject to two restrictions: that the taxation shall not be at any greater rate than is assessed upon other moneyed capital in the hands of individual citizens of such State, and that the shares of any national banking association owned by non-residents shall be taxed where the bank is located, and not elsewhere. The change made in Section 3608, with the omissions from Subdivision 6, Section 3641, will permit the assessment of national banks as other moneyed capital is assessed in this State.

Sec. 3642. When the Assessor has not received from the owner of a tract of land the statement required by section thirty-six hundred and forty-one, or when such statement does not sufficiently describe a tract of land to enable the Assessor to assess the same as required by law, and the owner or his agent, or in case they cannot be found, or are unknown, the person in possession thereof, neglects, for ten days after demand by the Assessor, to furnish said Assessor with such description, the Assessor shall cite such owner, or agent, or person in possession, to appear before the Superior Court of the county in which such land is situated, within five days after service of such citation; and the Superior Court shall, upon the day named in such citation, to the exclusion of all other business, proceed to hear the return and answer of the said owner, or agent, or person in possession, to the said citation, and if the court shall find that the land has not been surveyed or divided into subdivisions of six hundred and forty acres or less, so that each part, or parcel, may be accurately described by metes and bounds, and assessed as required by law, then the court shall, by order duly entered in open court, direct the County Surveyor to make a survey and define the boundaries and location of said land by parcels or subdivisions, not exceeding six hundred and forty acres each, and deliver the same to the County Assessor. The expense of making such survey and description by the County Surveyor shall be a lien upon the land, and shall, when approved by the said Superior Court, be certified by said court to the Tax Collector of the county where the land is situated, and be added to the taxes upon said land, and be collected as other taxes are collected.

Sec. 3643. All property shall be assessed in the true name of the owner thereof, if his true name be known to the Assessor. If the name of the owner of any property appears of record in the office of the Recorder of the county where the property is situated, the name so appearing of record shall be deemed to be the true name of such owner. If the name of the owner of the property does not appear of record as aforesaid, and cannot, after diligent inquiry, be ascertained by the Assessor, then, but not otherwise, such property must be assessed to unknown owners. Whenever any property, or any interest therein, stands upon the records of any county in the name of more persons than one, or whenever any person, other than the person in whose name the property stands upon the records of the county, or is being assessed, claims an interest therein, and desires to be assessed therefor, such property need not be described more than once upon the assessment book, but the names of all persons appearing of record, as aforesaid, and the names of all claimants to said land who desire to be assessed therefor, as aforesaid, must be inserted in the assessment of such property as owners thereof and must be separately indexed. In no case shall property be assessed to joint or other partial owners thereof, by a name in the form of a firm, or partnership name, except when such property is actually owned, or appears upon the records of the county as being owned, by a partnership, or firm; and in all cases, other than partnership ownership, property shall be assessed to the persons owning the same, or any interest therein, or desiring to be assessed therefor, by their individual names.

Sec. 3644. If the owner or claimant of any property, not listed by another person, is absent or unknown, the Assessor must make an estimate of the value of such property.

Sec. 3645. The Assessor, as soon as he receives the statement of any taxable property situated in another county, must make a copy of such statement for each county in which the same is situated or assessable, and transmit the same, by mail or express, to the Assessor of the proper county, who must assess the same as other taxable property therein.

SECTIONS 3646, 3647, 3648, and 3649 to be repealed.

NOTE.—The substance of these sections is included in preceding sections, treating of the same or like subjects.

Sec. 3650. The Assessor must prepare an assessment book, with appropriate headings, as directed by the State Board of Equalization, in which must be listed all property within the county, under the appropriate head:

1. The name of the person to whom the property is assessed;

2. Land, by township, range, section, or fractional section, not exceeding six hundred and forty acres in any one tract; and when such land is not a congressional division, or subdivision, then by metes and bounds, or other accurate description sufficient to identify it, giving an estimate of the number of acres (not exceeding in any tract six hundred and forty acres), locality, and the improvements thereon. When any tract of land is situated in two or more school, road, or other revenue districts of the county, the part in each such revenue district

must be separately assessed. The improvements shall be assessed against the particular section, tract, or lot of land upon which they are located;

3. City and town lots, naming the city or town, and the number of the lot and block, according to the system of numbering on the official map of such city or town, which must be referred to by the book and page of its official record, and the improvements thereon;

4. All personal property, showing the number, kind, amount, and quality; but a failure to enumerate in detail such personal property shall not invalidate the assessment;

5. The cash value of real estate, other than city or town lots;

6. The cash value of improvements on such real estate;

7. The cash value of city and town lots;

8. The cash value of improvements on city and town lots;

9. The cash value of improvements on real estate assessed to persons other than the owners of the real estate;

10. The cash value of all personal property, exclusive of money;

11. The amount of money;

12. The assessment of the franchise, roadway, roadbed, rails, and rolling-stock of any railroad, as apportioned to his county by the State Board of Equalization, and also such other apportionments of such franchises, roadways, roadbeds, rails, and rolling-stock as may be made by such board, and furnished to him for the purpose of taxation in any district of his county. Taxable improvements owned by any person, firm, association, or corporation, located upon any land exempt from taxation, shall, as to the manner of assessment, be assessed as other real estate upon the assessment book. No value shall, however, be assessed against the exempt land, nor under any circumstances shall the land be charged with or become responsible for the assessment made against any taxable improvements located thereon;

13. The school, road, and other revenue districts in which each piece of property assessed is situated;

14. The total value of all property;

15. When any property, except that owned by a railroad, or other quasi-public corporation, is subject to or affected by a mortgage, deed of trust, contract, or other obligation by which a debt is secured, he must enter, in the proper column, the value of such security, and deduct the same. In entering assessments containing credits the face amount thereof must be specified, and he must enter in the proper column the value thereof, as in the case of other personal property. Each franchise must be separately entered and valued in the assessment book without combining the same with other property, or with the valuation thereof, except in the column of totals.

NOTE.—Amended to conform to requirements of the preceding sections.

Sec. 3651. All property of persons, firms, or corporations conducting or operating gas supply lines, electric light, heat, or power supply lines, water supply lines, telegraph or telephone lines, street railway lines, wharf, ferry, toll-bridge or toll-road, or other business conducted or operated under a franchise granted therefor by any county, city and county, city, or town, or of this State, shall be listed in a book or books to be designated as "Book of Assessed Franchises," in which shall be shown, under appropriate heads:

1. All real estate and property described as real estate;
2. All other property except the franchise;
3. The franchise.

It shall be shown, in the manner directed by the State Board of Equalization, or should they fail to direct the manner of showing, then by the Assessor of each county, in the "Book of Assessed Franchises":

1. The gross earnings for each year of the person, firm, or corporation conducting or operating any of the gas, electric, water, telegraph or telephone, or street railway lines, or other business operated under a franchise, as aforesaid, for a year next preceding the first Monday in March;

2. The amount of the operating expenses;

3. The amount expended for betterments, extensions, and permanent improvements;

4. The amount expended for repairs and maintenance;

5. The amount of bonded indebtedness;

6. If a corporation, the amount of dividends declared and paid, whether in cash, stock, or other form, and what;

7. The amount of capital stock;

8. The amount of capital stock paid up, if any, or the amount of capital stock subscribed, and the amount assessed thereon and paid;

9. If a firm or person, the amount of money invested;

10. The gross income, and the sources of it.

All property of corporations, other than franchises mentioned in section thirty-six hundred and fifty-one, shall be listed in a book or books designated as "Corporation Assessments." All property of each corporation shall be described under appropriate heads, following the name of the corporation assessed.

The Assessor of each county shall keep a book, or books, designated "State License Tax," in which he shall keep a record of all corporations liable to payment of corporation state license tax, and of all persons, firms, or corporations liable to payment of state excise license tax.

Sec. 3652. On or before the first Monday in July of each year, the Assessor must complete his assessment book. He and his deputies must take and subscribe an affidavit in the assessment book, to be substantially as follows:

"I, ——, Assessor (or Deputy Assessor, as the case may be) of —— county, do swear that between the first Monday in March and the first Monday in July, eighteen hundred and ——, I have made diligent inquiry and examination to ascertain all the property within the county (or within the subdivision thereof assessed by me, as the case may be) subject to assessment by me, and that the same has been assessed on the assessment book, equally and uniformly, according to the best of my judgment, information, and belief, at its full cash value; and that I have faithfully complied with the duties imposed on the Assessor under the revenue laws; and that I have not imposed any unjust or double assessment through malice or ill-will, or otherwise; nor allowed any one to escape a just and equal assessment through favor or reward, or otherwise."

But the failure to take or subscribe such affidavit, or any affidavit, will not, in any manner, affect the validity of the assessment.

Sec. 3653. 1. On or before the first Monday in July of each year, the Assessor must furnish each incorporated city and town within the county a complete certified copy of his assessment book, so far as such assessment book pertains to property within the limits of said incorporated cities and towns, which certified copy shall be filed with the clerk of said city or town, and shall thereupon be and become the assessment roll of such city or town.

2. The Assessor must, on the first, tenth, and twentieth days of each month, file with the clerk of each incorporated city or town within the county, a description of all personal property, the name and address, by street and number, of the owners, and assessed value thereof, whenever the tax on such property is collected by the Assessor.

3. The Assessor may charge incorporated cities and towns —— cents per folio of one hundred words for each certified copy of his assessment book, and —— cents per folio of one hundred words for each description of personal property.

NOTE.—The county assessment is made the assessment of the city or town, subject to the local board of equalization.

Sec. 3654. As soon as completed the assessment book, together with the map books, statements, and military roll, must be delivered by the Assessor to the clerk of the Board of Supervisors, who must immediately give notice thereof to each member of the Board of Supervisors. In the meantime, the assessment book, map books, and statements must remain in his office for the inspection of all persons interested. After the Board of Equalization has completed its labors, the map books and statements shall be returned to the County Assessor's office, and shall be kept in such office for future reference.

Sec. 3655. On the second Monday in July of each year, the Assessor of each county must transmit to the State Board of Equalization, in such form as said board shall require, a statement showing:

1. The several kinds of personal property;

2. The average and total value of each kind;

3. The number of live stock, number of bushels of grain, number of gallons of wine or liquors, number of pounds or tons of any article sold by the pound or ton;

4. When practicable, the separate value of each class of land, specifying the classes and the number of acres of each;

5. A true statement of the agricultural and industrial pursuits and products of the county, with such other statistical information as said board shall require.

NOTE.—Subdivision five is added.

SECTION 3656. To be repealed.

Sec. 3657. Every Assessor who fails to complete his assessment book, or who fails to transmit the statement mentioned in section thirty-six hundred and fifty-five, to the State Board of Equalization, forfeits the sum of one thousand dollars, to be recovered on his official bond, for the use of the county, in an action brought in the name of the people by the Attorney-General, when directed to do so by the State Board of Equalization.

The Assessor is a civil executive officer, and liable personally and on his official bond for failure or neglect of duty; and is liable personally and on his official bond for all taxes on property within the county represented by him, which is unassessed through his neglect or willful failure.

At any time between the first and twentieth days of June, in any year, any taxpayer may file with the Assessor of the county, a complaint as to the excessive valuation, or under valuation, of the property of himself or another. Such complaint shall describe the property, and state the grounds upon which the complaint is made, in ordinary and concise language. Thereupon the Assessor shall fix a day, not later than the twenty-fifth day of June following, on which to hear the evidence and render his decision on the complaint. At the time of filing the maps, assessment book, and other records of his office with the clerk of the Board of Supervisors, he shall also transmit to said clerk the complaint, together with his proceedings, and his decision thereon.

ARTICLE III.

POWERS OF COUNTY ASSESSOR.

Sec. 3660. Every Assessor shall have power:

1. To require any person found within such Assessor's respective county to make and subscribe an affidavit, giving his name and place of residence, and to make the statement required by section thirty-six hundred and forty-one of this Code;

2. To subpœna and examine any person in relation to any statement furnished to him, or which discloses property which is assessable in his respective county; and he may exercise his power in any county where the person whom he desires to examine may be found, but shall have no power to require such person to appear before him in any other county than that in which the subpœna is served upon him. In case such affidavit shall show the residence of the person making the same to be in any county other than that in which it is taken, or the statement shall disclose property in any county other than that in which it is made, the Assessor shall, in the respective case, file the affidavit or statement in his office, and transmit a copy of the same, certified by him, to the Assessor of the county in which such residence or property is therein shown to be. Every person who shall refuse to furnish the statement hereinbefore required in this chapter, or to make and subscribe such affidavit respecting his name and place of residence, or to appear and testify when requested so to do by the Assessor, as above provided, shall, on application of the Assessor to the judge of the Superior Court of the county in which the statement, affidavit, or examination is sought to be made or had, be cited to appear, within five days after service of such citation, before said judge or court, on a day and at a place named, to show cause why such statement, affidavit, or examination should not be made. After such citation shall issue and service thereof be made, all examinations shall be conducted as ordered by the court, and the testimony taken shall be filed and acted upon by the Assessor, to ascertain the extent and value of said property, and such other information as may be necessary in making the assessment thereof according to law. The application of the Assessor to the court for the order of citation shall be by affidavit, setting forth that the party or parties, to be named in the citation, refuse to make the statement required, or to make and subscribe the affidavit respecting his name and residence, or that subpœna has been served upon the party or parties, as in this section provided, and that they disobey the same and refuse to appear and testify as to the statement furnished by, or as to any property owned or claimed by, or in possession of, any person, corporation, co-partnership, or association named in said sub-

pœna, and that the information sought is required by him, in the discharge of the duties of his office as Assessor, and not otherwise. If, upon the hearing, good and sufficient cause be not shown for such refusal, the court shall order the party cited to answer such questions as may be put to him by the Assessor, or his representatives, relating to the statement made by, or the property owned or claimed by, or in possession of, any person, co-partnership, association, or corporation named in the order; and for disobedience of the order of the court, it shall punish the party for contempt. The subpœna shall require the presence of the person named therein, at a time and place specified, to testify on oath, before the Assessor of the county of ————, as to a statement made by a person, co-partnership, association, or corporation named in the subpœna, of the taxable property of such person, co-partnership, association, or corporation, or as to the property owned, or claimed by, or in the possession of such person, co-partnership, association, or corporation, and to produce the books and papers of such person, firm, association, or corporation. A witness shall be entitled to the same fees as in civil cases, to be paid from the general fund of the county on order of the Superior Court. Personal service of the subpœna shall in all cases be made. The service of the subpœna shall be made only by the Sheriff or Assessor of the county, or his deputies, who shall make the return thereon required in other cases;

3. To enter any house, building, office, or warehouse during reasonable hours, and to examine the books and papers of any person, co-partnership, association, or corporation, in the discharge of the duties of his office, as Assessor, either in person, or by deputy.

NOTE.—The foregoing sections, 3607 to 3660 inclusive, contain all of the present law relating to taxable property, definitions, assessments of property, statement of property, duties and powers of Assessor, amended to conform to the provisions of the Constitution relating to revenue and taxation. Section 1, Article XIII, of the Constitution provides that all property in the State, not exempt, etc., shall be taxed in proportion to its value, to be ascertained as provided by law, and the word property, as used in the article, is designed to include moneys, credits, bonds, stocks, dues, franchises, and all other matters and things, real, personal, and mixed, capable of private ownership, and declares that the Legislature may provide, except in cases of credits secured by mortgage or trust deed, for a deduction from credits of debts due to bona fide residents of this State. It was evidently intended that the provision to be made by the Legislature for the deduction of debts from credits should be made in a manner that would not defeat the first declaration of the section, that all property (not exempt) in the State shall be taxed in proportion to its value. And the provisions of Subdivision 6 of Section 3629 of the Political Code are that, in case of banks, the statement is not required to show the debts in detail, and that the deduction may be made from solvent credits by the banks themselves, is clearly without the spirit and intent of this section of the Constitution. It was clearly intended by the Constitution to permit the Legislature to empower an Assessor, in the exercise of the discretion necessarily permitted in determining the value, to take from the credits (not solvent credits) such debts as were assessable as credits to other persons resident of this

State; for there is no authority in the Constitution for the Legislature to provide that every citizen may become his own assessor, as he practically does under the provisions of Section 3629, which empower him to determine which credits are solvent, which debts to deduct, and, in the case of banks, to permit an aggregate reduction of all debts or liabilities of any bank from the aggregate amount that it may determine to be solvent credits. This is made more apparent by the provisions of Section 8 of Article XIII of the Constitution: "The Legislature shall require each taxpayer in this State to make and deliver to the County Assessor annually a statement, under oath, setting forth specifically all the real and personal property owned by such taxpayer or in his possession or under his control at 12 o'clock M. on the first Monday in March." Thus the statement is to be made and delivered to the County Assessor, and is to set forth the real and personal property. The word "property" includes "credits" and "stocks," and both must be made to appear in the statement delivered to the County Assessor, if they are owned or in the possession or under the control of the taxpayer making the statement.

Section 3608 practically directs that stock is not property. This is against the decisions of the Supreme Court of this State, against the general law of this State, the laws of the United States, and the decisions of the Supreme Court of the United States, and in their relation to taxation only, are stocks declared to be not property. The effect of this declaration is farther-reaching than would appear from the statement of Section 3608; for, instead of being double taxation as therein stated, it exempts from assessment and taxation many millions of dollars of property in this State and makes it impossible to assess national banks, insurance corporations, and the like.

SECTION 3663.   To be repealed.

NOTE.—Its provisions are contained in Section 3626 as proposed herein.

SECTIONS 3674 and 3675.   To be repealed.

NOTE.—The two foregoing sections attempt to limit the powers and duties of County Boards of Equalization as fixed by the Constitution (Section 9, Article XIII).

SECTION 3676.   To be amended to read as follows:

Sec. 3676.   The board may direct, at any time during its session as a board of equalization, by order entered in its minutes, on petition or otherwise, that a hearing be had to determine the true value in money of any property appearing on the assessment roll, and upon any hearing relating to such value of property, the board may subpœna such witnesses, hear and take such evidence in relation to the subject pending, as in its discretion it may deem proper.

NOTE.—The question of the equalization of property given as security for loans of money made by the University of California should have consideration. The assessed value of such loan is deducted from the value of the property securing it, resulting in the payment of no tax by such property, unless it be assessed for more than the face value of the loan. It appears from the Auditor's report from Alameda that in that county in 1895 such loans amounted to more than $370,000, and in San Francisco to about $570,000. Taxes on this amount of assessed value must be borne by other property.

SECTION 3692.   To be amended to read as follows:

Sec. 3692.   The powers and duties of the State Board of Equalization are as follows:

1. To prescribe rules for its own government and for the transaction of its business;

2. To prescribe rules and regulations, not in conflict with the constitution and laws of the State, to govern Supervisors when equalizing, and Assessors when assessing; .

3. To make out, prepare, and enforce the use of all forms in relation to the assessment of property, collection of taxes, and revenue of this State; .

4. To hold regular meetings at the state capitol, on the second Monday in each month, and such special meetings as the chairman may direct in any county of the State;

5. To annually assess the franchise, roadway, roadbed, rails, and rolling-stock of all railroads operated in more than one county in this State, at their actual value, on the first Monday in March, at twelve o'clock meridian, and to apportion such assessment to the counties, and cities and counties, in which such railroads are located, in proportion to the number of miles of railway laid in such counties, and cities and counties, in the manner provided for in section thirty-six hundred and sixty-four of said Code;

6. To equalize the assessment of each mortgage, deed of trust, contract, or other obligation by which a debt is secured, and which affects property situate in two or more counties, and to apportion the assessment thereof to each of such counties;

7. To transmit to the Assessor of each county, or city and county, its apportionment of the assessments made by said board upon the franchises, roadways, roadbeds, rails, and rolling-stock of railroads, and also its apportionment of the assessments made by such board upon mortgages, deeds of trust, contracts, and other obligations by which debts are secured, in the manner provided for in section thirty-six hundred and sixty-four of said Code;

8. To meet at the state capitol on the first Monday in August, and remain in session from day to day, Sundays excepted, until the second Monday in September;

9. At such meeting to equalize the valuation of the taxable property of the several counties in this State for the purposes of taxation; and to that end, under such rules of notice to the clerk of the Board of Supervisors of the county affected thereby, as it may prescribe, to increase or lower the entire assessment roll so as to equalize the assessment of the property contained in said roll, and make the assessment conform to the true value in money of the property assessed, and to fix the rate of State taxation, and to do the things provided in section thirty-six hundred and ninety-three of said Code; *provided*, that no board of equalization shall raise any mortgage, deed of trust, contract,

or other obligation by which a debt is secured, money, or solvent credits, above its face value;

10. To visit, as a board, or by the individual members thereof, whenever deemed necessary, the several counties of the State, for the purpose of inspecting the property and learning the value thereof; and any order made or resolution adopted, or other official act performed by said board and duly entered on its minutes, shall in every respect have the same effect as though done at the office of said board in Sacramento;

11. To call before it, or any member thereof, on such visit, any officers of the county, and to require them to produce any public records in their custody;

12. To issue subpœnas for the attendance of witnesses or the production of books before the board, or any member thereof; which subpœnas must be signed by a member of the board, and may be served by any person;

13. To appoint a clerk, prescribe and enforce his duties. The clerk shall hold his office during the pleasure of the board;

14. To report to the Governor, annually, a statement showing:

First—The acreage of each county in the State that is assessed;

Second—The amount assessed per acre;

Third—The aggregate value of all town and city lots;

Fourth—The aggregate value of all real estate in the State;

Fifth—The kinds of personal property in each county and the value of each kind;

Sixth—The aggregate value of all personal property in the State;

Seventh—Any information relative to the assessment of property and the collection of revenue;

Eighth—Such further suggestions as it shall deem proper;

15. To keep a record of all its proceedings.

NOTE.—Amendment: Subdivisions 4 and 10 empower the chairman to call special meetings in any county, and give effect to the official acts at such meetings.

SECTION 3696. To be amended to read as follows:

Sec. 3696. On or before the first Monday in September of each year, the State Controller shall present to the State Board of Equalization a statement of all the license taxes that have been paid into the treasury of the State by the treasurers of the several counties. Between the first and second Mondays in September of each year, after having deducted from the specific amount required for state revenue, as provided by the Legislature, the amount of license taxes received, as shown by the Controller's statement, the board must determine the rate of state tax to be levied and collected upon the assessed valuation of the property of the State, which, after allowing five per cent for delinquencies in and costs of collection of taxes, must be sufficient to raise the

balance of the specific amount of state revenue directed to be raised
by the Legislature.   The board must immediately thereafter transmit
to the Board of Supervisors and County Auditor of each county a statement of such rate, and upon its receipt the clerk of said board and
County Auditor must each, in writing, notify the State Board of Equalization thereof.

Part IV, Title II, comprising sections from 4000 to 4348, inclusive,
relating to the government of counties, is to be superseded by an Act
now in course of preparation by this Commission, and to be entitled
"An Act to establish a uniform system of county and township governments."